other lang.

CW00408996

OBJECT-ORIENTED PROGRAMMING
IN EIFFEL

THE OBJECT-ORIENTED SERIES

OBJECT-ORIENTED PROGRAMMING IN

EIFFEL

Robert Rist
Robert Terwilliger

PRENTICE HALL
New York • London • Toronto • Sydney • Tokyo • Singapore
Mexico • New Delhi • Rio de Janeiro

© 1995 by Prentice Hall Australia

All rights reserved. No part of this publication may be reproduced, stored in a retrieval system, or transmitted in any form or by any means, electronic, mechanical, photocopying, recording, or otherwise, without written permission of the publisher.

Acquisitions Editor: Kaylie Smith
Production Editor: Katie Millar
Cover and text design: Nina Paine
Typeset by DOCUPRO, Sydney

Printed in Australia by Ligare Pty Ltd, Riverwood, NSW

1 2 3 4 5 99 98 97 96 95

ISBN 0 13 205931 2.

National Library of Australia
Cataloguing-in Publication Data

Rist, Robert.
  Object-oriented programming in Eiffel.

  Bibliography.
  Includes index.
  ISBN 0 13 205931 2.

  1. Object-oriented programming (Computer science).
  2. Eiffel (Computer program language).
  I. Terwilliger, Robert B. II. Title.

005.133

Library of Congress
Cataloging-in-Publication Data

This information is available from the Publisher

Prentice Hall, Inc., *Englewood Cliffs, New Jersey*
Prentice Hall Australia, *Sydney*
Prentice Hall Canada, Inc., *Toronto*
Prentice Hall Hispanoamericana, SA, *Mexico*
Prentice Hall of India Private Ltd, *New Delhi*
Prentice Hall International, Inc., *London*
Prentice Hall of Japan, Inc., *Tokyo*
Prentice Hall of Southeast Asia Pty Ltd, *Singapore*
Editora Prentice Hall do Brasil Ltda, *Rio de Janeiro*

 PRENTICE HALL

A division of Simon & Schuster

Must it be assumed that
because we are engineers
beauty is not our concern,
and that while we make our
constructions robust and
durable we do not also strive
to make them elegant?

Is it not true that the genuine
conditions of strength always
comply with the secret
conditions of harmony?

The first principle of
architectural esthetics is that
the essential lines of a
monument must be
determined by a perfect
adaptation to its purpose.

Gustave Eiffel
1887

From his response in the newspaper
Le Temps *to a petition by members*
of the literary and artistic
Establishment protesting his project
of elevating a tower of iron in Paris.

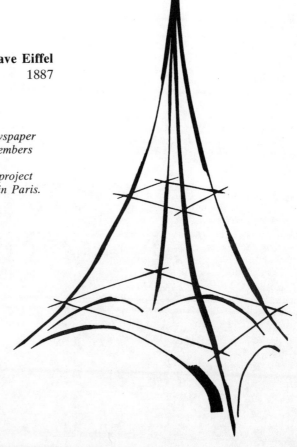

CONTENTS

To my mother, Norma Rist

Robert Rist

To life—got something better to do?

Robert Terwilliger

PREFACE

This text is written for two audiences. The primary audience is students learning a first language at university, so the text assumes no previous knowledge of programming. For this audience, the text contains the syntax and mechanism of statements in the Eiffel language, a set of examples, and a set of design rules and charts. The second audience is procedural programmers who want to learn about object-oriented design. For this audience, the text contains a comprehensive set of design rules and worked examples in Eiffel. In either case, the reader of this text will learn how to do object-oriented design and programming in the Eiffel language.

Eiffel can be divided into two part. The programming language Eiffel is covered in the first three parts of the text: first the concepts of object-oriented design, then data flow, control flow and data structures, and then inheritance. Assertions are used in Eiffel to define the abstract behavior of a routine or a class and thus support formal software engineering, and are covered in the fourth part of the book. A large case study of an automatic teller machine is provided in the fifth part of the book, to illustrate the Eiffel language, and as each new type of Eiffel statement is introduced in the text, it is applied in the case study to show how it works in a large system. Students are always asking to see examples of realistic Eiffel code, so the case study provides code to "flesh out" the text, that can be adapted and used in the design of other systems.

Eiffel can be taught in two main ways, either in two parts or in one integrated package. To teach Eiffel in two parts, the language part of the text and the case study can be used for the Eiffel language, and software engineering using assertions as formal specifications can be covered separately. To teach Eiffel as an integrated whole, the assertion part of Eiffel can be covered at the same time as each topic in the language, so the students covers both routines and assertions on routines (for example) in the same week.

The syntax of Eiffel is very simple. The basic language resembles Pascal, except that there are no semi-colons between statements; the Eiffel compiler is smart enough to recognize when a new statement has started, so the user need not write a semi-colon to tell the compiler. The number of statements in the language is very small, so there is little choice about how to implement a solution in code. For these reasons, writing code is very simple and easy, and the design of an Eiffel system is the main concern of the programme. Eiffel allows very clean, simple, and elegant solutions to be written, because it was designed from the ground up to support reuse. Traditional languages support reuse through routines, and a routine is tailored by passing data to it. Eiffel supports reuse through routines, though creating multiple objects of a single class, through inheritance of a class, and through the use of generic classes. In Eiffel, there is one very strong guideline for design: if you repeat code, then your design is wrong. In traditional languages, a solution with no repeated code is a goal that is attempted, but seldom achieved; in Eiffel, repeated code is a red flag that the design is wrong, and a new design will place the code where it can be defined once, then used and reused as needed.

The design of a solution in Eiffel is the hard part, and is the focus of this book. A solution must be clear, correct, and elegant. A clear solution can be easily understood by another programmer, and requires that the correct names be used for routines, data, and classes, that all comments be clear and simple, and that the code be formatted on the page in a way that is easy to read. A correct solution is defined by assertions (pre- and postconditions on routines, and assertions on data) that can be formally defined, added to each routine and class, and checked by the computer at run-time. An elegant solution is one that uses the principles of object-oriented design in Eiffel, and results in a system that is composed of many small and self-contained pieces, that are combined in the correct way to achieve the goal of the system. In such a solution, each part of the system is contained within its own class and routine, and the parts are then used and reused without change in other parts of the system, in extensions of the system, and in other systems.

Design is taught in a way that is new and powerful. First, a theoretical framework for design is presented and used to integrate procedural and object-oriented (OO) design. Second, a set of explicit design principles are defined and applied through the text, that convert a procedural solution to an OO solution. The basic idea behind the framework is very simple: plans and objects are orthogonal. A single plan can use many objects, and a single object can take part in many plans. Program design can be viewed as a planning task, where the goals of the system are defined in the specification, and the programmer then retrieves or builds a plan to achieve each goal, combines the plans, and then implements the combined plan in code. In a traditional language, the only step after this is to wrap routines around the repeated code. In an OO language, two additional steps are needed, to define a set of routines, and to place the routines in the appropriate class. In traditional languages, the objects are implicit in the code, but in Eiffel they are explicit and define the structure of the system as a set of objects or classes.

The basic problem that students face in designing an Eiffel system is how to cut up a long plan into pieces, and where to place the pieces; each piece of code must be placed in a routine in a class. A piece of code is a routine; call this a node. A system structure chart lists the classes across the top of the chart, the system goals down the side, and the nodes in the chart. Each goal has a plan that achieves the goal and the plan is implemented in code, so a circle or node can be drawn on the chart where a goal and an object intersect, to who where the code is located. A set of nodes that are called in sequences define the plan for that goal, so the system structure chart also defines the order in which parts of the system are executed; it is the OO equivalent of a procedural structure chart. The designer has enormous freedom in where to place the code, so a set of 30 design principles provide a powerful theoretical and practical framework for the design of OO systems in general, and the design of Eiffel systems in particular. The large case study used in the book shows how the design principles are applied to design a large, robust, and elegant solution to a realistic problem.

Each chapter of the book covers both understanding and design. First, the new language construct for that chapter is presented. The construct is then illustrated in a set of small examples, and applied to a large example that applied the construct to the design of a large system. For the language section of the book, the case study of an automatic teller machine provides the practice in design, where a case study of the design of a Coke machine provides the practice is design by assertions. In the language sections, a strong distinction is made between functions and procedures, where a function returns a value and changes nothing and a procedure changes one or more values and returns nothing. This design principle is not used in the assertion part of the book.

At the time, there are three Eiffel compilers: ISE, SiG (Eiffel/S) and Tower Eiffel. While the basic language is the same for all suppliers, there is great variability in the details of the language, in the number and content of the Eiffel library classes supplied with a compiler, and in the methods used to compile and run a system. The code in this book has been written and compiled under ISE Eiffel Version 3.2 for Unix machines, so there may be discrepancies with other Eiffel compilers, and with other versions of ISE Eiffel. The code in the text may be copied by anonymous ftp to the site *ftp.socs.uts.EDU.AU* in the directory */pub/users/rist/oopie.*

Acknowledgments

I thank John Hughes for his warmth and support; his constant encouragement allowed this book to be written. I thank Bertrand Meyer for designing the Eiffel language, and John Potter for explaining it to me; Eiffel is the only language I have ever used that makes me think harder than I want, and it has changed the way I think about system design. Finally, I thank J. Paul Tremblay, Grant Cheston, and Brian ven der Buhs of the Department of Computational Science at the University of Saskatchewan for their courageous use of, and excellent comments on, early versions of the book.

Robert Rist

I thank the Department of Computer Science at the University of Colorado, Boulder, for the support and facilities which made the writing of this book possible.

Robert Terwilliger

SERIES EDITOR'S PREFACE

Being able to program a computer is no longer an exceptional skill, and the fundamental notions are in fact quickly making their way into the standard school curriculum. Neither is it difficult, if you need to learn programming, to find a book that will guide you through the basics, The present book is about something else: its goal is to teach you how to program well — a different challenge altogether.

In the past decade a particular style of programming, known as **object-oriented** programming, has increasingly been recognized as better adapted to quality software development than the traditional approaches. Object technology, as it is also called, makes software development benefit from techniques of abstraction and systematic reasoning that have for a long time proven themselves in other scientific fields. It yields programs that are more reliable (have fewer *bugs*), easier to change, easier to explain to other people, easier to port to new machines. It supports **reusability**, that is to say the ability to build software by combining existing modules, the way electronic engineers build circuits by combining existing chips.

Object technology is not a single approach; it has a number of variants, each focusing on slightly different goals. Eiffel, C++ and Smalltalk, the most commonly used object-oriented languages, typify the principal approaches; C++ has endeavoured to retain compatability with earlier methods, as embodied in the C language; Smalltalk has emphasized fast prototyping. The Eiffel approach, used in this book, focuses on producing software of the highest possible quality.

Object technology has gained considerable attention in the software industry, and a growing number of companies are using it for projects of widely diverse nature. The fast growing Object-Oriented Series, of which this volume is the twenty-first, is testimony to the amount of research and applications that are happening in the field. The excitement about object technology was bound to raise the suggestion that it should be used for teaching as well, and a growing number of universities have for several years been introducing object-oriented elements, often using Eiffel, into their curricula. More and more of them, realizing that the best concepts should be introduced first, have reorganized their introductory courses to make full use of O-O techniques. One of the first universities in the world to take that route, at a time when it was far away from conventional wisdom, was UTS (the University of Technology, Sydney), which, as a result of the pioneering efforts of John Potter, introduced Eiffel into its undergraduate curriculum as early as 1988 and since then has trained hundreds of students in object technology. (As a visiting faculty member in 1992 I had the great pleasure of observing the impressive results of these efforts and trying to bring my share.) Robert Rist has been associated with this effort almost from the beginning, and has taught the beauties of systematic object-oriented programming to countless beginners.

This book is the result of his experience, complemented by the contributions of Robert Terwilliger (especially on the topic of assertions). Although many people have been talking about producing introductory programming textbooks using an all-O-O approach, this one is, as far as I know, the first to have delivered on the promise. It is also, with the exception of Robert Switzer's highly successful monograph also published in this Series, the first text to present Eiffel at an introductory level. On both counts I have no doubt it will be highly successful.

Eiffel will help you master the concepts both through what it provides — a small set of useful mechanisms — and, in spite of the apparent paradox, through what it does not have. One of the nicest comments I ever heard from students taking Eiffel-based courses was "But — there is no language!". What the students meant was that there was little if any linguistic baggage (such as might come for example from retaining compatibility with older languages, C or other) standing between the learner and the concepts. In other words, the correspondence between the language and the method (modern object-oriented software development) is one to one. The language will help you; it should never hinder you. Apart from a few inevitable details of syntax, to learn the language is to learn the method. This also means that you are not stuck with the language: as many people have remarked, learning programming through Eiffel is an excellent preparation for learning other languages.

If you are a student and are using this book to learn programming, either by yourself or as part of a course, you will benefit from the authors' considerable efforts at teaching you not just short-term tricks but fundamental skills that will help you throughout your career. Over and again, the book introduces clear and essential principles of design, which together provide a solid foundation for quality software development. In some cases, you may not immediately grasp why the principles are so relevant; this is because the concerns mentioned above — reliability, extendibility, reuseability — are not always crucial for small programs of the kind you may have to write at an introductory level, but take their full meaning in an industrial context, when you come to write software meant to last for many years, to be used and modified by many different people, and to satisfy the tough constraints of a corporate environment.

Rist and Terwilliger constantly have that industrial context in mind, repeatedly introducing techniques of quality design that will help you become not just a programmer, but a member of a much more rarefied group: a good programmer.

Bertrand Meyer

PART A
Object-oriented programming

CHAPTER 1

Object-oriented programming

Keywords

data
code
routine
behavior
data flow
control flow
object
class
system

An object-oriented system groups the data and the actions that use this data together. Computer code or instructions are placed inside a set of small routines, so the complexity of the code is hidden inside routines. A class contains both data and the routines that change and use this data, so a class encapsulates both data and code. An object is an instance of the general class, so each object has its own data but shares the routines for that class. The class is designed around the data it contains, and the routines define the behavior of the class. There is a strong distinction between external behavior and internal implementation: the behavior of a routine or class is shown, and the implementation is hidden. The behavior of the system is produced by executing a series of small, simple routines on the data in the objects.

1.1   Programming

Welcome to the wonderful world of object-oriented (OO) programming. It is hoped that, by the end of this book, you will be convinced that OO languages in general, and Eiffel in particular, are excellent tools for writing programs. Computer systems written in Eiffel can be clear, easy to understand, robust, reusable, elegant, powerful, and a pleasure to design and use. This first part of the book shows how

3

to design and understand an Eiffel system, and demonstrates the flavor, appearance, and behavior of Eiffel code. The detailed syntax is given later in the book.

A computer program is a series of instructions that can be understood by a computer and which tell it how to carry out a particular task. A program is like a recipe in a cookbook; it is a step-by-step description of how to combine the basic ingredients in order to make something delicious. A recipe normally consists of two parts: a list of ingredients, and a list of instructions explaining how to combine and cook the ingredients. Here is a recipe for chocolate cake:

4 oz margarine	1/4 teaspoon baking powder
2 oz sugar	A little milk, if required
2 eggs	
3 oz flour	
1 oz cocoa	

Mix the margarine and sugar together until light and creamy, then add the beaten egg gradually. Fold in the flour, cocoa, and baking powder, previously sieved. Add milk if necessary, to give a soft dropping consistency. Put the mixture into two greased sandwich tins. Bake the cake in a moderate oven (375 degrees Fahrenheit) for 25–30 minutes.

The goal of the task is to make a chocolate cake, and the instructions provide a plan for achieving this goal. If you follow the step-by-step instructions, then the result is a chocolate cake. More formally, a plan is a set of actions which, when executed in the right order, achieve the goal of the plan. The goal of making a chocolate cake is realized or achieved by executing the actions in the plan. The list of ingredients defines the objects used in the plan. Traditional languages such as Pascal, C, or COBOL emphasize the plan or instructions. OO languages such as Eiffel or C++ emphasize the objects used by the plan. Both instructions and objects are needed to carry out the task, of course, but the emphasis is different in the two approaches. A plan-based approach asks, "What is the plan?", or "What do I do?"; an OO approach asks, "What is the object?", or "What do I use?"

When a computer program is run, the instructions are executed one by one, from the first instruction to the last, just as the steps in a recipe are executed one by one in their listed order. Programming is the process of designing the program. Design is different from execution, so the design of a program is not so constrained; you can start the design with the first step, with the last step, or with any of the intermediate steps. Design is the creative part of programming.

Consider the task of designing a recipe for chocolate cake. The obvious place to start is to get some chocolate and combine it with a standard cake mix made from flour, eggs, and water. Four objects are needed for this first attempt at design (chocolate, flour, eggs, water), as well as objects such as a bowl and a spoon. The ingredients are combined by putting the flour in the bowl, and adding the eggs, the water, and the chocolate. The first step in executing this plan is to get the bowl and spoon, and the various ingredients, then combine them, put the whole lot in an oven and bake it. In this design, we started with the objects, worked out what to do with them, and then decided on an order for the various steps. Once the recipe is fully designed, the steps are executed in order. Of course, there is no guarantee that the recipe will work; looking at the real recipe, the errors in my first program design attempt are apparent.

The complete recipe given above is detailed enough for a person to follow and produce a cake. Some of the steps are quite vague ("Add milk if necessary"), and appeal to a person's general knowledge about how to prepare food. Unfortunately, computers do not have a great deal of general knowledge about the world, and they are not flexible. For this reason, the instructions you give a computer have to be given in exact detail, so that there is no possibility of error and the computer can carry out the task. An algorithm is a series of instructions which, when carried out or executed, are guaranteed to achieve the desired goal, so a program provides an algorithm for a task. When you instruct a person, you can leave out some of the steps because a person is smart enough to infer any missing information. Computers are dumb, however, so you need to write every step down in detail in a clear and simple language so that even a computer can understand it. The instructions in a computer program are known as computer code, because early computers were programmed in mathematical codes, not in the English-like instructions we use today. The process of writing these instructions is thus called coding. This book uses the Eiffel language to communicate with a computer, and shows how to write code in Eiffel. It also gives a set of guidelines for designing an Eiffel system so that the resulting code is clear, correct, and understandable.

There are two main approaches to design, called top-down and bottom-up design. Top-down design starts with a high-level or abstract decomposition of the plan, and develops the detailed plan forward from the first action to the last. The plan is gradually made more detailed until every step in the plan can be written down or coded as a computer instruction. Top-down design is the main tool used in the design of traditional, procedural systems. Top-down design can be used for an OO system, but it is also possible and common to start with the most basic or concrete objects and then work out how to combine the objects in the right way. Starting with the simplest and most basic objects allows you to try various ways of combining them, of defining the steps of the plan. This approach can be described as bottom-up design, in which the order of execution of the instructions is the last thing to be decided. Either approach can be used, as well as other approaches; people are very creative, and different people prefer different design methods. The end product of any design method is an executable algorithm, but there are many ways of getting to this final product.

The remainder of this chapter illustrates the bottom-up design of a simple banking system consisting of a single customer and a single account. First the account and its use are designed, then the customer, and then the bank. In the final system, the plan to deposit money is executed from the first action to the last, so the bank creates an account for the customer, and the customer then uses the account. Each step in the design is illustrated with Eiffel code, but the syntax rules of the language are not provided until Chapter 4. This first part of the book illustrates how to design an OO system, and shows how the solution can be implemented in Eiffel.

1.2   An object: a bank account

The basic idea behind OO programming is that the world is made up of objects that are used in various ways. When you wish to do something in the world, you first gather the materials or objects you need, then use these objects to achieve your goal. If you were building a large steel tower, such as the Eiffel Tower in Paris, you would need to design the various supporting and connecting beams, and decide how the beams are put together so that the resulting tower will be stable, strong, and aesthetically pleasing. Software design is just the same: a software system is built from objects connected in such a way that the resulting system is stable, robust, and elegant.

Consider a simple banking system consisting of a single customer with a single account. The account can be used in various ways: you can deposit money, withdraw money, add interest, or see the account balance. This specification lists four goals for the account: to deposit, withdraw, add interest, and display the account. The first step in functional or procedural design is to list the goals or requirements that the system must achieve. The first step in the design of an OO system, however, is to define the objects in the system.

Data is central to OO design, and the use of this data is secondary. An object is designed around the data stored in that object. An object contains or encapsulates data, and the data is central to the design and definition of an object. Once the data has been defined, then the routines that use the data are defined and stored with the data. This is the basic design principle for OO systems: an object contains data, and the routines that change or use that data.

OO PRINCIPLE 1: An object is designed around the data it stores.

The most basic object in the bank system is the bank account. For a bank account, the obvious data is the money in the account. In a computer system, data is stored in the computer's memory as a variable, a value that can be stored and changed. The money in an account is a real value, so in Eiffel the variable is declared by writing

    balance: *REAL*

This statement should be read as "the variable *balance* is a real number" or, more formally, "balance is of type *REAL*". This variable declaration tells the computer to allocate storage for a single real value, and to call this value *balance*. Formally, a variable consists of three parts: a name, a type, and a value. In the declaration above, the name is *balance*, the type is *REAL*, and the value is unspecified. In Eiffel, a real variable is initialized to the value 0.0, and then the balance is changed when the customer deposits or withdraws money, or the bank adds interest or subtracts bank charges from the balance.

Now that the basic data has been defined, the first step in OO design, we can look at how this data is used. When money is deposited into a bank account, the balance of the account is increased by the amount deposited. The Eiffel instruction that adds an amount to the balance is

    balance := balance + amount

This assignment instruction (:=) tells the computer to calculate the value on the right-hand side of the assignment and store this value in the variable named on the left-hand side of the assignment. The right-hand side of the statement tells the computer to get the current values of *balance* and *amount*, and add them together to calculate a new value. This value is then stored in the variable *balance*, thereby changing or updating the value of *balance*. When you read an assignment statement, call it "gets" or "is assigned", such as "balance gets balance plus amount". An assignment statement is an instruction that is executed in two steps: find the right-hand side's value, then store it in the left-hand side variable.

The Eiffel language was designed so that code is written once, then used and reused as needed. The simplest way to reuse code is to wrap a routine around the code, and execute the routine as a single operation; this is known as calling the routine. A routine may contain a single line of code, but often contains many lines of code. When the routine is called or executed, all the code inside the routine is executed. An Eiffel routine to deposit money into a bank account is

```
deposit (amount: REAL) is
        -- add amount to balance
    do
        balance := balance + amount
    end -- deposit
```

The name of this routine is *deposit*, because it contains the code to deposit money into the account. The routine name is followed by the values or arguments that are passed to the routine, which lists the values used by that routine; in this case, a single real value that is the *amount* of money to be deposited. A comment describing the routine is then given; in Eiffel, a comment is indicated by two minus signs "--". Any text after the comment indicator is ignored by the computer, so comments are used to communicate with people who read the code, and are ignored by the computer. The routine body is then coded, enclosed in the keywords **do** and **end**. The *deposit* routine takes a single argument, the amount of money to be deposited, and adds this amount to the current balance in the routine body.

The basic principle in the design of reusable software is to divide a complex task into small pieces, and to define each piece as a routine. Each routine is small, and does a single thing. An OO system carries out complex tasks by breaking the task into small pieces, and coding each piece as a small routine in the appropriate class.

OO PRINCIPLE 2: A routine is small and does a single thing.

The deposit routine does not show the new balance, it just deposits money. To display the new balance, a separate routine needs to be defined; this is a basic idea in Eiffel, where commands are defined as routines which are called as needed. The account balance is a single, real number, so the routine to display the balance can be coded as

```
display is
         -- display the balance
    do
         io.putstring ("The account balance is $")
         io.putreal (balance)
    end -- display
```

The *deposit* and *display* routines show how the account is used, but there is a step missing; the account must be created before it can be used. In Eiffel, an object is created by a special routine called the creation routine for the object; this routine is usually called *make*. For an account, the creation routine sets the balance to an initial value read in from the user, so the code to create the account and set the initial balance is

```
make is
         -- set the initial balance
    do
         io.putstring ("Enter the initial account balance: ")
         io.readreal
         balance := io.lastreal
    end -- make
```

The single variable declaration and the three routines define a basic bank account. The declaration defines the data stored in an account, and the routines show how the basic account is used. There are many other things we can do with a bank account besides put money into it (such as withdraw money or add interest), but we will continue with this simple example before looking at more complex code.

1.3   A class: class ACCOUNT

The code shown above allows us to store a single account balance in the variable *balance*, and to update this balance by a deposit. The variable *balance* is defined by the declaration, the account is created by the *make* routine, and the account is then used by the *deposit* and *display* routines. A normal bank, however, contains many different accounts, one or more for each customer. A specific account is an instance of a general class, so we can create many instances of a single class or type. This is the difference between an object and a class: the class defines the general behavior, and an object is an instance of a class.

OO PRINCIPLE 3: An object is an instance of a class.

Consider the class *CAR*; in Eiffel, a class name is written in upper case. The class *CAR* defines what is meant by a car, just as the class *ACCOUNT* defines what is meant by an account. If you look at a busy street, you see many instances of the class *CAR*, i.e. many objects that are cars. The class provides the definition or the general behavior, and an object is an instance of a class; you see many individual cars on the street, not the conceptual class *CAR*. A class (almost) corresponds to a type in computer science, so we can talk about different types or classes of objects; for the present, a class can be equated with a type. Every object in Eiffel is an instance or example of a class, so there are Eiffel classes for *INTEGER*, *REAL*, and so on. The class *INTEGER* defines what values can be stored in an integer, and what can be done with integers; every integer variable is an instance of an integer.

The data in class *ACCOUNT* (*balance*) and the code that uses this data (*make, deposit, display*) are all placed in the same class. This is the basic rule for designing a class: the data and the code that uses or changes this data are placed in the same class. Any code that changes a data value has to be placed in the same class as the variable that is changed, because Eiffel does not allow a value to be changed from outside the class. A value can be used outside its class, so there is a choice to be made about where to place the code that uses a value, but a value can only be changed by code within the class. Any code that changes a value must therefore be placed in the same class as the data.

OO PRINCIPLE 4: A value can only be changed by code in its class.

Code that uses a value may be located outside the class, but it is usually included in the same class as the value it uses. The code that changes and uses the data defines the behavior of the class, because it defines what the class can do and how the class can be used. In the design of a class, then, there are three basic rules. First, a class is designed around its data. Second, the data are usually hidden and only the behavior is visible. Third, the routines that use the data and define the behavior are placed in the same class as the data.

OO PRINCIPLE 5: The data and the code live in the same class.

Both data and code are called features in Eiffel. A feature can be data, in which case it is called an attribute of the class and stores some value. A feature can be a routine, in which case it changes or uses an attribute's value. A class is usually composed of a small amount of data and a large number of small routines. The definition for the class *ACCOUNT* is

```
class ACCOUNT
creation
    make
feature
    balance: REAL
    make is
```

```
                    -- set the initial balance
          do
                io.putstring ("Enter the initial account balance: ")
                io.readreal
                balance := io.lastreal
          end -- make
    deposit (amount: REAL) is
                -- add amount to balance
          do
                balance := balance + amount
          end -- deposit
    display is
                -- display the balance
          do
                io.putstring ("The account balance is $")
                io.putreal (balance)
          end -- display
    end -- class ACCOUNT
```

Look back at the format of the recipe for chocolate cake. The recipe first lists all the objects, then gives a set of instructions or a plan for how to use the objects; this is the traditional way to write a recipe, or a program, by separating the data from the code. An OO system takes the other approach, where each object comes with its own instructions, and the set of instructions have to be put together to make the cake.

A routine is described by its behavior, and the code or implementation inside the routine is hidden. The behavior of a routine is defined by the data flow into and out of the routine. Data flow itself is simply defined; data flow occurs when data is made in one place, and used in another. There are four main types of data flow: data flow from the user to the system (input), data flow from the system to the user (output), data flow passed from one routine to another, and data flow returned from one routine to another. Data flow may also occur within an object, when one routine sets a value in the object, and another routine in the object later uses this value. This internal data flow is not usually shown.

A routine can be drawn as a circle, and the data flow is indicated by an arrowhead going into or out of the circle; call each circle a node. An arrow going into the top of a node indicates that data is read from the user, and an arrow going out of the bottom of the node indicates that data is shown to the user. An arrow going into the left side of a node indicates that data is passed to the routine from another part of the system, and an arrow going from the left side of the node indicates that the routine passes data back to another part of the system. This notation is shown on the next page, where the data flow is indicated by a triangle arrowhead on each node.

data from user   data to user   data to routine   data from routine

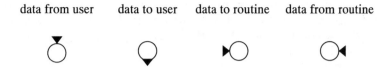

Looking at the code for class *ACCOUNT*, we can show the behavior of each routine in the class by drawing a node for that routine, and showing the data flow into and out of that node. The creation routine reads a single value, the initial balance, from the user. The *deposit* routine receives the amount to deposit from a customer. The *display* routine receives no data, but outputs a message and the value of the current balance to the terminal screen. The data flow for each routine is shown below.

An object is created by executing the creation routine for that class. To create an instance of an account, the class *ACCOUNT* is first defined, then a specific account is created by calling the *make* routine. The *make* routine tells the computer to allocate a piece of computer memory (here a single real variable called *balance*) and to set the initial value of this variable. If we both use the same bank and have the same type of account, then there is only a single class or type of account, but we each have our own balance for our own account. The class definition defines how an account behaves, and a specific account or instance of the class (an object) is created when the creation routine is executed.

In OO programming, an object is defined by its behavior, by the routines that act on the data contained in the object. All the code in an OO system is contained within a class, so a complex system is built from classes. An object is an instance of a class, and the objects are created and used when the system runs. More formally, a class definition exists when the code is written, but an object does not exist until run time, when the code is executed. An object contains its own data values, but shares its routines with all the other objects of that class. In a traditional language, the data is declared in one place and the code is written in another place, so a program is built from a chunk of data and a chunk of code. In an OO language, every class contains its own data and code, so a system is built from a set of classes.

1.4   A client: class *CUSTOMER*

A customer of the bank has an account, and uses that account. In Eiffel, a class that uses or calls the features of another class is called a client, and the class that supplies the services is called a supplier. The supplier class *ACCOUNT* was designed above, and the client class *CUSTOMER* is designed in this section.

A customer uses features or services that are provided by the account. When you use the services of someone else, such as a lawyer, a doctor, or a plumber, then you are a client of that person. In the same way, one class is a client of another if it uses the services provided by that second class. In the example here, class *CUSTOMER* is a client of class *ACCOUNT* because it uses or calls the account features. This is known as a client–supplier relationship, in which class *CUSTOMER* is the client using the services or features supplied by the class *ACCOUNT*.

A client–supplier relationship is defined when a client *C* declares a variable of type *S*. This relationship is shown by writing the two classes as ovals, with an arrow from the client to the supplier. An oval contains the class name, and an arrow is drawn from left to right, from client to supplier. The direction of the arrow indicates that the client calls or uses one or more features defined in the supplier; here, the *CUSTOMER* calls or uses features of an *ACCOUNT*. The client chart for the two classes is

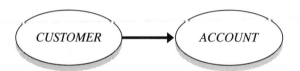

A class is designed around its data, so the basic approach in the design of class *CUSTOMER* is to start by asking, "What is the data in the object?" Once the class attributes have been defined, we then look at how this data is used by the object. A customer has a name and an account, so the data in a class *CUSTOMER* is thus

```
class CUSTOMER
    name: STRING
    account: ACCOUNT
```

The attributes of this class consist of two variables: one of type *STRING*, and one of type *ACCOUNT*. The customer name is a string, a sequence of characters such as "Alan Turing". A customer's account is an instance of the class *ACCOUNT*; in Eiffel, the name of a variable can be the same as the name of a class.

When a customer is created, the values of these variables are set by the creation routine. For a customer of a bank, these details are typed in by someone such as a bank clerk, and read in and stored by code inside the *make* routine for class *CUSTOMER*. The Eiffel code needed to read data from a user is quite long, because the data has to be read using one set of instructions (input–output, or *io* instructions) and then stored in the variable by an assignment statement. The *make* routine for a customer has to get the customer's name, store it in the variable, and then call the routine to create an account. The *make* routine in class *ACCOUNT* then gets the initial balance from the clerk. The Eiffel code to get the customer's name and create an account is

```
    make is
            -- set the name and create an account
        do
```

```
            io.putstring ("Enter the customer name: ")
            io.readline
            name := io.laststring
            !!account.make
        end -- make
```

When this code is executed, the bank clerk types in data which is read by the code in the system. Assume that the values "Alan Turing" and 1000.0 are entered into the computer. First, the customer name is read and stored in the variable called *name*. The routine then calls the account creation routine, which reads in and stores the initial balance. The code for creating a customer lives in class *CUSTOMER*, because it changes the value of *name*. The code for creating an account lives in class *ACCOUNT*, because it changes the account *balance*. The plan to create a customer and an account is thus split between the two classes, and each class contains part of the total plan. A customer has an account, so the *ACCOUNT* creation routine is called from the *CUSTOMER* creation routine.

The code to read and store the customer name and account balance defines a plan for the goal of creating a new customer. The goals or requirements of a system are usually explicit in the system specification, but may need to be inferred as the system is designed; here, the goal to create a customer and an account is not given explicitly, but we know that an account must exist before money can be deposited or withdrawn. The actions in the plan (get the name, store it, get the balance, store it) must be written as code somewhere in the system, but a programmer has enormous freedom in where the code is placed. This is the real challenge in program design—to decide where to place, and how to implement, the plan for each goal.

In a functional language such as Miranda or Lisp, the function is the basic computational unit, and a plan is coded as a function. In a procedural language such as Pascal or C, the procedure is the basic computational unit, so a plan is coded as a set of procedures that are executed in order. In an OO language such as Eiffel or C++, the object is the basic computational unit, so a plan is split or divided among the objects. The basic unit of planning or design, the plan, is thus implemented in different ways in each type of language. The actions in a plan can often be grouped in many different ways, at the discretion of the designer, which makes program design a difficult and creative process. All the actions must be coded somewhere in the system, and an order to execute the actions needs to be defined so that the computer can execute the code; however, there are usually many orders and organizations possible.

PLAN DEFINITION: A plan is a set of actions which, when executed in the right order, achieve the goal of the plan.

The specific order in which events happen in a computer system defines the control flow in the system. When one routine calls another, for example, we say the calling routine controls the called routine. Control flow can be shown by drawing a line between two routines, so the call from the creation routine in

CUSTOMER to the creation routine in *ACCOUNT* is shown as two connected nodes. By convention, the calling node is shown to the left.

Control flow is indicated by a line between two nodes. A routine call is indicated by a horizontal line, so the node on the left calls the node to the right. A routine call can "carry" data with it by passing data as an argument to the routine. A function can return a single value back to its caller. Sequence is indicated by a vertical line, so the node at the top of the line is executed before the node at the bottom of the line. This notation is shown below, where the diagram on the left shows a routine call, and that on the right shows two routines that are executed in sequence.

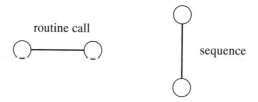

Data flow can be shown using arrows, so both the control and data flow can be shown on a single diagram or chart, called a system structure chart. In a system structure chart, the classes are listed across the top of the diagram in client order, the goals are listed down the left-hand side, and routine calls are shown by drawing a line between two nodes; a routine normally has the same name as its goal.

Data flow and control flow define the basic structure of a computer system. The code in class *CUSTOMER* calls the *make* routine in class *ACCOUNT*, but does not pass any data to it. The code in both *make* routines gets input from the user, however, so both nodes show that data is read in by the node. The system structure chart for this fragment of the system, together with the routine call and the routine header, is shown below.

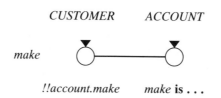

A routine is called by writing the name of the routine, followed by the data values passed to the called routine. The data values are called the arguments to the routine; for this example, no data is passed from the calling to the called routine. When a routine is called in another class, the caller writes the name of the object (*account*) followed by a dot (.), followed by the name of the called routine (*make*) and any arguments (none here). When a creation routine is called, all of this is preceded by two exclamation marks (*!!*); an exclamation mark is often called a "bang" in computer science. The account creation routine call *!!account.make* should be read as "bang bang account dot make". This code is contained in class

CUSTOMER, and calls the *make* routine in class *ACCOUNT*. The code in the account creation routine is then executed, creates an account with some initial balance, and control then returns to the caller.

To deposit money into the account, we call the *deposit* routine in the *ACCOUNT*. The customer chooses the amount to deposit, so code is defined in class *CUSTOMER* to read in a value from the user and pass it to the *deposit* routine in class *ACCOUNT*. Similarly, to show the customer details, we need to show the name of the customer and the balance of the account, so we need a *display* routine in class *CUSTOMER* and another *display* routine in class *ACCOUNT*. The first routine shows the name of the customer and calls the account's display routine to show the balance. In an OO system, the plan is split or divided among the objects it uses, so part of the code is placed in each class, along with the data used by the code.

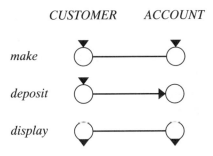

The behavior of these two classes is shown in the system structure chart above, where the caller is shown to the left of the diagram, and the called routine is shown to the right. A vertical line between two nodes indicates sequence, a horizontal line indicates a routine call, and an arrow indicates data flow. In the diagram, each routine in class *CUSTOMER* calls a routine in class *ACCOUNT*, but nothing in the system yet calls the code in class *CUSTOMER*.

In a system structure diagram, the goals, plans, and objects are explicitly shown: the class names at the top, the goals down the side, and the plans as a series of nodes in the chart. In traditional languages the objects are implicit in the code, but they are explicit in an OO language. It can be seen from the system structure chart that the structure of the system is defined by the interaction between the plans and objects in the system. The code for a plan must be included somewhere in the system, and a system structure diagram shows where the code is placed. A node is drawn where a plan and an object intersect, and shows that the code for that part of the plan lives in that object.

In general, plans and goals are orthogonal, because a plan can use many objects and an object can be used in many plans. This reflects the real world, where a plan can use many objects (the plan for a cake uses flour, eggs, sugar, and so on), and an object can be used in many plans (an egg can be scrambled, fried, boiled, and so on). The system structure makes this interaction explicit, and provides a tool to show the structure at a level higher than the system code.

OO PRINCIPLE 6: Plans and objects are orthogonal: a plan can use many objects, and an object can be used in many plans.

The behavior of the class *CUSTOMER* is shown by the diagram, while the code that produces this behavior is shown in the class definition below.

```
class CUSTOMER
creation
    make
feature
    name: STRING
    account: ACCOUNT
    make is
                -- set the name and create the account
        do
            io.putstring ("Enter the customer name: ")
            io.readline
            name := io.laststring
            !!account.make
        end -- make
    deposit is
                -- deposit money into the account
        do
            io.putstring ("Enter amount to deposit: ")
            io.readreal
            account.deposit (io.lastreal)
        end -- deposit
    display is
                -- show the customer details
        do
            io.putstring ("For ")
            io.putstring (name)
            io.putstring (": ")
            account.display
        end -- display
end -- class CUSTOMER
```

The *CUSTOMER* class definition contains five features: two of the features are attributes and three are routines. One of the attributes is a variable of type *STRING*, and the other is of type *ACCOUNT*. The first routine is the creation routine, which sets the name and account balance for the customer; the second routine allows money to be deposited into the customer's account; the last routine shows the customer name and account balance. The classes *CUSTOMER* and *ACCOUNT* work together to implement the plans for the system.

1.5   The root class: class *BANK*

The root class is the class that starts the whole system. The root class creates objects and calls their features as necessary, so it is the original client at the far left of a client chart. More formally, it is the class at the root of the calling tree. The root class for the basic banking system is class *BANK*. The bank has a single customer, and the customer has a single account. A root class usually has a single routine, which is the creation routine for the class and the system. The code in this routine then calls other routines, which in turn call other routines, and so on.

The complete system of three classes defines the bank system. The client chart for the *BANK* system is thus

because the *BANK* calls features in *CUSTOMER*, and the *CUSTOMER* calls features in *ACCOUNT*. Class *BANK* is the root class for the system, because it starts everything off.

The data in class *BANK* is a single customer, and the code to declare this customer is

> *me: CUSTOMER*

The bank creates a single customer, deposits money into the customer's account, and shows the new balance; this is done in the creation routine for the bank. The complete class definition for the class *BANK* is thus

```
class BANK
creation
    make
feature
    me: CUSTOMER
    make is
            -- create a customer, deposit money, show all details
        do
            !!me.make
            me.deposit
```

> *me.display*
> **end** – – make
> **end** – – class *BANK*

The calling structure between classes is shown in the system structure chart, where an arrow indicates data flow and a line indicates control flow. A node at the left of the chart is a routine call, a node in the middle is both called and calls, and a node to the right is the end of the line, a routine that calls nothing else.

The chart for the *BANK* system is shown below. In this system, the customer name is read in by code in class *CUSTOMER*, and the initial account balance is read in by code in class *ACCOUNT*. The amount to deposit is read in the class *CUSTOMER*, and passed as an argument to the deposit routine in class *ACCOUNT*, where it is used. The customer name is output by code in class *CUSTOMER*, and the account balance is output by code in class *ACCOUNT*. The root class controls the order in which events happen, by calling routines in the other classes. The plan to create objects is divided among the three classes, as are the plans to deposit money and display the object details.

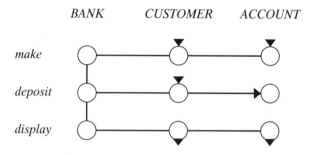

A class consists of data and the code that uses the data, so each class contains both data and routines. The system of three classes consists of three sets of data and routines. Each routine is quite small and simple, and the system works by calling the routines in sequence. In a system written in a traditional language, it is common to see large chunks of code; in an OO system, the code is split into small routines and distributed among the various classes. This makes the code simpler to understand, because each small routine does a single thing and can be easily understood. It also makes the code much easier to reuse, because it does not have to be changed when the system changes. Instead, the various routines are called as needed without changing the actions in each routine; only the caller has to change, not the routine definition.

1.6   System charts

The price for reusable software is that the code is distributed, between routines in a single class, and between classes. This can make it difficult to see and understand how the system hangs together as a whole, so diagrams or charts are used to show the links between classes. Three main types of diagrams are used in this book: client charts, data structure charts, and system structure charts. These charts can be used to design a solution before any code is written, or to describe the finished system at a higher level than the code.

A client chart shows the calling relation between classes and thus shows if one class uses features in another class. It is not very detailed, however; it does not show the data contained in a class, the routines defined in a class, or the order of routine calls. This section shows two types of detailed charts: a data structure chart and a system structure chart.

A data structure chart is built from the attribute declarations in each class, from the root class through the client and supplier classes to the most basic supplier class at the end of the client chart. It shows the data in each class, and the links between the data in each class of the system, and provides an overview of the system data structure. A variable has three parts: a name, type, and value. Simple variables such as real numbers, integers, and characters have a simple value. Object or reference variables, however, have a value that is a memory address, formally a pointer or reference to memory; the data contained in the object is stored at that location in memory. A client declares a reference variable, creates the object, and the value of the variable is a reference to the object in memory.

In the bank system, the root class contains a single variable of type *CUSTOMER*, whose name is *me*. A *CUSTOMER* contains two variables whose names are *name* and *account*, of type *STRING* and *ACCOUNT* respectively. An *ACCOUNT* contains a single variable called *balance*, of type *REAL*. The data structure chart for this system is shown below. In this chart, specific values have been given to the variables, simple values to the simple types, and reference values (shown as pointers) to the reference types. The actual values stored in an object depend, of course, on the actual values entered by a user or allocated by the system when the object was created or updated.

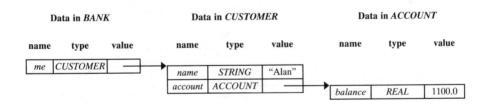

Objects are persistent. This means that the data stored in an object persists in memory, as long as the object exists, as long as the system runs or executes on the computer. Once a value has been set in an attribute, that value remains in the object until it is changed, so a value can be set by one routine, then used or changed by other routines. In the bank account, for example, the *balance* is set by the *make* routine, which then returns control to its caller. When the *deposit* routine is called at a later time, the code in that routine picks up the value of *balance*, adds an amount to it, and stores the new value. When the display routine is called at a later time, the persistent value of *balance* is again picked up, and shown to the user.

A system structure chart is built by listing the classes across the top of the chart in client chart order, the goals down the side of the chart, and then drawing a circle or node where a plan and an object intersect. The system structure chart is the OO equivalent of a structure or calling chart in a traditional language, and has the same function: it shows the calling structure in the system.

A node corresponds to one or more features in the same class; normally a node is a routine, but it may also correspond to an attribute, or to several features. Nodes are connected by horizontal lines to indicate that one routine calls a feature in another class; feature calls within the same class are normally not shown. The general rule is that a node is drawn when the control crosses an object (horizontal line) or a goal (vertical line) boundary.

A line to the right of a node indicates that the node calls a feature in another class. A line to the left of a node indicates that the node is called from another class. A node at the left side of a chart is the start of a plan, because it starts the series of calls. A node in the middle corresponds to a called feature which calls a feature in another class, so the node has a line both to the left (it is called) and to the right (it calls). A node at the far right of a chart indicates a routine at the end of the line that calls nothing, so it has only a line to the left (it is called). Nodes are connected by vertical lines to indicate that one routine is executed after another in the same class. A full description of how to build a system structure chart is given in Appendix C.

The system structure chart for the *BANK* system is shown below. The bank system has three classes (*BANK, CUSTOMER, ACCOUNT*) and three goals (*make, deposit, display*). For this system, there is a node at every intersection of goal and object, and every node corresponds to a single routine, but this simple pattern need not occur for more complex systems.

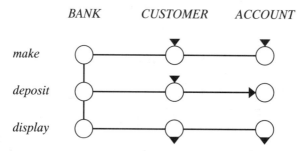

The first line of code in the creation routine of the root class *BANK* is a call to create a customer. This transfers control to the customer creation routine, which is then executed. The code in that routine reads the customer's name, and calls the account creation routine to initialize the balance of the account. The account is created, and the initial balance is stored in the variable *balance* in the account. The routine is then finished, so control returns to the caller in class *CUSTOMER*, and then to the caller in class *BANK*.

The next line of code in the root class creation routine, a call to the customer *deposit* routine, is then executed. This routine in turn calls the account *deposit* routine, and the code there updates the account balance. The routine is then finished, so control returns to the caller, which also finishes and returns control to its caller. The root class then calls the customer *display* routine, which then calls the account *display* routine. All the code in the root class has now been executed, so the bank system exits. This long sequence of routine calls is tedious to describe in words, but can be read directly and easily from the system structure chart.

The data and routines in an OO system are distributed throughout the system, one part in each class. This makes the parts of an OO system easy to reuse and makes each part easy to understand in isolation, but it can be difficult to see how all the parts connect in the complete system. Client charts, data structure charts, and system structure charts all help to give a global picture of the system. Each chart provides a true and accurate picture of the system code, which means that it can be used as a tool either in design or for documenting the system.

1.7   Class layout

A class has the basic format shown in the example classes in this chapter. The class definition begins with the keyword **class**, followed by the name of the class. The next entry in the class definition is the **creation** clause, which names the routine (usually called *make*) used to create an object. The rest of the class consists of a set of **features**, which may be data or routines. A routine may take arguments as input, or it may not, depending on the situation. The class is terminated by an **end** statement. The basic format of an Eiffel class is as follows:

1. The name of a class is CAPITALIZED. The names of all types are capitalized, both for classes you write (such as *ACCOUNT*) and for classes provided by Eiffel (such as *REAL*).
2. A space line is used to separate attributes from routines, and each routine in the class.
3. A space is written after every comma, colon, and semi-colon, and on either side of an assignment statement.
4. All features, both attributes and routines, are indented equally in steps of four spaces.
5. A header comment after the routine name describes what the routine does. Header comments are indented to the level of the code.
6. The routine body (**do . . . end**) is indented inside the feature.
7. The code is indented inside the routine body.
8. The name of the routine is written as a comment at the **end** of the routine.

These are the standard conventions for setting out Eiffel modules, and should be followed whenever you write code. The typefaces used in this book follow the standard Eiffel manuscript format (Meyer, 1992), where the executable code is shown in italics, Eiffel keywords (see Appendix B) are shown in bold face, and comments are shown in plain text.

1.8   Running an Eiffel system

The code that defines each class is stored in a separate text file. The name of the class is the name of its text file; the class *ACCOUNT*, for example, is stored in the file "account.e". A separate text file must be used for each class.

As the code in a text file is a series of characters and a computer only speaks binary, the text is not executable by the computer. It is converted to executable code by compiling the system. At the time of writing, there are three Eiffel compilers on the market (ISE Eiffel, SiG Eiffel or Eiffel/S, and Tower Eiffel), and each compiler has a slightly different form of compilation which changes slightly for each release of the language. The format of a compilation is idiosyncratic to the specific version of the Eiffel language you are using, and is not given here.

Essentially, you give the compile command for your version and tell the compiler the name of your root class, and the name of the creation routine in that class. When the Eiffel compiler is started, it finds the file for the root class; from the root class it automatically finds and links all the connected classes into a single executable file for the whole system. The name of this executable file is the name of the root class, so all the executable code for the bank example is stored in an executable file called "bank". When this file is executed, the creation routine in the root class is executed and calls routines in the other classes.

The system is executed when the executable file is run on your computer; this is done by entering the name of the file as a command. When you run the system, Eiffel creates an object for the root class and executes the creation routine of the root class, which then creates the other objects and calls their features as necessary.

The Eiffel compiler checks the syntax of your system, converts the Eiffel code to C code, and then converts the C code to executable code. The C code is kept in a special file created by the system, so a compilation can create many new files on your system. Eiffel has a smart compiler, so a class is recompiled only if it has been changed; any existing, unchanged classes are not recompiled. The Eiffel language is defined by Bertrand Meyer in *Eiffel: The Language* (1992) and is standard across all versions of Eiffel, but the Eiffel libraries supplied with a compiler may change from one version to another.

1.9   Case study: the *BANK* system

The design of a banking system has been introduced in this chapter, and is developed throughout the book from the basic class *ACCOUNT* to the final solution of 17 classes. The case study in Part E of this book illustrates each part of the Eiffel language introduced in the text; thus, the theory given in each chapter is applied in each part of the case study. The case study supplies a working example of each Eiffel construct, and shows how to combine the pieces to define a large system. It also shows how to design each new part of the system, by tracing the steps in design from the specification, through analysis, design, and then coding. You should look at the case study for each topic to make sure you understand how that topic fits into a complex system.

The first part of the case study is the design of a complete class *ACCOUNT* to define a bank account, that shows the specification, design, and solution for this task. The class *ACCOUNT* shows the form and structure of a complete Eiffel class.

Summary

- A program consists of both data and code. In a traditional system, the data is separate from the code. In an OO system, each class contains both data and code.
- A class is designed around its data (attributes), and contains both the data and the code (routines) that uses or changes that data.
- A class consists of a small number of attributes and a large number of small routines.
- The class defines the behavior of an object; an object is an instance of a class.
- Variables of reference types have pointers or references to objects as their values. They are shown on a client chart.
- Variables of simple types (INTEGER, REAL, DOUBLE, CHARACTER, BOOLEAN) have basic or simple values. Both reference and basic types are shown on a data structure chart.
- Routines are chunks of code that calculate or change a variable. They are shown on a system structure chart.
- The structure of an OO system is created by the interaction between the plans and objects in the system. Plans and objects are orthogonal, so the actions or code in a plan are divided among many classes. The code is placed in the class that contains the data used by that code.

Exercises

1. Define the following terms:
   - attribute
   - routine
   - class
   - object
   - supplier class
   - client class
   - root class
   - client chart
   - plan
   - data structure chart
   - system structure chart.
2. What is the format of a class definition?
3. What does a node (a circle) indicate on a system structure chart?
4. How is data flow shown on a node?
5. How is control flow shown on a system structure chart? How is sequence shown on a system structure chart?
6. How is a routine called?
7. How is a plan implemented in an OO system?
8. Write a system in which a customer has two accounts. Draw a data structure chart.

9. Write a system with three customers *me*, *him*, and *her*; each customer has two accounts. Draw a system data structure chart.

10. Extend the *bank* system so that you can withdraw money from an account. Draw a system structure chart for this new system. Add the code in class *ACCOUNT*, then add the code in class *CUSTOMER*, then in class *BANK*.

11. Add interest to the account. You need to add a variable *rate: REAL* to class *ACCOUNT*. Draw a system structure chart, a new data structure chart, and then code the system.

12. After each deposit and withdrawal, show the balance of the account. Use the existing display routine in class *ACCOUNT*. *Draw* a system structure chart.

CHAPTER 2

Reusable software

Keywords

function
procedure
signature
assertion
behavior
export
inherit

The Eiffel language was designed to build reusable software. The main way it does this is by defining a set of features, and a set of classes, that can be defined once and used as needed. The behavior of a routine is defined by its input and output arguments, and by assertions on the routine; the code that creates or implements the behavior is hidden inside the routine. The behavior of a class is defined by its exported features, which can be seen and called by other classes; some features can only be called within the class. A routine is reused by calling it multiple times. A class is reused as a client by creating many objects, or by inheritance.

2.1   Designing for reuse

An object is defined by its behavior; if it looks like a duck, quacks like a duck, and swims like a duck, then it is a duck. A chair is something that can be sat upon, a door is something that allows entry and exit, a window is something that you can look through. When you use a television, you push the buttons and the picture appears; you change the channel and a new picture appears. When you use a CD player, you put in the disk, push the buttons, and music comes out. When you use a car, you turn the key, put it in gear, press the accelerator, and off you go. For any of these complex objects, you use the object and ignore how the behavior is produced by the object.

The secret to designing a complex object is to hide the complexity inside the object, and provide a simple and standard interface. When the car was invented, each manufacturer decided on a set of controls that would be offered with that car, and decided where and how to place the controls in the cabin of the car. Each manufacturer usually made a different design decision, so driving a new car required a new set of skills and habits to be learned. Over the last 100 or so years, there has been an immense amount of time and effort devoted to the selection and layout of the controls in cars. Almost all cars now have the same set of controls, and the same layout of these controls, so the same skills can be used with little change from car to car. The interface between the driver and the car has been made so simple that any person is now expected to be able to drive. Even children who are too small to see over the steering wheel have been able to drive a car! In the same way, two- and three-year-old children can use a computer through a point and click interface with a mouse. When you use a computer, you type on the keyboard or use the mouse, and read what appears on the screen; the internal details of how the keyboard or mouse movement is converted to electric and magnetic signals which are sent through the computer chip and finally affect the screen can be ignored, as long as the behavior is reliable.

The simplest way to design reusable code is to hide the code inside a routine, call the routine, and treat the routine as a single instruction. If the behavior of the routine is clearly defined, then the internal details can be ignored by the user. A user does not want to know how the routine actually works, as long as it works correctly. The task of the designer is to define a clear and simple interface that precisely defines the input to the routine, and the output from the routine; this is known as the input–output behavior of the routine.

Object-oriented programming has taken this approach one step further by hiding both the code and the data inside the object. A routine hides or encapsulates its instructions, and an object encapsulates both data and routines, and shows only the behavior of the object. For this reason, both data and routines are called features in Eiffel, because you can't tell the difference between them from outside the object; they are all equally features of the object. A value may be stored as data inside the object, or calculated when needed, but from the outside the behavior is identical; you ask for the value and it is returned. An object with well-defined behavior and hidden implementation is known in computer science as an abstract data type, which allows the data type to be used reliably with no knowledge of how this behavior is implemented. Each class provides a set of features that can be used by a programmer, with no need to look inside the class to see how the behavior is caused.

The Eiffel language was designed for reusable software; in a computer system, the code and data are called software because they can be changed, while the actual equipment is called hardware. Software reuse in routines is supported by exactly defining the values that are passed to and from a routine through the arguments, and by defining the effect of a routine through assertions. An assertion is a statement of fact, such as "The balance of an account is never negative". In Eiffel, assertions can be attached to routines to assert or state what must be true when the routine is called, and what must be true when the routine exits. Software reuse in classes is supported by strictly defining the external behavior of a class, by defining a class and then creating multiple objects, and by allowing one class to inherit another. A class is reused by exactly defining the class interface or behavior, and then using the exported features of the class as needed.

2.2   Functions and procedures

The external behavior of a routine is defined by its input and output values (if any) and its pre- and postconditions. This section describes the input–output behavior of the two types of routine, called functions and procedures; assertions on routines are described in the next section.

A routine header lists the routine name, followed by zero or more declarations enclosed in a pair of parentheses; these are called the arguments to the routine. Values are passed from the caller to a routine through the arguments; the caller supplies a value for each argument, and the routine uses these values. The *deposit* routine in class *ACCOUNT*, for example, takes a single value as an argument, the amount of money to deposit. A routine can receive any number of arguments, including zero; the examples here take either no arguments or a single argument. The values supplied by the caller are called the actual arguments, and the values in the routine header are called the formal arguments. The actual arguments are matched or bound to the formal arguments when the routine is called.

There are two types of routine, called functions and procedures. A function returns a value, and changes nothing. A procedure changes one or more values, and returns nothing. These two rules are all you need to define the right type of routine, and give strong guidelines for the design of routines in Eiffel.

EIFFEL PRINCIPLE 1: A function returns a value and changes nothing.

An example of a function is a routine that calculates the absolute value of a number. This function takes a single real value as an argument, and returns the absolute value of that number (another real number). One way to write this function is

```
abs (number: REAL): REAL is
        -- absolute value of number
    do
        if number >= 0 then Result := number
        else Result := - number end
    end - abs
```

The caller passes a single real value to this routine, such as *abs (-45.7)*. This actual value is matched to the formal argument in the routine header, and used in the function. The value of the function is the value assigned to *Result* inside the function. No stored value is changed; instead, a new value is calculated from the argument and passed back to the caller. The caller then uses the returned value.

When a bank account receives interest, the interest is added to the balance. If interest is added daily, then the interest for one day is added each day. The interest may be a fixed amount, it may be a fixed percentage of the balance, or it may depend on the balance. Let us assume that an account receives interest daily, that the amount of interest depends on the current balance, and that there are two interest rates. A function in class *ACCOUNT* to calculate and return the daily interest rate, given the current balance and the yearly interest rate, is

```
class ACCOUNT . . .
    limit: REAL is 5000.0
    low_rate: REAL is 5.0
    high_rate: REAL is 6.0
    day_rate: REAL is
            - - daily interest rate for current balance
        do
            if balance < limit then Result := low_rate
            else Result := high_rate
            end
            Result := (Result / 365.25) / 100.0
        end - - day_rate
```

The function first finds the correct interest rate to use in three steps. First, it uses the class attribute *balance* to find the correct rate to use, then it converts the rate to a daily rate by dividing by the number of days in the year, then it converts the daily rate from a percentage to a fraction. This value is then returned as the result or value of the function. The header comment for the routine says nothing about how the result was calculated; it describes what the routine looks like from the outside. No stored value is changed by this function; instead, a new value is calculated from the current balance and the rate constants, and returned by the function.

EIFFEL PRINCIPLE 2: A procedure changes value(s) and returns nothing.

A procedure changes one or more values. The routine to add interest to an account is a procedure, because it changes the value of the balance. The *interest* routine calls the function *day_rate* to get the interest rate, then uses this value immediately to calculate the interest due, and adds this value to the balance. The code to do this is

```
interest is
        - - add daily interest to the balance
    do
```

```
          balance := balance + balance * day_rate
     end – – interest
```

The *interest* routine is very simple and easy to understand, because the rate calculation has been hidden inside the function *day_rate*. This is the key to designing simple, clear, and reusable software: a routine does a single thing, so each routine is small and simple. Note that the *interest* routine does not return a value to the caller; if the customer wants to see the new value of the balance, then a routine to display that value must be called. If a routine interacts directly with the user, either for input or output, then that routine is a command. The routine changes the state of the terminal screen, and may also change the values stored in the object, so any input or output routine is implemented in Eiffel as a procedure.

A routine can be identified as a function or a procedure purely by its external behavior, because a function returns a value and a procedure does not. The behavior of a routine is defined by its signature, and the signature defines the routine header: the arguments define the input types in the signature, and the returned type defines the output type in a signature. The routine header and the routine signature contain the same type information.

There are really only two types of behavior: queries and commands. A query returns information about the state of the object, while a command changes the state of an object. The behavior of an object is defined by the commands and queries that the object provides or supplies. This approach can be illustrated by thinking of an object as a big, black box with two sets of buttons, "query buttons" and "command buttons". If you push a query button, an indicator lights up on the button and gives you some information about the internal state of the machine. Pushing the button does not change the value, so if you push the button ten times in a row, you'll get the same answer each time (unless a command has changed the state in between queries). On the other hand, when you push a command button, the machine starts screeching and clicking but you do not get any information about what is happening inside the box. When the machine stops and you push a query button, the answer you get will usually be different from the answer you had before the command was given. The machine has changed state. The attribute values define the state of an object, so a command changes attribute values. A command is implemented by a procedure.

A query can be implemented by a function or by an attribute. Data values stored inside an object are called the attributes of that object; this corresponds to the idea of variables in traditional computer languages. When a value is returned from a query, the value may be stored in the object as an attribute or computed by a function. Attributes, functions, and procedures comprise the three types of features of an object. An attribute behaves identically to a function with no arguments; from the outside, it is impossible to tell if a returned value was stored inside the class as an attribute, or computed and returned as the value of a function. In the interest rate calculation, a value was calculated and returned by the feature. If there was only a single interest rate, this single value would be stored as an attribute, but the feature *daily_rate* behaves the same, whether it is implemented as a function or as an attribute.

The behavior of a feature is defined by its input and output; more formally, it is defined by the data flow within the system, not by the data flow into and out of the system. A feature can be drawn as a node, and the input and output can be shown on the node; data flow within the system is shown to the left and right of a node, and data flow into and out of the system are shown above and below the node. The possible behaviors of procedures, functions, and attributes are shown below. Reading data from the user changes the state of the I/O (input–output) system, as does writing data to the user, so input and output routines must be procedures. Procedures and functions are routines, so they may receive arguments from a caller. Functions and attributes implement queries, so they return a single value to the caller. Finally, a procedure may be called and change the value of an attribute, with no data flow into or out of the routine. Multiple data values may be read from the user, shown to the user, or passed to a routine.

	Procedure	**Function**	**Attribute**
data from user			
data to user			
data passed			
data returned			
no data flow			
total possible			

The signature of a feature is a list of the values that are passed to, and returned by, a feature; formally, it is a list of the types of these values. The signature of a routine can be read directly from the routine header, because the header lists the input values in its argument list, and the output values in the type of the feature. An attribute or function returns a value of a given type; most values discussed so far have been *REAL* values, but there are many other types. A signature consists of a set of input types, followed by a semi-colon, followed by the output type if any, so it has the form < input types; output type>.

The class *ACCOUNT* now contains eight features. Four of these features are attributes: one variable attribute (*balance*) and three constant attributes (the limit and two rates). Four of the features are routines: three procedures to *make, deposit*, and add *interest*, and one function to return the *day_rate* for interest. These eight commands and queries are all features of the class, so they are all indented equally in the class listing. The header for each feature is shown to the left on the next page, and the signature is shown to the right.

balance: REAL	< - ; REAL>
limit: REAL	< - ; REAL>
low_rate: REAL	< - ; REAL>
high_rate: REAL	< - ; REAL>
make (amount: REAL)	<REAL; - >
deposit (amount: REAL)	<REAL; - >
interest	< - ; - >
day_rate: REAL	< - ; REAL>

The feature header and the signature show the types of the input and output values for the feature. The signature may be defined before the routine is coded and thus define the external behavior of the routine; design then consists of implementing the behavior in code. If the correct way to divide a task into parts is not known initially, the complete plan may be written and then cut up into routines in each class; in this case, the signature is known only after the code has been written. In either case, the signature defines the precise, external appearance of the routine, and provides the clear division between internal and external that is essential for the design of reusable software.

2.3   Assertions

The signature and the assertions on a routine define the formal behavior of a routine. They can be used to specify the behavior of a feature before any code is written, and thus be used to design the system. The data flow shown on a node reflects the signature, so there is a simple transition from design, to formal specification, to feature header. The assertions may be used while the system is running, to check that the code really does do what was specified. Finally, the assertions can be used to communicate with a programmer who is looking for a routine to accomplish a task, and scans through the class to find if such a routine already exists.

An assertion is a statement of fact that must be true when the assertion is executed. There are two main types of assertion in Eiffel, called pre- and postconditions. A precondition is an assertion that must be true when a routine is called, so we require the precondition to be true upon routine entry. The precondition is tested after the arguments have been bound, but before the routine body is executed. A postcondition is an assertion that must be true when a routine exits, so the routine ensures that the postcondition is true upon exit. The postcondition is tested after the code has been executed, but before control is returned to the caller. The approach of defining the behavior of a routine before the code is known as design by contract: the signature and assertions define a contract for the routine, and the routine has to obey this contract and provide the defined service. The assertions define the action of the routine, and can be used to check that the routine really does implement the contract correctly.

When money is withdrawn from the account, the signature is <REAL; - >, because an amount of money is passed to the routine, deducted from the balance, and no value is returned to the caller. Three conditions can be defined on this routine to ensure that it works correctly. First, the amount of money to withdraw should be greater than zero; you cannot ask for a negative amount of money. Second, the value of the balance should be reduced by this amount, after the routine has been executed. Third, the balance should never be negative. A routine that implements *withdraw* is shown below, with assertions on its input and effect; multiple assertions are separated by semi-colons.

---

withdraw (amount: REAL) **is**
       -- deduct this *amount* of money from the *balance*
  require
       positive: amount > 0;
       funds: amount <= balance
  do
       balance := balance − amount
  ensure
       changed: balance = **old** *balance − amount*
  end -- withdraw

In the *withdraw* routine, the routine header shows the signature: a single *REAL* value is passed to the routine from its caller, and no value is returned. The precondition defines what must be true when this routine is called: the *amount* to withdraw must be positive. The postcondition defines what must be true when the routine exits: the current *balance* must equal the old *balance* plus the *amount* withdrawn, and the *balance* must never be negative. These facts completely define the behavior or action of the routine, and can be used to design the routine, to check that it is correct, and to describe the routine to a programmer.

The *withdraw* routine does not contain code in the routine body to test if it has been called correctly. In Eiffel, design by contract says: "If you call me in the right way, then I guarantee to return the correct answer." If the client calls the routine incorrectly and violates the contract, however, the contract is broken by the client and the routine no longer guarantees anything. This is an important principle in the design of an Eiffel system: it is the responsibility of the client to call the routine correctly.

EIFFEL PRINCIPLE 3: The client is responsible for calling a routine correctly.

A routine does not test if it has been called correctly; that is the responsibility of the client. If the routine was called incorrectly, then the assertions on that routine should fail and notify the caller. When an assertion fails, the user is told the name of the assertion that failed (the name shown before the colon above), as well as the assertion itself (shown after the colon). This is how assertions are used as a debugging aid, because Eiffel tells the user exactly what went wrong when the routine was called.

Assertions are discussed in detail in Part D of this book. They provide a formal specification of a system that says what the system should do, without saying how to do it. The formal specification can be used to assist a programmer to write the code, and to check the code when it has been written, and thereby prove that the code is correct. It is hoped that, in the future, the task of programming can be based on such formal specifications, and that the code can be generated automatically and correctly from a set of precise, logically correct assertions.

2.4   Classes

The class contains data and the code that uses or changes that data. Each feature in the class is defined by its behavior, and a class is defined by the aggregate behavior of its features. The external behavior of a class is exactly defined by the signatures and assertions of the features in the class. The assertions and signatures define an abstract data type for the class, in which the behavior is known and the implementation is ignored.

The class is the main unit of reuse in an Eiffel system, because objects are created as instances of a class, and these objects are used in the system to provide behavior. If a customer has three accounts, for example, then three objects of type *ACCOUNT* are created as attributes of a customer. Each account contains the data values specific to that account (here, the current balance and interest constants), but all the accounts share the routines defined in the class. The code to create three accounts in class *CUSTOMER* might be

```
class CUSTOMER
    . . .
feature
    first, second, third: ACCOUNT
    make is
            -- set customer attributes, create three accounts
        do
            . . .
            !!first.make
            !!second.make
            !!third.make
        end -- make
```

Here, the code to read in the customer details has been omitted for simplicity. As a result of running the creation routine *make* to make a customer, three objects of type *ACCOUNT* have been created within the single customer. Each account has a different name, so each account can be used separately by giving the name of the object and calling features on that object. Each account can have a different balance, but will behave in the same way.

A feature of an object can always be called from inside that object; some features can only be called from inside the object. A class has an export policy which defines those features that can be seen by the outside world external to a class, and which features can only be seen inside the class. This policy defines the external behavior of the class, by specifying which features or services are available to a client. The export policy is defined when the feature is defined, by attaching one or more class names to the **feature** keyword that precedes the feature definition. The named classes can use the features listed under that export policy. If no names are placed after the feature keyword, then anybody can use the features. The main export policies that can be set on a feature are

Export clause	Meaning
feature *{}*	exported to no class
feature *{NONE}*	exported to no class
feature *{X, Y, Z}*	exported to classes X, Y, Z
feature	exported to all classes
feature *{ANY}*	exported to all classes

The **feature** keyword can appear many times in a class definition, as many times as needed to define the export policy of that class. The policy is set by the feature clause, and is in effect until the next clause. All features exported to a specific class are written under the feature keyword with that class, then the next set of features is defined with its own export policy, and so on. Hidden features are listed in the class under a **feature** *{NONE}* policy. The export policy provides two advantages for system design. First, it provides a clean, precise definition of the behavior of a class; the class behavior is defined by the behavior of its exported features. Second, it provides security for the system, because only the listed clients can use the features of that class. In the *BANK* example, it is crucial for the security of the bank that only a small, specified set of classes can actually create a new bank account, or deposit money into it.

The **creation** clause may also contain an export policy to list the classes that are allowed to create an object. The creation and the export status of a routine are independent, so a routine can be called as a creator (using !!) or as a normal feature (no !!). The creation clause lists the classes that can call the routine as a creator. The format of the export is the same as a normal feature, such as

creation *{A, B}*
    make

A creation routine can also be called as a normal feature, if the user wishes to reset or re-initialize the attribute values. A routine call by a client to create an object is shown in the first line on the next page, and a routine call by a client to reset the values stored in an existing object is shown on the second line. !! is used only to create objects, but the creation routine can be used to create objects, or to set or reset attributes as needed.

!!object.make	execute *make* as the creation routine
object.make	execute *make* on existing object

Several creation routines may be listed in a **creation** clause, separated by commas; these will all have the same creation export policy. There may also be several creation clauses, if the designer wants a different export policy for each creation routine.

A class is designed around the data that it contains, but is defined by its behavior. The actual way that the data is stored or represented is usually hidden, and only the behavior is exported. This allows us to change the way that the data is stored, without affecting the behavior of the class. If the attributes of the class are exported, then every time an attribute changes, the class and its users have to be changed; a simple change can thus have large effects on the system. In order to insulate as much of the system as possible from change, the attributes are normally hidden. It is possible to export an attribute, and there are situations where this is necessary, but it should be avoided if possible; it makes the code less reusable, because a client has to know the exact form of the data, and the client and the supplier have to be amended when the representation changes. Eiffel supports data abstraction and the definition of abstract data types by exporting the behavior and hiding the representation.

EIFFEL PRINCIPLE 4: Export the behavior and hide the representation.

The function that calculates the interest rate and its associated constant values cannot be called from outside the class *ACCOUNT*; they are private to that class. The balance is also hidden, so all access to the balance is provided by the class's routines. The other routines can all be called by the class *CUSTOMER*, so they are exported to that class. The export policies for the class are thus

```
class ACCOUNT . . .
feature {NONE}
    balance: REAL
    limit: REAL is 5000.0
    low_rate: REAL is 5.0
    high_rate: REAL is 6.0
    day_rate: REAL is . . .
feature {CUSTOMER}
    make is . . .
    deposit (amount: REAL) is . . .
    withdraw (amount: REAL) is . . .
    interest is . . .
```

```
    display is . . .
  end – – class ACCOUNT
```

A large library of common, useful classes is supplied with the Eiffel compiler for everything from mathematical operations, to data structures, to window systems and graphical interfaces. These classes have been extensively tested by the Eiffel designers and can be safely used by any programmer. The Eiffel class library shows how an OO system directly supports reuse, because the library classes were defined by someone else and they come with the Eiffel compiler. You use these library classes in exactly the same way as classes written by you.

Eiffel provides a tool called **short** that shows the exported features of a class; this is called the short form of the class. To find out which features are available, you run the tool on that class (by typing something like **short** *ACCOUNT*) and the tool goes through the class and finds all the exported features. For each exported feature, it shows the name, arguments, comment, and assertions, but no code. These four pieces of information are all that you need to use a feature, because they define its exact behavior; how the behavior is implemented can be ignored, because you just want to use a feature and not look inside it.

To use a feature, look at the class documentation, and then use the library class like any other class: create an object, and call the features of that object. If a feature is called correctly, its contract is in force, and the correct behavior is guaranteed. If a feature is called incorrectly, then an assertion on that feature is violated and an error message appears to show the violated assertion. Eiffel is thus self-documenting, because the documentation is derived directly from the code. No separate documentation is needed, and the documentation always describes the system code.

2.5   Inheritance

There are two ways to use a class in any OO language. The first way is to declare a variable of a given type or class, and then create an object and use its features; in Eiffel, this is the client–supplier relationship discussed above. The second way to use a class is to inherit that class and use its features; in this case, no separate object has to be created.

The meaning of inheritance in an OO language is very close to the meaning of inheritance in evolution. Consider the class *ANIMAL*; an animal is born, moves around, eats, breathes, has babies, and so on. The class *MAMMAL* is a more specific type of animal which has all the features of an animal, plus specific features of its own: the babies are born alive, and live on the mother's milk when they are young. The class *MARSUPIAL*, in turn, is a specific type of mammal which inherits all the features of a mammal and adds its own unique features: the baby lives in the mother's pouch for the first months of its life. The class *HUMAN* is another specific type of mammal which inherits all the features of a mammal and adds its own unique features, such as having the ability to use fire and to drive a car.

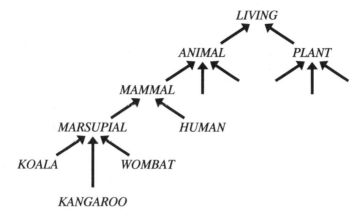

The inheritance chart for this example is shown above. In an inheritance chart, the parent class is shown above the child class, with a single arrow from the child to the parent. Of course, there are other types of animals and plants, and more specific types of kangaroo and human; the full inheritance hierarchy for life on earth is huge. This chart serves the same function as a client chart, to give an overall picture of the links between the classes in a system. The inherit relation is different from the client relation; inherit means "is" (a human is a mammal, a customer is a human, a savings account is an account), whereas client means "has" (a person has a name), "contains" (a bank contains a set of customers), or "uses" (a customer uses an account). You need to draw two separate charts for a system, one to show the client links and another to show the inheritance links.

One class inherits another by writing the keyword **inherit**, followed by the name of the parent. In Eiffel, all features of the parent are inherited by the child; more formally, all features of the parent are features of the child. When a class is inherited, the child behaves exactly as though the parent code was written in the child; there is literally no difference in the way the child and parent features are used. From outside the child class, it is impossible to tell whether the features were newly coded in the child, coded in the parent, or coded in some distant ancestor; they are all treated identically. This is a strong technique for code reuse, because the code is defined once and then inherited as needed, without change. It is a technique used in any OO language, not just in Eiffel.

OO PRINCIPLE 7: Write code in a parent, and reuse it by inheritance.

Consider a new class that is a *CHECK* account. This is a specific type of account, with different rules for adding interest; a check account gets no interest. There are now two types of account, a savings account and a check account. These are both a type of account, so they should inherit an abstract class *ACCOUNT* and add or change any features as needed. The only difference in this example is the interest rate, so the abstract class *ACCOUNT* contains the common code, but each specific type of account has its own rules for calculating the interest rate. The inheritance chart for the accounts is

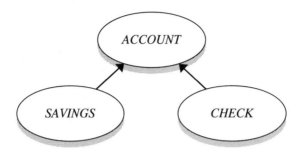

The new parent class *ACCOUNT* contains 90 percent of the code presented above, but the interest rate is not defined; instead, it is deferred for each child to define. This is done by defining the external behavior of the parent, but leaving the body of the feature empty. Each child class then supplies its own body for that feature. The changed interest rate code in class *ACCOUNT* is shown below: the daily rate has been deferred, so all the constants (limit and rate) are omitted from the parent and placed in the child class *SAVINGS*. The deferred calculation routine is

```
class ACCOUNT
    . . .
feature {NONE}
    day_rate: REAL is
                -- daily interest rate
        deferred
        end -- day_rate
    . . .
end -- class ACCOUNT
```

Class *ACCOUNT* now has an attribute to store the balance, plus routines to make an account, deposit and withdraw money, add interest, display the balance, and a deferred calculation of the interest rate. The parent class thus has seven features: an attribute, five routines coded in the class, and one deferred routine whose body will be defined by the child classes. The class has no creation clause, because no object of type *ACCOUNT* will ever be created; only objects that are check or savings accounts are created and used in the system. The class *ACCOUNT* captures the common behavior and code, which is inherited and used in each specific type of account.

The complete definition for a check account which provides object creation, deposit, withdrawal, display, and (no) daily interest is shown below.

```
class CHECK
inherit
    ACCOUNT
```

```
    creation
        make
    feature {NONE}
        day_rate: REAL is 0.0
    end -- class CHECK
```

The complete definition for a savings account which supports object creation, deposit, withdrawal, display, and daily interest is shown below. The interest rate for a check account is stored as a constant, while the interest rate for a savings account is calculated as needed by a function. From outside the class, the behavior is identical: a client simply asks for the interest rate, and the correct value is returned. The fact that one value is stored and one value is computed reveals the power of separating the behavior from the implementation.

```
    class SAVINGS
    inherit
        ACCOUNT
    creation
        make
    feature {NONE}
        limit: REAL is 5000.0
        low_rate: REAL is 5.0
        high_rate: REAL is 6.0
        day_rate: REAL is
                -- daily interest rate for current balance
            do
                if balance < limit then Result := low_rate
                else Result := high_rate end
                Result := (Result / 365.25) / 100.0
            end -- day_rate
    end -- class SAVINGS
```

All the features of the parent are inherited by the child, so each child inherits six features from the parent class ACCOUNT. The routine day_rate is defined in the child to return a value of zero for a check account, and the appropriate rate for a savings account. Each child uses the parent features, and supplies its own definition of day_rate which implements the inherited, deferred feature.

The features of the three classes are shown on the next page, first for the parent class ACCOUNT, then for the two child classes CHECK and SAVINGS. All features except the attributes (balance, limit, low_rate, high_rate) and the day_rate feature are exported; the exported features are shown in bold face. The day_rate is a deferred feature in the parent which is implemented or effected in each of the children.

ACCOUNT	CHECK	SAVINGS
balance	balance	balance
make	make	make
deposit	deposit	deposit
withdraw	withdraw	withdraw
display	display	display
interest	interest	interest
day_rate	day_rate	day_rate
		limit
		low_rate
		high_rate

The class *ACCOUNT* has seven features: six effective features and one deferred feature. The class *CHECK* has seven effective features: six inherited unchanged, and one inherited and defined in the child. The class *SAVINGS* has ten features: seven inherited unchanged, one inherited and defined, and three added in the child. The interface to each type of account is identical, because all the exported features have the same names and behaviors. The actual calculation of the daily rate for a savings and a check account is hidden inside the routine; from the outside, you just call the routine and the rate is calculated and the interest is added.

A customer with a savings and a check account simply creates each account as needed, then uses each account by calling routines on the account. The code in class *CUSTOMER* to create two accounts, add interest, and show the balance for both accounts might look like that shown below; note that this is different from the class *CUSTOMER* shown in the last chapter.

```
class CUSTOMER
feature
    savings: SAVINGS
    check: CHECK
    make is
            -- for both accounts, make the account, add interest, and
            -- show the balance
        do
            !!savings.make
            savings.interest
            !!check.make
            check.interest
            savings.display
            check.display
        end -- make
```

The client chart for a banking system for a bank with a single customer with two accounts, one savings and one check, is shown below; the inheritance chart was shown on the previous page. Note that there is no class *ACCOUNT* in this chart, because the customer has one check account and one savings account; no abstract object of type *ACCOUNT* is used by the customer.

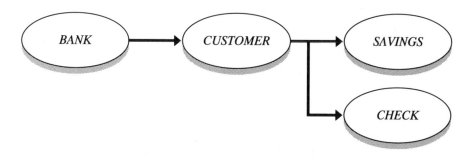

Almost all the code used in class *SAVINGS* and class *CHECK* was defined in class *ACCOUNT* and inherited unchanged; one feature was inherited and made specific to the specific type of account. This is reflected in the system structure chart, because the chart shows where the code lives for each plan. For the goal of creating a savings or a check account, all the code is in the abstract class *ACCOUNT*, as is the code to deposit money and display the balance; for these goals, the plan terminated at the parent class. The code to add interest is shared between the parent and the children, because the parent adds the interest but the children supply the interest rate. The rate is calculated in one child and stored in the other, but each class has a called feature, so the classes are shown in the chart. The system structure chart for the bank with a single customer, and the customer with the behavior shown above, is

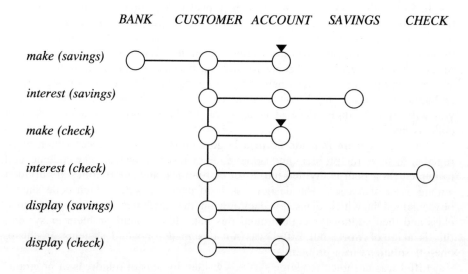

The definition of inherited classes with the same parent and the same external interface but different implementations is known in Eiffel as polymorphism (poly = many, morph = shape). It allows a client to treat the classes identically, by calling features on each child class having the same name and signature but different actions. Each class defines its own specific behavior, and from the outside this behavior appears identical; more formally, the interface to each class is the same. This supports strong code reuse, because most of the code is defined once in the parent and inherited; only the code specific to each child class has to be written in each child.

Inheritance allows the code to be defined once, and then inherited and used where needed; it is another form of reuse. You need to define the behavior of an animal once, and then use this class as needed, either as a client of a class (as in "George has a pet koala") or by inheritance (as in "George is a real animal"). Any child class simply inherits the parent, and the child then has access to all the code in the parent. Inheritance is transitive, so features defined in class *ANIMAL* are features of the classes *MAMMAL*, *MARSUPIAL*, and *KANGAROO*.

2.6   Code reuse

The key idea in Eiffel that supports strong code reuse is the clear and explicit line between the external behavior of a feature and its internal implementation. For a routine, the behavior is defined by the signature and assertions of the routine. For a class, the behavior is defined by the behavior of its exported features. The code in a class is reused when a client calls features of a class, creates multiple objects from a class, or inherits features from a class.

EIFFEL PRINCIPLE 5: If you repeat code, your design is wrong.

In Eiffel, there is never any need to repeat code; code is defined once, and then used as a client or by inheritance. In other languages, code reuse is a goal to be aimed at, but in Eiffel it is a basic design tool. If you repeat the same code in an Eiffel system, then you have almost certainly designed your system incorrectly. This is a very strong guide for design, because it is easy to notice if you are rewriting the same code; whenever you notice this red flag, stop designing or coding at once and re-think your design. The new solution will be better, because you will write a single piece of code, once, to do a single task, and reuse this code as needed.

An Eiffel system is made up of a large number of small pieces which work together to solve the problem and achieve the goal of the system. The code needed to implement a plan is divided into a set of routines, and the routines are divided among a set of classes. The design task is to decide exactly which code should be contained in which class, by deciding on the attributes that are stored in a class and then adding the code around this data. For a small problem or system, this is a lot of work, but Eiffel was not designed for small systems or cheap, one-off solutions to a problem.

Eiffel was designed for large systems written by tens or hundreds of programmers, and used and reused over a period of years or decades. Experienced programmers will notice that an Eiffel listing is very long; what can be done in a page of Pascal, C, or C++ may take several pages of Eiffel code. Part of this is the physical layout of an Eiffel class on the page, as it uses a lot of white space in order to make each feature easy to read. Another reason is that an Eiffel class contains a lot of small routines, and rarely has a routine longer than ten lines or so. The problem solving is distributed in an OO system between classes, where each class supplies a little code and then calls routines in another class.

When a system becomes large, then code reuse really makes sense. In a large Eiffel system, programmers need not write a lot of code; rather, they browse through the class library, see which classes they need, and then use the existing code in these classes. The existing code is expected to be correct, because it is part of an existing, working system, so new systems do not require as much work to debug and test. Ideally, a new system requires no new code; it is built by combining existing, working, correct classes.

Summary

- Reusable software defines the external behavior, and hides the implementation.
- The behavior of a feature is defined by its signature and its assertions.
- The behavior of a class is defined by its exported features.
- A function changes nothing, and returns a single value.
- A procedure changes one or more attributes, and returns nothing.
- A precondition asserts what must be true when a routine is called; a postcondition asserts what is then guaranteed to be true when the routine returns control.
- Assertions support design by contract: if the preconditions are true, then the routine guarantees that the postconditions will be true on routine exit.
- A routine is reused by defining it once, then calling it multiple times.
- A class is reused by creating multiple objects of that class. A client creates and thus has objects of the supplier class as attributes; client means "has", "uses", or "contains".
- A class is reused by inheritance. The child inherits all the features of the parent, and can then alter the inherited features as needed, and add new features. A child is of the same type as its parent; inherit means "is".
- If you repeat code in an Eiffel system, your design is probably incorrect.

Exercises

1. What is the basic principle behind the design of reusable software?
2. What is the behavior of a function? of a procedure?
3. How is a value returned by a function? by a procedure?
4. Name and describe the three types of features in a class. Why are attributes and routines indented equally in a class listing?
5. What is a signature? Why is a signature important?

6. List the signature of every feature in the class *ACCOUNT*, defined in the first part of the *BANK* case study in Part E of this book.
7. What is an argument to a routine? Give an example, showing both the code in the caller and the called routine. What are arguments used for?
8. Can a creation routine have arguments? Can the creation routine for the root class have arguments? Why (or why not)?
9. What is an export policy? How is the export policy for a feature set? What are the different types of export policies? Can a feature have two export policies? Can a class have two export policies?
10. What is meant by design by contract?
11. Where are assertions defined in a routine? When are assertions tested? How are assertions used in design? in debugging?
12. How is the behavior of a routine defined?
13. How is the behavior of a class defined? What are the different types of export policies?
14. What is meant by inheritance? How is an inheritance chart drawn? Draw an inheritance hierarchy for (1) primates, including monkeys, apes, and humans, and (2) motor vehicles, listing the main attributes in each class.
15. How can a client tell if a feature was inherited, or coded in the child class?

CHAPTER 3

System design

Keywords

design
top-down
bottom-up
procedural
functional
object-oriented (OO)
evaluate
code

This chapter discusses the process of system design. The difference between novice and expert design is presented to provide an overall framework, and then design is discussed within two dimensions: direction (top-down versus bottom-up), and perspective (procedural versus functional versus OO). The first part of the chapter defines the terms and notation needed to describe each approach. A system specification is then presented, and each approach is used in turn to convert the specification from English words to Eiffel code.

3.1   The process of design

Design is the central process in programming. It is a creative process. There are many methods in the computing literature that prescribe an approach to design, and enormous variability in how people use each method. Real design is guided by these methods, but not bound by them; there are a myriad of ways to design a computer system, because there are many different ways of viewing a complex artifact, and each perspective defines a different way of looking at the system during design. In programming, it is rare for two people to produce the same solution to a problem. Even when two solutions are similar, the process used to design each solution can be very different.

The basic process of design is to start with some aspect of the solution, and build the system around this initial idea or focus. The various design methods differ in where they start to design a solution, and in the way that one step leads into or links with the next part of the solution to be designed. The key idea in design is to decompose a complex problem into small pieces, solve each piece of the problem, and then put the pieces together to make the final solution. The two general approaches to program design, top-down and bottom-up design, differ in how the problem is decomposed into pieces, and in how the pieces are combined.

In top-down design, an initial abstract solution is gradually made more detailed, until the actions or steps can be implemented in code. In this approach, the behavior of each step is described with no internal mechanism, then each step is refined or expanded to specify the mechanism. Design by contract is thus a form of top-down design, in which the behavior of each step is defined before its implementation. Top-down design is often used when the problem is simple or familiar, and the designer has a good idea about how to break the problem into smaller parts. In this approach, pieces of the final solution are developed from first to last, from the start of the solution to the end.

In bottom-up design, the problem is immediately decomposed, one small part is chosen, and a detailed solution is designed for that part. Given this initial, detailed solution for that part of the problem, other steps are added around this detailed code until the complete solution has been constructed. Bottom-up design occurs when the problem is new or difficult, so the form of the solution is not known until late in the design process. In this approach, the initial, detailed piece that begins design may be the first action, the last action (the goal), or the most important, central, or focal action. Each choice of where to start defines the order in which pieces are added to the evolving solution.

A common design strategy is to choose a goal, and design a plan that achieves the goal. A goal is an output defined in the problem specification, and the system is written to produce this output and thus achieve the problem goal. The plan is a sequence of actions that are executed in order. If the designer writes a detailed plan as a series of lines of code, then that plan is not reusable. To make the parts of the plan reusable, the actions must be divided into a set of discrete pieces that become routines, and the routines divided among the different classes. The process of allocating the parts of a single plan into routines in different objects can be extremely difficult, but it is the key problem in converting a bottom-up solution into reusable OO code. The process of splitting the plan into pieces, which are implemented as a set of class features, defines the structure of the final OO system. Novice programmers see a system as code; experts see it as a set of interacting nodes.

Beginning programmers favor a concrete, procedural approach to design. They start with the inputs to the system, and design forward from the inputs to the outputs, at the level of concrete or detailed code. First the inputs are coded, then the calculations, and then the outputs. This approach has the advantage that there is always detailed code that can be examined and executed, instead of vague, general abstractions. It has the disadvantage that decisions about the form of the solution are made as the code is written, with little knowledge of the overall structure of the solution. Novice programmers equate construction and design.

When a house is built, you have to lay the foundations as the first step in construction. Design, however, is not so constrained; often, the last part of the house to be designed is the foundation. You should know the layout of the house, how many floors it has, how much weight needs to be supported, and so on, before you lay the foundations. If you start to build before the design is complete, then you have to continually tear down what you have already built as you realize that your structure is wrong for the house you want. Software is easier to change than hardware, but it is still time-consuming and frustrating to have to keep changing your code.

Expert programmers have two kinds of knowledge not possessed by novices: knowledge about solutions, and knowledge about design. The first of these is knowledge about the standard solutions that are used in computer science, and in each specific domain of expertise. A standard solution provides a high-level or abstract chunk that can be used as a single piece during design, because the internal details are known; the expert has coded that piece before, and simply retrieves it from memory. Novices do not have a large set of known programming solutions (program clichés or schemas), so they are forced to design at the concrete level; as they learn more solutions, they can design using these abstract pieces.

The second type of knowledge possessed by expert designers is knowledge of how to design. Experts can look at a problem, decide how to analyze it, retrieve a very rough solution, and then focus on the parts of the solution that have to be worked out in more detail. These are the unknown parts that can affect the structure of the whole system, so they are examined in more detail than the known and therefore simple parts that can be coded by a retrieved solution or schema. Experts know that the constraints in a solution flow backward from the goals of the problem, and often design backward from the goals to the plans to the inputs, or outward from the central idea to both the input and the output. They make at least two passes over the system during design, a first pass to work out what the overall solution will look like, and a second pass to code the system.

The key task of a novice programmer is to build up knowledge of how the language works, use this knowledge to build small parts of the solution, then tie these parts together to make a complete system. There are two tricks or heuristics that are invaluable to the novice. The first heuristic is to build a small and simple part of the solution at a time, and to ensure that the simple part works before you make it more complicated. If you have a complex solution, then break it down into parts, check that each part works in isolation, then check that they work together. If you have a problem, write a small piece of code to test your ideas; indeed, write as small a piece of code as possible in order to test the part of the solution that doesn't work. Ignore the complete solution, and write a code fragment that tests the single problematic part. The skill of decomposing a large task into small pieces is essential for building large systems.

PROCESS PRINCIPLE 1: Decompose: solve a small part of the solution first.

The second heuristic is to evaluate your solution. Never accept your first solution. The typical behavior of a novice is to write code that works (produces the output), and then to stop with this first attempt. This behavior has two consequences. First, your solution will probably be bad stylistically, hard to understand, and hard to modify and reuse; this is what happened when cars were first invented and their controls were designed. Any code you write should be designed for the next person to use it, not for you to write and forget. Seeing the world through someone else's eyes is hard — children cannot do it, and some people never master it — but this ability really separates the expert from the novice. A good solution is designed for someone else to use. It is the result of many iterations or repetitions, each version improving on the last. If you don't bother to evaluate and improve your code, then you will not learn from your mistakes, and you will never become a good programmer.

> **PROCESS PRINCIPLE 2:** Iterate: evaluate your solution, then improve it.

The process of design can be described as a series of move-testing experiments (Schön, 1983), in which you make a move and then see the consequences of the move. Sometimes the consequences of a move are good, the solution is adequate, and the process of design then stops. Sometimes the move leads to unfortunate consequences and creates a bad design. An expert can string a long series of moves together and evaluate each solution mentally, picking and choosing alternate solutions until the final solution is considered to be good. A novice often has trouble seeing that there are any choices at all, that there are alternate ways to design a solution. The novice design strategy can be called "grab and run" design, in which the first idea to appear is grabbed and used without further thought. To change yourself from a novice to an expert you must become aware, first that there are choices to be made during design, and second that each choice has consequences for other parts of the system.

3.2   Design strategies

Three types of design are discussed in this chapter: top-down, bottom-up, and OO design. These are based on the three main types of computing, called procedural, functional, and OO programming. The basic idea behind all three strategies is to break the problem into pieces, and solve each piece in relative isolation. The three methods differ in how they decompose the task into pieces or chunks, based on order, plan, and object respectively. Each strategy is reflected in the order in which parts of the solution are designed and added to the growing system.

A program is a plan to achieve the goals or requirements defined in the problem specification. A plan is a set of actions which, when executed in the right order, achieve the goal of the plan. When I get up in the morning, I have the goal of getting ready for work. This abstract goal breaks down into three more specific goals: to eat breakfast, have a shower, and get dressed. I have a well-developed plan for each of these goals, because I have been achieving these goals for several decades now.

The traditional way to design a procedural program is by top-down design using a top-down structure chart, in which a single abstract goal is listed at the top of the chart; this is broken down or decomposed into more specific goals, and so on until the bottom level of the chart corresponds to basic actions that are implemented as code. The chart is developed from the top, down. In a structure chart, each label corresponds to the name of a routine, and a routine calls one or more other routines; the detailed code at the bottom level is not shown in the chart. A routine call is shown by an arrow from the caller to the called routine, and calling order is indicated by the left to right order within each level of the chart. Data flow is not shown explicitly in the chart, but it is implicit in the left to right order; a routine uses data produced by another routine somewhere before it in the system. Because the chart explicitly shows the order in which events occur, it provides a procedural view of the system, and a routine is usually a procedure.

A partial structure chart for the task of getting ready for work in the morning is shown below. A procedural calling or structure chart explicitly shows the control flow in a system, by showing the order in which routines are called. Often, however, there is no necessary, single order in which the events have to happen. I have to shower before I get dressed, but I can eat breakfast before I shower, between showering and dressing, or after dressing. I have to pick some order of the actions, of course, but I have great freedom in choosing this order. I have chosen an order that works for me, based on my particular situation; someone else may choose another order for the events.

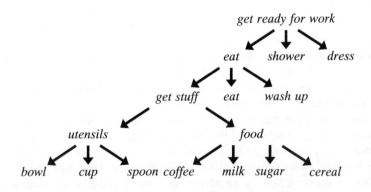

In the chart shown above, one step is to get the utensils I need, and the next step is to get the food, but I could equally well have chosen to get the food first, then the utensils. Alternately, I could get the utensils and food I need to make coffee as a single chunk or routine, then get the utensils and food I need to make my cereal. The exact order chosen for these actions basically depends on the layout of my kitchen, and the ease with which I can do the actions first thing in the morning, while I am still half asleep. This detailed reasoning is not shown in the chart, only the final order of the events.

In a strict top-down approach, we have to choose a specific order of events at each level, before we know what the detailed links are between the actions. This is known as premature commitment, because we commit to a specific order or structure before we really have any basis for choosing that order. If the order turns out to be wrong, then the detailed actions cannot be executed in the predicted order, and we have to patch the solution or work out a new order. Dividing a task into progressively smaller pieces is the great advantage of top-down design, because it provides an overview of the system, and then allows you to concentrate on one small part of the task at a time. Premature commitment is the great disadvantage in top-down design, because you are forced to make decisions about structure and order before you have any informed basis for the choice. If the task is easy or familiar, then the right order can be easily predicted; if the task is new or difficult, we have to guess the order and hope that our guess turns out to be right.

A bottom-up approach to design does the initial planning at the level of detailed actions, often at the level of lines of code. At this detailed level, design may occur forward from the inputs to the outputs; this is based on the order of actions, so it is concrete, procedural design, and is the typical novice strategy. Detailed design may also start with the goal, in which case the plan is designed by working backward from the goal, through the plan actions, at the code level. This design strategy is based on working out one plan at a time, so it is concrete, functional design. Whatever strategy is used, the end product is a detailed plan that must then be divided into parts, each part enclosed in a routine, and each routine placed within the appropriate class.

Functional or plan-based design is defined by taking each goal (eat, shower, dress) in isolation, working out a plan for each goal, and then deciding how to abstract and combine the plans to give a single order for the actions in the three plans. Each goal is broken down into sub-goals, and a plan for each sub-goal is defined with a minimal commitment to how the plans are to be combined and executed, so bottom-up design provides a least commitment approach.

A plan can be described by drawing a plan structure chart which shows how the actions in the plan depend on each other; pouring cereal into a bowl depends on having the cereal packet and the bowl, for example. A plan dependency chart is constructed by starting with the goal, and working backward from the goal, through the plan, to the initial inputs or the initial state. Each link in a dependency chart links a precondition to an action, because it defines what must be done before the action can be executed. In the breakfast example, the dependencies are defined by the state of the materials, so each plan produces an object that is in the desired state. In a computer system, the dependencies are mainly defined by the data flow in the system, so each plan produces a data value that is used by the next part of the plan, and each plan can be coded as a function. In a plan structure chart, the arrows point away from a goal to its prerequisites. If the arrows are turned around, then an arrow reflects the data flow in the system, from the inputs to the outputs or goals; this diagram is called a data flow chart.

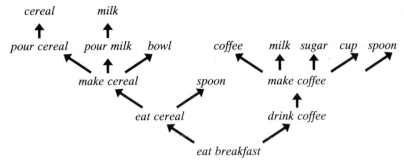

A partial dependency chart for eating breakfast is shown above. The single goal to eat breakfast breaks down into two goals, to eat my cereal and drink my coffee. To eat the cereal, I need to have the cereal and milk in a bowl, and a spoon in my hand. To make the cereal, I need to pour the cereal and the milk into the bowl, and before I can do this I need the cereal, milk, and bowl. The dependencies flow backward from the goal, as I discover what is needed to achieve the goal and add these actions to the plan. To achieve the goal of drinking the coffee, I need to make the coffee first. To make the coffee, I need to get the ingredients, the cup, and a spoon. A further step, not shown in the partial dependency chart, is to make the water hot; this requires a whole plan of its own, which fits into the top of the plan dependency structure shown.

The order of the actions is roughly defined by reading from the top of the chart, but there are many ways to order the actions while still obeying the essential dependencies. The chart shows that several ingredients are shared between the two plans, such as the spoon and the milk. When the plan is executed, the same object is used each time, and thus only need appear once in the structure chart. The common dependency can be shown by joining the arrows at each object, but that is a later step; first you work out what each plan needs in isolation, then you combine the plans and order the plan actions.

The third approach to system design is object-oriented design, in which the task is broken down into objects, and actions are defined on each object. The links between classes in an OO system are described by a client chart and an inheritance chart, and in more detail by a system structure chart. A class is described in isolation by listing its features; the usual convention is to list a set of attributes and a set of routines (Booch, 1994; Coad and Yourdon, 1990; Rumbaugh et al., 1991). Eiffel does not follow this practice, because it sees the behavior as primary, and the implementation by attributes and routines as secondary. A graphical class description for the two classes *CUP OF COFFEE* and *BOWL OF CEREAL* is shown below; *CUP* and *BOWL* are known as container classes.

CUP [COFFEE]	
coffee	milk
sugar	water
make	
carry	
drink	

BOWL [CEREAL]
cereal
milk
make
carry
eat

A description of each class in isolation does not show how the classes are used when the system is executed; this is provided by a system structure chart, shown below. In that chart, a cup of coffee is made first and then a bowl of cereal, the coffee is drunk and then the cereal is eaten; a system could be built in which these actions are divided into smaller chunks and interleaved, but that amount of detail is not needed here.

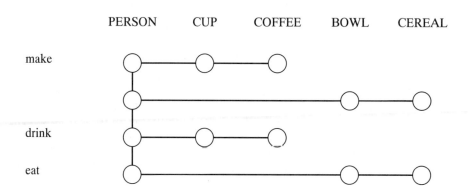

An object-based approach tries to design and code a complete class at a time. A class is chosen as the focus for design, and the designer chooses the attributes for that class and adds the routines that use these attributes. The routines define how the class is used, and thus define the plans in which the class can take part. Before we can design and code the class, we need to know what behavior is required; this behavior is defined by tracing out the plans for that class. Before a complete class can be coded, the behavior of the whole system may have to be worked out. In an OO system, a single goal can be chosen as the focus for design, and the code defined in each of the required classes for that single goal; this is a plan-based approach to OO design, and is the main strategy used in this book. For this example, a pure bottom-up OO design would code first the *CEREAL* class, then the *BOWL* class, then *COFFEE*, *CUP*, and *PERSON*; a top-down OO design would define the classes in client order, from left to right of the chart.

Each design strategy concentrates on a different aspect of the final solution, so each perspective groups or chunks the problem in a different way. A strategy based on the order of the actions is a procedural design, so a chunk is a procedure. A strategy based on the plan dependencies defines plan-based or functional design, so a chunk is a function in a functional language, or a plan in other languages. A design strategy based on the object defines OO design, so a chunk is a class that encapsulates both data and actions. These three views or aspects of a solution are combined and integrated in the final system code: the plan actions are placed in a set of routines in a set of objects, then executed in the defined order.

It is unusual for design to follow just one strategy, however, because a single move in design can have implications for the plan, the procedural, or the object structure of a system. Each move or step in design creates its own consequences, and insights are discovered, applied, and explored wherever they occur.

3.3   Problem specification

The rest of this chapter applies each of the three design methods to a simple problem. Top-down procedural design is presented first, then bottom-up plan design, and finally bottom-up OO design. The general design principles given in the previous chapters are applied to this specific problem, to illustrate how they are used during design. Each strategy provides a framework for design, but we will deviate from the strategy whenever a new insight has to be explored. To allow the design methods to be easily compared, a system structure chart is used to show the order in which parts of the solution are designed for each method. Only a very basic and simple solution is presented here, because the example is intended to show the process of design, without the complexity seen in real problems.

The problem specification is:

> Build a simple interactive graphics system. A single triangle is created first by the system, then the triangle is moved and its area and perimeter displayed under the control of the user. The system reads a series of menu choices from the user and executes each choice, until the user says to exit the system.

3.4   Goals, plans, and objects

The first task in converting a problem specification to a solution system is to identify the objects and goals in the system. The obvious object, and thus class, is the class *TRIANGLE*. The single triangle object is controlled by menu choices, so a separate client class is needed to control the triangle, class *MENU*. A triangle is created, then moved and its area and perimeter are calculated. This first attempt at design has identified two classes and five goals (make, move, display, area, perimeter); other classes and other goals may be needed in the system.

The system structure chart at this point in time is shown below; a circle at the left edge of the chart indicates a feature call, and the other circles indicate feature definitions in the class, usually routine definitions. Selection or choice is indicated by a double circle; the triangle has to be created, but the next operation is selected from the menu by the user.

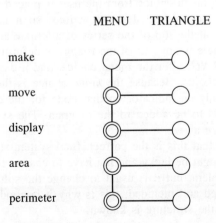

MENU   TRIANGLE

make

move

display

area

perimeter

This chart provides an object to think with; it captures the structure of the system and is easily translated into Eiffel code, but is much easier to change than the code. Given the initial design, the data flow can now be added to each node, to flesh out the initial solution structure. The basic rule used to decide where to place the code is that the code lives with the data.

When the triangle is created, the initial location has to be input; this is done in class *TRIANGLE*. When the triangle is moved, the displacement has to be read in; this is done in class *MENU*, and the data is passed to the triangle. Displaying the triangle requires an output; this is done by the *TRIANGLE* code. Showing the area and perimeter also require outputs, and these will also be done in class *TRIANGLE*. Each of the nodes either reads data from the user, outputs data to the user, or changes the value of an attribute, so they are all procedures. Since most of the data is in class *TRIANGLE*, most of the code is placed there.

MENU   TRIANGLE

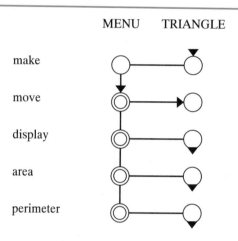

make

move

display

area

perimeter

The code to read a menu choice from the user is placed in class *MENU*. The user command selects one of the alternate actions, so it is read in before the selection and is shown at the top of the series of alternate actions. The displacement to move the triangle is not part of the triangle's definition, so it is also read in by code in class *MENU*, after the menu choice, and a data flow indicator has to be shown for that choice. Because the *move* choice is the first choice listed, however, there is already an indicator on that node for the command choice, so no new indicator needs to be added to the diagram. The system structure chart with data flow is shown above.

No claim is made that this is the correct, final system structure; it is simply the first attempt. We might be lucky and not have to change the solution structure as we explore the problem, but it is usual to change the solution as more of the constraints are identified and included; this is why it is good to design first, and only write code when the structure is known.

3.5   Top-down design

Top-down design starts by working out the sequence of events that happen in the system at a very high or abstract level, and then refine or expand each of these abstract routines. The main order of events in the system is to first create the triangle, then manipulate it through the menu until the system exits. There is a single creation call, followed by a loop around the menu choices; the loop exits when the user decides to exit the system.

This analysis reveals an important point: the triangle is created before the menu is entered. The menu thus does not create the triangle; it exists already, when the menu starts up. Another class is therefore required to create the triangle, and then call the menu; this new class will be the root class for the system; we will call it class *GRAPHIC*. The analysis also shows that an extra goal is needed, as well as the main five goals, to exit the system; this is part of the menu processing. The system structure chart at this point in the development of the solution is shown below.

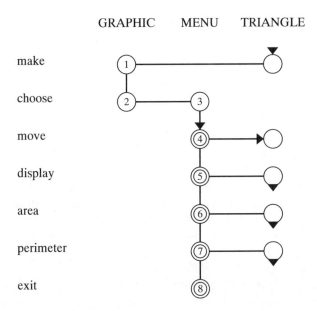

Class *GRAPHIC* creates a triangle, then creates the menu. Class *MENU* gets choices from the user until the user enters a command to exit; for each choice except the exit choice, it calls the required routine. Class *TRIANGLE* contains the basic data and routines. The system now appears to be complete from our perspective of top-down design. The abstract structure of the solution has been designed based on the main control flow in the system, and the nodes have been defined with no internal detail. The order in which we added the nodes to the system using top-down design is shown by the numbers in the nodes of the system structure chart.

We will show the code first for class *GRAPHIC*, then for class *MENU*, and leave the code for class *TRIANGLE* until later. The root class has to create the triangle, then create the menu. The menu will then operate until the system exits. Because the triangle is created in the *GRAPHIC* class and used in the menu, the object has to be passed as an argument from the *GRAPHIC* class to the menu, so that it can be used there.

The complete Eiffel code for the root class of this system is shown below. Because this is the root class, the export policy does not matter, so we have chosen to export all the features. A root class has no clients to worry about, because it is called directly by the computer when the system is executed.

```
class GRAPHIC
creation
    make
feature
    tri: TRIANGLE
    menu: MENU
    make is
            -- create the triangle
            -- create the menu, pass the triangle as an argument
        do
            !!tri.make
            !!menu.make (tri)
        end -- make
end -- class GRAPHIC
```

The behavior of the menu class has now been described, but little has been said about its implementation. There are many kinds of menu system, ranging from single character commands to point and click graphical interfaces. For simplicity, we use a simple character interface, in which the menu commands and actions are

'm'	move the triangle
'd'	display the position of the triangle
'a'	display the area of the triangle
'p'	display the perimeter of the triangle
'q'	quit or exit the system

The heart or focus of the menu system is the code that gets and executes a user choice. The code to get a choice from the user simply prompts for, and reads in, a single character. The code that executes this choice examines the input, and calls the appropriate routine in class *TRIANGLE* to execute the choice. When the choice is to move the triangle, a displacement also has to be read in, before the triangle is moved. The code to read and execute choices is repeated inside a loop, until the user says to quit the system.

A character is read from the user each time through the loop in the *get_choice* routine; this routine must be a procedure, because it is an input routine and thus changes the state of the screen and the system buffers. The *do_choice* routine is also a procedure, because it changes the position of the triangle or the state of the screen. The routine uses an **inspect** statement, which inspects the value of a variable and executes code, depending on the value of that variable. The *exit* routine returns a Boolean value (**true** or **false**) and changes nothing, so it is a function. The routines communicate through a variable in the system buffer that stores the user input, called *io.lastchar*. When Eiffel reads a character using the command *io.readchar*, the character is stored in the feature *io.lastchar*, so this system variable contains the last character read from the screen. The two-step process maintains the strong distinction between commands and queries in Eiffel: a command is issued to get a character from the screen, then a query is issued to find the value of this character.

One possible solution for class *MENU* is shown below. The creation routine receives a triangle from its client, and stores the triangle in the object. It then contains a loop to get and execute user choices, until the user quits the system. These actions define the high-level behavior of the class, and the details are contained and thus hidden in the *MENU* routines *make*, *get_choice*, *do_choice*, and *exit*.

```
class MENU
creation
    make
feature {NONE}
    tri: TRIANGLE
feature {GRAPHIC}
    make (triune: TRIANGLE) is
                -- store the argument in a class attribute
                -- get and execute menu choices until exit
        do
            tri := triune
            from
            until exit
            loop
                get_choice
                do_choice
            end -- loop
    end -- make

feature {NONE}
    get_choice is
                -- read a single character from the user
```

```
        do
                io.putstring ("Please enter your choice of m, d, a, p, or q: ")
                io.readchar
        end -- get_choice
  do_choice is
                -- execute the user choice
        do
                inspect io.lastchar
                    when 'm' then tri.move
                    when 'd' then tri.display
                    when 'a' then tri.show_area
                    when 'p' then tri.show_perimeter
                end -- inspect
        end -- do_choice
  exit: BOOLEAN is
                -- did the user input the quit command?
        do
                Result := io.lastchar = 'q'
        end
  end -- class MENU
```

The triangle object is created by the *GRAPHIC* class, and passed as an argument to the menu creation routine, which stores a pointer or reference to the object. The class *MENU* has a single exported feature, the creation routine. The creation routine calls three other routines in the class; these are only called from inside the class, so they are not exported. The *MENU* class calls four routines in the class *TRIANGLE*, so these four routines have to be exported by that class.

3.6   Plan-based design

Plan-based design uses the goal and its plan as the basic unit of design. Design starts by choosing a single system goal, and traces out the code that is needed to achieve this goal; the code defines a plan for achieving the goal. When the plan for the first goal has been designed, a new goal is chosen and the process repeats until all the system goals have been achieved, and the system has been designed and coded.

We have chosen the goal of moving a triangle as the first goal to begin design, so we will now develop all the code needed to move a triangle. A more intuitive place to start plan design would be to choose the goal to create a triangle, but we want to include some code in the menu; as we can now see, triangle creation does not use any code in the class *MENU*.

We have chosen a bottom-up, plan-based approach for the design of the plan for this goal. A bottom-up approach starts with the most basic, detailed code that is the heart or focus of the plan. The goal is to move a triangle. Before we can decide on a plan for this, we need to know how the triangle is represented or stored by the computer. There are many ways to represent a triangle. One way is to store the triangle as three points, so we need to store six real numbers, three x-coordinates and three y-coordinates. Another method is to store an angle and two sides, two angles and a side, or three sides. In an OO system, the exact way we choose to represent a triangle is hidden from the client, and only the behavior is exported: in bottom-up design, however, we start at this detailed level. We choose to store the triangle by storing the location of each vertex, so we need to store three sets of x and y coordinates.

We have made a design choice in the previous paragraph. We chose a Cartesian coordinate system based on x and y coordinates. A vertex could also be stored in polar coordinates as an angle and a distance from the origin, rather than in the Cartesian coordinate system chosen. Fortunately, this choice has few consequences because we will hide the representation and export the behavior, so the exact representation is a detail internal to the class.

The basic operation to move a triangle is to move each of its vertices by the given distance. The distance to move a vertex will thus be given as x and y (Cartesian) distances, called *delta_x* and *delta_y*. The basic, focal code to move a single vertex is thus

```
x := x + delta_x
y := y + delta_y
```

We need to read in these two distances from the user, and the user has to choose the move option from the menu by entering the character 'm'. We can now write the code for this plan: select move, get the distances, and move the three vertices. We designed the plan by bottom-up and backward design (first move, then get distances, then choose option); once the plan has been designed, the actions in the plan (the code) are executed in forward order.

The code that defines a complete plan for moving a triangle is shown below. The code reads in a menu choice from the user, tests that it is a move command, reads in the distance to move the triangle, and then moves the triangle by adding the distances to each vertex. Two *REAL* variables are used to store the displacements, and six *REAL* variables are used to store the three vertices, $x1$, $x2$, and $x3$ and $y1$, $y2$, and $y3$. The complete, detailed Eiffel code for the plan is

```
io.putstring ("Please enter your choice of m, d, a, p, or q: ")
io.readchar
if io.lastchar= 'm' then
    io.putstring ("Enter x distance to move: ")
    io.readreal
    delta_x := io.lastreal
    io.putstring ("Enter y distance to move: ")
```

```
    io.readreal
    delta_y := io.lastreal
    x1 := x1 + delta_x
    x2 := x2 + delta_x
    x3 := x3 + delta_x
    y1 := y1 + delta_y
    y2 := y2 + delta_y
    y3 := y3 + delta_y
end
```

This is a complete plan, but it is not a good OO solution, even though it is written in Eiffel code. The plan is a single chunk of code, but we know that a plan can include or use many objects. To convert this plan into reusable, OO code, the code has to be divided into a set of routines, and the routines placed in the appropriate class.

The representation chosen for the triangle was six *REAL* values, to store the locations of the points at the three vertices. Looking at the previous sentence, we can see that another object has been used in design, but does not appear in the solution: a *POINT*. A *POINT* consists of two *REAL* numbers, which denote x and y coordinates. A triangle is moved by moving each of the three points in the triangle.

The partial system structure chart for the goals of moving a triangle is shown below, so it is clear that the plan extends over four classes; there is code in each class to implement the plan. The nodes that define the plan to create a triangle are also shown in the chart. The order in which code was developed by bottom-up design of each plan is indicated by the numbers on the chart. First the goal to move a triangle was chosen, its plan was designed, and then the plan was converted into routines in a set of classes. The goal to create a triangle was then chosen and the actions in that plan were abstracted to define two routines, placed in two classes.

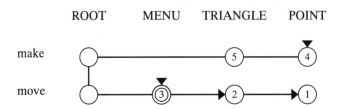

The code in the plan has been divided into a set of routines which are strung together like beads on a string. The complete plan consists of the code in each of the nodes, which are connected by horizontal lines. All the code in the plan has to exist somewhere, but a designer has great discretion about where to place a particular line of code. The correct location of the code is the main design decision in an OO system, because it defines the signature of each routine and thus the behavior of the class.

PROCESS PRINCIPLE 3: Abstract the code to define routines in classes.

There are many OO, Eiffel, and general design principles that suggest how a series of concrete actions should be abstracted into a series of routines, but there is one general principle that is very strong and useful: push the code to the right of the chart. In this example, the code to move a triangle was pushed out of class *TRIANGLE* and into class *POINT*, resulting in a better, more reusable system. The typical novice error in design is to write the code where the programmer first discovered the need for it, instead of making a conscious, explicit decision about where to place the code. If the code shown above was implemented as a single chunk, it would be placed in the class *GRAPHIC* instead of distributed among the three objects it uses. If you use a concrete, plan-based approach, then the first step is to work out the actions you need in the plan; the second step is to decide where and how to place the actions in each class.

PROCESS PRINCIPLE 4: Push the code as far right as is reasonable (client).

The general idea is to let each object do its own work, so each object contains the code that changes or uses the attributes of that object. This may require defining a new object, and then placing the code in the new class. An attribute can only be changed by code within its class, so there is no choice here. Code which uses an attribute value, without changing it, can be placed in the same class or in a client, or even further away in a client of a client. As a rule of thumb, it is reasonable to push the code to the right in a client chart, but in rare cases this rule can lead to a worse, more complex design that repeats code; this is why we use the word "reasonable" instead of "possible".

The corresponding guideline for inheritance is to place the code as far up the inheritance hierarchy as is reasonable. This rule was illustrated in the design of the savings and check accounts, by defining a general class *ACCOUNT* and two specific types of account, *SAVINGS* and *CHECK*. The rule can be stated very simply: push the code as far up the hierarchy as is reasonable. Again, strict adherence to this rule can lead to a solution that is more complex than necessary, so the guideline cannot be followed blindly; it is a useful guide, not an iron-clad rule.

PROCESS PRINCIPLE 5: Push the code as high as is reasonable (inheritance).

The foundation of reuse in general, and of Eiffel in particular, is to define a piece of code once, and place that code where it can be used by whoever needs it, without change. A plan is separated into parts, and each part is placed in a class. The major portion of your time in system design should be spent in deciding where to place the attributes and routines, both in the client and in the inheritance structure of your system.

3.7   Object-oriented design

The class *POINT* was discovered during the analysis of the plan to move a triangle, so we need to examine the other goals to see if they, too, use the class *POINT*. The focus of attention now is on an object of type *POINT*, so the goals and plans in which a point is used have to be examined. The process of searching from an object to the plans that use it defines pure OO design; a single class at a time is designed and added to the system.

Three points have to be created to create a triangle. To display the position of the triangle, the three points are displayed. The plans to display the area and the perimeter may, or may not, require code in class *POINT*. Two solutions are reasonable, because we can store each value or calculate it as needed; it is unclear which choice is better at this point in design. If we calculate the area and length of the perimeter when the triangle is made and store these as attributes of the triangle, then the values are stored in each triangle and both plans stop at class *TRIANGLE*. If, on the other hand, we choose to calculate the area and perimeter as needed, using the location of the three points to give the distance of the sides, then we need to use the three points in the calculations. We have chosen the second solution, so the class *POINT* is used in the plan for every goal in the system.

Pure OO design takes a single class, and designs it in isolation by defining the signature of all its exported behaviors. Many of these behaviors are obvious from the specification, but it should now be clear that defining the complete behavior of a class depends on knowing all the plans in which that class participates. Often, this requires a complete analysis of the system.

A bottom-up OO design approach selects the most basic object, and designs that class first. In this example, the most basic class is the class *POINT*. A point has to be created, moved, and displayed when a triangle is created, moved, and displayed (actually, three points have to be created, moved, and displayed for each triangle). To calculate the values of the area and perimeter, the distance between two points has to be calculated, so an additional feature is required in class *POINT* to find the *distance* between one point and another. This function takes a target point as an argument, finds the distance between the target and the current point, and returns the distance.

The system structure chart for the complete graphics system is shown on the next page. The order in which nodes of the system structure were designed and coded in a bottom-up, OO approach is indicated by the numbers in the nodes.

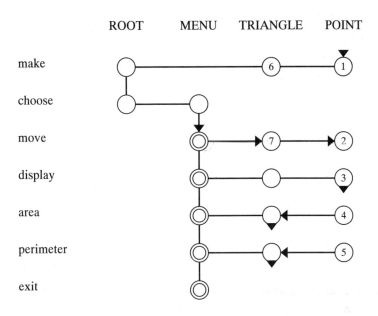

The complete code for the class *POINT* is shown below. Most of the code is fairly clear and uses knowledge that has been presented already, but two parts need to be explained. First, the *POINT* class inherits class *SINGLE_MATH*, a class supplied in the standard ISE Eiffel library. *SINGLE_MATH* provides a host of mathematical functions that use single-precision real values; there is a corresponding class, *DOUBLE_MATH*, in the library that provides double the precision. The function *distance* in class *POINT* takes a single argument that is a point, and returns the distance between that point and the current object. The routine uses the *sqrt* function from class *SINGLE_MATH* to calculate this distance; the distance is needed to calculate the area and perimeter of the triangle. Because the class is inherited, the feature *sqrt* is called just as though it was coded in the child class.

The second point to note in the code is that the *x* and *y* values are exported to class *POINT*, and thus are not completely hidden. These two values are used to calculate the distance, because the current point needs to know the location of the point passed as an argument. The export clause formally applies to objects, so *x* and *y* have to be exported from the target object to the current object. Even though both objects have the same type or class, they are different objects. The rule of thumb is to hide the representation, but there are times (such as this one) when there is no choice; an attribute has to be exported. The design guideline is to hide the representation unless there are compelling reasons to export it.

```
class POINT
inherit
    SINGLE_MATH
creation {TRIANGLE}
```

```
        make
feature {POINT}
    x, y: REAL
feature {TRIANGLE}
    make (x_init, y_init: REAL) is
            -- store the initial coordinate values
        do
            x := x_init
            y := y_init
        end -- make
    move (delta_x, delta_y: REAL) is
            -- move the point by delta_x horizontally, by delta_y vertically
        do
            x := x + delta_x
            y := y + delta_y
        end -- move
    display is
            -- display the location
        do
            io.putchar ('(')
            io.putreal (x)
            io.putstring (", ")
            io.putreal (y)
            io.putchar (')')
        end -- display
    distance (target: POINT): REAL is
            -- distance of the current point from the target
        do
            Result := sqrt ((x - target.x)^2 + (y - target.y)^2)
        end -- distance
end -- class POINT
```

The attributes, creation routine, and the move routine in class *TRIANGLE* are

```
class TRIANGLE
creation
    make
feature {NONE}
    top, left, right: POINT
feature {GRAPHIC}
```

```
      make is
              -- create the triangle
          do
              !!top.make
              !!left.make
              !!right.make
          end -- make
feature {MENU}
      move is
              -- get two displacements from the user, and move the triangle
          local delta_x, delta_y: REAL
          do
              io.putstring ("Enter x distance to move: ")
              io.readreal
              delta_x := io.lastreal
              io.putstring ("Enter y distance to move: ")
              io.readreal
              delta_y := io.lastreal
              top.move (delta_x, delta_y)
              left.move (delta_x, delta_y)
              right.move (delta_x, delta_y)
          end -- move
      . . .
end -- class TRIANGLE
```

The only part of the complete system that has not been coded at this point is the routines in class *TRIANGLE* to display the position of the triangle, and the area and perimeter of the triangle. The *display* routine simply consists of three calls to display each point. The *perimeter* is found by adding the distance between each pair of points on the perimeter, and outputting the result. The *area* calculation is complex mathematically, because it has to derive the height of the triangle from the three vertices. The construction of these routines is left as an exercise.

3.8   Design versus execution

This chapter has demonstrated the difference between the process of designing a system, and the process of running or executing the final solution. The code in a system defines an algorithm which, when the actions of the algorithm are executed in the defined order, guarantees to produce the desired result. These actions do not have to be designed in the order in which they are executed. Novices tend to develop detailed code forward from the inputs, but experts know there are better ways to design, based on the focus of the solution and its plan structure. Experts use their knowledge of abstract solutions and the design process to separate design from execution.

Top-down design works out the abstract steps, from the first to the last, then refines each step to show more detail; a step roughly corresponds to a routine. Bottom-up design starts with a detailed, concrete piece of code which defines the focus for the algorithm, and adds code backward from the focus to support it and to ensure that it is executed correctly. With bottom-up design, there is no abstract structure, so the code has to be abstracted, placed in routines, and the routines placed in classes.

Procedural design is based on the order in which events occur in the system, and works forward from the first action to the last. In this approach, code often has to be rewritten as the plans and goals are discovered, explored, and evaluated. Functional design is based on plan dependencies, so it often works by starting with the most basic focus of the plan, and adding code backward from the goal or focus to support that code and to ensure that it works correctly. Object-oriented design is based on the classes in the system, and tries to define a single class at a time. A plan defines a horizontal slice of a system structure chart, and a class is a vertical slice of the chart. By searching outward from a class to discover how the class is used, the designer explores the plans for each object, and can then define the behavior of the class.

Because the code in an OO system is distributed among many classes, each class can be developed in relative isolation, so there is no need to design from the first executable instruction to the last. A top-down approach can be taken to design, but this approach forces you to make decisions about the structure of a system very early in the design process, before you have explored the problem. A bottom-up approach is a least commitment approach to design, because it allows you to define the pieces you need with little commitment about how those pieces will be connected in the final solution. You can define a routine in a class, and then later decide when that routine should be called.

3.9   Design versus coding

Design is an iterative process. An initial solution structure serves as a basis for design, but it is usually changed as the problem is explored and the problem constraints are discovered. For this reason, it is better to use a two-pass strategy in design, the first pass to explore the problem and design the solution structure, then a second pass to code and test the solution. Structure charts provide an invaluable tool for writing down the form of a solution, without writing detailed code; nodes on a chart can be defined and moved much more easily than Eiffel code. Once the system structure has been defined, the data flow for each node can be defined on that structure. The data flow from one node to another defines the signature of each node, as well as the arguments that are passed to and returned from each feature. The arguments and the feature name define a feature header, so the code can then be written for the full system.

The classic design strategy of a novice programmer is forward, detailed design with instant coding. There is no previous design phase, so the code is written from the first instruction to the last in a single pass, then the whole system is compiled and executed. This strategy is caused by a lack of abstractions; novices see the system as code, rather than as a set of routines and classes. It is a losing strategy. Most coding problems are actually design problems that are found for the first time when code is written. If there is no design stage, then all the problems are found while coding.

A powerful strategy for system development is to code and test a small part of the system at a time, to ensure that part of the system works before the next part is added. This approach is known as stepwise development, because code development occurs in small steps. The opposite approach is to design and code the whole system before running any of it. When the whole system is finally run, the result is often a mess that doesn't work, and you have no idea where the error lies; this is particularly true when you are learning the language at the same time as you are designing the system. Stepwise development helps you find the place where an error can occur: any error must lie in the code you just added to the system. This is a very simple tool, but it saves an immense amount of time and effort during system development.

> **PROCESS PRINCIPLE 6:** Code and test part of the system at a time.

The key to stepwise development is choosing a small part of the system that can be designed, coded, and executed in isolation. This part can be a complete if small class, the plan for a single goal, or the abstract structure of the solution with no internal details. Because an OO system works by connecting small pieces, and supports a least commitment or bottom-up approach to design, it is easy to do stepwise development in Eiffel.

3.10   Design framework

System structure provides an overall blueprint for an Eiffel solution which is easily developed and changed during design, and easily converted to Eiffel code when the design is complete. To build the system structure, the designer must be able to specify the classes in the system, their attributes, and the goals and plans in the system. A decision must then be made about the location of the code in each plan.

Design can be top-down, where an initial abstract idea is gradually made more concrete. Design can be bottom-up, where a detailed plan is developed and must then be abstracted into routines, and the routines placed in classes. Design can be based on the order in which events happen, in which case the solution is developed from the first to the last action. Design can be based on the plan dependencies and data flow in the system, in which case a single goal at a time is selected and its plan derived. Finally, design can be based on the objects in the system, in which case a single object at a time is explored and developed. An individual usually adopts one of these strategies to provide a global framework for design, and deviates from this strategy as opportunities arise to explore the problem.

Four questions are given below that allow a designer to map out the system structure and define the behavior of each node in that structure. These questions must be answered when a solution is designed, but the exact order in which the questions are asked, and pieces of the system appear, is determined by the individual's design strategy.

1. What are the objects?
    Objects are designed around their data; an object name is a noun. Attributes store the data in an object; an attribute name is a noun. A real object has many attributes, only some of which are relevant to the goals of the system. Some attributes that are obvious from general knowledge may be defined at this point.
2. What are the goals?
    Object behavior is defined by the plans in which an object is used; a goal is a verb.
3. What are the plans?
    A plan is a set of actions which, when executed in the right order, achieve the goal of the plan. A plan may require additional attributes to be stored in each object, depending on what is done in the plan. The actions in the plan use data, so both routines and attributes are implicit in the plan and can be identified at this stage.
4. What is the behavior of each node in the system?
    A system structure chart shows the objects that are used in the plan for each goal. The behavior of a node is defined by its data flow. A node can use data read in from the user, passed as an argument, or stored in the object. Only the first two types of data flow are shown on a system structure chart.

These questions provide the basic information that is used in the design of an OO system. The behavior of each feature in each class is the result of applying the many design principles to this basic, essential information. The exact structure of the final system depends on the choices made by the designer during the process of design.

Summary

- Novice programmers use forward, concrete design with few abstractions.
- Expert programmers know abstract solutions, and they know how to design.
- Top-down design is abstract to concrete; bottom-up design is concrete to abstract.
- Procedural design is based on the order of actions in a system, functional design is based on the data flow, and OO design is based on the class. Each basis provides a different way of viewing the complex artifact that is the system.
- Expert procedural designers use top-down (abstract to concrete) or focal (key or most basic code to details) design.
- Experts use a two-pass development strategy. First, they design the system using charts. When the design is complete, they code a piece of the solution and test it.

- There are many ways to design a system, many variants within a single approach, and many possible solutions that can be evaluated and improved. Design is iterative.
- Design the complete system before you code any of it, if possible. Write code in small chunks and test each part as you add it.

Exercises

1. For the task of making coffee, (a) list the ingredients needed, (b) list the actions needed, and (c) draw the dependencies between the actions in the task. How many orders can you find for executing these actions?
2. Draw a top-down structure chart for the task of withdrawing money from an ATM (automatic teller machine). The bottom level of the chart should be the basic actions, such as putting in the card, entering the password, and so on.
3. For the task of withdrawing money from an ATM, draw the data dependencies between the actions. How many orders are possible for executing the basic actions?
4. Consider the goal of making your favorite sandwich. How do you do this? List the actions in the plan that you follow.
   (a) Identify the abstractions; build a procedural structure chart.
   (b) Identify the dependencies between the actions; build a dependency diagram.
   (c) Identify the objects used, and the way that you use them; draw a system structure chart.
   (d) Identify the signature for each object; show the attributes and operations for each class.
5. What is a goal? What is a plan? How do you build the system structure? What does the system structure show?
6. How is the order of events shown in a system structure chart? How is a plan shown in a system structure chart? How is a class shown in a system structure chart?
7. What is the difference between a feature definition and its implementation?
8. How is the data flow in a system structure chart reflected in the feature headers?
9. For the triangle system, show where and how each principle — object-oriented, Eiffel, and design — was applied to build the final solution.
10. Write a data structure chart for the triangle system.
11. Define the behavior of each class in the triangle system by listing the signatures of the exported features.
12. Choose a design strategy and apply it to the following, very incomplete, specification. Where the specification does not provide the information you need, make any reasonable decisions and assumptions.

THE LIBRARY PROBLEM

"Write a simple library system. The library has books, journals, and magazines. Books and magazines can be borrowed, but not journals. Magazines and journals are published every month. A patron of the library can borrow up to three items.

All items are stored on a single list, which is indexed by the name of the item and its call number. A patron can examine the list by name, to see if the library holds that item. The list can also be examined by call number, to see if a copy is in the library at the moment, and thus can be borrowed."

PART B
The Eiffel language

CHAPTER 4

Data flow

Keywords

declaration
creation
input
output
assignment
expression
value
reference

This chapter presents the Eiffel syntax and mechanism for the topic of simple data flow: declaration, creation, input, output, and assignment. A declaration reserves storage for a variable and gives the variable an initial, default value. The creation routine is then called to give the class variables a useful value. The input commands get a value from the user, the output commands show a value to the user, and the assignment statement stores a value in a variable. The value of a variable may be a simple value that can be used immediately, or it may be a reference to an object. For two references, we must distinguish between the same reference value (point to the same object) and the same content value (different objects, same content); two copies of this book, for example, contain the same content but are not the same object.

4.1 Declaration

A variable declaration reserves storage in the computer's memory for a variable. It gives the variable a name, a type, and an initial value. A variable declaration may list one or more variables of the same type; multiple names are separated by commas. A variable declared as a feature of a class is called an attribute. An attribute value is stored persistently in an object, so one routine can store the value and another routine can later use the value. If a value is defined in the declaration, the variable is a constant, and the value cannot be later changed; a constant must be declared as an attribute.

A variable declared within a routine is called a local variable, because it is local to that routine. A local variable is created on entry to the routine, exists while the routine is being executed, and is deleted when the routine exits. A local variable may be declared using the local keyword, or it may be declared in the routine header as an argument to the routine. The area or region in which a variable can be used is called the scope of that variable. An exported attribute can be used in a client or in its own class, a hidden or private attribute can be used only within its class, while a local variable can be used only within its routine.

The four types of declaration are

variable attribute	*length: REAL*
constant attribute	*length: REAL* **is** *4.5*
local variable	**local** *length: REAL*
argument	*move (delta_x, delta_y: REAL) is*

A class, variable, or routine name in Eiffel is a sequence of one or more characters. The first character must be a letter ('a' to 'Z'), but the other characters may be letters, digits ('0' to '9'), or the underscore character ('_'). The convention in Eiffel is to create a compound name by linking simple names with an underscore, such as tax_rate, first_name, and top_score. Two variables in the same class may not have the same name, because the computer needs a unique name for each variable; this situation is known as a name clash. A variable may have the same name as a class. This is not a name clash, because there are not two variables with the same name: there is a single variable and a class with the same name. Eiffel has a set of reserved words, listed in Appendix B, that have a special meaning in the language and cannot be used as names.

The type of a variable is written after the name, separated from the name by a colon. All types in Eiffel correspond to a class, except for generic classes, so there are Eiffel classes for *INTEGER*, *REAL*, and so on. A generic class such as *ARRAY* can produce many specific types, such as *ARRAY [REAL]*, *ARRAY [INTEGER]*, or *ARRAY [CUSTOMER]*. By convention, class names are written in upper case in Eiffel. The simple or basic types of variable in Eiffel are *INTEGER*, *REAL*, *DOUBLE* (double precision real numbers), *CHARACTER*, and *BOOLEAN*. All other types are known as reference types, because the value is a reference or pointer to an object; most variables in an Eiffel system will be reference types.

Eiffel variables are given a default value when they are declared. Integer, real, and double precision variables are initialized to zero. Boolean variables can have the value **true** or **false**; their default value is **false**. Character variables are initialized to a space ('Δ'). Characters are written inside single quotes ('a', 'b'), while strings are written inside double quotes ("This is a string"). Reference variables are set to an initial value of *Void*, which means they refer to nothing, and the value is set to a reference to an object when the object is created.

Declaration	Default value	Example values
age: INTEGER	0	12, -94, 1066
cost, tax: REAL	0.0	12.89, -94.86, -0.00001
interest: DOUBLE	0.0	12345.678901234
in, found: BOOLEAN	false	true, false
reply: CHARACTER	'∆'	'a', '*', '?'
name, address: STRING	Void	"hi", "who?" "77 Sunset Strip"
triangle: TRIANGLE	Void	<reference>

A local variable is a variable declared within a routine, and can only be used inside that routine. A local variable is declared as a formal argument to a routine (discussed in the next chapter), or in a **local** declaration. A local variable may not have the same name as an attribute, because this creates a name clash. The declaration of a local variable has the same form as an attribute declaration, but it is listed in the argument list of a routine or preceded by the word **local** and declared before the routine code.

Attributes are persistent, so a value stored in an attribute persists as long as the object exists. A local variable only exists inside the routine where it is declared; when the routine exits, the variable disappears and the computer storage is reused. If a value is created, used, and then discarded, the value should be stored in a local variable, or returned by a function and used immediately. Attribute values define the state of an object, so they are used to store values that are used over a period of time. Local variables should be used whenever possible, in order to keep the number of attributes small.

A constant is declared by giving the name, type, and value in the attribute declaration. Local constants are not allowed in Eiffel; constants are considered to be part of the class definition, and thus have to be declared as attributes. Examples of constant declarations are

> *days_in_year: INTEGER* **is** *365*
> *tax: REAL* **is** *3.5*
> *found: BOOLEAN* **is true**
> *end_choice: CHARACTER* **is** *'q'*
> *name: STRING* **is** *"Anna Karenina"*

Unique constants represent a set of unique values. The series of names in the declaration are given a series of *INTEGER* values that are guaranteed to be unique and increasing, but whose exact value is unknown. They are used to represent enumerated types, when the set of possible values can be enumerated and no further detail is needed. The declaration has the form

> *Red, Orange, Yellow, Blue, Green, Indigo, Violet: INTEGER* **is unique**

Each name is a constant, so it can be assigned to an *INTEGER* variable, and that value can be tested, as in *if colour < Yellow then . . . .*

4.2   Creation

A variable has a name, a type, and a value. A simple or basic variable has a value that is immediately useful, such as a *REAL* number. The value of a reference variable is an address in memory, a pointer to the location of an object in memory. A reference variable is initialized to the special value *Void*, which is replaced by a pointer to the object when the object is created.

An object is created by calling its creation routine, preceded by the creation command *!!* (bang bang). When an object is created, a series of things happen. First, an area of memory for the new object is allocated by the operating system, then the attributes in the new object are set to their default values. The object's creation routine is then executed (if it exists), and finally a pointer to the allocated storage is attached to the name of the object. An object has to be declared before it can be created, so that Eiffel knows how much storage to allocate for an object of that type. Creating an object results in the following events:

1. *Allocate storage for the attributes of the object.* For the class *POINT*, there are two real-valued attributes, so enough storage for two *REAL* numbers is allocated.
2. *Set the attributes to their default values.* When attributes are created, they are set to a default value. *INTEGER, REAL,* and *DOUBLE* numbers are set to zero initially, a *CHARACTER* to the value space ('Δ'), a *BOOLEAN* to the value **false**, and a reference variable to *Void*.
3. *Run the creation routine if it exists.* The creation routine usually sets the attributes of the object to more specific values. In the *POINT* class, for example, the *make* routine sets the attributes to the initial location of the point, wherever that location might be.
4. *Set a pointer from the name to the storage.* Every attribute has a value. For the basic attributes (*INTEGER, REAL, CHARACTER, BOOLEAN*), this value is the stored value of that field. For objects, the value is a pointer to the allocated storage for that object.

A point located at position (3, 4) is shown below. The name of the object is *p*. It is of type *POINT*, so the value of the name is a reference to the area of main memory (shown here in hexadecimal notation) where the object's attributes are stored. At that location in memory, the allocated storage for the attributes can be found; here, two real values with names *x* and *y* and values 3.0 and 4.0.

Data in *TRIANGLE*   Data in *POINT*

name	type	value
p	*POINT*	A032F440

name	type	value
x	*REAL*	3.0
y	*REAL*	4.5

If the point *p* is moved, then the values of *x* and *y* may change, but the value of p will not change; it is still the same point, and the name still refers to the same piece of storage where the x and y values are stored (the hexadecimal memory address AO32F440 here). A different object of type *POINT* is allocated a different piece of storage, and can thus store different x and y values. The name of an object refers to a piece of storage, so its value is a reference or a pointer. The pointer is used to look up memory, and then get values to use. If you try to use a name that does not refer to anything (usually because you forgot to create it), then Eiffel flags an error for using a "Void reference". An object of a basic type need not be created. An object of a reference type has to be created or assigned a value; the class may or may not have a creation routine, however. The class *STRING* is a reference type, because a string is a complex object that contains a series of characters. A string is usually not explicitly created, however, because it is assigned a string value directly.

A class may have no, one, or many creation routines listed under the **creation** keyword; multiple creation routines are separated by commas. By convention, the single or main creation routine is called *make* in Eiffel, and the routine can have any number of arguments. The creation routine for the root class usually has no arguments, but may have a single argument of type *STRING*. A creation clause has an export policy, just like any other feature of the class, so only the listed clients can create an object of that type. An object is created by calling the creation routine for the class, preceded by *!!* (bang bang), such as *!!point.make*; if there is no *make* routine, then the object is simply created by writing *!!point*, and the attributes retain their default values. A make routine can be called without creation (no*!!*) to reset the values in an existing object.

To use an object, then, you must do four things:

1.	Define the class	**class** *POINT* . . .
2.	Declare the object in a client	*p: POINT*
3.	Create an object in the client	*!!p.make*
4.	Use the object in the client	*p.move (1.0, 1.0)*

The whole process starts when the creation routine of the root class is executed; the root class usually consists of a single, small creation routine. Eiffel creates an object for the root class, and the code in the root class creation routine creates other objects, which in turn create other objects, and so on.

4.3   Input

Input and output operations are controlled by a special system object whose name is *io*; thus, every input and output command uses the object *io*, and is of the form *io.feature*. Eiffel is strict about the type used in an operation, so there is not a single command to read or to output values in Eiffel; instead, there is a different command for each type of input and output.

Input requires a command to read a value from the user, followed by a query to return the value that was just read. To read an object, you issue a command of the form *io.read<type>*. This command gets a value from the user, but doesn't return anything. To find out what the value was, you must ask for the last value read in, using the query *io.last<type>*. To get a single, integer value from the user thus requires three lines of code:

```
io.putstring ("Please enter your age in years: ")
io.readint
age := io.lastint
```

The three string read commands read a word, a sequence of *n* characters, or a complete line from the screen. The string is then available from *laststring*. The input commands, the input queries, the type that they read, and a sample input for each, are

io.readint	*x: INTEGER*	12
x := io.lastint		
io.readreal	*x: REAL*	43.6
x := io.lastreal		
io.readdouble	*x: DOUBLE*	43.6
x := io.lastdouble		
io.readchar	*x: CHARACTER*	a
x := io.lastchar		
io.readline	*x: STRING*	hi there you cute computer
io.readstream (10)		hello Dave
io.readword		hello
x := io.laststring		
io.next_line		move to next input line

Some versions of Eiffel use the read command *io.readstring* in place of the three commands to read a line, stream, or word. The command reads the whole input line; the line is then returned by the query *io.laststring*. The commands and queries given above are based on ISE Eiffel Version 3; other compilers may use different, but similar instructions.

Every input from the user should be preceded by a prompt, so that the user knows what to type. You don't need to use quotes to input values; the computer finds out how to treat the input by looking at your input commands. Note that the input commands do not mention a variable. Eiffel stores the input in a set of buffers, one buffer for each type of object. To access the buffer, you issue a query to get the last value read into the buffer. Getting the last value does not change the value of the buffer, it only reads that value. This means you can get the last value input as many times as you want. The input will only change when you read in a new value for that type of object. Reading in a new value changes the value stored in the buffer, so any input value must be used by your system before the next value is read in from the user.

A variable of type *STRING* is a reference variable, so the name of a string has a pointer or reference as its value. The function call *io.laststring*, however, does not return the string stored in the string buffer; it makes a copy of that string, and returns the copy. A new string can be read and stored in the input buffer without affecting the value of any existing strings.

4.4 Output

To output an object, you issue a command of the form *io.put<type>*; an output operation is a command, because it changes the state of the screen. The output commands, the type they output, and a sample output for each command, are

io.putreal (x)	*x: REAL*	43.6
io.putint (x)	*x: INTEGER*	12
io.putbool (x)	*x: BOOLEAN*	false
io.putchar (x)	*x: CHARACTER*	a
io.putstring (x)	*x: STRING*	hello
io.new_line		go to a new line

Each command outputs a single value of the relevant type, so an output of a string and three real numbers needs four output statements. Special characters are written as two symbols, the special symbol '%' and a following symbol; a new line character, for example, is denoted by '%N'. The single character '%' thus has to be written as '%%'. The list of special characters is shown in Appendix B. An unprintable character can be specified as an ASCII value using the special character form '%/code/', where the code is the ASCII (decimal) value of the character. A new line character, for example, has an ASCII code of 13, so it can also be specified as '%/13/'.

A long string may be written on two lines by starting every line but the first with a '%' and ending every line but the last with a '%'. Any number of blanks or tabs may be placed between the '%' signs with no effect on the format of the output. An example of a long string output is

io.putstring ("Having a wonderful time.%
% Wish you were here.%
% Please send money")

This command produces the screen output

Having a wonderful time. Wish you were here. Please send money.

A real number is printed with six decimal places by default. The appearance of the output can be tailored by converting a number to a string, and then printing the string. The features to do this are supplied by class *FORMAT*. The formatting commands take a value as an argument as well as a format specifier, and return a string of the specified format. The main features of class *FORMAT* and a short comment for each feature, based on the Eiffel/S library class *FORMAT*, are shown on the next page.

b2s (b: BOOLEAN): STRING	– – Boolean to string
c2s (c: CHARACTER): STRING	– – character to string
i2s (fmt: STRING; i: INTEGER): STRING	– – integer to string
r2s (fmt: STRING; r: REAL): STRING	– – real to string
s2s (fmt, s: STRING): STRING	– – string to string
s2b (s: STRING): BOOLEAN	– – string to Boolean
s2c (s: STRING): CHARACTER	– – string to character
s2i (s: STRING): INTEGER	– – string to integer
s2r (s: STRING): REAL	– – string to real

The format specifier follows the convention used in Pascal, by specifying an output field length and the number of decimal places, so the format specifier has the form "length.precision". The length is the length of the returned string. A correct output value is always returned. If the specified field length is too small, Eiffel uses as large a field as necessary to print the value. If the specified length is too large, then spaces are added before the output value, to make up the length. If the length specifier starts with the character zero ('0'), then zeroes are used to fill out the length, instead of spaces.

For integers, the precision gives the number of decimal places to use; the decimal values will always be zero. For real numbers, the precision gives the number of decimal places to show, so a format specifier of "5.2" produces a string of length 5 (two integer places, the decimal point, and two decimal places) in which there are two decimal digits. For a string, the precision defines a maximum total string length. The precision may be omitted for integers and strings.

Several examples of format conversion and their formatted output are shown below.

i2s ("1", 12)	returns the string	"12"
i2s ("3", 12)	returns the string	"Δ12"
r2s ("5.2", 432.6895)	returns the string	"432.68 "
r2s ("10.2", 1234.5678)	returns the string	"ΔΔ1234.56"

The format specifier may be a literal or a variable, but must be of type STRING. Class FORMAT is inherited by the class that wants to use the formatting features.

Every output should be preceded by a label, so that the user of the system knows what the output means. Showing the current tax rate as a percentage, in a nice format, requires the following code:

```
class X
inherit
    FORMAT

        . . .
        io.putstring ("The current tax rate is ")
```

```
io.putstring (r2s ("5.2", tax_rate))
io.putstring ("%%N")
```

The simplest Eiffel system that does something useful is a single class with a single output. The single class is, of course, the root class for the system; in fact, it is the system. In programming, the sample program that prints a message is usually called the "Hello world" program. Here is the Australian version:

```
class HELLO
creation
    make
feature {ANY}
    make is
            -- say hello to the world
        do
            io.putstring ("%NG'day mate%N")
        end -- make
end -- class HELLO
```

The effect of coding, compiling, and running this system is to produce the message

```
G'day mate
```

on your terminal screen; more complex systems are possible.

4.5   Example: class *PERSON*

Input from the screen is tedious in Eiffel. You print a prompt message, read in a value, then assign the value from the buffer into the variable you want; each input therefore requires three lines of Eiffel code. As an example, assume that you want to read in a person's name. To do this, you define a class *PERSON* with attributes *first_name*, *last_name*, *sex*, and *born*, create an object of this class, and read in a value for each attribute. Statements to read and display this data are shown in the features *make* and *display* in the class:

```
class PERSON
creation
    make
feature {NONE}
    first_name, last_name: STRING
    sex: CHARACTER
```

```
        born: INTEGER
feature
    make is
            -- set the attributes from input data
        do
            io.putstring ("Enter first name: ")
            io.readline
            first_name := io.laststring
            io.putstring ("Enter last name: ")
            io.readline
            last_name := io.laststring
            io.putstring ("Enter sex (M/F): ")
            io.readchar
            sex := io.lastchar
            putstring ("Enter year of birth: ")
            io.readint
            born := io.lastint
        end -- make
    display is
        -- display the name and year of birth
        do
            io.new_line
            io.putstring (first_name)
            io.putchar (' ')
            io.putstring (last_name)
            io.putstring ("Δ was born in the year Δ")
            io.putint (born)
            io.new_line
        end -- display
end -- class PERSON
```

To use this class definition, you need a client to declare an object of type
PERSON, then create the person and display the details for that person. The client
looks like

```
class X
creation
    make
feature
    you: PERSON
```

```
      make is
               -- create and display a person
          do
               !!you.make
               you.display
          end -- make
  end -- class X
```

4.6   Assignment

A variable is given a value by an assignment statement of the form

```
      variable := expression
```

A value is produced when the expression on the right-hand side of this statement is executed or evaluated, and the value of the expression is then stored in the variable listed on the left-hand side. Examples of assignments are

```
      name := io.laststring
      tax_rate := 0.12
      total_cost := air_fare + bus_fare + hotel
      area := 0.5 * length * height
      count := count + 1
      sum := sum + io.lastreal
```

Assignment is a two-step process. The assignment statement *count := count + 1* is both correct and common; the variable *count* is incremented by 1, so that the value of the variable is larger by one after the statement has been executed. This is very different from an equality test; it is impossible for a value to be larger than itself. The assignment operator should be called something like assigns, gets, or is. The operator should never be called equals; it does not test for equality, it assigns a value to the variable.

The two sides of the assignment must have compatible types. Two types are compatible if they are the same type, or one can be converted to, and thus stored in, the other; you cannot store a *REAL* value in an *INTEGER*, for example. For simple values, this means that an *INTEGER* value can be stored in a *REAL* variable, and a *REAL* variable (single precision) can be stored in a *DOUBLE* (double precision) variable. Going the other way, a *REAL* value has to be rounded or truncated before it can be stored in an *INTEGER* variable. Functions to do this type of conversion can be found in the Eiffel library class *SINGLE_MATH*.

4.7   Expressions

Expressions are used to calculate the value that is stored in an assignment statement, or to calculate a value that is used immediately in the code. An expression is a sequence of values connected by operators. The values may be variables, constants, or literals; a literal is a value written as part of the code, such as 0.5. Operators are defined on certain types, so they can only be used on values of the correct type. The numeric operators are covered in this chapter, while relational and Boolean operators are covered in the next chapter.

The *INTEGER* operators are divisor (integer division, written as //) and modulus (integer remainder, written as \\), which take two integers as arguments. The divisor operator returns the number of times that one integer divides into another, so 47 // 10 = 4, 53 // 25 = 2. The modulus operator returns the remainder after an integer division, so 7 \\ 10 = 7, 53 \\ 25 = 3. The result of these operators is of type *INTEGER*. The operators, their names, and a sample expression, are

| // | divisor | 365 // 30 |
| \\ | modulus | hours \\ 12 |

The numeric operators (defined on *REAL* and *INTEGER*) are

+	plus	3.6 + total_cost
–	minus	gross_pay – tax
*	times	hours * rate
/	divide	assets / people
^	exponent	pi * radius ^ 2

The result of an expression that uses these operators may be an *INTEGER*, a *REAL*, or a *DOUBLE* number. The rule is that all numeric types in an expression are first converted into the "heaviest" type in the expression; the expression is then evaluated. A *DOUBLE* (double precision) value is heavier than a *REAL* value, which in turn is heavier than an *INTEGER* value. If two *INTEGERs* are added, the result is an *INTEGER*; if an *INTEGER* and a *REAL* number are added, then the result is of type *REAL*. Minus, times, and divide are similar in the types they produce. Any number of operators can be combined within a single expression.

Because each operator is defined on a given type, the effect of the operator can differ depending on the type of its arguments; this technique is called overloading. We have already seen an overloaded operator, the operator *make*. This operator has the same name in each class, but does different things depending on the object that it creates. In the same way, the divide operator "/" has different effects depending on whether its arguments are *INTEGER* or *REAL*. For integer arguments, divide is the integer division operator called "divisor" above, and produces an integer result; for two integer arguments, the "//" and "/" operators have the same effect or semantics. For any other legal combination of arguments, "/" is the normal division operator that produces a real number (*REAL* or *DOUBLE*).

When an expression is evaluated, some operators take precedence over others. There is a strictly-defined operator precedence order for any computer language; the numeric operator precedence order in Eiffel is, from highest to lowest precedence

+ –	unary plus, unary minus
^	exponent
* / // \\	times, divide, divisor, modulus
+ –	plus, minus

Unary plus and minus take a single argument, such as "– 6" or "+ 42"; all other operators take two values, so they are called binary operators.

For a flat expression (one without brackets), all exponents are calculated before any multiplication is done, and all multiplication is done before any addition, in precedence order. Operators at the same level of precedence are executed from left to right in the expression. Brackets are used to force evaluation, because expressions within brackets are evaluated before unbracketed ones. Several example expressions, the order of evaluation, and their results, are shown below.

---

1 + 2 * 3 ^ 3 – 4 / 5
-> 1 + 2 * 27 – 4 / 5
-> 1 + 54 – 4 / 5
-> 1 + 54 – 1
-> 55 – 1
= 54

1 + 2 ^ 2 * 3 / 4.0
-> 1 + 4 * 3 / 4.0
-> 1 + 12 / 4.0
-> 1 + 3.0
= 4.0

(1 + 2 ^ 2 * 3) / 4.0
-> (1 + 4 * 3) / 4.0
-> (1 + 12) / 4.0
-> 13 / 4.0
= 3.25

-73 \\ 12 // 5 + 3 ^ 2 / 4.0
-> -73 \\ 12 // 5 + 9 / 4.0
-> -1 // 5 + 9 / 4.0
-> -1 + 9 / 4.0
-> -1 + 2.25
= 1.25

Brackets should be used to make the expression clear where there is any possibility of confusion. Whenever you write code, you should always write it with the next person in mind, who has to read and understand your code.

Sophisticated mathematical functions such as *sqrt* and *sin* are provided by the *MATH* class of your Eiffel compiler. Depending on your version of Eiffel, this class may be called *MATH, SINGLE_MATH*, or *DOUBLE_MATH*. This class must be inherited by the class that wants to use the features of class *MATH*. The exact content of this class differs between compilers; the basic Eiffel language is fairly standard, but any other Eiffel library classes are free to vary between suppliers, and between versions within a supplier.

4.8   Example system: *HOUSE*

A simple system is developed in this section to illustrate basic data flow. The system uses only *REAL* data values to find and display the volume of a simple house. The code is developed by backward, detailed design to discover the data flow in the plan. The data flow is shown by a data flow chart, which defines the necessary order of the actions; a data flow chart is a plan structure chart with the arrows pointing down instead of up, to indicate data flow instead of the need for a value. The data flow defines a set of piecewise dependencies, and any correct solution must obey these piecewise dependencies. The code in the plan is then divided into routines and the routines are placed in classes.

4.8.1   Specification

"Find the volume of a house consisting of a living area and an attic. The living area is a box or rectangular prism, and the attic is a triangular prism."

4.8.2   Problem analysis

The volume of the house is composed of two parts, the attic and the living area. The volume is thus given by the Eiffel statement

> *volume := box_volume + attic_volume*

The volume of the living area is given by the statement

> *box_volume := length * height * width*

which uses three values input by the user. The volume of the attic is given by

> *attic_volume := 0.5 * length * attic_height * width*

so the height of the attic has to be input (the length and width are the same as the box). This problem thus requires the user to input four values, and the program outputs a single value; all values are *REAL* numbers. The data flow in the solution is indicated in the dependency chart below, where a name indicates a variable, and an arrow indicates a data flow from one variable to another. This chart defines the essential structure of the solution; any additional structure depends on the choice and skill of the designer.

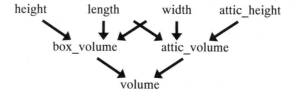

In the design, we started at the goal and worked backward to add the code that the final calculation needs or depends on; these are the dependency links. When the plan is executed, the data flows forward from the inputs to the output. Data flow means that one line of code produces a data value that is used in a later line; the two lines play the role of producer and consumer of data.

This pattern can be seen in the calculation of the total volume by the three calculations

> $box\_volume := length * height * width$
> $attic\_volume := 0.5 * length * attic\_height * width$
> $volume := box\_volume + attic\_volume$

The value of the box volume is produced by the first line, and the value of the attic volume is produced by the second line. The third line uses or consumes these two values, and produces a value for the house volume. It doesn't matter if the box or the attic volume is calculated first, just as long as they are both produced before they are used in the third line. There is no necessary ordering of these actions; producing the box and then the attic volume is just as good as producing the attic and then the box volume. The order shown in the code is "intuitive" for a person reading the code, but the computer doesn't care which order is used, so long as data is produced before it is used.

The same pattern may be seen within each sub-goal, to calculate the box and attic volumes. We need to read in three values to find the box volume, but there is no necessary order in which we have to code the three inputs. This is a general characteristic of data flow; a producer must precede a consumer, but the order of the producers is undefined. In the field of artificial intelligence, this is known as a non-linear plan, because no single linear order is defined by the problem. Some serial order must be chosen so that the solution can be executed on a serial computer, but that order is only partly defined by the structure of the problem.

The problem has the overall behavior that four values are input from the user, and one value is output to the user; this is shown below, where the arrows represent data flow from and to the user. The code in the system reads the input from a terminal screen, and writes the result to the screen.

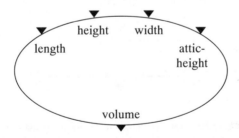

Lines of code connected by a data flow link are piecewise ordered by that link, because the producer must precede the consumer. Where there is a network of such dependencies, as shown in a data flow chart, there is no necessary complete order for these actions. A large part of design is spent in working out the best way to place and organize the code, within the constraints defined by the necessary dependencies. A good designer first works out what is essential in a solution, and then makes an informed, explicit choice about the procedural structure of the final solution.

4.8.3   Solution design

The obvious place to start OO design is with the definition of the class *HOUSE*, which creates and finds the volume of a house. Is a separate root class required, or can we use only the class *HOUSE*? All the data is contained within the class, so a system consisting of a single class is possible.

We have used a separate root class, so that class *HOUSE* contains the called routines and a client *START* uses these features. The root class calls the creation routine for a house, then ask for the volume to be shown to the user. If a single class was used for the system, then its creation routine would do more than create a house, and the modularity of the system would be incorrect. A creation routine creates the object, in this case a house. The client chart for our system is thus

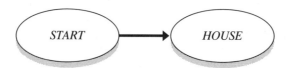

The behavior of the two classes is shown in the system structure chart below. The root class *START* contains a single creation routine that creates the house and calls the display routine. The *HOUSE* class contains two exported features, one to create the house and the other to show the volume of the house. Class *HOUSE* also contains a private function to calculate the *volume*, which is called only within the class. We have shown the internal calling structure of class *HOUSE* to provide a clear picture of the system, but usually a system structure chart does not show internal routine calls within a class.

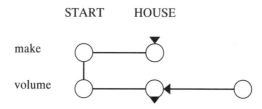

The creation routine for class *HOUSE* must be a procedure, because it changes the values of the house attributes. We have separated the calculation of the volume from its display, because the house volume may be used (in a future system) without displaying it. The feature that calculates the *volume* is a query, because it returns a single value and changes nothing. It could be implemented by an attribute or by a function; we have chosen to make it a function, so that we can keep the number of attributes as small as possible.

4.8.4 Solution code

An implementation for this system is shown below. The code for the root class *START* is shown first, then the code for the supplier, class *HOUSE*.

class *START*

```
creation
    make
feature
    house: HOUSE
    make is
            -- create the house, show its volume
        do
            !!house.make
            house.show_volume
        end -- make
end -- class START

class HOUSE
creation
    make
feature {NONE}
    length, height, width, attic_height: REAL
feature {START}
    make is
            -- read in and set the values of the attributes
        do
            io.putstring ("Enter the height of the living area: ")
            io.readreal
            height := io.lastreal
            io.putstring ("Enter the length of the living area: ")
            io.readreal
            length := io.lastreal
            io.putstring ("Enter the width of the living area: ")
            io.readreal
            width := io.lastreal
            io.putstring ("Enter the height of the attic: ")
            io.readreal
            attic_height := io.lastreal
        end -- make
    show_volume is
            -- show the volume of the house
        do
            io.putstring ("%N%NThe volume of the house is: ")
            io.putreal (volume)
        end -- show_volume
    feature {NONE}
```

```
    volume: REAL is
            -- volume of the house
        local box_volume, attic_volume: REAL
        do
            box_volume := length * height * width
            attic_volume := 0.5 * length * attic_height * width
            Result := box_volume + attic_volume
        end -- volume
    end -- class HOUSE
```

The plan for showing the volume of a house defines the underlying, necessary actions that must be executed. To convert a plan into reusable Eiffel code, the actions in the plan must be divided into routines, and the routines divided into classes. The plan could be coded in three lines in a language such as Pascal, one line to prompt for the inputs, one to read the data, and one to calculate and write the result; as you can see, the Eiffel code is considerably longer. The Eiffel code in this solution is reusable, however—a far more important criterion than brevity. A short solution is good, and you should always try to write simple and concise code, but the number of lines of code is way down the list of factors that are used in designing a reusable OO solution.

4.9   Reference and value semantics

The previous parts of this chapter have dealt with simple data types; the rest of the chapter deals with reference types. Variables of type *INTEGER*, *REAL*, *DOUBLE*, *BOOLEAN*, and *CHARACTER* have simple, immediate values, whereas reference types have a value that is a pointer to memory. Eiffel uses this pointer to access memory, and then uses the object found there. The difference in the value of a variable affects the way in which a variable is used, so different rules are needed to describe the meaning or semantics of value and reference types.

Every object in Eiffel is an instance of a class, so there are classes for the simple data types as well as for complex objects; the name of the class is given in the variable declaration. A class may be stored in two different ways, however, called reference and expanded types. If a class is defined as a reference type, then its value is a reference that is set to *Void* when the object is declared, and set to a reference when the object is created. If a class is defined as an expanded type, then the values of an object of that type are not references, but the objects themselves, and the object does not need to be explicitly created.

The basic types *INTEGER*, *REAL*, *DOUBLE*, *BOOLEAN*, and *CHARACTER* are expanded types; all other types are reference types. Expanded types improve the efficiency of an Eiffel system, because the value is used immediately and does not require tracing through a reference to a location in memory, then using the value at that location. A type is defined as expanded by writing the keyword **expanded** as the first word of the class definition. The class *INTEGER*, for example, has the class header

> **expanded class** *INTEGER*

If the keyword **expanded** is not included in the class header, then the class is a reference type. A class may be defined as a reference type and declared as an expanded type, by using the keyword in the declaration, such as

> *x:* **expanded** *X*

The interaction between expanded and reference objects of the same type has subtle implications that are not discussed in this text. The interested reader is referred to *Eiffel: The Language* (Meyer, 1992) for further details.

4.9.1   Assignment

An assignment of the form $a := b$ stores the value of b in the variable a. This is an assignment of values if a and b are expanded types. It is an assignment of references if the variables are reference types. To illustrate this difference, consider two points and two real values that are declared and created by the code shown below; here, the initial location of the point is passed to the creation routine as two real values.

```
a, b: REAL
p1, p2, p3: POINT
    !!p1.make (12.6, −3.4)
    !!p2.make (12.6, −3.4)
a := p1.x
b := p1.y
```

Points *p1* and *p2* now exist, with their *x* and *y* coordinates set to the same values. These are different objects, because the values of the names *p1* and *p2* (the location of the coordinates in memory) are different; the values of *a*, *b*, *p1*, and *p2* are indicated by the data structure chart shown below.

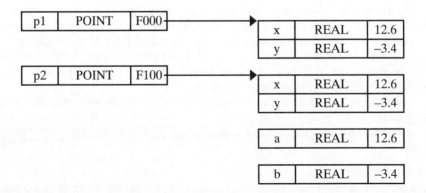

The feature call *p1.x* returns the value of the *x* coordinate of the object *p1*, and the feature call *p1.y* returns the value of the *y* coordinate of the object. The *x* and *y* values can be assigned to the *REAL* variables *a* and *b* because *a*, *b*, *p1.x*, and *p1.y* are all of the same type, *REAL*. If the point *p1* is now moved, the values of *a* and *b* are not affected, because they are expanded types; the value has been stored in those variables, and is not affected by any change to *x* and *y*.

The point *p1* can be assigned to *p3* by the code

---

    p3 := p1

---

because they are both of the same type, *POINT*. A point is a reference type, however, so the assignment of *p1* to *p3* assigns a reference. The name *p3* now contains the same reference value as the name *p1*; they both refer to the same point, as shown in the diagram below. Changing the content of *p1* by the code

---

    p1.move (4.2, 12.8)

---

changes the content of *p3*, because both names refer to the same object. The value of *p3* is not changed; its value is still a pointer to some location in memory. The value stored at that location has changed, however, indirectly affecting the variable *p3*.

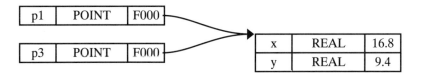

Care must be taken to separate the name of a reference variable from its value. For basic types, the story is simple: a basic variable has a simple value, which can only be accessed through the name of that variable. For reference types, however, an object can have any number of names, and the single object can be accessed through any of these names. To be completely clear and accurate, we should say, "the object that is referred to by the name *p1*", but for most purposes we can use the shorthand form of this statement and refer to the object *p1*. An object can have multiple names if it is created and then assigned to other variables. For simplicity, we will talk about an object with a name, unless we need to explicitly separate the name from the object.

As a consequence of the different values in reference and expanded types, assignment and equality work differently. Formally, we say that the meaning or semantics of assignment and equality are different for the two types of value.

4.9.2 Equality

An equality test using the "=" operator compares two values. Thus, if you compare two points that have the same location, such as *p1* and *p2*, they will not be "=" because you are comparing references, not contents, and the references are different. There are now two meanings of equality that need to be separated: "prints the same" and "identical". Equality of content is called equal and is tested by the operator *equal*. Equality of reference is called identical and is tested by the operator "=". The two *POINT* objects *p1* and *p2* are equal but not identical, because they have the same content but different values, whereas the two points *p1* and *p3* are both equal and identical.

Eiffel provides a special function that is defined on all objects to test if two objects have the same content. The function *equal* takes two objects and does a field-by-field comparison to determine if the fields are equal, and thus if the objects are equal. The two points *p1* and *p2* can be compared to see if they have the same location by calling the Eiffel *BOOLEAN* function

```
     equal (p1, p2)
```

which returns a Boolean value (**true** or **false**) saying whether the objects are field-by-field equal, using the "=" operator to compare each field.

It is usual for a class to define its own equality operator, so that the meaning of *equal* is tailored to each type of object. This more specific function is usually called *is_equal*, and it is called on an object by passing the test object as an argument. For the class *POINT*, for example, the equality function could be called in the client and defined in the class *POINT* as

```
     if p1.is_equal (p2) then . . .
     is_equal (test: POINT): BOOLEAN is
             – – is the location of test the same as the location of Current?
         do
             Result := (x = test.x) and (y = test.y)
         end – – is_equal
```

This function in class *POINT* tests each coordinate of the two points, and returns true if the *x* and *y* coordinates of both points are equal. Object equality may be tested using the Eiffel function *equal*, or by a more specific function called *is_equal* within a class, which tests specific fields in that class for content ("=") equality.

4.9.3   Copy

Assignment of values means that a new value is stored in the new variable. Assignment of references, however, means that two variables with different names now refer to the same object. Assignment therefore cannot be used to get a copy of an object, so Eiffel supplies a command *copy* to copy objects, which is defined for all classes. It is called on the object to be copied, and takes a name of the correct type as an argument. It makes a field-by-field copy of the object, and attaches it to the name given as the argument. A copy of the point *p1*, for example, can be made and given the name *p4* by declaring both names to be of type *POINT*, and writing the code

> *p4: POINT*
>   *p1.copy (p4)*

As a result of executing this command, the name *p4* now refers to a new object that is a field-by-field copy of the object *p1*. An object must have a reference to be copied; a name with a *Void* reference cannot be copied, because there is no object on which to call the command, so *p1* here must have a (non-*Void*) reference as its value.

The function *clone* is also defined for all classes. It is passed an object as its argument, and returns a field-by-field copy of the object. The object can be *Void*; in that case, a *Void* reference is returned. A copy of the point *p1*, for example, can be made and given the name *p4* by writing

> *p4 := clone (p1)*

As a result of executing this command, the name *p4* now refers to a new object that is a field-by-field copy of the object *p1*. While there are other, subtle differences between the two operators (see Meyer, 1992, for details), objects are normally cloned rather than copied because *clone* handles *Void* references with no problems.

4.9.4   Eiffel definitions

In Eiffel, behavior is described by the name and signature of a feature, and the pre- and postconditions on a routine. Pre- and postconditions allow programming by contract: if the routine is called when the precondition is true, then the routine guarantees that the postcondition is true when the routine exits. Preconditions define any constraints on the input arguments to the routine, which are required to be true when the routine is entered; they are listed under the keyword **require** in the routine definition. Postconditions define what must be true after the routine has executed; they are listed under the keyword **ensure** in the routine definition.

Eiffel uses preconditions to check that a feature has been called correctly; if the precondition fails, then the system halts and displays an error message giving the class, routine, and assertion that caused the system to crash. In the same way, Eiffel uses postconditions to check that a feature has the correct effect. The combination of signature, comment, and assertions about the routine provide a complete description of the routine interface, and supply all the information needed to use that feature.

To illustrate how useful such documentation can be, the short definitions (output by running the tool **short** on the class *ANY*) for the routines *copy*, *clone*, and *equal* are given below. The routine header gives the type of the input data passed to the routine, and output data passed back from a function; this defines the signature of the feature. The interface provides all the information needed to use these routines, with no knowledge of the implementation. The interface definitions are

> *copy (other:* **like** *Current)* **is**
>   −− Copy every field of *other* onto

```
                    -- corresponding field of current object
            require
                    other_not_void: other /= Void
            ensure
                    is_equal (other)
            end -- copy
    clone (other: ANY): like other is
                    -- Void if other is void.
                    -- Otherwise, new object is field-by-field identical
                    -- to object attached to other
            ensure
                    equal (Result, other)
            end -- clone
    equal (some: ANY; other: like some): BOOLEAN is
                    -- Are some and other either both void
                    -- or attached to field-by-field identical objects?
            ensure
                    Result = (some = Void and other = Void) or
                             (some /= Void and other /=Void and then
                             some.is_equal (other))
            end -- equal
```

The three routine definitions use several advanced Eiffel features that have not yet been covered. In brief, the keyword **like** allows the type of an argument to be defined as "like this one", the keyword *Current* refers to the current object, and the class *ANY* matches a class of any type; the topic of inheritance must be covered before a more detailed explanation can be given. Because the routines can be applied to an object of any type, the object received as an argument can be of any type. Defining one argument to be **like** another (to be of the same type) means that the routine can declare and use a local variable of the appropriate type, no matter what type of object was passed to it.

4.9.5 Deep versus shallow operators

The Eiffel operators *equal, copy,* and *clone* described above are called shallow *copy, clone,* and *equal*, because they only look one level inside the object; they do a field-by-field operation on each object. If an object contains other objects, then the fields of that object are references, so a true comparison of the content is not done. The operator only looks one level down the chain of pointers, instead of following the chain down to the bottom level.

Consider two objects of type *TRIANGLE*, both created with their vertices at the same location, such as the equilateral triangle with vertices at (0, 1), (–1, 0), (1, 0); the data structures for the triangles are shown on the next page. The two objects are not = (tested by *tri1* = *tri2*), because the value of *tri1* (the memory address F000) is not the same as the value of *tri2* (the memory address F050).

The two triangles are not *equal* (tested by *equal* (*tri1, tri2*)), because *equal* does a field-by-field comparison one level down. A triangle has three points (*top, left,* and *right*), and a point is a reference type, so the value of each field (each point) refers to a different memory location and thus the values are not "=". A field-by-field comparison of two triangles looks one level down the data structure and compares point references. Looking at the first field (*top*) of each object, the value F008 does not "=" the value F058.

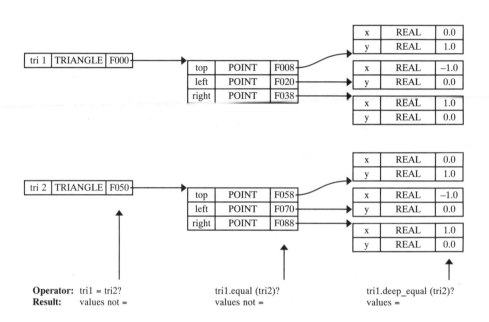

The problem of shallow testing can be overcome by using deep versions of *copy, clone,* and *equal,* called *deep_copy, deep_clone,* and *deep_equal.* These routines are defined on all Eiffel classes, and are called in the same way as their shallow versions. The deep version traces down the references to the very end of the chain, deep within each data structure, and then copies or compares the values at the end of each reference chain. Looking at the first field at the end of each chain, the value of *tri1.top.x = tri2.top.x.* Looking at the next field, *tri1.top.y = tri2.top.y,* and the comparison continues, with the eventual decision that *deep_equal* (*tri1, tri2*). The exact hexadecimal values of the pointers can be ignored in practice; they have been added in the diagram to make clear that the pointer values are different, because they refer to different objects located in different places in memory.

The Eiffel rules for variable declaration, and object creation, assignment, copying, and comparison have now been presented in detail. Variables receive their values when the variable is declared, when an object is created, or when a value is assigned to the variable name. Basic variables provide the ground or basic level, from which complex objects are built; they receive a value from their default values, from user input, or from assignment in the system. The basic values can be directly displayed by output to the user; to display a complex object, each basic field in the object has to be displayed. Objects can be copied or cloned, but this is unusual; more often, the unique object is passed around the system by assigning its reference to a new name as required.

4.10   Case study: the *BANK* system

The code for a banking case study is developed in Part E of this book, from the initial version of one class to the final version of 17 classes. The case study is used to illustrate each new aspect of the Eiffel language, as that aspect is presented in each chapter. The case study thus provides an example of correct, complete, and working Eiffel code, which can be examined if you are unclear about any of the theory or examples presented in each chapter. It also shows how code is reused in Eiffel, because the system is extended many times with almost no alteration to the existing code. This is the promise of Eiffel, that code can be written once and reused, even when the specification of the system changes.

The simple bank system introduced in Chapter 1 used a single class *ACCOUNT*. The complex case study developed through the rest of the book begins in this chapter with a more complex account. The system specification for this first part of the case study is:

> Money is deposited into and withdrawn from a bank account, and the balance can be displayed. Interest is added daily on the current balance; the interest rate is 4.5 percent a year.

Now that the detailed syntax and mechanism of object creation and data flow have been defined, look at the first part of the case study again, to check that you understand how the code works. The case study is extended in Section 2 of Part E to include classes *CUSTOMER* and *BANK*; it is then extended again to illustrate the topics of selection, iteration, data structures, and simple and complex inheritance.

Summary

- The basic Eiffel types are *INTEGER*, *REAL*, *DOUBLE*, *BOOLEAN*, and *CHARACTER*.
- An input command *io.read<type>* stores an input value in a buffer for each type of object. The last value of that type read from the user is returned from the query *io.last<type>*.
- An output command of the form *io.put<type>* shows a data value of that type.
- An assignment statement evaluates the expression on the right-hand side, and stores the value in the variable on the left-hand side.
- One variable produces a data value that is used by another variable, so we say that the two variables are connected by data flow.
- Operators are defined on types, so an operator can have different effects by overloading.

- Operators have a strictly defined precedence order; this precedence order can be overridden by parentheses.
- A basic or expanded type has an immediate value and need not be created. A reference type has a reference as its value. The semantics of assignment and equality are different for expanded and reference types, and are called reference and value semantics.
- Eiffel provides special operators to test objects for equality (*equal*) and to copy objects (*copy*, *clone*) in both shallow and deep versions.

Exercises

1. How is an attribute declared? How is a constant declared? Can an attribute have the same name as a class?
2. What is the value of an attribute after it has been declared, but before it has been created?
3. How is a local variable declared? What is the scope of a local variable? What is the scope of an attribute? Can a local variable have the same name as an attribute of the class? Can a local constant be declared? What is the difference between a literal and a constant?
4. What are the basic Eiffel classes? What is the structure of a basic type? What is the structure of a reference type? Give an example of each.
5. What happens when an object is created? State what happens when there is a creation routine for the class, and when there is not a creation routine for the class.
6. Look at the code for a customer that has a single account, presented in Chapter 1. Draw a structure chart showing the values stored in a customer at three points in time:
   (a) Before the *CUSTOMER* creation routine has been executed.
   (b) Before the *ACCOUNT* creation routine has been executed.
   (c) After the *CUSTOMER* creation routine exits, and the customer has been created.
7. Write down a command to read in
   - an integer
   - a real number
   - a character
   - a string.

8. An input command gets a value from the user, and stores it in a buffer. How do you get the value from the buffer? How many instructions are there to get a value from an input buffer? Is the instruction a command or a query?
9. Describe the general method for getting a value from the user. Write the declarations and code needed to read and store
   - two integers
   - two strings
   - a string and an integer.

10. Write down the command to output
    - an integer

- a real number
- a character
- a Boolean
- a string.

11. When do you need a prompt? a label?
12. Explain, step by step, how an assignment statement works.
13. What is meant by operator precedence? What is the numeric operator precedence order?
14. Evaluate the following expressions, showing each step:
    - 1 + 2 * 3 / 4.0
    - 1 // 2
    - 34 // 4.5
    - 1 // 2 \\ 3
    - 1 \\ 2 * 3 // 4 / 5.0
    - -43 // 4 ^ 2
    - -((12 / 3.0) * (0 // 7) + 2)

15. Write a class X that consists of a single make routine, plus attributes. Write a make routine to read in the weight of an object in pounds, convert the weight to kilograms, and show the answer. The program should print out both the weight in pounds and in kilograms. One pound is equal to 0.453592 kilograms.
16. Write a class X that consists of a single make routine, plus attributes. Write a make routine that reads in an employee's hourly rate, the number of hours worked, and the tax rate. It then finds and shows the gross salary (before tax) and net salary (after tax) for the employee.
17. Write a class X that consists of a single make routine, plus attributes. Write a make routine that converts degrees in Fahrenheit to degrees in centigrade. Fahrenheit degrees range from 32 degrees F (freezing point of water) to 212 degrees F (boiling point of water); centigrade degrees range from 0 (freezing) to 100 (boiling).
18. Write a class X that consists of a single make routine, plus attributes. Write a make routine that finds the time and cost of a car trip. The input data is the distance covered on the trip, the average speed, the number of gallons of petrol used per 100 kilometers, and the cost of a gallon of petrol. Draw a data flow chart for this problem.
19. Write a class X that consists of a single make routine, plus attributes. The specification is:

> You have decided to become a rock concert entrepreneur and want to use your knowledge of computing to help with the accounting. Write a system that calculates your individual profit and the total attendance for a rock concert.
>
> There are three ticket prices: the cheap seats are $10, the standard seats are $20, and the special seats are $100 each. The special ticket holders sit in the front row and get a pair of autographed sunglasses, plus a chance at a backstage pass. You must pay rent on the stadium, and the cost of the band, security, and insurance. The security is calculated at 32 cents per person attending. The insurance is 3.6 percent of the income.

You have two partners in this venture, and must split the profits evenly between all three partners. You must pay 12.5 percent tax on any profits made from the concert. Show the net (after tax) profit per person, and the total attendance at the concert.

20. A farmer has three pigs. A pig has a name, weight, and age. Write a system that creates the three pigs, then shows their average weight. Write your system in the following stages:
    (a) List the classes.
    (b) Draw a client chart.
    (c) Draw a data flow (data dependency) chart. This chart shows the complete data flow from input to output that is needed to produce the average pig weight.
    (d) Draw a system structure chart with data flow shown.
    (e) For the class *PIG*, define the attributes and the signature and header for each routine.
    (f) For the root class *FARMER*, define the attributes, signatures, and headers.
    (g) Draw a data structure chart for the system.
    (h) Code the system.
    (i) Run the system.

CHAPTER 5

Routines

Keywords

routine
procedure
function
argument
Result
operator
once

A routine is called by listing the name of the routine in the code. When a routine is called, control is transferred to the called routine, the routine's code is executed, and control is returned to the caller. Data is passed to a routine from the caller through an argument list. The caller supplies actual values, which are bound to the variables declared in the argument list in the listed order; these local declarations are called the formal arguments of the routine. Actual and formal arguments must agree in number, order, and type; names are irrelevant. Once a value has been bound to a formal argument, that value cannot be changed in the routine. A single data value is passed back from a function, and no value is returned from a procedure. A feature may be called from inside the same class, or from a client class.

5.1 Routine syntax and mechanism

A routine is called when Eiffel encounters the routine name as part of the code it is executing. Eiffel then finds the routine via its class definition, and executes the code in the routine. When all the code has been executed, the routine exits and control is returned to the caller immediately after the routine call. Data is passed to a routine through the argument list in the routine header; these formal arguments are local variables for the routine, so they can only be used inside the routine. The caller supplies values that are bound to each argument, in the order they are listed in the routine call. Once it has been bound, the value of an argument cannot be changed; Eiffel enforces this rule. A single value is returned from a function, by assigning a value to the special variable *Result* inside the function. A procedure returns nothing. A feature (attribute, function, or procedure) can be called within the class where it is defined, or a client can call a feature.

A routine definition consists of two main parts, the routine header and the routine body. The routine header defines the signature of the routine, by listing the type of each data value received from the caller and, for a function, the type of the value returned to the caller. The routine body provides the code that is executed in the routine. Comments and local variables are listed after the header and before the body, and assertions are listed before and after the body; assertions are discussed in detail in Part D of this book.

The format of a procedure is shown to the left below, and the format of a function to the right. Arguments and local variables are optional, and are included only if they are needed.

Procedure	Function
name (arguments) **is**	*name (arguments): TYPE* **is**
– – description of change	– – description of value
local *declarations*	**local** *declarations*
do	**do**
routine code	*routine code*
end – – name	*Result := expression*
	end – – name

A procedure header consists of a name, any input arguments, and the keyword **is**. The header comment describes what the procedure does, with no mention of how this behavior is implemented inside the routine; it is indented to the level of the code. Any local variables are then declared after the keyword **local**. The procedure body is then coded, first the keyword **do**, then the routine code, then the keyword **end**. The name of the procedure is written as a comment at the end of the procedure.

A function header consists of a name, any input arguments, a colon, the type of the function, and the keyword **is**. A function has a type and returns a value, like an attribute. Eiffel uses the function type listed in the header to define a local variable called *Result* for that function. When this local variable is created, it is given the default value for that type of object: zero, space, **false**, or *Void*. The value that is returned by the function is the value that is assigned to *Result* inside the function. Apart from this difference, a function has the same format as a procedure.

There are three types of function in Eiffel: the normal function described above, plus prefix and infix operators that are defined and called without the normal dot notation. An infix operator is called by listing its object before the operator name and its argument after the name; no dot is required. A prefix operator is called by listing its object after the operator, again with no dot. The standard numeric, relational, and Boolean operators are defined as operators, so they can be called using the normal mathematical notation (such as "3 + 5", "x > 3", and **169not** (x > 3)") instead of the Eiffel dot notation (which would be

"3.+(5)", "x. > (3)", and "(x > 3). **not**" respectively). They provide no additional functionality, but give the programmer syntactic sugar that make expressions easy to write. An example of each type of routine header is shown below.

procedure	*move (x, y: REAL)* **is**
function	*height: REAL* **is**
infix operator	**infix** "+" *(n: REAL): REAL* **is**
prefix operator	**prefix** "not": *BOOLEAN* **is**

The feature header shows the signature of that feature, by listing the type of every value passed in to and returned back from the feature. An attribute accepts no arguments, and returns a value, so its signature shows no input and a single returned value. A function has any number of input arguments and a single returned value. A procedure has any number of input arguments and no returned value.

In rare cases, a routine can have multiple names; one name is usually a shorter form of the other, more meaningful name. When this occurs, the names are simply listed in the routine header before the arguments, separated from each other by a comma. The routine can then be called by any of these names.

5.2   Passing data to a routine

Data is passed from the caller to the called routine through the argument list. The calling code contains the values or variables to be passed as actual arguments, and the routine header has a matching list to receive these values, which define the formal arguments to the routine. The data values passed by the caller, and received by the routine, must agree in number, order, and type. Once a formal argument has been bound, you are not allowed to change its value; if you try to do so, the system will not compile.

To illustrate how arguments are passed, consider the command *move* in the class *POINT*. In the example system presented in Chapter 3, the x and y distances to move the point were read in by code in class *MENU*, and passed as arguments to the *move* routine in class *TRIANGLE*, which then passed them to the *move* routine in class *POINT*. The routine call in class *TRIANGLE* is shown to the left below, and the routine header in class *POINT* is shown to the right.

class *TRIANGLE*	**class** *POINT*
feature	**feature**
top, left, right: POINT	*x, y: REAL*
top.move (x, y)	*move (delta_x, delta_y: REAL)* **is**

The *move* procedure call in class *TRIANGLE* has two arguments, and is called on an object of type *POINT* (the name of the object is *top*). The *move* procedure header in class *POINT* says that the name of the routine is *move*, and two arguments are expected from the caller, both of type *REAL*; the argument list consists of two *REAL* numbers. No value is passed back from the procedure. The argument list is a local declaration, so the variables in that list (*delta_x* and *delta_y*) are local variables in the routine *move*. When the routine is called, the variables are initialized to the values passed in by the caller, and the routine uses these values. If the values supplied by class *TRIANGLE* are 4.2 and 6.9, for example, then these values are passed as arguments to the routine, the formal arguments are bound to the values, the code in the routine is executed, and the location of the point is moved by 4.2 and 6.9.

Because the use of routines is so common in computer science, there is a special language for describing it. The values that are passed in the routine call are called arguments. The variables in the routine header are called formal arguments; the header lists the name and type of each formal argument. The values passed to the routine are called actual arguments. When the routine is called, the value of each formal argument is set to the value of the corresponding actual argument; this is called argument binding, and we say that the actual argument is bound to the formal argument. The first actual argument is bound to the first formal argument, the second actual argument is bound to the second formal argument, and so on until all the arguments are bound. Formal arguments of the same type may be grouped in a single declaration, with the names separated by commas; formal arguments of different types are separated by semi-colons. Examples of routine headers with multiple, single, and no arguments are

---

make (name: STRING; height, weight: REAL; age: INTEGER) **is** . . .
move (x, y: REAL) **is** . . .
distance (target: POINT): REAL **is** . . .
area: REAL **is** . . .
display **is** . . .

For binding to work, the formal and actual arguments must agree in number, order, and type. The formal arguments define what the routine looks like from the outside. A user of the routine then has to provide actual arguments that match the routine's arguments. This is much like a child's puzzle where you have a set of blocks of different shapes, and a board with holes of different shapes. You can only put a block in a hole if they have the same shape. In the same way, the shape of the calling routine (the block) has to match the shape of the called routine (the hole) or the two will not fit together. Binding is done purely on the order in which the arguments occur. The names of the actual arguments may be the same as the names of the formal arguments, or they may not. The name is irrelevant; only the shape, defined by the signature of the feature, matters when the actual and formal arguments are bound.

5.3   Getting data back from a function

5.3.1   *Syntax and mechanism*

A function returns a value back to its caller. This value defines the type of the function, and the type is written in the function header, after any arguments. The function *area* from the class *TRIANGLE*, for example, receives no arguments and returns a single *REAL* value; the header is

```
area: REAL is
```

When a function is called, any arguments to the function are bound, the local variable *Result* is created and initialized, and the function code executes and returns a single value that is used by the calling routine. The value of a function is set by assigning a value to *Result* inside the function. The function *area* from the class *TRIANGLE*, for example, may be implemented as

```
area: REAL is
        -- area of the triangle
    do
        Result := left.distance (right) * height * 0.5
    end -- area
```

No arguments are passed to this function. The area of the triangle is calculated, and assigned to the variable *Result* inside the function. Assigning a value to *Result* sets the value of the function and is the only way to return a value from a function. Because there is only one line of code in this routine, the function then terminates and returns the value to its caller.

The variable *Result* is like any local variable, except that Eiffel creates it automatically from the type listed in the function header and sets the variable to its normal default value. You can then use the variable to store a value, or to provide a value; in particular, you can do such things as *Result := Result + value*. It is a local variable, and the value of that variable when the function exits is the value of the function. If the value is not set inside the function, then the variable retains its default value of zero, space, false, or *Void*.

5.3.2   Examples

The function *distance* in the class *POINT* receives a *POINT* as an argument and returns a *REAL* number. The function header and body are

```
distance (target: POINT): REAL is
        -- distance of the current point from the target
    do
        Result := sqrt ((x–target.x)^2 + (y–target.y)^2)
    end -- distance
```

Many standard arithmetic functions, such as *sqrt* (square root) and *sine* (sine of an angle) are functions that receive a single value and return a single value. Examples of function calls are shown to the left below, and the function header is shown to the right. Without knowing anything about how these functions are implemented, the function headers can be defined for these routines, because the signatures are known; a single *REAL* value is passed in, and a single *REAL* value is passed back.

length := sine (30)	*sine (angle: REAL): REAL* **is**
answer := sqrt (36 / 7.4)	*sqrt (value: REAL): REAL* **is**
io.putreal (sqrt (hypotenuse))	

The routines are defined in the Eiffel library class *SINGLE_MATH*, which supplies features for single precision mathematics; there is a corresponding class *DOUBLE_MATH*. The code for the two arithmetic functions above return a real value, so the functions must include the code shown below, as well as any other code needed to actually calculate the result.

sqrt (value: REAL): REAL **is**	*sine (angle: REAL): REAL* **Is**
–– square root of *value*	–– sine of the *angle*
do	**do**
Result :=	*Result :=*
end –– sqrt	**end** –– sine

When you code a routine, you can write the header name and arguments and the outline body as shown above, without thinking about what happens inside the routine. In the approach defined by top-down design with formal specification, the signature and assertions are defined before any code is written, so the code must then implement the defined behavior.

5.3.3   Programming by side-effect

While it is possible for a function to change an attribute (the code to do so can easily be written as part of the function's body), such an action should be avoided, as it contradicts the whole idea of the function: a query (function or attribute) changes nothing.

This style of programming is called programming by side-effect. You call a function to return some value, and the code in the function returns the value, but also changes something "on the side". This can lead to code that is immensely hard to test and understand, because you are changing a value without admitting that you are doing so. If you admitted it explicitly, the function would be split into a procedure and a function, and your code would be clean and wholesome. Avoid side-effects in Eiffel. Other languages, especially C++, use side-effects as a basic programming tool, but it can be argued with some force that such a practice is error-prone, and creates complex and non-reusable code. The argument can be made formal when assertions are used to enforce programming by contract, discussed in Part D of this book; C++ does not use assertions.

A seductive piece of code to write in Eiffel is a function that accepts a string, uses the string as a prompt, reads in a value from the user, and returns that value. This small routine allows you to ignore the tedious sequence of events needed to get user input. Of course, you actually need several functions, because each will return only one type of value (real, integer, character, or string). The (bad and politically incorrect) code looks like

```
get_real (prompt: STRING): REAL is
        -- get a value from the user and return it
    do
        io.putstring (prompt)
        io.readreal
        Result := io.lastreal
    end -- get_real
```

The problem is that this code is a procedure masquerading as a function. It is a function, because it returns a value. It is a procedure, because it changes the "value" of the terminal screen, as well as the value of the feature *io.lastreal*. Another routine might wish to use the last input value, and expects that the value has not changed; a user would expect the value to still be accessible, because a function was called and, since functions change nothing, the value should be unchanged. This routine uses programming by side-effect, by changing a value inside a function, and thus is misleading and error-prone. The correct way to implement this task is to use a command and a function, like Eiffel does for input; a command which displays the prompt and gets a value from the user, and a function which returns that value. Unfortunately (or fortunately, depending on your perspective), this is only slightly less clumsy than writing the straight code.

A strong implication for design of this approach is that a function cannot call a procedure, because the procedure changes values. More formally, a function can change the state of the world as long as it replaces the state afterward; the state of the world is then the same on exit from, as it was on entry to, the function. For this reason, a function can set and change the values of local variables, because they do not exist outside of the function; looking from outside the function, nothing has changed. A procedure can call a function and use the returned value, because that does not violate the design rules for commands in Eiffel.

5.4   Calling a feature from a client

A feature may be called from within the same class, where it is called by giving its name and arguments. It may also be called from a client class, where the client has to supply the name of the object, as well as the feature name and arguments. The action is identical in both cases. The general form of a feature call is *object.feature* (pronounced "object dot feature"). If there is a feature call without an object, then Eiffel assumes that the current object is being used and looks inside the current object for the feature definition. A call within the same class thus has the implicit form *Current.feature*; the reserved word *Current* denotes the current object.

It is common to have features with the same name in different classes; this is known as overloading a routine name. This does not create a name clash, because Eiffel can deduce that the routines are defined in separate classes, and find the correct class for each call. In the *TRIANGLE* system, for example, the *move* routine is called on three points

> *top.move (delta_x, delta_y)*
> *left.move (delta_x, delta_y)*
> *right.move (delta_x, delta_y)*

but both the classes *TRIANGLE* and *POINT* contain a routine with the name of *move*. How does Eiffel know which is the correct routine to use?

When a feature is called, the Eiffel compiler looks at the object on which it is called. The name of the object is located to the left of the feature call, on the other side of the dot, or is *Current*. Given the name, Eiffel can find the type of the object from the variable declaration. Given the type, it can find the class definition. Given the class definition, it looks inside the class for a feature with that name. There is never any confusion; a feature is called on an object of some type, and that class must contain a feature of the correct name. The sequence of events for the feature call *object.feature* is listed and diagrammed below.

1. Find the object to the left of the dot; if there is no dot, use *Current*.
2. Find the class of this object from the declaration.
3. Find the feature defined in that class definition.
4. Execute the feature on the object.

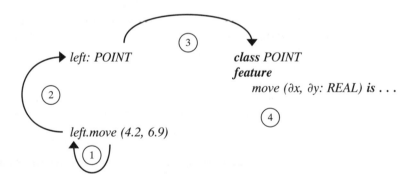

A feature must be exported if it is used in a client. An export clause formally allows two objects to communicate, so it is possible for a class to be a client of itself. An example of this was shown in the function *distance* in the class *POINT* in Chapter 3, which received a point as an argument and returned the distance from the target to the current point. Because the current point used the *x* and *y* values of another object, the target point, these features had to be exported to class *POINT*.

It is possible to nest routine calls, so that a feature is called remotely by a class that is not a direct client; the general form of the call is "*object.feature1.feature2. . .*". A remote call such as this is evaluated left to right. The first feature is called on the object, and returns a value. The second feature is then called on this value, and returns another value. The third feature is then called on this value, and so on. The features within the sequence must be queries, so that an object is returned by each feature. Each object is used to call the next feature, until the end of the chain; the last feature may be a query or a command.

The same result can be achieved by storing each value returned from successive calls, but temporary variables are then needed to store each returned object. A sequence of feature calls is shown to the left below, and the equivalent nested call is shown to the right.

```
b := a.feature1
c := b.feature2
d := c.feature3
d.feature4                    a.feature1.feature2.feature3.feature4
```

A remote call that returns the last character on the third line of the fourth page of a book, for example, could be done using the sequence of calls *book.page (4).line (3).last*. Remote calls should be treated carefully, however, because a remote call can indicate that your design is wrong. It may be better to move the code further down toward the base class (to the right in a system structure chart), than to call the feature high up the chart and have to pass through several intermediate objects.

5.5   Operators

An operator is a function that is defined and called slightly differently from a typical function. Operators are written in two forms, called infix and prefix operators. Infix operators, such as "+", are written in the middle of their arguments, as in "*3 + 5*". Prefix operators, such as "**not**", are written before their arguments, as in "**not** *(x > 3)*". An operator is a function, so it returns a value and has a type; the returned value from "+" is of type *INTEGER, REAL,* or *DOUBLE,* and the returned value from "**not**" is of type *BOOLEAN.*

A normal function call lists the object, a dot, the function name, and then any arguments, but the object and arguments for an operator are written without the normal dot notation. For a prefix operator, the function call lists the operator name, then the object. For an infix operator, the function call lists the object, then the operator, and then the single argument. Operators provide syntactic sugar so that the usual mathematical notation can be used when writing expressions.

To define an operator, the name of the operator is enclosed in double quotes and preceded by the keyword **infix** or **prefix**. The argument (if any) is then written, the type of the operator is coded, and the local variables and routine body follow. The standard numeric, relational, and Boolean operators in Eiffel are all defined as operators in the relevant class. A free operator is an operator whose name begins with one of the characters '@', '#', '|', or '&'; any user-defined operator is a free operator, so it must begin with one of these four special characters. A free operator is defined and called like any operator, but it has a higher precedence than other operators; free operators have the highest precedence of all operators. The complete operator precedence order is given in Appendix B.

Consider an infix operator named "*#percent*" which is called on a real number and takes a real number as argument. It returns the percentage value of the expression, so the operator call

---

    percent := 10 #percent 34.5

---

would return a value of 3.45. The operator would have to be defined as part of the class *REAL*, because it is called on real values. The operator definition would look like

---

infix *"#percent" (value: REAL): REAL* **is**
         – – Current percent of value
     do
         *Result := value * (Current / 100.0)*
     end *– – #percent*

This operator uses the current value of the object (here a *REAL* value) to provide the percentage to calculate. The argument provides the value to take a percentage of. The returned value is the *Current* percent of the argument. Operators provide no extra power to the language, because they behave the same as functions. They are used so that the normal arithmetic and logical notation can be retained and implemented within the same framework as other routine definitions.

5.6   Once routines

A routine may be defined so that it executes only once, no matter how many times it is called. A once procedure may be called many times, but the code inside the procedure only executes the first time it is called; subsequent calls have no effect. A once function executes its code the first time it is called and returns a value, and all subsequent calls return that same value. Once routines allow a value to be initialized once, and then shared across objects, and play the same role as global variables in conventional languages. A once routine is defined by replacing the keyword **do** with the keyword **once** at the start of the routine body.

The input–output system uses a once routine so that all objects share the same I/O system. The object *io* is of type *STANDARD_FILES*. Every client that calls this object should use the same I/O system, so that the creation routine for the I/O system is executed once, and the same I/O system is used by all subsequent calls.

5.7   Example system: the postal system

The stage has now been set for the design of a complete system that uses data flow within and between objects. A simple postal system is developed in this section to show how an object can be created in one class, passed as an argument to another class, and then used in that second class. In the system, an object of type *LETTER* is created, passed as an argument, and the value of that argument (a pointer to the letter object) is then stored in a letter box and retrieved by the owner of the box.

5.7.1   Specification

"The system simulates a postie delivering a letter. The location of the letter box is known to both the postie and the occupant. A letter is generated and given to the postie, who delivers it to the letter box of a house. The owner of the box then gets the letter from the box and reads it."

5.7.2   Analysis

The focus of the system is the code that simulates a postie delivering the letter. This is accomplished by passing the letter as an argument to the box, and storing the letter as an attribute of the letter box; more formally, a reference to the letter object is stored. At some later time, the owner picks up the letter stored in the box. The key code is thus the routine *deliver* in the class *BOX*, shown below.

```
class BOX
feature
    letter: LETTER
    deliver (mail: LETTER) is
            -- store the letter in the box
        do
            letter := mail
        end -- deliver
end -- class BOX
```

Both the postie and the occupant know about the letter box, so both objects require a reference to the box. Neither the postie nor the occupant makes the box or the letter; in fact, the world generates all the objects. An outline of the code in the class *WORLD* (the root class) is

```
class WORLD
creation
    make
feature
    letter: LETTER
    box: BOX
    postie: POSTIE
    me: OCCUPANT
    make is
            -- set up the world for letter delivery
            -- deliver the letter and get the occupant to pick it up
```

```
          do
                  !!box
                  !!postie.make (box)
                  !!me.make (box)
                  !!letter
                  postie.deliver (letter)
                  me.pickup
              end -- make
      end -- class WORLD
```

The creation routine of the root class defines the top-level order of events. The box is first created, then a postie and an occupant are created with knowledge of the letter box. The letter is then created and given to the postie, who delivers it to the box. The occupant then picks up the letter from the box.

5.7.3   Solution design

There are five classes in the system: *WORLD, POSTIE, OCCUPANT, BOX*, and *LETTER*. Both the postie and the occupant are people, but they have far more specific roles in this example, specific enough to require different classes. The world creates a postie, occupant, box, and letter, and gives the postie and the occupant the address of the letter box. It then gives the postie a letter, which the postie delivers to the box. The occupant then looks in the box, retrieves the letter, and reads it. There are three main goals embedded in this sequence of activities: to *make* the world, *deliver* the letter, and *pick up* the letter. The system structure chart for the postal system is shown below.

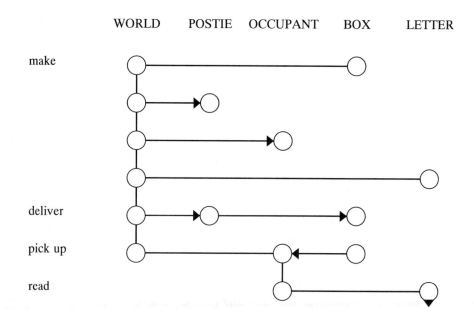

5.7.4   Solution code

Solution code for this problem is shown below. The root class *WORLD* was presented above, and is not repeated here. The other four classes are listed in client order: *POSTIE, OCCUPANT, BOX,* and *LETTER*. The classes *LETTER* and *BOX* have no creation routine, because none is required. Class *LETTER* has a single attribute, the content of the letter, which is defined as a constant. Class *BOX* has a single attribute, the letter, which is *Void* initially and is set to the letter passed in as an argument when the letter is delivered. Only the occupant can read a letter, so the feature to read the letter is exported only to that class.

```
class POSTIE
creation {WORLD}
    make
feature {NONE}
    box: BOX
feature {WORLD}
    make (target: BOX) is
            -- store the letter box
        do
            box := target
        end -- make
    deliver (letter: LETTER) is
            -- put the letter in the box
        do
            box.insert (letter)
        end -- deliver
end -- class POSTIE

class OCCUPANT
creation {WORLD}
    make
feature {NONE}
    box: BOX
    letter: LETTER
feature {WORLD}
    make (target: BOX) is
            -- store the letter box
        do
            box := target
        end -- make
    pickup is
            -- pick up and read any mail
```

```
            do
                if box.has_letter
            then
                    letter := box.letter
                    box.empty
                    letter.read
            end
        end -- pickup
end -- class OCCUPANT

class LETTER
feature {NONE}
    content: STRING is "%NHaving a great time. %
                %%NWish you were here. %
                %%NPlease send money.%N"
feature {OCCUPANT}
    read is
                -- show the contents of the letter
            do
                io.putstring (content)
            end -- read
end -- class LETTER

class BOX
feature {NONE}
    letter: LETTER
feature {POSTIE}
    insert (mail: LETTER) is
                -- put this letter in the box
            do
                letter := mail
            end -- insert
feature {OCCUPANT}
    has_letter: BOOLEAN is
                -- the box has a letter
            do
                Result := letter /= Void
            end -- has_letter
    empty is
                -- delete any mail in the box
            do
```

```
                letter := Void
            end -- empty
    end -- class BOX
```

The postal system runs when the system file *world* is executed. Eiffel creates an instance of the root class *WORLD* and executes its creation routine. The creation routine then creates the other objects and calls features in them, which call other features as necessary. Security is provided by the export policies of the features in each class. When all the routines have executed, control returns to the root creation routine, that routine then finishes, and the system exits.

5.8   Case study: the *BANK* system

The banking system case study begun in Chapter 1 with the design of class *ACCOUNT* can now be extended to a full system of three classes. The specification for the extended system is:

A bank has a single customer, and the customer has a single account. A customer has a name, sex, address, and a bank account. Money can be deposited into and withdrawn from the account, and the balance can be displayed. Interest is added daily on the current balance; the interest rate is 4.5 percent a year. For this version of the system, the customer executes a single transaction of each type.

The analysis, design, client chart, structure chart, and Eiffel code to implement this specification are given in Section 2 of the case study (see Part E).

Summary

- A routine is called by listing the name of the routine, plus any arguments. When Eiffel encounters the name, it transfers control to the routine and executes the routine's code. When the code has been executed, control returns to the caller.
- A routine receives data values through the argument list. A function returns a value by assigning it to the special variable *Result* in the function. A procedure returns nothing.
- Actual and formal arguments must agree in number, order, and type; names are irrelevant. A formal argument is a local variable, but its value cannot be changed once it is bound.
- When a feature is called, it applies to the object to the left of the dot. If a feature is called without an object, it applies to the *Current* (containing) object.
- An operator may be an infix or a prefix operator. It has the same behavior as a function, but it is called using infix or prefix notation, not the normal dot notation.
- A routine may be defined to execute once only. For a once procedure,

subsequent calls have no effect. For a once function, subsequent calls return the same value as the first call.

Exercises

1. Describe the format of
   - a procedure
   - a function
   - an infix operator
   - a prefix operator.
2. Describe the behavior of
   - an attribute
   - a procedure
   - a function.
3. How is a routine called? What happens when a routine is called?
4. How is data passed to a routine from its caller? How is data returned by a routine?
5. How is data read from a user in a routine? How is data shown to the user?
6. Describe the format of an argument list. Define what is meant by
   - formal argument
   - actual argument
   - argument binding.
7. What are the values of the formal arguments in the following examples? Assume that the class contains the following attribute declarations and no intervening code:

   local *a, b: REAL*
   local *p, q: POINT*

   (a)   *a := 12.6*
           do_it (a, a + 32)   *do_it (b, c: REAL)* **is . . .**
           do_it (b, a)
           do_it (a, b)

   (b)   *!!p.make_input*
           do_that (p, q, a)   *do_that (a, b: POINT; p: REAL)* **is . . .**
           !!q.make_input
           do_that (q, p, 134/6*3 − 1)

8. List the signature of every exported feature in the classes *BANK, CUSTOMER,* and *ACCOUNT* from the banking case study (see Part E, Sections 1 and 2).
9. The class *X* has a *REAL* attribute called *number* and four routines. The first routine (*make*) receives the initial value of number as an argument. The second routine (*add3*) adds 3 to the number and displays the new value. The third routine (*add*) takes an integer as argument, adds this to *number*, and displays the new value. The fourth routine takes an integer and two strings, and

displays the first string, then the sum of *number* and the integer, then the second string. Define the signature of every feature. Code the class.

Write the client (class *DRIVE*) for *X*, that creates an object and calls each routine once.

10. Add two new features to class *X*. The first feature (*square_num*) returns the square of *number*. The second feature (*formula*) accepts two integer values and a real value (call the arguments *i, j, a*) and returns the value ((*number* + *i*) / *j*) * *a*. Define the signatures of these routines. Code the header for both routines, then the body of each routine.

Add code to the class *DRIVE* to call each of these functions, and display the value returned by each feature.

11. What is a side-effect? Why are side-effects bad for reusable software?

12. Describe the mechanism used by Eiffel to find the code needed to execute a feature call from one client to another (*object.feature*). What happens when there is no explicit object mentioned (*feature*)? What is the value of *Current*?

13. What is the difference between an operator and a function? What is an infix operator? What is a prefix operator? Give three examples of operators in Eiffel.

14. Show the format of an **infix** operator definition. Write a definition for the infix operator *#mod* (modulus). What is the signature of this operator?

15. Draw a client chart for the postal system. Draw the data structure for the system. Simulate the system, showing how the value of every attribute is set.

CHAPTER 6

Control flow

Keywords

control flow
if
inspect
loop
action

The control flow in a system dictates the order in which actions are executed. Sequence, selection, and iteration define the control flow in a system. Sequence is given by the listed order of actions within a routine and by routine calls. Selection means choosing which path of action (which block of code) to perform as the next step of a plan. There are two selection statements in Eiffel, the **if** and the **inspect** statement. Iteration means that a set of actions is repeated or iterated until some result is achieved. There is only one Eiffel iteration statement, the **loop** statement.

6.1   Sequence, selection, and iteration

A computer executes actions in the order they are listed in the code, unless told to do something different. There are three ways to change the flow of control in a system from the simple listing order of code. Calling a routine transfers control to that routine. Selecting a block of code transfers control to that block. Iteration controls how many times a block of code is repeated inside a loop. In all three cases, control returns to the code immediately after the routine, the selection statement, or the loop. Any program can be built from sequence, selection, and iteration; the approach of using only these three components to build a program is called structured programming.

    A control flow chart shows the order in which actions are executed when the code is run. Because a control flow chart was the first type of chart in general use, it is often referred to as a flow chart. Control flows from one line of code to the next if actions are executed in sequence; this is shown to the left of the following diagram. Control may be split so that several next actions are possible, depending on the value of a test; such a pattern is shown in the middle of the diagram. Control may return to a previous action or not, depending on the value of a test; this pattern is shown to the right of the diagram. A test evaluates to either **true** or **false**, so it is implemented as a Boolean variable, expression, or function.

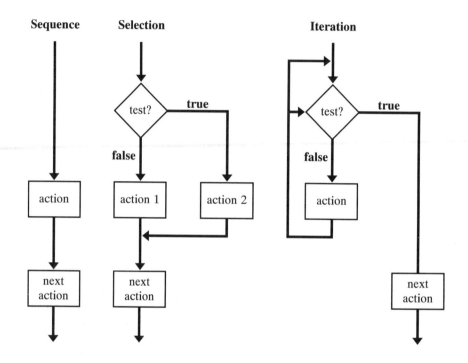

In a flow chart, there are three main symbols. A small circle (not used here) indicates the start or end of the program, a box represents one or more lines of code, and a diamond represents a Boolean test. The arrows that connect these symbols indicate the flow of control. The standard conventions are to draw the control flow from top to bottom and left to right in the chart, and to draw each box so that it has only a single entry point. In Eiffel, the loop condition is tested before the loop action is done. If the condition evaluates to true, the action is not executed. If the condition is false initially, then the action is repeated until the test becomes true.

6.2   Selection: the if statement

6.2.1   Syntax and mechanism

A selection operator selects an action to execute, depending on the value of its condition. The basic selection or conditional operator in Eiffel is the **if** statement. An **if** statement begins with the keyword **if**, and ends with the keyword **end**. The statement is executed and either zero or one actions are selected, then control passes to the statement following the **end** of the selection.

There are three variants of the **if** statement; you must have a final **end**, no matter which form is used. Zero or one actions may be executed in the first two variants, but the last variant has to execute exactly one of the alternative actions. An action may be a single line of code, but more often is multiple lines of code, which may include routine calls.

The three variants of the **if** statement are as follows:

(i) *Single condition*

```
if condition then
      action
end
```

If the condition is true, then the enclosed action is executed. If the condition is false, then no action are done.

(ii) *Multiple conditions*

```
if condition1 then
      action1
elseif condition2 then
      action2
elseif condition3 then
      . . .
end
```

If *condition1* is true, then *action1* is executed, and control passes to the statement after the **end** of the compound **if** statement. If the first condition is false, then the **elseif** part of the statement is tested, and the same rules are applied: if *condition2* is true, then *action2* is executed, and if *condition2* is false, then the alternate part (**elseif**) of that statement is tested. The conditions are tested one by one until some condition evaluates to true, or all the conditions have been tested. If none of the conditions evaluate to true, then none of the actions are executed.

(iii) *Default final action*

```
if condition1 then
      action1
. . .
else
      default action
end
```

One of the actions must be executed in this form of the statement. The conditions are tested in the listed sequence. If one of them is true, then its action is executed. If none of the conditions are true, then the final

else keyword is reached, and the final action is executed; thus the final action provides a default if none of the conditions turned out to be true.

The **if/elseif** and **then** are written on the same line in the code, and the **end** is placed on a new line. If the action fits on the same line as the condition, it is written on that line. If the action is too large to fit on the line, or if there are multiple actions, take a new line and indent a number of spaces; four spaces is the usual number. Indenting the code is an invaluable aid in seeing the flow of control in code; it is a simple trick, and a powerful aid in understanding and debugging. Because indenting is so useful in design, debugging, and understanding code, it should be done when you write code, not added as an afterthought. An indentation in the code makes the control flow obvious; if you have actions controlled by a condition, then the controlled actions are indented to show that control.

Because the action can be compound, it is possible to code an **if**, **inspect**, or **loop** statement as part of the selected action. This practice is known as nesting code, because one complex action is contained or nested in another. It is common in traditional languages, but uncommon in Eiffel. In Eiffel, a routine provides the basic unit for action, and any complexity is hidden inside the routine. The Eiffel practice is to enclose complex code in a routine, and to select and call that routine rather than writing the code "in-line" as part of the control statement.

6.2.2   Client and system structure charts

Selection is not shown on a client chart. If there is a feature call, then that call defines the client relation between two classes. The relation is true whether or not a particular run of the system executes that feature call. The client relation therefore does not reflect conditional actions.

Selection is shown in the system structure chart as a double circle, instead of a single circle; more formally, a conditional feature call is shown as a double circle. In a menu, for example, there may be three options that can be chosen: show the menu, perform an action, or quit the menu. The system structure chart for this fragment of the system is shown below. A menu choice is read from the user, then the choice is used to select an action. If no other input is required, the chart shows a single data input for all the selection nodes. If a choice requires additional data from the user (such as the distance to move the triangle in the *TRIANGLE* example), then an input marker is shown on the node that reads in that data.

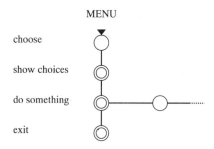

A double circle in a system structure chart means that the feature call is optional or selected, so a set of connected double circles shows the alternate goals that can be selected.

An object may be selected in the same way that a goal is selected. A customer can withdraw money from a savings account or from a check account, for example, and has to select the object to use. Object selection is shown by a filled circle in the node, and the alternate objects are shown to the right of the choice node. No line is drawn to these nodes, because a line indicates that the connected code is executed. In this case, only the code for one object is executed, so there is no line. The nodes to the right of the object selection node show the set of alternate class features.

A portion of the system structure chart for an ATM system is shown below. In this example, a user is shown the balance of an account, and has to select the account (the object) to display. In this scenario, there is no goal choice, because the display is automatic; an account has to be displayed, and the user can only choose which account to display. A choice for object selection would look like

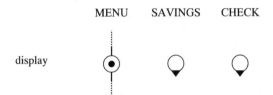

Both a goal and an object may be selected. In the bank system case study, for example, a customer first selects which goal they want (deposit, withdraw, show balance, etc.) and then the object they want (savings or check account). A selection of both goal and object is indicated by combining the two symbols, to create a filled double circle.

A menu that asks the user to select a goal and an object, and executes the code for that goal on that object, is indicated on a system structure chart by the symbols shown below. The first choice is a pure goal selection which displays the possible menu choices; this choice calls a routine within the menu. The second, third and fourth choices select both goal and object, so the objects are alternates and no line from the selection node is shown.

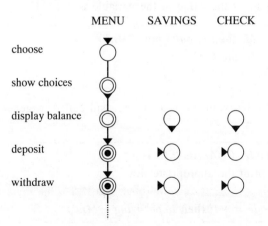

The data flow is shown in the diagram in the usual way, by data flow markers. The first marker on the top node indicates the code to read in a menu choice for the goal. The first choice listed is a display, so it is shown with an output. The second choice requires no additional data, and simply calls routines to show the balance. The third and fourth choices require the user to select an account and to enter an amount to deposit or withdraw; this amount is then passed to the selected object, as indicated on the diagram.

Only selection between goals, between objects, or between both, are shown in a system structure chart. Choices that do not cross one of these boundaries, and thus do not affect any other part of the system, are hidden within a single node.

6.2.3   Examples of the if statement

The first example of selection uses the gender of a person to generate a title for their name. The task is to examine the value of a character variable ('M' or 'F'), and produce a string output ("Mr." or "Ms."). There are many ways to do any task in programming, and the selection of the best alternative separates the good from the bad designer. All the variants shown except the first are reasonable solutions for this problem.

The first solution is shown below. This is a bad solution. It does the task but is error-prone, because the two statements are independent. First, this solution does not reflect the logic of the problem, because one of the alternates must be chosen; the choices are not independent. Second, you should not test a value twice, because you run the risk of getting it wrong the second time. If the valid values for *sex* are changed, it is possible that the person modifying your code would change the first line, consider the change to be finished, and produce buggy code by not seeing and fixing both tests.

```
if sex = 'M' then io.putstring ("Mr.") end
if sex = 'F' then io.putstring ("Ms.") end
```

A better solution is to have a single test, with two actions, where the second action is the default if the value of the variable is not 'M':

```
if sex = 'M' then io.putstring ("Mr.")
else io.putstring ("Ms.")
end
```

This code can be wrapped in a routine, and called to generate the title. The procedure is

```
print_title (code: CHARACTER) is
        -- print the appropriate title
    do
        if code = 'M' then io.putstring ("Mr.")
```

```
        else io.putstring ("Ms.")
        end
    end – – print_title
```

The print routine is not responsible for checking that it has been called correctly; this is the responsibility of the caller. If the gender code was input by a user, however, it may be incorrect and the input has to be validated before it is stored. One way to validate the gender is to use a *BOOLEAN* function, which returns **true** for a valid sex code and **false** otherwise.

```
valid_gender (code: CHARACTER): BOOLEAN is
        – – is code a valid sex code?
    do
        if sex = 'M' then Result := true
        elseif sex = 'F' then Result := true
        end
    end – – valid_gender
```

There is no need to set *Result* to be false, because *Result* is here a Boolean variable that is initialized to **false**; if the value is not changed in the routine, then its value is still **false** when the routine exits. This solution is the obvious way to produce the title and solve the problem, but the obvious solution is often not the best solution. Design is iterative, so your first solution should be just that: the first and worst solution. Other, better solutions to this problem are shown below, when the **or** operator and the **inspect** statement are presented.

The next example shows how multiple actions may be controlled by a single test, by enclosing the actions in a block; when the condition is true, then all the actions are executed in sequence. The task is to calculate the gross pay where there are two pay rates, one for normal hours (*hours* <= 35) and one for overtime (*hours* > 35). Overtime is paid at time and a half (1.5 times the normal rate). Two solutions are given for this task. The first solution is shorter, the second is clearer; the clearest solution is the best. A short solution is good, and brevity is always to be encouraged, but not at the expense of clarity. You should always write your code with the next person in mind, and clear code is easier to understand and modify.

```
gross_pay (hours, rate: REAL): REAL is
        – – gross pay for hours at this pay rate, including overtime
        – – this is the collapsed version of the feature
    do
        if hours <= 35 then Result := hours * rate
        else Result := 35 * rate + (hours – 35) * rate * 1.5
        end
    end – – gross_pay

gross_pay (hours, rate: REAL): REAL is
```

```
            -- gross pay for hours at this pay rate, including overtime
            -- this is the explicit but long version of the feature
    local
            normal_pay, overtime, overtime_pay: REAL
    do                                          -- normal rate
            if hours <= 35 then
                normal_pay := hours * rate
            else                                -- overtime rate
                normal_pay := 35 * rate
                overtime := hours - 35
                overtime_pay := overtime * rate * 1.5
            end
            Result := normal_pay + overtime_pay
    end -- gross_pay
```

The normal pay and the overtime pay are calculated separately here, and added in the last line to get the total pay. If the hours worked is zero, then the normal pay is calculated to be zero. If the hours worked is less than 35, then the overtime pay is not calculated but is used in the final result. The overtime pay is zero if a value is not explicitly assigned, because REAL variables are initialized to zero. This example has used a literal value for the normal time limit of 35 hours, and another for the overtime rate of 1.5. As you can see from the code, the normal time value is used three times in the code, violating the heuristic that something should be done once. A better solution would define and use a constant, so that any change to the value needs a single line change (the constant definition) instead of multiple lines scattered through the code.

The last example of selection shown below illustrates a common use of selection, where a range of values is divided into a series of adjoining intervals that cover the range. In this example, a grade has to be calculated based on a student's mark. There are five possible grades, of which only one can be given. The grades are

```
 0 <= mark <  50, "Fail"
50 <= mark <  65, "Pass"
65 <= mark <  75, "Credit"
75 <= mark <  85, "Distinction"
85 <= mark < 100, "High distinction"
```

The obvious solution for this problem is to write a series of five **if** statements, one for each range. In this solution, each statement tests if the value is greater than the minimum and smaller than the maximum, so the total solution would use five statements, each with two tests. This first and worst solution is needlessly long and complicated, because the **elseif** can be used to test each range in turn. The best solution for this task is

```
grade (mark: REAL): STRING is
        - - grade for this mark
    do
        if mark < 50 then Result := "Fail"
        elseif mark < 65 then Result := "Pass"
        elseif mark < 75 then Result := "Credit"
        elseif mark < 85 then Result := "Distinction"
        else Result := "High distinction"
    end - - grade
```

Only a single boundary value is tested in each line. There is no need to explicitly test if the mark is greater than 50 and less than 65 (for example), because the second test (*mark < 65*) is executed only if the first condition failed. The mechanism of the **elseif** statement guarantees that, if the mark is compared to the value 65, then that mark has already failed the previous test and therefore has to be greater than or equal to 50. For the same reason, there is no need for a final condition; if the **else** clause is ever executed, then no previous condition was true, and the mark must be greater than 85. Explicitly testing both ends of the range in each line is bad, because each boundary is tested twice. The mechanism of the **elseif** form allows short, clear, and safe code.

There is also no need to include code for the cases when the argument value is less than zero, or greater than 100, because that is not the responsibility of the routine; it is the responsibility of the client to call the routine in the right way. If the routine is called in the right context, then it guarantees to return the right result; if it is not, then the software contract is broken and no result is guaranteed.

6.3   Relational operators

Relational operators take two values as arguments, compare the values, and produce a *BOOLEAN* result. The operators, their names, and an example of each, are

Operator	Meaning	Example
=	equal	hours = 8
/=	not equal	reply /= 'q'
<	less than	weight < maximum
>	greater than	value > minimum
<=	less than or equal	my_wage <= your_wage
>=	greater than or equal	discriminant >= 0.0

All the relational operators are infix or binary operators, because they are placed between the two values they use. Relational operators have lower precedence than the numeric operators, so the numeric values in a flat expression are calculated first and then compared; the total precedence order for all operators is given in Appendix B. Relational operators all have equal precedence, so they are evaluated left to right in an expression unless the precedence is overridden by brackets.

6.4   Boolean operators

Boolean operators take one or two Boolean values as arguments, and return a Boolean value. The Boolean operators are **not, and, and then, or, or else, xor**, and **implies**; the behavior of each operator is given by the truth tables shown below. In the table, the symbol T means **true**, F means **false**, and ? means don't care.

The operator **not** takes a single argument, so it is a unary, prefix operator; all other Boolean operators take two arguments, so they are binary and infix operators. The operator **xor** is the exclusive or operator; the expression is true if one or the other, but not both, of its arguments is true. The operator **implies** is the logical implication operator, which has the formal behavior that a false premise (the value of *a* here) implies anything.

not	a	not a
	T	F
	F	T

and	a b	a and b	**and then**	a b	a and then b
	T T	T		T T	T
	T F	F		T F	F
	F T	F		F ?	F
	F F	F		F ?	F

or	a b	a or b	**or else**	a b	a or else b
	T T	T		T ?	T
	T F	T		T ?	T
	F T	T		F T	T
	F F	F		F F	F

xor	a b	a xor b	**implies**	a b	a implies b
	T T	F		T T	T
	T F	T		T F	F
	F T	T		F ?	T
	F F	F		F ?	T

The operators **and then**, **or else**, and **implies** are lazy operators, because the second argument is evaluated only if necessary. In *a* **or** *b*, for example, if the value of *a* is true then it doesn't matter what the value of *b* is; **true or** *anything* evaluates to **true**. In the normal form of the operator, the value of both arguments is tested, so the value of *b* is always evaluated, and tested in *a* **or** *b*. For the lazy operators, the first argument is always evaluated, but subsequent arguments are only evaluated if they are needed to find the value of the expression. In *a* **or else** *b*, for example, the value of *b* is not tested if *a* is **true**, because there is no need; if *a* is true, then the expression must evaluate to **true**.

Arguments in a Boolean expression can be literals (**true**, **false**), variables, or expressions. The precedence order for the Boolean operators is shown below, using the precedence levels given in Appendix B; a high level means that an operator is applied before an operator at a lower precedence level.

Precedence level	Operator		
11	**not**		
5	**and**	**and then**	
4	**or**	**or else**	**xor**
3	**implies**		

The precedence order for numeric, relational, and Boolean operators given in Appendix B states that **not** is evaluated first in a flat expression, then the numeric operators are evaluated, then the relational operators, and finally the remaining Boolean operators. Complex expressions are evaluated using this default operator precedence order, unless it is overridden by brackets. Several examples of complex Boolean expressions and their order of evaluation are given below; the values of the variables in each expression are given above the examples.

a = **true**, *b* = **false**, *c* = **false**	$x = 12, y = 3, z = 6.5$
a **and** *b* **or not** *c*	**not** $(x > y)$ **and** $(x >= z)$
= *a* **and** *b* **or true**	= **not true and** $(x >= z)$
= **false or true**	= **false and** $(x >= z)$
= **true**	= **false and true**
	= **false**
not *a* **and then** *b* **or** *c* **implies** *b*	$(x \ / \ 3 \ * \ y) \ /= z + 6$
= **false and then** *b* **or** *c* **implies** *b*	= $(4 * y) \ /= z + 6$
= **false**	= $12 \ /= z + 6$
	= $12 \ /= 12.5$
	= **true**

A better solution to the title problem (Mr. or Ms.) can now be given using Boolean operators. The solution simply sets *Result* to be **true** if the code is valid; if the code is not valid, then the function returns its default value of **false**.

```
    valid_gender (code: CHARACTER): BOOLEAN is
            -- is code a valid sex code?
    do
            Result := sex = 'M' or sex = 'F'
    end -- valid_gender
```

This solution assigns a Boolean value directly to *Result*, with no need for an **if** statement. The solution is short, simple, and crystal clear.

6.5   Selection: the inspect statement

The **inspect** statement allows a multi-way branch for discrete variables; it is similar to a case statement in other languages. An expression is tested at the top of the statement, and a list of possible values is given within the statement; a selection value cannot be listed twice within the statement. When the statement is executed, the expression is evaluated and the value matched to one of the listed values in a **when** clause; the corresponding action is then taken. An optional **else** clause may be included to deal with cases that do not match any of the listed values. The format of the inspect statement is

```
    inspect expression
    when values then
        action
    when values then
        action
    . . .
    else
        action
    end
```

The **inspect**, **when**, and **end** keywords are indented equally, and the **when** and **then** are placed on the same line. If the action can also be placed on the same line, then it follows immediately; if it cannot, then the action is indented on the following line. A block of actions may be controlled by a single test. The **else** keyword is placed on a new line, and its action follows on that line, or is indented on the next line. All the possible values of the expression must be enumerated in the statement, or an **else** clause has to be included. If the expression has a value that is not listed in the statement, then the system will crash with a run-time error.

The **inspect** statement can only be used when the values of the expression are of type *INTEGER* or *CHARACTER*. Because **unique** values are of type *INTEGER*, inspect can be used to select from a set of unique values. There are three ways to denote possible values for selection:

(i)   A single value: **when** *3* **then . . .**
(ii) A set of values: **when** *'a', 'e', 'i', 'o', 'u'* **then . . .**
(iii) A range of values: **when** *1 . . 12* **then . . .**

Multiple values are separated by commas, such as **when** *1, 2, 6 . . 7, 43, 99 . . 112* **then . . .**

The **inspect** statement can be used to validate the gender code and to generate a title (Mr. or Ms.), and provides the best solution for this task. The possible values are listed together in a single statement, and the action for each value is shown immediately to the right of that value. In the solution shown below, either upper or lower case codes are valid.

```
valid_gender (code: CHARACTER): BOOLEAN is
        -- is code a valid sex code?
   do
        inspect code
        when 'M', 'm', F', 'f' then Result := true
        else Result := false
        end
   end -- valid_gender
```

Here, there needs to be an explicit **else** clause, because the user can input values other than the correct ones. The code to print a title can also be implemented with an inspect statement, which clearly shows the action for all four of the valid sex codes. The best solution for this task is shown below.

```
print_title (code: CHARACTER) is
        -- print the appropriate title
   do
        inspect code
        when M', 'm' then io.putstring ("Mr.")
        when 'F', 'f' then io.putstring ("Ms.")
        end
   end -- print_title
```

An example of the inspect statement showing multiple actions for one of the choices is shown below. In this example, the code examines a grade (fail, pass, credit, distinction, high distinction) produced from a mark, and prints a friendly message for the student.

```
   inspect grade
   when 'F' then io.putstring ("Too bad")
   when 'P' then io.putstring ("OK")
   when 'C' then io.putstring ("Good work")
```

```
when 'D', 'H' then
     io.putstring ("%NOh frabjous day")
     io.putstring ("%NCalloo, Callay!")
else
     io.putstring ("I know I've made some bad decisions lately, %
     %but I'm feeling much better now.")
end
```

In this example, the usual grades are covered by the explicitly listed choices; any unusual but valid grades are covered by the default action.

6.6   Iteration: the loop statement

Iteration or repetition allows a set of actions to be repeatedly executed inside a loop, until a test forces the loop to exit. After the loop exits, the next statement after the **end** of the loop is executed. There is only one iteration instruction in Eiffel, the **loop** statement.

6.6.1   Syntax and mechanism

The **loop** statement is made up of a series of clauses. The format of the statement is

```
from
     initializations
until
     exit condition
loop
     action
end
```

Each keyword starts a new line. If the remainder of the clause can be placed on the same line, then it is; usually, it is placed on the next line and indented. If there are no initializations, the **from** keyword is still coded, but it is immediately followed by the **until** keyword. The loop's mechanism is as follows:

1. The initializations are performed, if there are any.
2. If the exit condition is true, the loop action is skipped.
3. Otherwise, the loop instructions are repeated until the exit condition becomes true.

If the loop is entered, then the test value must be set to true by the action in the loop. If the test is not made true at some point, then the loop will never exit, and it will execute forever; this is known as an infinite loop. In an infinite loop, it is often the case that no output appears on the screen, but the computer is busy executing the loop actions until it is abnormally terminated by either the user or the operating system.

6.6.2   Iteration and charts

Iteration is not shown on a client or a system structure chart. The client chart shows which class uses the services of another, so the number of times that a service is used (above zero) is not relevant. The system structure chart shows that a feature is called, but the number of times the feature is called is not shown in that chart either.

6.6.3   Examples

The first loop example is a function that sums the numbers from a start value to an end value, inclusive; these values are passed as arguments. It is the responsibility of the caller to pass the correct values, so a call to the following routine could result in an infinite loop if *finish* is initially larger than *start*; this could be checked with a precondition. The loop is controlled by a counter, so it is called a counter-controlled loop. Counters are very common in computing. The variables *i, j, k, l, m,* and *n* are often used as counters, because these names are often used as a counter or index in mathematical notation.

```
sum_between (start, finish: INTEGER): INTEGER is
        -- sum the integers from start to finish, inclusive
    local i: INTEGER
    do
        from i := start
        until i > finish
        loop
            Result := Result + i
            i := i + 1
        end
    end -- sum_between
```

The second example finds the average rainfall in a period. Rainfall is recorded each day of the period, and end of input is signalled by the special sentinel value of -999. This type of loop is called a sentinel-controlled loop. The input buffer is used to store each input; the buffer can be tested to see if it is the sentinel or a valid rainfall value. If the first input is the sentinel value, the code inside the loop should not be executed, so a value has to be read in before the loop and this value tested by the loop condition. If the value is not the sentinel, it has to be processed (added to the sum here), and then the next value read in at the bottom of the loop. The code inside the loop thus has the form "process, then read". The intuitive form of a loop is "read, then process", but this form will not work in this case, because a read has to be placed before the loop test.

The input routine prompts the user and stores a value in the input buffer, here in the buffer *io.lastint*. The routine is a procedure because it changes the state of the terminal screen and the input buffer. The main routine below loops around getting input and processing it by incrementing the value of *sum*, and the day counter *days*. The day counter has to start at zero, because there may be no input and the counter should then contain the value zero. The function to calculate the average rainfall value from the sum and count is shown below the input routine.

```
rainfall, days: INTEGER
end_of_input: INTEGER is -999

get_all_rainfall is
        -- get all the rainfall for the period
        -- record the sum and the interval
    do
        from
            io.putstring ("%NEnter the rainfall values for the period")
            io.putstring ("%NTo finish, enter the value -999%N");
            get_rainfall (days)
        until
            io.lastint = end_of_input
        loop
            rainfall:= rainfall + io.lastint
            days := days + 1
            get_rainfall (days)
        end
    end -- get_all_rainfall

get_rainfall (today: INTEGER) is
        -- prompt the user for today's rainfall value
    do
        io.putstring ("Enter the rainfall value for day ")
        io.putint (today + 1)
        io.putstring (": ")
        io.readint
    end -- get_rainfall

average_rainfall: REAL is
        -- average rainfall for the period
    do
        if days > 0 then Result := rainfall / days end
    end -- average_rainfall
```

A third variety of loop may be called a result-controlled loop, in which the loop repeats until some flag is set to be true. The number of times that the loop executes is not known initially, so the loop cannot be controlled by a counter. The loop is not controlled by the input, so it is not a sentinel-controlled loop either. A common pattern in programming is to have a loop that executes until either a flag is set or a counter exceeds a test value; thus, the exit test for a loop may itself be a complex construct. In such a case, it is usual to define the test as a Boolean function and hide the complex test in that routine.

Eiffel was designed to have a very simple syntax, so that there is only one iteration construct, the **loop** statement. The language Pascal, in comparison, has three iteration commands: for, while, and repeat. The Eiffel **loop** construct corresponds to the Pascal *while* statement, because the test is placed at the top of the loop, before any code in the body of the loop is executed. In Eiffel, most of the effort in system building is devoted to designing a correct solution; the implementation language has therefore been kept very simple.

6.7   Input validation

It is the responsibility of the client to provide the correct data to any routine called by the client. A computer system cannot rely on the user to always input the correct data, however, so input from the user should be validated before it is allowed into the system. The standard way to validate input in Eiffel is to use the I/O system buffers (*io.last<type>*) to store the input until a valid input has been entered.

User input is read inside a loop, until a valid input is received. The loop exits when a Boolean test for valid data returns true, at which time the buffer contains a valid value. This value is then queried and used by the system. The standard input validation technique therefore needs three parts: a loop to get the data, a function to validate it, and a function to return the valid value.

Consider the task of getting a menu choice from the user, where the choice consists of a single character. The menu system gets the choice and executes it by calling the appropriate routine in another class. In selecting a choice from an automatic teller machine (ATM) menu, for example, a *MENU* class will get a valid choice and call the appropriate account routine. Class *ACCOUNT* contains all the code used to manipulate an account, but has nothing to do with *MENU* handling, because there are many ways to interface with an account, through a character or graphical menu or directly from the bank. This separation of objects and concerns is crucial to the design of an OO, reusable system.

The main control structure needed to get and execute a choice in the class *MENU* shown below is provided by two routines, one called *get_choice* and one called *do_choice*. The *get_choice* routine must be a procedure, because it changes the state of the screen and the value of the input buffer. Because it is a procedure, it cannot return a value, so *do_choice* picks up the valid value directly from the I/O buffer, in this case from the feature *io.lastchar*. The routine *do_choice* must also be a procedure, because it calls other procedures that change the balance of the account or display data on the screen.

A customer has a single account in this example. The menu choices on that account are

D, d	deposit money
W, w	withdraw money

B, b	show balance
H, h	show choices (help)
Q, q	quit the system

The system structure chart for this code fragment is very similar to the menu system used in the *TRIANGLE* system in Chapter 3, so it is not provided here. An outline of the code in class *MENU* is shown below.

```
class MENU
creation
    make
feature
    account: ACCOUNT
    make is
            -- display the menu, execute the choice
        do
            from show_choices
            until end_chosen
            loop
                get_choice
                do_choice
            end
            io.putstring ("%NY'all have a nice day, hear%N")
        end -- make

feature {NONE}
    get_choice is
            -- get a valid menu choice from the user
        do
            from
                io.putstring ("%NEnter menu choice: ")
                io.readchar
            until valid_choice
            loop
                io.putstring ("That is not a valid choice. Please try
                again")
                io.putstring ("%NValid choices are D, W, B, Q, and
                H%N")
                io.putstring ("%NYou may use upper or lower case letters")
                io.putstring ("%NEnter menu choice: ")
                io.readchar
            end
```

```
            end -- get_choice
        valid_choice: BOOLEAN is
                -- has the user entered a valid choice?
            do
                inspect io.lastchar
                when 'D', 'd', 'W', 'w', 'B', 'b', 'H', 'h', Q', 'q' then
                    Result := true
                else Result := false
                end
            end -- valid_choice

        do_choice is
                -- execute the choice made by the user
            do
                inspect io.lastchar
                when 'D', 'd' then
                    io.putstring ("Enter the amount to deposit: ")
                    io.readreal
                    account.deposit (io.lastreal)
                when 'W', 'w' then
                    io.putstring ("Enter the amount to withdraw: ")
                    io.readreal
                    account.withdraw (io.lastreal)
                when 'B', 'b' then
                    account.show_balance
                when 'H', 'h' then
                    show_choices
                end -- inspect
            end -- do_choice

        end_chosen: BOOLEAN is
                -- has the user chosen to finish?
            do
                Result := io.lastchar = 'Q' or io.lastchar = 'q'
            end -- end_chosen

        show_choices is
                -- show and explain the menu choices
            do
                . . .
            end -- show_choices
    end -- class MENU
```

In this solution, class *MENU* is a client of class *ACCOUNT*, because it uses the features of the account; the creation or assignment of the account has not been shown above. Such a solution is strange, because it implies that the menu has an account (client means "has", "uses", or "contains"), when we normally think that an account has a menu. Getting the choice and executing it have to be separated to make a reusable system, so two classes are required; the menu defines the interface, and the account supplies the actions. Since the account routines have to be called from inside the menu, there is no choice in how the solution is coded at this point in time. A much better solution is provided by the use of inheritance; however, presentation of this solution must be deferred until the topic of inheritance has been covered.

6.8   Recursion

A sequence of actions can be repeated by iteration in a loop, or by recursion in a routine. A recursive routine is one that calls itself. The routine is initially called by a client, does some work on the problem, and then calls itself. The called copy of the routine then does some work, and calls itself again. At each step, part of the problem is solved, so eventually the problem is completely solved and no further calls are needed. At that point, the last copy of the routine returns control to its caller, which in turn returns control to its caller, and so on until control is returned to the original client.

Input validation provides a simple example of recursion. The input routine gets a value from the user. If the value is correct, then the routine exits. If the value is incorrect, then the routine calls itself to get a new value. Calling continues until a correct value is input, at which point the last called version exits, returns control to the caller, that exits, returns control to the caller, and so on. The code for a routine that gets a valid menu choice is

```
get_choice is
        -- get a valid menu choice from the user
    do
        io.putstring ("%NEnter menu choice: ")
        io.readchar
        if not valid_choice then
            io.putstring ("That is not a valid choice. Please try again")
            io.putstring ("%NValid choices are D, W, B, Q, and
            H%N")
            io.putstring ("%NYou may use upper or lower case letters")
            get_choice
        end
    end -- get_choice
```

Most recursive routines are functions, not procedures. A recursive function receives an argument, does some work, and passes on a smaller argument to the next copy of the function. Recursion continues until the argument is basic or empty; this is known as the base case in recursion. When the base case is reached, there may be many copies of the routine in memory, each waiting for the next to return control. The last copy of the routine then returns the basic answer to its caller, which returns a value to its caller, and so on.

A recursive function has three parts:

1. The action: at each call, the function does some of the work and passes on a simpler value.
2. The recursive call: the simpler value is passed as an argument to the next copy.
3. The base case: when the base case is reached, control returns back up the stack of routines.

The classic example of recursion is the factorial function, which returns the value of n factorial (written n!). The factorial of an integer is the integer multiplied by all smaller integers, down to 1; four factorial, for example, is given by

> 4! = 4 x 3! = 4 x 3 x 2! = 4 x 3 x 2 x 1!

This is a clear case for recursion, because the value of n! is defined in terms of a simpler problem, that of finding (n-1)! The code is

```
factorial (n: INTEGER): INTEGER is
            -- n x n-1 x n-2 x . . . x 1
    do
        if n = 1 then Result := 1
        else Result := n * factorial (n - 1)
        end
    end -- factorial
```

The factorial function is an example of tail recursion, because the recursion is the last code in the function. In tail recursion, the routine does some work and passes on a simpler problem. Some problems are more easily handled by head recursion, in which the recursive call is followed by the routine's processing; in head recursion, the routine passes on a simpler problem, then does some work with the returned value.

The factorial function is an example of one-way recursion, because the routine only calls a single copy of itself. Two-way recursion is common, and multi-way recursion is possible. A good example of two-way recursion is the quicksort algorithm, in which a list of values is split into two and each half of the list is sorted—by splitting each half and sorting each quarter of the values. This is two-way recursion, because each call to quicksort generates two recursive calls, one for each half of the argument list.

Recursion is an extremely powerful tool that can produce very compact and powerful code; this is especially useful for scanning data structures such as lists and trees. In some languages, such as Lisp, recursion is the basic form of looping and iteration is quite rare. Traditionally, functional languages tend to use recursion, and procedural languages tend to use iteration; Eiffel is a procedural, OO language.

6.9   Case study: the *BANK* system

The *BANK* system case study is extended by adding password processing and a menu-based interface to the bank account. A customer enters a password into the system, and if the login is successful, a menu of commands for the customer's account is presented. The customer then chooses commands, and the system executes them, until the customer exits the system. This version of the system simulates the action of an ATM. The current specification is:

Build a simple banking system, in which the bank has a single customer, and the customer has a single account. A customer has a name, sex, address, and a bank account. Money can be deposited into and withdrawn from the account, and the balance can be displayed. Interest is added daily on the current balance; the interest rate is 4.5 percent a year.

The customer has access to the account through an interactive menu, such as that used by an ATM. The system starts up and waits for the customer to enter a password. The customer is allowed three attempts to enter a valid password. If no correct password is entered after three attempts, then the system terminates. If the password is correct, then the customer is shown a menu of account choices, and the system reads and executes the choices. Any number of transactions may be made; processing on the account continues until the customer chooses to exit the system.

The valid menu choices (upper or lower case) are

D	Deposit
W	Withdraw up to the total amount in the account
B	Show the balance
Q	Quit the system
H	Help: Show the menu choices

Interest is added to the account after the system exits.

The analysis, design, client chart, system structure chart, and solution code for this version of the banking system are shown in Section 3 of the case study (see Part E).

Summary

- The basic selection statement in Eiffel is the **if** statement. It has three forms:

  if . . . then . . . end
  if . . . then . . . elseif . . . elseif . . . end
  if . . . then . . . elseif . . . else . . . end

The selection executes zero or one of the actions, depending on the value of the conditions.

- The **inspect** statement provides a simple multi-way branch for selection, but it can only be used for expressions with discrete values. Its form is

> **inspect** *expression*
> **when** *values* **then** *action*
>
> **. . .**
>
> **else** *action*
> **end**

All possible values of the expression must be included in one of the tests.

- The iteration statement in Eiffel is the **loop** statement. It has the form

> **from**
>   *initializations*
> **until**
>   *exit condition*
> **loop**
>   *action*
> **end**

- The Boolean operators are **not, and, and then, or, or else, xor,** and **implies.** The operators **and then, or else,** and **implies** are lazy, so their second argument is only evaluated if necessary.
- Operator precedence is **not,** then the numeric, relational, and Boolean operators. Brackets are used to override the default preferences and to make an expression clearer.
- Input validation uses the input buffer to store values until a valid value is found.

Exercises

1. What is meant by structured programming?
2. What symbols are used in a flow chart? What conventions are used in a flow chart? How many lines of code are in a box?
3. Draw a flow chart for dining at a restaurant.
4. Which part of structured programming does an **if** statement implement?
5. What are the three forms of an **if** statement? How many times does **end** occur in each?
6. Write the code to show whether you need an umbrella or not. Read in the rainfall for the last half hour. If it is raining, then you need (output) an umbrella; if not, take your sunglasses.
7. Write a class *SHOP* that sells teddy bears. The shop stores the number and

price of a teddy bear. The user inputs a number, you check if you have enough, and reply "OK" or "Nope". If you have enough bears, then sell that number to the happy shopper (decrement the number of bears and increment the money). Develop the code in four steps:

(a) Code the class template and feature headers.

(b) Code a routine to process a single user input.

(c) Wrap a loop around the test, and exit the loop when all the bears have been sold.

(d) Add the ability to exit the loop at any time. Show the number of bears left at that time.

8. Using the **if** statement, implement a routine to display the following advice:

Age	Reaction
16	child
17	eager
18	hardworking
19	let me out of here
20+	not to be trusted

Do not consider values other than those shown here; that is the responsibility of the caller.

9. Name the relational operators. What arguments are taken by the relational operators? What is returned? What is the precedence order of the relational operators?

10. List the Boolean operators. What arguments are taken by Boolean operators? What is returned? What is the precedence order of the Boolean operators?

11. What is the precedence order for the numeric, relational, and Boolean operators?

12. Evaluate the following expressions:

- 32 * 6 <= 9 / 43 + 5 **and** 'a' > 'A' **or** "cat" /= "category"
- **not** (33 // 3 = 11 * 8 \\ 8) **xor** "myHeight" > "yourHeight"
- 4 − 6 ^ 2 / 3 < 5 **and then** 't' < 'z' **and then not** (p = Void)
- (i = 0) **or** (j / i) = k, where i = 0, j = 3, k = 2
- (i = 0) **or else** (j / i) = k, where i = 0, j = 3, k = 2
- (i = 0) **or else** (j / i) = k, where i = 3, j = 3, k = 1

13. What is the format of an **inspect** statement? What is the restriction on its use? What are the three ways to specify selection values? Can these be combined? What happens if the current value of the test does not match any listed value?

14. Use an **inspect** statement to implement the following selection and output:

Age	Reaction
15–20	child
21–25	eager
26–30	hardworking

| 31–35 | let me out of here |
| 36+ | not to be trusted |

15. Write a routine *factorial* to calculate n! (n factorial) using a loop.
16. Write code to produce the following pattern; use routines for modularity.

```
    *
   ***
  *****
   ***
    *
```

17. Adapt your code to produce the following pattern:

```
    *
   +++
  - - - -
   ^^^
    !
```

18. Write the code needed for a simple menu system. The menu gets a single character, and outputs a message or takes some action. The choices and actions are

a, A	"eh?"
d, D	ask for a number, double it, and display the result
e, E	exit the menu

19. Validate the user input. If the user's choice is not valid, tell them and get a new choice; repeat this until a valid choice is entered.
20. Write a recursive routine to find the power of a number. The arguments will be the number (*REAL*), the power (*INTEGER*), and the function returns a *REAL* value.
21. The Fibonacci numbers begin with the sequence 1, 1, 2, 3, 5, 8, 13, 21, 34, 55, and so on. Each Fibonacci number is the sum of the previous two numbers; the first two are defined to be the value 1. Write a two-way recursive routine to show the first ten Fibonacci numbers (tricky).

CHAPTER 7

Designing for reuse

Keywords

principles
contract
precondition
postcondition
STRING
antibuggingRdebugging

Reusable software is based on the idea that you never rewrite code: you just use it in different ways, and add code as necessary. The most important technique for designing reusable code is to design for reuse from the very beginning, and write a solution for future users, not just for the current use. Reuse will fail if you design a minimal solution to the current problem. Some basic principles for designing reusable software are presented in this chapter, and illustrated with the Eiffel library class *STRING*. The advantages of reuse principles in avoiding bugs in the first place, and recovering from any bugs that do arise, are then discussed.

7.1 Design by contract

The foundation of reusable software in Eiffel is design by contract. A feature is defined to behave in a certain way. If the feature is called with the correct input, then it guarantees to produce the correct output; this is the contract between client and supplier. If I am a supplier of some service (like a doctor or a plumber) and you contract me to do a job, then you define the job and leave me to do it. As a client, it is your responsibility to define the job and give me all the information I need to accomplish it. As a supplier, it is my responsibility to do the job correctly, given the right information. This clear separation of the responsibilities of client and supplier defines a contract between the client and supplier, so that they both know what to do and can interact simply and cleanly.

> **DESIGN PRINCIPLE 1:** Design by contract: behavior is defined by a contract, so the implementation is hidden.

The precise definition of the behavior of a class or type, divorced from any particular implementation, is known as the definition of an abstract data type, or ADT. This approach allows many different implementations to be used, without affecting the semantics or meaning of the type, because all the implementations have the same behavior. A designer simply wants to use the features of a class, and does not care about how they are implemented. Any complexity is invisible to the designer or the user, because it is hidden inside the class definition.

One part of design by contract is the definition of an explicit interface between features; such an interface is defined by the signature of the feature. If a feature is passed the correct arguments, then it should use those arguments (and any other data) to do the job and make the correct change to a stored value or return the correct result to the client. This is why a class is composed of a large set of small features; the interface between the client and supplier is well-defined, and each feature "does its own thing". The power of OO systems for supporting reuse comes from the definition of features that do a single task, and can be relied on to do one, simple task. A feature does a single thing, and does it well. It is often difficult to define what is a "single thing", however; the major part of the effort in OO design is spent in working out how to separate a complex problem into its basic elements, and in placing the code for each element in the correct routine in the correct class.

> **DESIGN PRINCIPLE 2:** A feature does a single thing.

The approach of building a system from small parts is in strong contrast to the typical novice approach, in which a large chunk of code is written with no internal divisions. An example of this monolithic approach to design was shown in the plan for moving a triangle (Chapter 3), where a large chunk of code was written, then decomposed into small pieces. A part of the task cannot be done in such a solution; it is all or none. Another example was shown in the discussion of an input–output routine that prompts for an input and returns that input value to the caller (Chapter 5). Such a routine does two things: it changes the value of the input buffer and returns a value. If a client later wishes to do only one of these things, such as using the input value a second time, then the value cannot be returned separately. The routine has to be decomposed and rewritten to deal with this new situation, and any existing, working software has to be changed to use the new solution.

Complex tasks are done by calling a sequence of small features, so that the decomposition of the task into simple pieces is explicit. Decomposition is a basic tool for system design, because it defines a set of small tasks, each of which is easy to code and test. It is also a basic tool for reuse, because the solution structure makes each task explicit so that it can be used without rewriting it. Consider the task of adding interest to a bank account. This task was decomposed in Chapter 1 into a procedure that added the interest, and a function that returned the daily interest rate. When a new type of account, the check account, was added to the system, the procedure was reused without change, because a new function for a new interest rate could be added. If these two tasks had been placed in a single routine, then that code would have to be decomposed and rewritten to deal with two interest rates. Reuse is based on designing for the future, so that future changes can be added to the system without changing the existing, working code. This is difficult, much more difficult than writing a "throw-away" solution to the current problem, but it pays off in the long run.

The construction of an Eiffel system has a high initial cost, but a low maintenance cost. Careful consideration has to be given to the initial definition and coding of the classes. Once defined and tested, however, the code never has to be changed. It is reused by calling each feature as necessary. A new client may call and combine the features in a different way than the existing clients, but the features themselves are not changed. The initial investment in a correct feature pays off every time that feature is used. This approach is known as "designing for change", and Eiffel makes change easy by implementing a change as an addition, so that the existing software is reused in the new version, not changed.

The strong division in Eiffel into two types of features is a result of this rule. A command changes one or more values, and returns nothing; it is implemented by a procedure. A query changes nothing, and returns a single value; it is implemented by a function or by an attribute. Programming by side-effect violates these rules; the code pretends to be a function, but violates the condition that nothing is changed. Eiffel does not allow you to change the value of an argument to a routine, so it is impossible to use the argument list as a *Return* mechanism. The only way to get a value back to the caller is to return it as the value of a function.

There are some situations where you cannot avoid changing an attribute inside a function. You can, however, maintain the contract that a function doesn't change the world. The key insight is that the world has to be in the same state before and after the function call. This means you are allowed to make any changes within the function, as long as you restore the initial state at the end of the function. As far as the rest of the world is concerned, nothing has changed, so the contract is maintained. Local variables are one way to implement this, because they are created when the function is entered, and disappear when the function is exited. There are other, more sophisticated techniques that save the state of the world initially, and restore it before the function returns.

The separation of changing the state of an object, and finding out what the new state is, produces sets of paired routines: a command (procedure) to change the state, and a query (function or attribute) to return any new value. This is the pattern seen in the input routines, where you issue a command to get a value from the user, then issue a query to find out what that value was. To illustrate this idea, consider the situation where you turn on the lights of your car during the daytime. You issue the command to turn on the lights (by pulling/pushing/turning a knob/button/lever), but then you cannot see if the lights are actually on or not. To discover the state of the lights, you have to get out of the car, move to the front of it, and look. This is a command to change the state, followed by a query to discover if the command succeeded, a very common pattern in Eiffel.

A good design solution to the separation of command and query which is now common in modern artifacts is to build in a feature to display the current state. In a car, turning on the lights now also turns on a light on the car dash, providing instant feedback. The trend toward WYSIWYG ("what you see is what you get") computer interfaces is another example of this approach, where the effect of a command is instantly visible on the screen. For every command, there is a matching query that shows if the command succeeded.

The definition of features allows an explicit interface between parts of a system. A caller must pass the right arguments to the feature, because actual and formal arguments must agree in order and type. The definition of arguments says nothing about the values of those arguments, however; it just defines their type. In most cases, there are also restrictions on the values that are passed to and received back from a routine. The contract between client and supplier is enforced by setting preconditions and postconditions on a routine.

A precondition is a condition that must be true before the routine is executed; we say the condition is asserted to be true on entry to the routine. If we wish to calculate the average, for example, the appropriate code is *average := sum / count*. Before this code is executed, we must be assured that the value of *count* is non-zero, because a divide by zero is undefined and will crash the system. Thus, a precondition of this routine is that *count* be non-zero. If this precondition is satisfied (if it is true), then the routine guarantees to return the correct value for the average. The correct value of the average is a postcondition on the routine; it is an assertion that must be true when the routine exits. Pre- and postconditions can be explicitly defined, and checked when the routine is entered and exits. If the precondition is violated, then the software contract becomes void, and no result is guaranteed. If the precondition is true and the postcondition is violated, then the code in the routine is incorrect. Assertions enforce the software contract. For two assertions *pre* and *post*, the contract is defined by testing the *pre* assertions on entry to, and the *post* assertions on exit from, the routine.

The general form of an assertion is a Boolean; it may be a Boolean value, expression, or function call. An assertion may be preceded by a name that is used to make the meaning of the test clear. The general form of an assertion is thus

---

name: boolean expression

Multiple assertions in a pre- or postcondition are separated by semi-colons.

The general form for a routine with assertions is shown below, where an optional *TYPE* is shown for functions; procedures do not return a value. The routine requires the preconditions to be true before the code is executed, and will test them on entry, after argument binding. If the preconditions are satisfied, then the routine ensures that the postconditions are true, and tests them before exit from the routine. The assertions are written so that they can be evaluated like any other Eiffel code, and their results used to enforce the software contract.

```
     name (arguments) <:TYPE> is
           -- header comment
        require
           precondition(s)
        local
           declarations
        do
           code
        ensure
           postcondition(s)
        end -- name
```

Programming by contract, or programming by assertion, is a very powerful technique for software engineering; the use of this technique in Eiffel is discussed in Part D of this book. Assertions define the assumptions that are made by the routine (the preconditions) and by the caller of the routine (the postconditions). Without going into detail about how assertions are defined and tested, we can derive a basic rule for designing by contract: it is the responsibility of the caller to satisfy the preconditions of a routine.

DESIGN PRINCIPLE 3: The client is responsible for calling a routine correctly.

The code in the called routine should not check that it was called in the right way. The precondition can be checked, and may well fail if the contract was broken, but the precondition is separate from the code in the routine. A routine should not validate its arguments; this is the responsibility of the client. In the *average* example, the caller must contain code to test that the value of *count* is non-zero, before passing that value. If the value is zero, then the *average* function should not be called. A routine guarantees that it will produce the correct result if it is called correctly, so the *average* routine needs a precondition to test the value and thereby check that the contract is still in force.

An example of design by contract was given in Chapter 2, when the *withdraw* routine was discussed, and its code and assertions were presented. The code is repeated below. Two preconditions are defined on the routine. First, the amount to withdraw must be positive; you cannot withdraw zero or a negative amount. Second, the balance can never go below zero, so the amount to withdraw must be less than or equal to the balance. These assertions are both preconditions of the routine, because they must be checked before the code is executed. If they are satisfied (if they both evaluate to true), then the code is executed. If the code is correct, then the new balance must be changed by the amount; this is defined as the postcondition and is checked before control is returned to the caller.

```
     withdraw (amount: REAL) is
```

```
┌─────────────────────────────────────────────────────────────┐
│            -- deduct this amount of money from the balance    │
│    require                                                     │
│        positive: amount > 0                                   │
│        funds: amount <= balance                               │
│    do                                                          │
│        balance := balance - amount                            │
│    ensure                                                      │
│        changed: balance = old balance - amount                │
│    end -- withdraw                                             │
└─────────────────────────────────────────────────────────────┘
```

In design by contract, the client defines the contract and leaves the details to the supplier. A strong implication of this rule for design is that control should be given to the supplier; more generally, control should be pushed down the client chart, so that any decision making is local. An object contains the data and the code to make a decision, so it should make that decision; the client should not do the work of the supplier. This principle is called delegation of authority. An office manager delegates authority to the line staff, and these people handle as much of the work as possible, so control is delegated as far as possible. This is the reason to be careful with remote feature calls: it is possible for the manager to bypass the chain of command, but then the details are not handled at the lowest possible level, and the clean separation between levels is lost. This approach is called centralized authority or kibbitzing, where the people doing the work do not have the authority to make decisions.

DESIGN PRINCIPLE 4: Let the supplier do the work.

A plan uses many objects, so the code for the plan spans many classes. It is possible to place all this code in the top-level class and avoid objects altogether; Eiffel cannot stop you from designing a bad system. You have to decide how to decompose the plan, and where to place each element of the plan. Your decision is made simple by using the design principle to push the code down the client or system structure chart. The class that contains the data also contains the code that uses or changes that data, so the decision to move code may lead to the design of a new class, as was seen in the design of the class *POINT* in Chapter 3.

The system structure chart shows that the code in a plan can be viewed as a set of nodes connected by control flow; think of these as beads on a string. The code must be placed in the system somewhere. The system designer decides where to place the code by pushing all the beads to the left (all the code is written at the top level of control), or pushing each bead as far to the right as it will go, and thus stringing the beads out evenly.

7.2   Features of a class

A system should always be written in such a way that it can be reused: it should be modular, simple, and clear. Code should always be written so that the next person can use it, not so that you can write and forget it. Software is used and reused over a period of years or decades, and it is unusual for the original author of the code to be the person who wishes to reuse it. Code must always be designed with the next person in mind, so that someone unfamiliar with the code can read and understand it.

Good design is hard. A good design is simple, pleasant, and obvious to use. The car is now such a common artifact that we don't think twice about using it, and expect everyone to be able to drive a car. The controls of a car have been designed so that anyone can use them; the control panel in a car has taken over 100 years to design, with many bad decisions made during that time. The classic mistake made by a designer is that the user understands as much about the system as the designer. This assumption is ludicrous; most people are not experts in a field, and do not wish to be. A good designer tries one solution after another, each time evaluating if this is the correct decomposition of the problem into its basic elements, and evaluating if the solution is simple and obvious to someone who has never seen it. Good design is the end product of a series of solutions, where each version is evaluated and thrown away. The mark of a really expert designer is that their first solution is a good one. Most of us are not experts, so we need to try many solutions before a good solution emerges.

Bad design is easy. Bad design is infuriating and depressing to use. A sure sign of bad design is that it is hard to use, hard to understand, and requires a lot of explanation or comments (Norman, 1988). It is almost certain that your first solution will be a bad one, because it has not been thought out and tested. The first solution is usually a bad solution because it is designed as a "one-off" solution that will never be reused. Whenever you design a system and write code, you have to take the position of someone who has never seen the code before, and ask yourself if that person could understand your code with no help from you. It is difficult, but essential, to take a different viewpoint from yourself. When you write code, you know the problem and the solution intimately. A future user of the system, and of the code, does not and does not want to; they simply want to pick up a component and reuse it. As much of the internal complexity of the system as is possible should be hidden within the routines. Only the behavior of the routines should be visible; this is the principle of information hiding.

DESIGN PRINCIPLE 5: Hide the complexity inside a routine.

The basic method for hiding the complexity is to define a set of features and export only the behavior. How does the designer know the best way to define a set of features? How should a complex problem be split into smaller processes? How do you know what should be a routine? Object-oriented design gives strong guidelines about what should be a routine, and where that routine should be placed. The rule (though not its interpretation) is simple: routines that use an attribute live in the same class as that attribute. In Eiffel, routines that change the value of an attribute have to be coded in the same class, because an attribute acts like a query; its value cannot be changed outside of the class.

DESIGN PRINCIPLE 6: Routines that use an attribute live in that class.

Consider the problem of finding the total wall area in a room. A room has four walls, and a wall has a number of windows and doors. The wall area for the room is calculated by finding the area of the windows, the area of the doors, and the area of the four walls of the room, then deducting the window and door areas from the total area. In this simple specification, there is a single goal: find the wall area. Four objects are used to find this area: windows, doors, walls, and rooms. The code to find the area of a window lives in the class *WINDOW*. The code to find the area of a door lives in class *DOOR*. The code to find the area of a wall lives in class *WALL*. The code to find the area of a room lives in class *ROOM*.

The client chart for this system is shown below, followed by the relevant code fragments in each class.

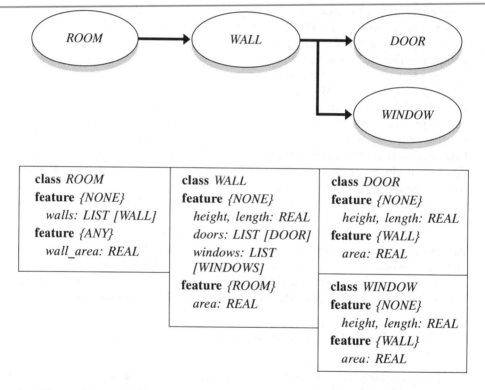

class *ROOM*	class *WALL*	class *DOOR*
feature *{NONE}*	**feature** *{NONE}*	**feature** *{NONE}*
walls: LIST [WALL]	*height, length: REAL*	*height, length: REAL*
feature *{ANY}*	*doors: LIST [DOOR]*	**feature** *{WALL}*
wall_area: REAL	*windows: LIST*	*area: REAL*
	[WINDOWS]	
	feature *{ROOM}*	class *WINDOW*
	area: REAL	**feature** *{NONE}*
		height, length: REAL
		feature *{WALL}*
		area: REAL

The code to calculate each area uses the dimensions of each object (wall, door, window), so there are a set of *area* routines, each defined within the relevant class. The attributes for each class, and the routine header for the *area* routines, are shown on the next page. The code uses a class *LINKED_LIST*, which is described in the next chapter; for the present, all we need to know is that a list can store many objects of the same type, such as a list of four walls or a list of windows.

The code that changes or uses an attribute is placed in the same class as that attribute. The attributes are hidden (not exported) whenever possible, by exporting them to no class; more formally, to the class *NONE*. A class exports its behavior, and hides its internal representation. Code to change the value of an attribute must be in the class that contains that attribute. There is no choice, because the value of an attribute can only be changed by code within that class. The decision about where to place the code that uses an attribute, without changing it, is more complex. If the code that uses an attribute is placed outside the class that contains that attribute, then the attribute has to be exported. It is possible to export an attribute, and there may be occasions when it is reasonable to do so, but an attribute should be exported only after long and careful thought has led to the conclusion that there is really no choice about the export.

DESIGN PRINCIPLE 7: Hide the attributes whenever reasonable.

One of the most powerful methods for keeping the attributes hidden is to strictly define the behavior. Often, what might at first glance look like a need for exporting an attribute is really a behavior. In the *ROOM* system, for example, there may be a need to test if the size of a door is less than some value. The obvious code to do this is something like

```
if door.height < limit then . . .
```

The correct way to test if the door is high enough is shown below. Logically, the client wishes to know if the door is high enough for a particular use; this should be implemented as a test to see if the door is high enough, as a function in the class *DOOR*. With this technique, the height of the door is not known to the client, so this attribute need not be exported. As an added advantage, the meaning of the test is now obvious from reading the code.

```
class WALL
    . . .
    if door.higher (limit) then . . .
end -- class WALL

class DOOR
    . . .
feature {NONE}
    length, height: REAL
    . . .
feature {WALL}
    higher (limit: REAL): BOOLEAN is
            -- is the door higher than limit?
        do
            Result := height > limit
        end -- higher
```

The second solution requires more code than the first, but this is not a valid criticism of the solution. An OO system is written so that it is reusable, not so that it is short. If the reusable code is also short, then that is excellent. If it is a choice between brevity and reuse, however, then reuse wins every time. If the class *DOOR* ever changes so that *height* is no longer stored as a single attribute with the name *height*, then the obvious, first solution above requires two classes to be changed. The second solution localizes the change to a single class, the class *DOOR*. For reusable design, export the behavior and hide the representation.

Attributes define the essential features of a class and store the state of the object. Keep the number of attributes as small as possible. Local is beautiful, so local variables should be used whenever possible. If the same variable occurs in several routines, then several local variables should be used, one per routine. Attributes are not meant to make the code short, or to improve efficiency; they define the state of an object. The design principle is very simple: try to make a variable local. If a variable cannot be local, then and only then do you declare it an attribute.

> **DESIGN PRINCIPLE 8:** Keep the number of attributes small; use local variables where possible.

In an OO system, data is stored in an object, and the features of the class manipulate that data. There is thus little need to pass data around a system; some argument passing is inevitable, but this should be kept to a minimum. If a lot of data is passed around a system, then data encapsulation has probably failed and the system should be redesigned.

> **DESIGN PRINCIPLE 9:** Don't pass around a lot of data.

An object may be passed around by using the object reference as an argument and storing the reference in the called routine; the postal system in Chapter 5 used this technique. In that system, there was no choice, because the letter was created in one place and used in another. Only a single value was passed as an argument, however, so a large amount of data was not passed around. Passing around many items of data is usually a red flag which indicates that the code that gets the data should be moved into the class that uses or stores the data.

7.3   Understandable code

Every name (class, attribute, procedure, function, or local variable) in a system should help the reader understand your code. Clear, simple, and meaningful names tell the reader what each variable stores in a routine, what each routine does, and what each class contains. Meaningless names (such as *a, b, c, x, ttl_wt, value*) give no help to the reader; to understand what these variables contain, the reader has to read the code, infer what it does, and then infer what role each of the variables plays. The process should work the other way, so that the names help the reader infer what the code does. It is possible to make a name too long, and the code then suffers because it cannot be seen at a glance, so a name should be as short as reasonable and as long as necessary.

DESIGN PRINCIPLE 10: Names are clear, simple, and meaningful.

The only thing worse than a name with no meaning is a name that is misleading, so great care should be taken in getting the names right. When I write code, one of my main reference books is a thesaurus, so that I can try various alternatives before deciding on the best name. A name should indicate exactly what a feature does; words are a very powerful aid in communication.

Because a feature lives in a particular class, that class can be used to provide a context for the feature name. In the *ROOM* system, for example, there are many features called *height*. There is no need to call them *door_height, window_height,* and *wall_height,* because they are features of the appropriate class. If they are used internally, the feature is obviously a feature of that class. If they are exported and used externally, then the name of the object indicates the class, such as *door.height, window.height,* and *wall.height.*

Every routine should have a header comment; this comment describes what the routine does. It is written from the perspective of someone using the routine, and describes what the routine looks like from the outside; how the routine implements the specification is an internal matter to that routine. No implementation details should appear in the routine header comment. If such detail is required, it can be placed inside the routine.

A comment is set in the present tense, not the future; the routine does something, so the comment should not say it "will do" something. The language is imperative; the routine does something, so you don't hope that it "should" do something. There is no need to tell the reader a fact that is obvious from the code or from the context, so comments can be short and clear. There is no need to tell the reader that a routine is a function ("This function . . .") or a procedure ("This procedure . . . "); this is obvious from the routine header. For the same reason, you need not specify that a function "returns", "finds", or "calculates" something; this is what a function does by definition. The language of a comment is simple, active, and declarative.

7.4   Choices in design

The principles given in this chapter provide a strong basis for the design of a solution, and should be used as the basic rules for design. The world is complex, however, and two principles for design may support different choices; there are valid situations where slavishly following a single guideline produces an inferior solution. The design principles embody the default rules for Eiffel system design, and should be used and applied unless there is a compelling reason to do otherwise.

Design is about making choices, where each choice has a consequence for the structure of the solution. For the typical problem, many solutions are possible, and each solution may have a reasonable supporting argument. In such a case, the value of each competing argument has to be compared and a decision made about how to implement the solution in code. This process of creating and comparing alternative solutions is common in design, and reveals why design is such a hard process, requiring an enormous amount of experience and knowledge. The beauty of Eiffel is that it offers far more formal and strict design guidelines than most languages, but even in Eiffel design is more heuristic than algorithmic. Bertrand Meyer, the author of Eiffel, characterizes the skills of a programmer as "somewhere between Bertrand Russell and a plumber". Russell was a pure mathematician who set out the foundations of modern mathematics in the *Principia Mathematica* (Russell and Whitehead, 1913), and who reflects the logic and elegance seen in the design of a good computer system. A plumber has to make things work, using the tools and materials at hand. Programming requires both sets of skills.

Design is as much an art as a science, so it is almost impossible to give rules for every situation. Far more is understood about the process of design now than was known ten years ago, but there is far more to learn. This does not imply that design has no place in science; the mathematician Poincaré noted that "The defining characteristic of a scientist is aesthetic, not logical".

7.5   Documentation: the short form of a class

It is a commonplace in computing that the documentation for a system never keeps pace with the system itself. When the system changes, any existing documentation has to be changed to reflect the new system. If this is done, it is a constant drain on resources for the company. If it is not done, the documentation is out of date. Eiffel solves this problem by storing the documentation in the code, and provides a set of tools to derive class and feature definitions directly from the code.

The **short** tool is an executable program that takes a class as an argument (in Unix, we type **short** *filename.e*) and produces a document from that definition. The tool reads the class file, and shows the external interface of every exported feature in the class. Non-exported features are not listed, because they are not part of the external interface. The external interface of a feature is defined by the header of that feature, the header comment, and the pre- and postconditions. The **require** keyword in the output indicates a precondition, and defines any assumptions about the value of the input arguments. The **ensure** keyword indicates a postcondition, and defines the effect of calling the routine. An assertion has the form of an optional name, followed by a colon, followed by the assertion itself, such as *funds: balance >= 0* from the account withdrawal routine in Chapter 2.

7.6   The Eiffel library class *STRING*

Eiffel supplies a set of classes with the Eiffel compiler, known as Eiffel library classes; the exact names and number of library classes depends on the version of Eiffel you use. Library classes directly support reuse, because the class has already been written, and you can simply use that class. We have already seen some of these classes; there are Eiffel library classes for *INTEGER*, *REAL*, *CHARACTER*, *BOOLEAN*, and *STRING*. The Eiffel library class *STRING* is discussed in this section as an example of well-designed, reusable code.

The short form of a class lists the name of each feature, the name and type of its arguments, the header comment for that feature, and the preconditions and postconditions on each feature. A precondition asserts what has to be true about the values of the input arguments. A postcondition asserts what has to be true when the feature returns, if the precondition was satisfied.

An abbreviated version of the short form of the ISE Eiffel Version 3 library class *STRING* is shown below. The class offers many more features than these; the full list may be found by referring to the Eiffel Version 3 Library Manual, which lists the features of over 100 library classes, or by running **short** on the class in your system. The selected features are shown below; some of them are then described after the short listing.

```
-- Character strings
class interface STRING creation procedures
    make (n: INTEGER)
            -- Allocate space for at least n characters
        require
        non_negative_size: n >= 0
        ensure
        capacity = n
exported features
    infix "<=" (other: like Current): BOOLEAN
            -- Is current string less than or equal to other?
        ensure
        Result implies not (Current > other)
    infix "<" (other: STRING ): BOOLEAN
            -- Is current string lexicographically lower than other?
    infix ">=" (other: like Current): BOOLEAN
            -- Is current string greater than or equal to other?
        ensure
        Result implies not (Current < other)
    infix ">" (other: STRING ): BOOLEAN
            -- Is current string greater than other?
        ensure
        Result implies not (Current <=other)
    append (s: STRING)
            -- Append a copy of s at end of current string
        require
```

> *argument_not_void: s /= Void*
>
> **ensure**
>
>   *count* = **old** *count* + *s.count*
>
> *capacity: INTEGER*
>
>   -- Number of characters guaranteed to fit in space
>
>   -- currently allocated for string
>
> *copy (other: STRING)*
>
>   -- Reinitialize with copy of *other*
>
> **require**
>
>   *other /= Void*
>
> **ensure**
>
>   *count* = *other.count*
>
>   -- For all *i: 1 .. count, item (i)* = *other.item (i)*
>
> *count: INTEGER*
>
>   -- Actual number of characters making up the string
>
> **ensure**
>
>   *Result >= 0*
>
> *empty: BOOLEAN*
>
>   --Is string empty?
>
> *fill_blank*
>
>   -- Fill with blanks
>
> **ensure**
>
>   -- For all *i: 1 .. capacity, item (i)* = *Blank*
>
> *is_equal (other: STRING): BOOLEAN*
>
>   -- Is current string made of the same character sequence as *other*?
>
> *item,* **infix** *"@" (i: INTEGER): CHARACTER*
>
>   -- Character at position *i*
>
> **require**
>
>   *index_large_enough: i >= 1;*
>
>   *index_small_enough: i <= count*
>
> *put (c: CHARACTER, i: INTEGER)*
>
>   -- Replace by *c* character at position *i*
>
> **require**
>
>   *index_large_enough: i >= 1;*
>
>   *index_small_enough: i <= count*
>
> **ensure**
>
>   *item (i)* = *c*
>
> *remove (i: INTEGER)*
>
>   -- Remove *i*-th character
>
> **require**

> *index_large_enough:* $i >= 1;$
> *index_small_enough:* $i <= count$
>
> **ensure**
>
> $count =$ **old** $count - 1$
>
> *resize (newsize: INTEGER)*
>
> $--$ Reallocate if needed to accommodate at least *newsize* characters
>
> $--$ Do not lose any characters in the existing string
>
> **require**
>
> *new_size_non_negative:* $newsize >= 0$
>
> **ensure**
>
> $count >= newsize;$
>
> $count >=$ old $count$
>
> *substring (n1: INTEGER, n2: INTEGER): STRING*
>
> $--$ Copy of a substring of current string containing all characters
>
> $--$ at indices between *n1* and *n2*
>
> **require**
>
> *meaningful_origin:* $1 <= n1;$
>
> *meaningful_interval:* $n1 <= n2;$
>
> *meaningful_end:* $n2 <= count$
>
> **ensure**
>
> $Result.count = n2 - n1 + 1$
>
> $--$ For all $i: 1 .. n2 - n1,$ $Result.item\ (i) = item\ (n1 + i - 1)$
>
> *to_lower*
>
> $--$ Convert string to lower case
>
> *to_upper*
>
> $--$ Convert string to upper case
>
> **end interface** $--$ class *STRING*

The first feature in the listing is the creation routine for a string which allocates enough storage to store n characters, where n is the single input argument. The precondition states that n must be non-negative, and the postcondition states that the string can now contain n characters.

The operator "$<=$" is an infix operator which compares the content of two strings on the basis of lexicographic order. Lexicographic order compares characters in the two strings from the first (leftmost) to the last, stopping when the characters are not equal. The value used for comparison is the ASCII value of the character, so 'a' $<$ 'b' $< \ . \ . \ .$ 'A' $<$ 'B', and so on. Because it is an infix operator, it is called by writing "*s1* $<=$ *other*" instead of using a normal feature call of the form "*s1.*$<=$ *(other)*". The feature is called on a string, and takes a string as argument (the argument is **like** the current object). There is no restriction on the value of the input argument. If a value of **true** is returned, then the current string is not greater than the string passed as an argument.

The *append* operator takes a string as an argument, and appends the argument to the end of the current string. It requires that the argument not be *Void*, so the passed reference must actually point to an object of type *STRING*. If this precondition is satisfied, then the routine guarantees that the new value of the current string has a total length of the old string and the string passed as an argument; the **old** operator shown in the listing refers to the value of the current object on entry to the routine.

The feature *substring* takes two integers as arguments. It returns a value of type *STRING* that is the part of the current string between positions *n1* and *n2* in the string. Consider the strings *s1* and *s2* shown below, where a substring of *s1* ("der") is assigned to the string *s2*.

```
s1: STRING is "Wonderful time"
s2: STRING
     s2:= s1.substring (4, 6)
     io.putstring (s2)                    ==> "der"
```

The function returns a string of length 3, guaranteed by the postcondition *Result.count = n2 − n1 + 1*). The returned string is a copy of the string containing all the characters from the fourth to the sixth position, as stated in the header comment and the commented postcondition

```
−− For all i: 1 .. n2 − n1, Result.item (i) = item (n1+ i − 1)
```

This is a comment rather than an executable postcondition, because the Eiffel proof machinery to process assertions cannot handle the logical quantifier "for all"; a discussion of this topic would take us far beyond Eiffel, however, into the field of automatic proof checking.

The preconditions of each feature are used to check that the feature has been called in the right way; this is the part of the assertion checking that enforces programming by contract. If a precondition is violated, then the label to the left of that precondition is displayed as an error message. If a client called the feature *substring* to get a part of the current string and passed values that were invalid, then the name of the violated precondition (*meaningful_origin, meaningful_interval*, or *meaningful_end*) would be displayed as part of the error message to tell the user exactly what went wrong.

There are two names for the function that returns a character from a string, given the position of the character. The first name is *item*, a function that is called using the normal dot notation, such as *s.item (3)*. The second name for the function is the infix operator @, which is called using the normal infix format, such as *s @ 3*. Both names refer to the same function body, and are thus names of the same feature.

The documentation shows that *STRING* is a reference class (see the class header), not an expanded class, so it uses reference semantics. An input string need not be cloned, however, because the function *io.laststring* returns a new object that is a copy of the input string, and not a pointer to the buffer. Once a

string has been passed from the I/O system, it is a normal reference object. For
the three strings *s1, s2, s3*, the operations shown on the left have the effect stated
on the right:

io.readline	
s1 := io.laststring	*s1* is a copy of the last string read in
s2 := io.laststring	*s2* is a copy of the last string read in
s1 = s2	**false**; *s1* and *s2* have different references
equal (s1, s2)	**true**; *s1* and *s2* have the same field-by-field content
s1.is_equal (s2)	**true**; *s1* and *s2* contain the same character values
s3 := s1	*s3* is the same string (same reference) as *s1*
s3.copy (s1)	*s3* now has the same field-by-field content as *s1*
s3 := clone (s1)	*s3* has the same content as *s1* (which may be *Void*)

The class interface definition for class STRING given in this chapter
illustrates how reusable software is built and reused. A programmer need not write
code for any of these features; simply find the appropriate feature in the class,
examine the interface to see how it is used, and then use it.

7.7   Dealing with errors

Errors can occur at three levels in the design and coding of a computer system;
errors in a program are commonly called bugs. The first and simplest level is that
of syntactic errors, where the syntax of a statement is incorrect; an error in the
syntax is flagged when you try to compile the system. The second level includes
type and interface errors, where each part of a system is correct in isolation, but
the pieces don't fit together; in Eiffel, this level is also discovered and flagged
at compile time. The third level includes semantic errors, where the system
compiles and executes but produces the wrong result. A system may also be
stylistically wrong or badly designed, but no compiler can yet catch this type of
error. Eiffel tries to catch as many errors as possible at compile time, because it
is better to fix bugs as soon as possible in system development.

The best solution to the problem of errors is to avoid them in the first place
(antibugging). All the design and layout rules given in this book are antibugging
tools; they are the products of long experience in making code easier to write and
understand. If, after designing the system in parts, using classes and routines to
define small modules, and coding and testing each part as it is added, your system
is still buggy, then it is time for debugging; this is the most infuriating, unpleasant
aspect of programming.

7.7.1 Antibugging

Antibugging is the use of tools and techniques to avoid the generation of bugs.
The most common novice error is to forget an **end** statement. Every routine, every
if statement, every **inspect** statement, and every **loop** statement requires an **end**.
Because the **end** is not the focus of attention during coding, it is easy to forget

it. The compiler will discover that an **end** is missing, and generate an error message that specifies a line number, but the error may not be in that line.

The Eiffel compiler generates an error message when it cannot parse the current statement; this is what the compiler means by an error. For this reason, the actual error will be at or before the flagged line. If an **end** is omitted from an **if** statement inside a **loop**, the compiler will probably not notice the error at that point, because the code can still be parsed. The statements following the "missing" **end** are simply added to the code under the control of the **if** statement, as if they were part of the **if** statement. The **end** of the **loop** is then interpreted as the **end** of the **if**, and the **end** of the routine is interpreted as the **end** of the **loop**. The first time the compiler realizes that something is wrong is when it sees the next routine header inside the "current" routine. At that point, the compiler gives up and generates an error message, but the real error may be long before the line flagged by the compiler.

The best way to avoid this error is to check that every compound statement is terminated by an **end**. The best way to ensure this is to indent the code to show flow of control; a missing **end** then visually "jumps out" at the programmer. Indenting should be done when the code is written, not as an afterthought; it is a simple, powerful aid to the programmer.

The second level of errors involves inconsistent code, where two pieces of code are correct by themselves, but do not fit together. This type of error is normally found by the compiler as a result of Eiffel's strict type checking. One example of type checking is that actual and formal arguments must agree in number, order, and type; if they do not, then the calling and called pieces of code don't fit together. Eiffel catches a large number of errors during the compilation stage, errors that in a less strict system would not be found until run time. Finding errors at the compilation stage is a great advantage, because the compiler tells you where the error is, and what the error is; you don't have to track it down.

7.7.2   Debugging

The third and most difficult type of error is one that occurs at run time, when the compiled code is executed. The error may cause the system to crash with a run time error, or the system may run to completion but produce the wrong output. This last type of bug is the hardest to find, because there is no obvious place to look for it; the system executes and terminates normally. The hardest part of debugging is finding the bug; once found, it is comparatively easy to fix.

When Eiffel detects an error at run time, the system terminates with an exception message. The message says that an exception was generated because an assertion was violated; the name of the assertion is usually shown, to indicate what was wrong. Eiffel also shows the location of the error by displaying the calling stack at the time the error occurred. When a routine is called, it is placed on a stack; more formally, a record of the routine call is placed on the call stack. When the routine exits, the record is taken off the stack. The current feature is thus at the top of the stack, the feature that called it is second on the stack, and so on down to the creation routine for the root class at the bottom of the stack. By looking at the routines on the stack, it is easy to find which routine contained the run-time error. By looking at the assertion that was violated, it is easy to find what the error was in that routine.

In the current version of the banking system (see Section 2 of the case study in Part E), the *make* routine in *BANK* calls the creation routine in *CUSTOMER*. The *make* routine in *CUSTOMER* creates an account, then executes one transaction of each type on the account. In the scenario used here, assume that an error occurs when the *withdraw* routine is executed in class *ACCOUNT*, because the *funds* precondition is violated. At that point, Eiffel will halt the system and show the current state of the calling stack. While each version of Eiffel uses a different format, the run-time error output should look something like

Class	Routine	Error
ACCOUNT	withdraw	funds: balance >= 0
CUSTOMER	withdraw	Assertion violation
BANK	make	Assertion violation

The bug that caused the crash is shown at the top of the stack of routine calls. The table says that the *funds* assertion was violated in the withdraw routine of class *ACCOUNT*. This routine was called from the *withdraw* routine of class *CUSTOMER*, which in turn was called from the *make* routine of class *BANK*. Knowing that the balance was wrong, it is a simple step in this example to find the error; the code in the *withdraw* routine of class *CUSTOMER* did not check that the withdrawal was legal before executing it. It is the responsibility of the caller to do this, so new code has to be added in class *CUSTOMER* to validate the user input and fix the bug.

If the system runs but produces the wrong output, your code is syntactically correct but it solves the wrong problem. In this case, the location of the bug can be very hard to find. Few things are more frustrating than staring at code for minutes . . . hours . . . days, and then realizing that the bug was in a different part of the system entirely! Don't stare at code for more than a couple of minutes; if you don't find the bug in that period, it is time to work smarter, not harder.

There are two standard debugging tools: be the computer, and see the data. The first tool requires you to play the role of the computer, and see what the code actually does, as opposed to what you think it does. Pretend that you are really dumb, as dumb as a computer, and that you can understand nothing except very simple instructions; but you know exactly what to do with each instruction. Go through the code using actual data values, and see if the code behaves the way you expected. This technique is known as hand execution of the code, because you execute the code "by hand" and use paper and pen to write down the values made by the code.

The second standard debugging tool is the use of debugging output to locate the bug. If your system is hundreds or thousands of lines long, then the first task is to work out where the bug is not, so that you can narrow down the location of where the bug must be. The technique of writing a series of small routines is the antibugging solution to this problem, because the bug must be located in the small amount of code inside the routine. If your routine is large, then you should think strongly about making it more modular by breaking it into a number of simpler pieces. This technique also makes the code reusable, and allows you to test a set of small, easy to understand routines. If you have examined the code in the small routine and still can't find the bug, then collect more information by placing output statements in the code. If the output is correct, then the error must occur after that position in the code; if the output is incorrect, then the error must occur before that statement. When you don't know the answer to a question, seek more information, don't stare at the code; debugging output gives you that information.

To be able to use debugging output, you must know the correct or expected value of the output so that you can compare the actual to the predicted value. For this reason, test values should be as simple as possible so that you can easily calculate the correct answer; values of 0 and 1 are good candidates. In testing the *gross_pay* routine in Chapter 6, for example, you might enter 40 for the number of hours and 1 for the pay rate; if you entered 53.72 for the hours and 12.346 for the rate, then it is hard to even calculate the correct answer, and thus hard to see if your code is correct. A good place to check that the code is correct is at the boundaries of a routine; Eiffel uses pre- and postconditions for just this purpose.

Summary

- The first foundation of reusable software is design by contract, which defines the behavior and assertions of a feature. The second foundation is OO programming, which places the data and the features using that data in the same class and defines an abstract data type.
- A class usually has a small number of attributes and a large number of routines. The attributes define the state of an object, and the routines define the behavior.
- Attributes should be hidden inside the class, and only the behavior exported.
- A routine does a single thing. If given the correct input, it guarantees to produce the correct output. It is the responsibility of the caller to give a routine the correct input.
- Every line of code has to be clear, simple, and meaningful. Code should be written with the next person in mind, not as a minimal solution to the current problem.
- Bad design is easy. Good design is hard. Good design requires you to take the perspective of a client who knows little about the features, and cares only about their behavior. Good design is usually the end product of a series of solutions.
- Antibugging is the prevention of errors by careful design and good habits. The best habit is to define a set of small, simple, reusable routines that are easy to understand and check.
- The worst part of programming is debugging, and the hardest part of debugging is finding the error. The most powerful debugging tools are hand execution and the use of debugging output.

Exercises

1. What is a precondition? What keyword precedes the precondition in a feature?

2. What is a postcondition? What keyword precedes the postcondition in a feature?
3. How does Eiffel use preconditions to generate error messages?
4. What is the complete interface definition for a feature?
5. What is the ouput from running **short** on a class?
6. Define assertions for every feature of class *ACCOUNT* in the case study, Section 1. Run **short** on your class to show the interface.
7. Define assertions on each feature of each class in the case study, Section 3. Run **short** on each class to show the class interfaces.
8. Consider the following specification:

Bill the builder

Bill the builder has come to you for help. He has a job to convert a tool shed into a shrine to Elvis Presley, and needs to know how much he should charge for the building job. Write a system that prompts him for input and shows him the amount of material he needs and the amount of money he should charge for the job.

The tool shed consists of one large, rectangular room. It is 3 meters high, 2.8 meters wide, and 5.6 meters long. The owner, Mr. Prince, wants to cover the walls in an expensive wallpaper made of crushed red velvet, with silver outlines of Elvis on it. The windows he wants are specially glazed with frosted outlines of angels. The doors are covered with mats of Kentucky blue grass.

Show Bill how much wallpaper, glass, and matting he should buy, and how much (total) he should charge Mr. Prince. Wallpaper comes in rolls of 50 square meters, and costs $299.99 per roll; you cannot buy partial rolls. Glass is cut to size, so Bill can buy exactly as much as he needs; glass costs $89.99 per square meter. Matting is bought in units of a square meter, and costs $312.00 per square meter; you cannot buy it in smaller pieces. Bill charges $45 an hour for his labor.

Unfortunately, Mr. Prince keeps changing his mind about how many windows and doors he wants, and how large they are. Thus, you have to read in all the relevant data as input, since the plans can change without notice. When he took the job, Bill insisted that all the doors in a wall were the same size, and all the windows in a wall were the same size. Read in the number of windows in each wall, and their dimensions, read in the number of doors in each wall and their dimensions, and calculate the amount of material that Bill has to buy. After all the room details have been input, ask Bill how many hours he thinks he will need to do the job. Show the amount and price of each material needed, the amount and price of labor needed, and the total price for the job.

Program details

The program reads in, for each wall, the number and size of the windows, and the number and size of the doors. It also reads the estimated number of hours needed for labor. The program calculates the amount of each material needed, and the cost of buying the materials. Bill can cut the wallpaper and matting to size, so you need not worry about whether a window cuts Elvis in half, or not. The program also finds the cost of labor, and the total cost of the job. Assume that all measurements are accurate to two decimal places. A sample output from the program looks like this:

Bill's Building Bill

	Amount	Cost	Buy	Total
Wallpaper	41.67	299.99	1 roll	$299.99
Glass	0.57	89.99	0.57 sq. meters	$51.29
Matting	4.80	312.00	5 sq. meters	$1560.00
Labor	18.00	45.00	18 hours	$810.00
				$2721.28

(a) Draw a data flow chart for this task in order to produce the total cost. At each node of the chart, write the expression that converts the input values to the output value.

(b) Define the objects in the system.

(c) Define each class in the system. For each class, first choose the attributes of the class, then define the exported and hidden features.

(d) Draw a system structure chart for the system. Pick a design strategy, and note if you deviate from the pure strategy as you design a solution. List the design principles you use to decide where the code should be placed.

(e) For each class, define the signature for each feature. Define the behavior of each class by showing the feature interface for all the exported features.

(f) Code and test the system.

CHAPTER 8

Data structures

Keywords

ARRAY
index
content
store
retrieve
parameter
LINKED_LIST
key
scan

The Eiffel library classes *ARRAY* and *LINKED_LIST* provide container or data structures that allow many objects of the same type to be stored in and retrieved from the data structure. An element of an array is indexed by its position in the array, and an element of a list is usually indexed by a unique identifier or key.

8.1   The definition of an array

An array is an ordered set of elements of the same type, so each element is an object. An element is stored at a given position in the array, such as first, second, third, and so on. Each element thus has an index (1, 2, 3, and so on) that is used to store and retrieve the element.

    A *STRING* is an array of characters; a character can thus be stored in, and retrieved from, each location in the string. A street may be represented as an array of houses, or as two arrays, one on each side of the street. Each element of the array is a *HOUSE*. A book may be represented as an array of pages, a page may be represented as an array of lines, and a line may be represented as a *STRING*. There are two basic operations on arrays: store an element in a specified location, and retrieve the element from a specified location. The location of the element is called its index, and the value of an element is called its content.

An object has a name, a type, and a value. This is also true of arrays, because an array is a (compound) object, but now there is an extra level to get to the content of the array. An element of an array has a compound name, because it is located by both the name of the array and the index of the element. Consider an array of 37 integers, whose name is *roulette_wheel*. To find the value of the first element in this array, you give the name of the array and the index of the element, using a notation such as *roulette_wheel*(1). The value of this element is usually 27 on the standard roulette wheel. An element of an array has a compound name, a type, and a value.

8.2   Using an array

A variable is declared to be an array of a specific or base type, so an array of integers is declared as *ARRAY [INTEGER]*. The array is declared to be of type *ARRAY*, then the type of the array elements is listed in square brackets. An array of *INTEGER* numbers, an array of *POINT*s, and an array of *ACCOUNT*s, for example, are declared by the Eiffel code

```
roulette_wheel: ARRAY [INTEGER]
triangle: ARRAY [POINT]
accounts: ARRAY [ACCOUNT]
```

Because we can declare an array to be of any type—more formally, the array can contain objects of any type—the class *ARRAY* is called a generic class in Eiffel. The array is a class, and the type of its elements is called the base class of the array. The base class is defined in the array declaration, and passed to the array definition as a parameter; to avoid confusion, a type passed in a declaration is called a parameter, and a value passed in a routine call is called an argument. The actual parameter is passed to the class header, and bound to the formal parameter in the header; the header for class *ARRAY* is

```
class ARRAY [G] . . .
```

Inside the class *ARRAY*, the code simply refers to a variable of type *G*, so the code in the class is generic; it works for anything. Parameter binding occurs at compile time, when the declaration is checked and compiled. Argument binding occurs at run time, when the argument value is known. The difference between a type and a class can now be stated: a non-generic class is a type, but a generic class can produce many types of objects, such as objects of type *ARRAY [REAL]*, *ARRAY [POINT]*, and so on.

An array is created by calling the *ARRAY* creation routine *make*. The creation routine has two arguments that specify the lower and upper bounds of the array, such as

```
!!roulette_wheel.make (1, 37)
```

Arrays often have a lower bound of 1 (the first index is 1), but this is not essential; if you wanted, you could create an array with indices 123 to 947, or even -32 to 43. The upper bound has to be greater than the lower bound, and the index must be an integer, but there is no other restriction on the values of the bounds. When an array is created, the contents of the array are set to the element default value, such as 0.0 for *REAL* numbers and *Void* for reference types.

An element is placed in an array by the *put* operator, which takes two arguments: the element to be put, and the position to put it in. The value 27 is placed in position 1 of *roulette_wheel*, for example, by the command

```
roulette_wheel.put (27, 1)
```

An element is retrieved from the array by the *item* operator, which takes the position of the element as its single argument. The value at location 6 of the roulette wheel, for example, is returned by the query

```
roulette_wheel.item (6)
```

A string is an array of characters, so the same feature names are used to store (*put*) and retrieve (*item* or *@*) elements in the class *STRING*, as are used for any array class.

The code to declare, create, and manipulate an array of *REAL* numbers is shown to the left below, and the array is shown to the right. The array is an object with the name *example*, the type *ARRAY [REAL]*, and a reference value that points to the location in memory where the array contents are stored. In the example, an array of six real numbers is created, so the initial values of the contents are six values of 0.0.

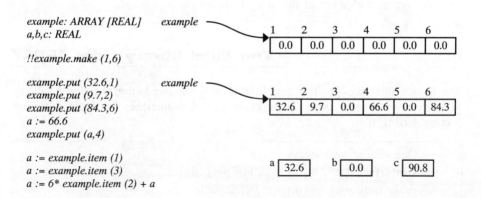

When a client uses a generic class such as an array, the actual parameter is shown in a client chart between the client and the generic class, by writing on the arrow between the client and the supplier. Using this convention, the class

EXAMPLE which uses an *ARRAY* of *REAL* numbers has the client chart shown below.

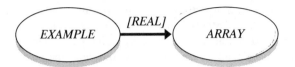

A generic class is shown in the system structure chart by placing it between its client and the base class. For simplicity, the common Eiffel library classes *INTEGER, REAL, DOUBLE, BOOLEAN, CHARACTER, STRING, ARRAY,* and *LIST* are usually not shown in a system structure chart.

Values are normally stored in and retrieved from the array one at a time, but it is possible to store a series of values into an array in one operation by using a manifest array. A manifest array is a series of values separated by commas, and enclosed by the symbols "<<" and ">>". A manifest array may be used in an assignment as shown below, where the elements of the manifest array are stored in the array *a*, starting from the first element of *a*.

```
a: ARRAY[INTEGER]
    !!a.make (1, 5)
    a := <<1, 2, 43 + x>>
```

A manifest array may be passed as an actual argument to a routine, if the formal argument is an array of the correct type. This technique allows a routine to have any number of arguments, because the whole sequence of actual values is bound to the elements of the formal argument of class *ARRAY*. Arrays of higher dimensions can be declared and used, such as *matrix*: ARRAY [*ARRAY* [*REAL*]]. In a *matrix*, each element of the array is an array.

8.3   The Eiffel library class *ARRAY*

The feature interfaces for the class *ARRAY* may be found from the Eiffel Library Manual, or by running **short** on the class. The class interface for the ISE Version 3 class *ARRAY* is

```
    −− One dimensional arrays
    class interface ARRAY [G] creation procedures
        make (minindex, maxindex: INTEGER)
                −− Allocate array; set index interval to minindex . . . maxindex
                −− (empty if minindex > maxindex).
            ensure
            minindex > maxindex implies count = 0;
```

> *minindex* <= maxindex **implies** count = maxindex – *minindex* + 1

exported features

    copy (other: ARRAY[G])

        – – Make current array an element by element copy of *other*.

      require

        other /= *Void*

      ensure

        lower = other.lower; upper = other.upper;

        – – For all *i: lower . . . upper, item (i) = . other.item (i)*

    count: INTEGER

        – – Number of available indices

    empty: BOOLEAN

        – – Is array empty?

    is_equal (other: ARRAY [G]): BOOLEAN

        – – Is current array element by element equal to *other*?

        – – (Redefined from *ANY*)

      ensure

        – – *Result* true if and only if, for all *i: other.lower . . . other.upper,*

        – – *item (i) = other.item (i)*

    item, **infix** *"@" (i: INTEGER): G*

        – – Entry at index *i*, if in index interval.

      require

        index_large_enough: lower <= i;

        index_small_enough: i <= upper

    lower: INTEGER

        – – Minimum index

    upper: INTEGER

        – – Maximum index

    put (v: G; i: INTEGER)

        – – Replace *i*-th entry, if in index interval, by *v*.

      require

        index_large_enough: lower <= i;

        index_small_enough: i <= upper

    resize (minindex, maxindex: INTEGER)

        – – Rearrange array so that it can accommodate indices down to *minindex*

        – – and up to *maxindex*. Do not lose any existing item.

      ensure

```
                    lower <= minindex; maxindex <= upper
        wipe_out
                    – – Empty the array: discard all items.

            ensure
                    wiped_out: empty
        invariant
            consistent_size: count = upper – lower + 1;
            non_negative size: count >= 0
        end interface – – class ARRAY
```

The basic operations are to create the list using *make*, store an element using *put*, and retrieve an element using *item*. The lower (start) and upper (end) bounds of the array are given by the features *lower* and *upper*, and the size of the array is given by *count*.

8.4   Array examples

Three examples of array usage are shown in this section. The first example demonstrates storage and retrieval from a one-dimensional array, the second shows how an array is used for sorting, and the third shows that reference as well as basic types can be stored and retrieved.

The first example stores integers in an array, writes them to the screen, and then finds the largest value in the array. The index of each element in the array is an integer, and the square of the index is stored as the content of each element. This example shows a very common pattern in array usage, where an index or count is used to access each element of the array. The index starts at the first element of the array, and is incremented by 1 inside a loop until the end of the array is reached. It is essential to increment the index in the loop, or you will generate an infinite loop, which never terminates. This general pattern can be used to fill an array, or to scan through the array. It is used in the *make* routine to fill the array, and in the *largest* routine to scan the array.

```
    class X
    creation
        make
    feature {NONE}
        a: ARRAY [INTEGER]
        size: INTEGER is 20
    feature
        make is
                    – – create the array of size size
```

```
                    -- fill each element with the square of its index
                    -- show each element
            do
                !!a.make (1, size)
                fill
                display
            end -- make

    fill is
                    -- fill each element with the square of its index
            local index, content: INTEGER
            do
                    from index := a.lower          -- start at front of array
                    until index > a.upper          -- stop at end of array
                    loop
                        content := index * index
                        a.put (content, index)     -- put value at position
                        index := index + 1         -- increment the index
                    end
            end -- fill

    display is
                    -- display each element of the array
            local i: INTEGER
            do
                    from i := a.lower
                    until i > a.upper
                    loop
                        io.putint (a.item (i))
                        io.new_line
                        i := i + 1
                    end
            end -- display

    largest: INTEGER is
                    -- largest value in the array
            local i: INTEGER
            do
                    from i := a.lower
                    until i > a.upper
```

```
        loop
            if a.item (i) > Result
            then Result := a.item (i)
            end
            i := i + 1
        end
    end -- largest
end -- class X
```

The second example shows how an array is used to sort a set of real numbers into ascending order. The smallest number is first in the array, the largest is last in the array, and each number is greater than or equal to its predecessor; formally, *array (i) <= array (i + 1) for i from 1 to n − 1*. The sorting algorithm shown here is an insertion sort. Each number is read from the user and placed in the array in its correct position, so the array is always sorted. There are hundreds of sorting algorithms, because sorting and scanning are among the most common operations in business computing.

The algorithm has four main parts. First, a value is read from the user. Second, the array is scanned to find where that value should be placed; it should be inserted when a value is found in the array greater than the input value. The new element cannot be simply stored in the array, however, because it would overwrite the value already stored in that location. The third part of the algorithm moves all the later elements down one location, opening up a space in the array. Finally, the input value is stored in its correct location, and the size of the used part of the array is incremented by one. This algorithm means that the array is initially empty and values are added in their correct position one at a time, so the array is always sorted and gets larger as new values are added. The key steps are the second (find location) and third (move values) steps; these are illustrated in the diagram below.

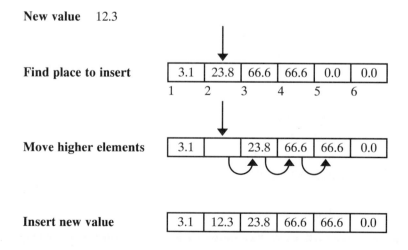

The code for an insertion sort is shown below. This code has to be placed in some class, but the class wrapper is not shown here.

```
a: ARRAY [REAL]
length: INTEGER

insertion_sort is
            place inputs into the sorted array, until user is finished
    do
        from
            !!a.make (1, 100)
            length := 0
            io.putstring ("%NEnter the numbers to be sorted. Finish
            by typing -999%N")
            io.putstring ("%NEnter a real number: ")
            io.readreal
        until finished
        loop
            position := find_insert (io.lastreal)
            insert (io.lastreal, position)
            length := length + 1
            io.putstring ("%NEnter the next number: ")
            io.readreal
        end
    end -- insertion_sort

finished: BOOLEAN is
        -- was the sentinel just input?
    do
        Result := io.lastint = -999
    end -- finished

find_insert (new: REAL): INTEGER is
        -- place to insert new number
    do
        from Result := 1
        until Result > length or else new > a.item (Result) -- look
                                        until found or finished
        loop Result := Result + 1
        end
```

```
        end – – find_insert

    insert (value: REAL, index: INTEGER) is
            – – insert value into the array at index
        local i: INTEGER
        do
            from i := length              – – from last value
            until i = index               – – until place to insert
            loop
                a.put (a.item (i), i + 1)   – – move value to next position
                i := i – 1
            end
            a.put (value, index)          – – insert new value
        end – – insert
```

In the *insert* routine, elements of the array have to be moved one at a time, starting at the end of the array and moving backwards to the insertion point. Moving elements one at a time forward from the insertion point will not work. In the example, the value 23.8 has to be moved from position 2 to position 3. Simply moving it will destroy the value at position 3 (66.6), however, so the value at that position has to be moved first. The same story can be told for every value to be moved, so the last value must be moved first, then the second last, and so on until the desired value can be moved safely. The new value can then be inserted in its correct position, and the size of the used array incremented.

The third example stores complex objects in an array, then displays each object. The routine that generates and stores the people uses a single local variable of type *PERSON*. A person is created and stored, then the next person is created using the same variable. This destroys any existing pointer from the variable name to the object, but that is no problem; the pointer to the old object is now stored in the array.

The sequence of operations is illustrated below in four steps. First, the array is declared and created (1), then a person is declared (using a local variable) and created (2). At this point in time, there is a reference from the name *person* to the object (call this first person person-a). The object is then placed in the array (3); more formally, the value of *person* is placed in the array, so the array now contains a pointer to the object person-a. Person-a is now referenced from two places, from the name of the local variable and from the array. A new person (call this person person-b) is then created (4), breaking the link between the local variable *person* and person-a, but person-a can still be accessed by retrieving the third element of the array. The new object (person-b) may now be stored in the array.

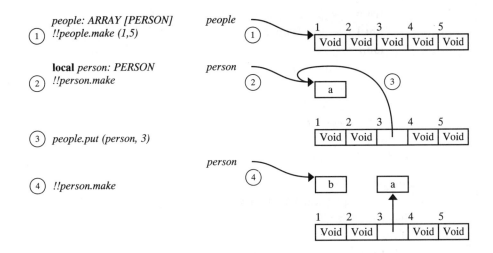

The code for this example is very similar to the first example, which used an array of integers. The array of size 5 is created, five people are stored in the array, and then the people are displayed. The creation and display routines for class *PERSON* are not shown here; they were listed in Chapter 4.

```
class CROWD
creation
    make

feature {NONE}
    people: ARRAY[PERSON]
    size: INTEGER is 3

feature
    make is
            -- create the array, fill it with people, display each person
        do
            !!people.make (1, size)
            insert_people
            display_people
        end -- make

    insert_people is
            -- fill the array with people
        local
            i: INTEGER
            person: PERSON
```

```
        do
            from i := people.lower
            until i > people.upper
            loop
                !!person.make
                io.new_line
                people.put (person, i)
                i := i + 1
            end
        end -- insert_people
    display_people is
            -- display each customer in order
        local i: INTEGER
        do
            from i := people.lower
            until i > people.upper
            loop
                io.putstring ("%NPerson number ")
                io.putint (i)
                io.putstring (": ")
                people.item(i).display
                i := i + 1
            end
        end -- display_people
end -- class CROWD
```

In the code shown above, several routines each used a separate local variable to index the array. This is the correct way to use a local variable, because each routine is self-contained, and local is beautiful. It is incorrect to use the same (attribute) variable each time, because an attribute is not meant to increase efficiency. Attributes are used only if a local variable cannot be used. Attributes store the state of the object, so the number of attributes should be kept small.

8.5   The definition of a list

A list is a data structure composed of a series of cells or elements of the same type. Each cell contains a value (such as an integer or a person) and a pointer to the next element on the list. The last cell has a value, but no pointer; more formally, it has a null pointer. The name of the list points to the head or front of the list. To find an element on the list, you start at the front and check each element in turn until you find the cell you want, or get to the end of the list and run out of places to look. A list is normally shown from the left of the page to the right; a list built from linked elements can be shown as a series of linked cells. The name of the list points to the first cell, and each cell in the list points to the next except for the last cell, which has a null pointer.

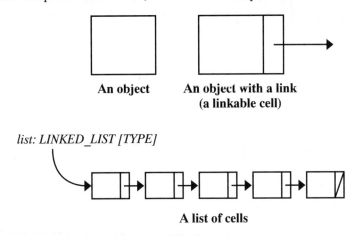

An object   **An object with a link**
                    (a linkable cell)

list: LINKED_LIST [TYPE]

A list of cells

A singly-linked list, such as that shown, can only be scanned from start to end, because there are no backward pointers from a cell to the previous cell. The doubly-linked lists discussed in this chapter can be scanned in both directions.

8.6   The Eiffel library class *LINKED_LIST*

The list data structure is implemented by the ISE Eiffel library class *LINKED_LIST*. The ISE Eiffel implementation defines a cursor to be a part of the list; the cursor points to the current element in the list. The cursor can move up and down the list, so it can be used to scan the list. To find if an element is in the list, for example, the cursor is set to the start of the list initially, and moved down the list one element at a time until the target has been found, or the end of the list has been reached.

8.6.1   Description

An ISE Eiffel list (henceforth just a list) is illustrated on the next page, showing the cursor and associated features of the list. An Eiffel list is an object with an internal state; this state is defined by the contents of the list itself, and by the position of the cursor. There are commands to change this position, and queries to find out where it is. There are commands to change an element of the list at the current cursor position, and queries to look at its value. The routines that change or return list elements use the element at the current cursor position, or the element immediately before or after the cursor. There are also features to combine or separate whole lists of objects.

The first element of the list is returned by calling the query *first* on the list, and the last element is returned by *last*. The element before the current cursor position is returned by *previous*, the element at the cursor is returned by *item*, and the element after the cursor is returned by *next*. The position of the cursor can be tested to see if it is *before* or *after* the list; if the cursor is *before* or *after* the list, then it is not pointing to an element of the list.

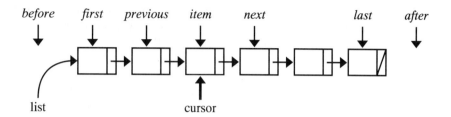

By convention, a list grows by adding elements to the right. Thus, the front of the list is shown at the left of the page, and the end at the right. You can move the cursor forward one position in the list by the command *forth*, and move it backward one position by the command *back*. If the cursor is moved too far to the left, it goes *before*; too far to the right, it goes *after*.

A *LINKED_LIST* is a generic class, because it can contain elements of any type. As we saw for an array, a client chart shows the name of the client and the generic class, connected by an arrow that shows the parameter. A bank that has a list of customers, for example, has the client chart shown below.

The bank is declared by the code shown below; a single object of type *CUSTOMER* has also been declared.

---

patrons: LINKED_LIST [CUSTOMER]
me: CUSTOMER

A list is created by calling the creation routine in the list class, called *make*. This creates an empty list into which values can be placed. When the list is created, the cursor is *before* and *after* the empty list. The code to create an empty list of customers is shown below; no bounds are given, because the list is empty when created, and grows as new cells are added to the list.

!!patrons.make
!!me.make

A cell may be inserted into the list before, at, or after the current cursor position. If it is added before or after, then the list is one cell larger after the insertion. If it is added at the current position, it replaces the existing cell. The three commands to add a customer to the list are

patrons.add_left (me)	– – add as previous element
patrons.add_right (me)	– – add as next element
patrons.replace (me)	– – replace current element

A cell is retrieved from the list by positioning the cursor, and then calling the query *item* to return the current object, such as

patrons.item	– – current value

A cell may be removed from the list by placing the cursor at a suitable position, and then removing the cell before, at, or after the current cursor position. The commands to remove a cell from the list are

patrons.remove_left	– – remove previous element
patrons.remove_right	– – remove next element
patrons.remove	– – remove current element

A cell can be inserted into or deleted from a list without moving the existing elements, because only the pointers in the previous or the current cell are changed. This is a great advantage over the array, where many elements often have to be moved when a single element is deleted or inserted; this pattern was illustrated in the insertion sort routine.

An illustration of how to remove the current cell in the list is shown below; the state of the list before deletion is drawn first, then the state of the list after the element has been deleted. The only action required is to reset the pointer in the previous cell, so that it points to the cell after the deleted element. Because the Eiffel implementation uses a cursor, and the cursor cannot point to a cell not in the list, the cursor position also has to be modified to point to the cell following the deleted element. The deleted cell disappears from the list, because no pointer in the list points to that cell. At some later point in time, the now unused cell is garbage collected, and the storage at that location is reused.

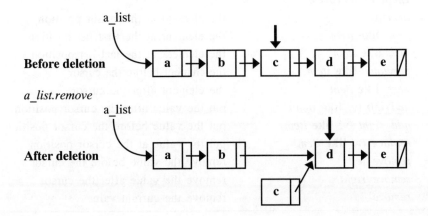

List insertion is done by changing the previous pointer so that it points to the new cell, and setting a link from the new cell to the next cell. No objects need be moved; only the values of the links that connect cells are changed.

8.6.2   Features

A selection of the ISE Version 3 *LINKED_LIST* features is shown below; a full list of features may be found by looking up the class in the Eiffel Library Manual, or by running **short** on the relevant class. There are three kinds of features: those that deal with the list itself, with the cursor, and with the elements of the list.

List features

make	make an empty list
count: INTEGER	the number of elements in the list
merge_left (*other:* **like** *Current*)	add the other list to the left of the cursor
merge_right (*other:* **like** *Current*)	add the *other* list to the right of the cursor
wipe_out	remove all elements in the list

Cursor features

forth	move the cursor forward one element
back	move the cursor backward one element
start	move the cursor to the first position
finish	move the cursor to the last position
go_to_ith (i: INTEGER)	move to position *i* in the list
before: BOOLEAN	is the cursor pointing before the list?
after: BOOLEAN	is the cursor pointing after the list?
off: BOOLEAN	*before* **or** *after*
isfirst: BOOLEAN	is the cursor at the first position?
islast: BOOLEAN	is the cursor at the last position?

Element features

item: G	the element at the cursor position
first: **like** *item*	the element at the first list position
last: **like** *item*	the element at the last list position
previous: **like** *item*	the element before the cursor
next: **like** *item*	the element after the cursor
add_left (v: **like** *item)*	put the value after the cursor position
add_right (v: **like** *item)*	put the value before the cursor position
replace (v: **like** *item)*	put the value at the cursor position
remove_left	remove the value before the cursor
remove_right	remove the value after the cursor
remove	remove the current value

There may be additional features in your Eiffel library list class, or the features may be different. The feature headers given above do not show how the cursor is affected by each operation. To find out the correct and current details of your list class, run **short** on your version.

8.7   Using a list

This section of the chapter illustrates the basic list operations of inserting elements in a list, and scanning the list for an element. In the example, each element has a unique key that is used to identify that element, so this section shows how to use an indexed list.

8.7.1   Scan routine

The basic piece of code used in list manipulation is a routine to scan through a list, such as a list of people. The declarations for a list of people and a single person, and the code to add people to the list, look like

```
crowd: LINKED_LIST[PERSON]
make is
            -- create a list of five people
      local    p: PERSON
               i: INTEGER
      do
          !!crowd.make
          from
          until i = 5
          loop
              i := i + 1
              !!person.make
              crowd.add_right (person)
          end
      end -- make
```

A list of five elements called *crowd* now exists. Each element is a complex object, a person, so the value of each cell of the list is a pointer to the object. A list is scanned by starting at the front, then moving the cursor forward by one position until the end of the list. The basic operation in the routine is thus *forth*, repeated as necessary.

```
from crowd.start          -- set cursor to start of list
until crowd.after         -- stop scan at end of list
loop crowd.forth          -- move forward one cell
end
```

To find a specific person, the list is scanned until the person is found, or there are no more places to look. The value of each element in the list is a reference to an object, so a list element cannot be compared with the "=" operator. If each person has a unique name, then the name can be used to identify the person and each list element is compared using the name as the key; a key is a unique identifier for an object. The name cannot be tested with the "=" operator, because it too is a reference type; the test for equality is *is_equal* from the class *STRING*. A procedure that finds a person, if they are in the list, is

```
find (name: STRING) is
            -- cursor points to the person with this name, or after
    do
        from crowd.start
        until
            crowd.after or else crowd.item.name.is_equal (name)
        loop crowd.forth
        end
    end -- find
```

If a person with the given name is in the list, the loop stops when the cursor is moved to the element that contains that name. If the name is not in the list, the cursor will be *after*. If the cursor moves *after*, then the first part of the **or else** is true and the second part is not executed; an **or** test would result in an error, because the code would attempt to look at the value of the element *after* the list. When designing a scan loop, the entry and exit conditions are often the focus of attention, as may be seen here, so the most common scan bug is an infinite loop; the *forth* operation is often left out of the loop, so the loop never terminates.

A function that searches the list and returns the matched element is incorrect Eiffel, for two reasons. First, the function has a side-effect because the position of the cursor is moved. If some other code relied on the position of the cursor, then this function would create untold havoc by changing the state of the list, and the bug would be very difficult to find because it is hidden and disguised inside the function. The second reason is the value that is returned if there is no matching object. The header of the function would be

```
match (name: STRING): PERSON is
```

An expert Eiffel programmer would look at this header, and instantly conclude two things. First, nothing is changed by calling the routine. Second, the routine returns an object of type *PERSON*; more formally, it returns a pointer to the object. If there is no such person on the list, then what is returned? Certainly, a person is not returned. The *Void* value could be used to indicate that no match was found, but then the caller would be in trouble, because *Void* is not of type *PERSON*.

8.7.2   Cause and effect: matched routines

A correct and efficient solution for finding an element is to copy the solution that Eiffel uses for reading input: have a command that scans the list for the person, then a query to test the value of the scan. The scan command causes a change, and the query checks the effect of the change. If the person was in the list, the scan command places the cursor in the correct position, so the person can be returned.

> **DESIGN PRINCIPLE 11:** Use matched routines: a command to make a change, and a query to test the effect of the command.

The code that scans a list to find a person with a given name is shown below. A procedure is called to scan the list, then the position of the cursor is tested. If the cursor points to an element in the list, then the person has been found and is returned by the query *item*, which returns the element at the current cursor position. If the cursor is *after* the list, then no matching person was found.

```
find (name)
if crowd.after then io.putstring ("No such person")
else target := crowd.item
end
```

This is correct and efficient, but obscure; the relation between *scan* and *crowd.after* is not visible in the code. To understand how this code works, the reader would have to examine the mechanism of *find*, which violates the idea of information hiding. To make the link clear, a function *found* is defined to check the location of the cursor:

```
find (name)
if found then target := crowd.item
else io.putstring ("No such person")
end

found: BOOLEAN is
        -- check if the person was found in the list
do
        Return := not crowd.after
end -- found
```

In this solution, all the stylistic constraints have been satisfied: queries and commands are correct, the code in the caller is simple, clear, and understandable, and the processing is hidden inside the routines. The code is also efficient, because the list is scanned only once to find the person.

The pattern of matched routines is very common in Eiffel, due to the strict division between procedures and functions. The general principle is that the command makes a change, and the query tests if the command succeeded. Often, you want to test if an element is in a list, and if it is, do something with it. The correct implementation is to scan the list with a command, and then test the effect of the command with a query.

8.8   Array or list?

An array is a good data structure in which to store a series of objects if the objects are stable. It is computationally cheap to find an element of the array from its index, so array access is, in general, faster than list access. If the data is volatile (elements are often added or removed), then the list is a more efficient data structure because its elements don't need to be moved when the list length changes. A choice between the array and list data structures basically depends on the volatility of the data, where low volatility implies an array, and high volatility implies a list.

8.9   Case study: the BANK system

The *BANK* system is extended in Section 4 of the case study (see Part E) so that the bank can have many customers. To allow a customer to be identified, each customer needs a unique key; this key is an integer, and successive numbers are used for each new customer. The additional specification for this part of the case study is

> The bank can have many customers. Each customer has a unique integer key; successive integers are used for every new customer. The bank runs over an extended period. At the start of each day, a bank teller adds interest to every existing account and then creates new customers; customers are never deleted. The ATM then runs all day, handling multiple customers. To use the ATM, a customer enters their unique key and password. Any number of transactions may be made on the account, until the customer is tired of playing with their money and exits the system. The ATM then waits for the next customer, until a special key of 666 is entered; this exits the ATM system for the day. The cycle then resumes for the next day: the teller adds interest and new customers, and the ATM system runs. Entry of the special key value of 999 into the ATM shuts down the whole system.

Summary

- An array is a data structure that stores a sequence of elements of the same type. Each element has an index which is used to store and retrieve the content of that cell.
- An array is declared by passing a parameter in the *ARRAY[. . .]* declaration. This actual parameter is bound to the formal parameter (usually called *G*) in the class header.

- If an element is inserted into the middle of an array, then the existing value at that location is overwritten. To save the existing value, all later values may be moved up one cell. If an element is deleted from the array, that cell may be marked with a special value, or all the later cells may be moved down by one.
- A list is a data structure that stores a sequence of elements of the same type. An element often has a unique key that is used to identify that element.
- A list is declared by passing an actual parameter in the *LINKED_LIST[. . .]* declaration. The actual parameter is bound to the formal parameter in the class header.
- A list allows you to insert and delete objects at any point in a list by changing at most one link pointer.
- The Eiffel class *LINKED_LIST* has a cursor, which is used to move around in the list. The class offers three kinds of features: those dealing with the list, with the cursor, and with the elements of the list.

Exercises

1. Write a program to create and display an array of integers. The content of each cell is read in from the user.
2. Execute the insertion sort program using real data; use an array of ten integers. Simulate the operation of the sort on paper, by hand.
3. Write a program to sort an array of people into alphabetical order, by name. Assume that a *PERSON* has a field *name: STRING*.
4. Write the code to create and display a list of integers. Use a list of size 10.
5. Adapt the insertion sort code to sort the list of integers.
6. Implement the Unix command **finger**. **finger** takes a single name, and searches the list of system users for the user with that name. It returns their name and login name, so that you can send mail to the login name.
   (a) Assume that a single name is supplied, and search the family names.
   (b) Assume that a single name is supplied, and search both the personal and family names.
   (c) What happens when there is a space in the supplied name?
7. Consider the following system specification:

The FeedMe Plant Nursery

The FeedMe Plant Nursery has employed you to design a simple inventory and accounting system for them. They want to keep track of the money and the amount of stock on hand.

The nursery sells fruit trees, such as apple, orange, plum, and apricot trees. The nursery has to keep track of how many trees of each type it has on hand. Money is divided into three categories. First, there is the money in the nursery's bank account. Second, there is money owed to the nursery from credit sales to customers. Third, there is the money owed by the nursery to its suppliers. At any time, the total capital of the nursery can be calculated from these sources.

There are two basic transactions in the system: selling trees to customers, and buying them from suppliers. The transactions change the amount of stock on hand, and may change the amount of money on hand. Trees are moved immediately the transaction is complete. If a customer pays cash, then the bank balance is also changed immediately. If a transaction is on credit, the money will not change until four days later. Suppliers get the same deal.

A NURSERY has the attributes: name: STRING

balance: REAL

trees: LIST [TREE]

An instance of a TREE is not a single tree. It is a record of the nursery's stock of that tree. In particular, the instance contains a count of the number of trees on hand of that type.

A TREE has the attributes: name: STRING

season: STRING   – – season when fruit is ripe

buyPrice: REAL

sellPrice: REAL

stock: INTEGER

Customers owe money to the nursery; this is money coming in. Suppliers are owed money by the nursery; this is money going out. The lists of credit and debit transactions have to be stored, so that money can be transferred four days after the transaction. A transaction has the form

A TRANSACTION has the attributes: amount: REAL

delay: INTEGER

When a credit transaction is made, a transaction object is added to the appropriate list. Four days later (a day is indicated by an 'N' message), the money is added to, or subtracted from, the bank balance of the nursery. Cash transactions change the bank balance instantly.

The system is interactive, and offers a menu of choices to the user. The user makes a choice, the choice is executed, and control then returns to the menu. The menu choices are

S   Sell any number of trees, of one or more types, to a customer, using cash or credit.

B   Buy any number of trees, of one or more types, from a supplier. The transaction can be cash or credit. There is no requirement that the nursery already has the tree type.

D   Display a list showing all the stock on hand. Show the type of tree, the number of trees on hand, and the selling price of the tree.

T   Show all the details of a single tree type.

C   Show the capital of the nursery at this instant in time. To find this, take the bank balance, add the money owed to the nursery, and deduct the money owed by the nursery. Show the three subtotals, then the balance.

N   This transaction simulates a new day; it is included so that you do not have to access a system clock. When the user chooses this option, it means that a new day has started. As stated above, credit transactions do not change the money until four days after the transaction.

E   Exit the system.

?   Show and explain the menu choices.

For each menu choice, you may need more details. If a customer buys some trees, then you must get the relevant details from the user. For each type of tree purchased by the customer, you will need to prompt for the type of tree and the number wanted.

(a) Choose a system design strategy: top-down, bottom-up, procedural, plan, or object.

(b) Design the system using this strategy; note if and when you deviate.

(c) Write the signatures for each feature in each class.

(d) Debate the location of the transactions. There are at least three "reasonable" solutions.

(e) Code and test the system using staged development.

PART C
Inheritance

CHAPTER 9

Single inheritance

Keywords

open–closed
inherit
parent
child
rename
export
redefine

Inheritance provides a new way to reuse a class in an OO system, separate from the client–supplier relationship. When one class inherits another, all the features of the old class are features of the new, inheriting class; the existing class is called the parent, and the inheriting class is called the child. This means that an existing class can be extended with no change to its code; a child class inherits the parent class and adds new features of its own. Existing users of the parent class are not affected, because the parent is not changed.

9.1 The need for inheritance

Inheritance supports a style of software development different from traditional approaches. Instead of trying to solve a new problem from scratch, existing solutions are inherited and extended. The benefit of this approach may be explained in terms of the open–closed principle, which states that a good module structure is both closed and open; in Eiffel, the module is the class. A module should be closed so that clients are protected from any changes in the working system. A client uses the services supplied by a module, and once these services have been defined the client should not be affected by the introduction of new services they do not need. A module should be open so that it can be changed and extended as needed. There is no guarantee that every service offered by a class can be defined once and never changed. Successful software systems continually undergo change, as the needs of the users change and develop.

This double requirement looks impossible, but it is solved by inheritance. A class is closed, because it may be compiled, stored in a library, and used by clients. A class is open, because any new class may inherit it as a parent, and add new features as desired. When the child class is defined, there is no need to change the original class or to disturb its clients. New code often contains errors, and a user does not want to deal with errors caused by new software for some other, new user.

Inheritance provides a powerful way to extend code by adding new features to an existing class without changing that class at all. This feat is accomplished by allowing one class to inherit another; the new class can use everything in the original class, plus any additional features defined in the new class. Assume we have an existing class A; this will be the parent class. If B (the child) inherits from A (the parent), then all features of A are available in B, with no need to define them. The child is free to add new code for its specific purposes, or to use the inherited code in other ways. The child class treats all the inherited features exactly as though they were written inside the child. A client of the child sees no difference between the inherited and the new features; they are simply features of the child.

9.2   Inheritance chart

In Eiffel, a child class inherits services or features from its parent classes. Two examples of inheritance are shown below, using an inheritance chart. In the example to the left, the class *SAVINGS* inherits the class *ACCOUNT*, because a savings account is a specific type of account. The class *SAVINGS* thus has all the normal features of an account, plus whatever features are particular to a savings account. In the inheritance chart shown to the right, there are two specific types of account, *SAVINGS* and *CHECK* accounts. Again, each child class has all the features of its parent, plus any specific features that separate the child from the parent.

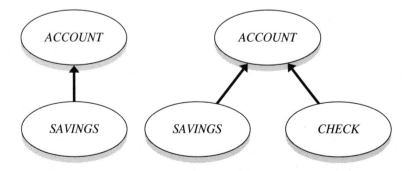

In an inheritance chart, a single arrow is drawn from the child to the parent; by convention, parents are drawn above their children in the chart. Unlike the real world, a child class chooses its parents; this is indicated by an arrow pointing from the child to the parent. The parent class cannot know which class might later inherit it, just as a supplier cannot know which class might later use its services.

A more complex inheritance chart of seven classes is shown below. Class A is inherited by both B and C, so A is the parent of the two children B and C. Classes D and E inherit from class B, so D and E are children of B. Classes B, C, D, and E inherit from a single parent, so they show single inheritance. Class F inherits from both class C and class G, so it has two parents and uses multiple inheritance. In general, a class can inherit from any number of parents. Inheritance from a single parent is discussed in this chapter, while multiple and repeated inheritance are discussed in Chapter 12.

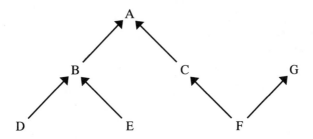

Inheritance is transitive, so class E has all the features inherited from its parents (B here), its grandparents (A here), and so on up the inheritance hierarchy. Any feature defined in A is a feature of B, and any feature of B is a feature of D, so class D can contain features from A, from B, and new features added in D. Class F contains features of its own, plus features inherited from C and from A. We say that any parent of a class is an ancestor of that class, possibly many links removed from the base class. In turn, any child of a class is called a descendant, possibly many links removed from the original class. In the inheritance chart, Class A is the ancestor of classes B to F, so classes B to F are heirs or descendants of A. Class F is also a descendant of class G, just as class G is an ancestor of class F. A child is a descendant one link down, and a parent is an ancestor one link up the chart.

A feature may be inherited, or defined in the child. If it is coded within the class, then it is called an immediate feature of that class. All the other (non-immediate) features of a class are inherited.

9.3   Syntax and mechanism

One class inherits another by writing the keyword **inherit**, followed by the name of the parent class. The keyword is written immediately after the class header; if several classes are inherited, the class names are separated by semi-colons. The general syntax is shown below, where A is the new, child class; class A is free to define its own features, in addition to the features inherited from its parents (classes B, C, and D here):

```
class A
    inherit
        B; C; D
```

When one class inherits another, the code in the child works exactly as though the parent code was written in the child. As far as the operation of the child class is concerned, there is no difference between features inherited from the parent and features defined in the child. Feature calls treat all features of the class identically, and the source of a feature is invisible.

The basic **inherit** statement states that a class is inherited, so the child has all the features of the parent. The **inherit** statement contains a series of clauses which modify the status of an inherited feature in various ways. The full form of the inheritance statement is shown below, where capital letters indicate a class and small letters indicate a feature. A child may inherit all features of a class and use them unchanged. If a clause is used to change the status of an inherited feature, then the set of clauses is terminated by an **end**.

```
class A
    inherit B
        rename                      -- new name in child
            m as n
        export                      -- new export policy in child
            {C, D} o, p
        undefine                    -- no definition in child
            q
        redefine                    -- new body in child
            r, s
        select                      -- select active feature
            t
        end;
    inherit C
        . . .
```

The **rename** clause gives an inherited feature a new name in the child; the feature body and signature are retained, but the feature has a new name. The export policy is inherited as part of a feature; the **export** clause gives a new export policy to a feature. A feature's signature may be changed if it is **undefine**d; discussion of this clause is deferred to Chapter 10. The name of a feature can be retained, but its body may be changed if the feature is **redefine**d in the child. Finally, if there are several features in the child with the same name, one of them can be **select**ed to be the active feature; discussion of this clause is deferred until Chapter 11.

A class inherits features from its parent, so it inherits the parent's creation routine as one of these features. The child does not inherit the creation status of this routine, however. The child must explicitly state its creation routine in its **creation** clause; it is the responsibility of the child to choose its creation routine. A class cannot inherit itself either directly or through a chain of other classes; such a situation is known as a cycle. Cycles are not allowed in the inheritance hierarchy.

A class does not inherit the expansion status of a parent. If the parent class was expanded, and you wish the child to also be expanded, then the child class header or the child object declaration should contain the keyword **expanded**. The base class (that is expanded) must have either no creation routine, or a single creation routine with no argument.

The **short** documentation tool shows only the immediate features of a class. A class often contains many features that are inherited from its parents, however, so these features do not appear in the short output. All the features exported by a class can be seen by running the **flat** tool on a class to get the collection of features, then using **short** to print the total class interface. In a Unix system, this is done by piping the output of **flat** into **short** with the command

---

flat *filename.e* | **short**

This command shows all the exported features in a class, both inherited and immediate.

9.4   Inherit or client?

An existing class can be reused in two ways, as a supplier and as a parent. When should you buy, and when should you inherit? The general answer is that inheritance means "is", and client means "has", "uses", or "contains". Looking at the *BANK* system, a customer has an account; a customer is not a type of account. A customer is a person; a customer does not contain a person.

A good question to ask if the relation is unclear is, "Can the class have two of them?" If the class can have two objects of some type, then the client relation is appropriate; if it cannot, then inheritance is likely. It is possible, for example, to define a bank customer as a bank account that is a person, so the class *CUSTOMER* would inherit from *PERSON* and *ACCOUNT*; from the person's perspective the customer is a person, but from the bank's perspective the customer is an account. A customer can easily have two accounts, however, so a customer cannot be a (single) account.

Inheritance is appropriate if an instance of B may also be seen as an instance of A (a square is a rectangle, a rectangle is a polygon; a cat, dog, or bird is an animal). The client relation is appropriate when an instance of B uses an object of type A. A useful question to ask is, "Does it have to be this way?", or "Is this temporary or permanent?" If the relationship is permanent and can never be changed, then inheritance should be used. If the relationship can change from one system to another or one use to another, then a client relation should be used.

The decision about how to structure a particular system involves many issues, and a discussion about this topic is left to more specialized texts on OO system analysis and design such as Booch (1994), Henderson-Sellers and Edwards (1994), and Rumbaugh et al. (1991). The basic idea is to define the behavior and code you need once, at one place in one class only, and then use this class by inheriting or by calling its features.

9.5   Inherit example: class *WORKER*

A worker is a person who works. The class *WORKER* can thus be split into two parts, one part defining what it is to be a *PERSON*, and one part adding the extra features that define a *WORKER*. A person has a name, address, and sex. A worker is a person with extra attributes (and routines that use those attributes) that deal with the pay rate, the hours worked, and so on. The dual role of a worker can be neatly captured through the inheritance relation.

    The class *PERSON* may be defined by the code shown below; some of the routine bodies have been omitted, because the code for the routines was given in Chapter 4.

```
class PERSON
creation
    make

feature {NONE}
    name, address: STRING
    sex: CHARACTER

feature
    make is
            -- set the values of the attributes
        do
            io.putstring ("%NEnter the personal details%N")
            io.putstring (" Name: ")
            io.readline
            name := io.laststring
            get_sex
            sex := io.lastchar
            io.putstring (" Address: ")
            io.readline
            address := io.laststring
        end -- make

    display is
            -- show the customer's personal details
        do
            print_title
            io.putstring (name)
```

```
                io.putstring (" lives at ")
                io.putstring (address)
         end - - display
   feature {NONE}
      get_sex is
            - - loop until the user enters a valid sex
         do
            from
               io.putstring (" Enter the sex (M/F): ")
               io.readchar
            until valid_gender
            loop
               io.putstring ("Valid codes are M or F. Try
               again%N")
               io.putstring (" Enter the sex (M/F): ")
               io.readchar
            end
         end - - get_sex

      valid_gender: BOOLEAN is . . .
            - - has a valid sex code been entered?
      print_title is . . .
            - - print an appropriate title

   end - - class PERSON
```

The class PERSON can be inherited and used by other classes. The new class WORKER inherits PERSON, and adds the additional fields *pay_rate, hours, gross,* and *tax*, plus their associated routines. The first part of the code for class WORKER is shown below, and the remainder of the code is developed in the rest of this chapter.

```
class WORKER
inherit
   PERSON
creation
   make

feature {NONE}
   pay_rate, hours, gross, tax: REAL
```

The new class has seven attributes, three inherited from the class PERSON (*name, sex, address*) and four immediate features defined within the class WORKER (*pay_rate, hours, gross, tax*). It also contains two routines inherited from class PERSON (*make* and *display*), plus any new routines defined within the class. A client of the class *WORKER* does not know if a feature was inherited, or defined within the class; the client simply uses a feature of *WORKER*.

All the inherited routines can be used in the class *WORKER* unchanged, but some need to be extended. In particular, the creation and display routines do not set or use the new attributes of a worker, so code has to be added to these routines. Applying the open–closed principle, the existing code should not be changed; instead, it should be used "as is" and then the additional code should be executed. This is done by renaming the existing parent routines, and calling them as a part of the *WORKER* processing.

9.6   Rename

In the *WORKER* example, the creation routine inherited from class *PERSON* only sets some of the worker attributes; in particular, it does not set the pay rate. A new creation routine could be defined within class *WORKER* to read in the name, sex, address, and pay rate, but this repeats the code defined in class *PERSON*; code should be reused, not repeated. Code reuse is central to the design of Eiffel. This principle can be used as a strong design rule: if code in a system is repeated instead of reused, then the design is probably wrong.

> **DESIGN PRINCIPLE 12:** Never repeat code. If code is repeated instead of reused, then the system design is wrong.

The creation routine for a worker should execute the creation routine for a person, and add the extra code required to use the extra fields in the worker. The *WORKER* creation routine thus needs the ability to call the *PERSON* creation routine. This ability is already provided by inheritance, because the class *WORKER* inherits the *make* routine from class *PERSON*. The creation routine in *WORKER*, however, should use the standard name *make* for its own creation routine. The solution is to inherit the parent's creation routine, and give it another name within the child class, such as *make_person*; this renaming is done by the **rename** command.

The **rename** keyword allows an inherited feature to have a different name in the child class. The keyword is written after the class that is inherited; the syntax has the form

```
class A
inherit
    B
        rename
            x as y,
            p as q,
            r as s
        end
```

An inherited feature is renamed by writing the old name, the keyword **as**, and the new name. Multiple features inherited from a class may be renamed; if multiple features are changed, then the renamed features are separated by a comma.

9.7   Rename example: class *WORKER*

The creation and display features from the class *PERSON* are inherited by *WORKER*, and renamed. Class *WORKER* will then define its own features *make* and *display*, and call the renamed *PERSON* features as part of these routines. The code to rename the inherited features is

```
class WORKER
inherit
    PERSON
        rename
            make as make_person,
            display as display_person
        end
```

The name of a feature in the class where it is first defined is called the original name, and the name of the feature in the child class is called the final name of the feature. When a feature is renamed, the name of the feature is changed in the child, so it can be called by this name in the child. When the child class is inherited, then the new name is inherited, because that is the name of the feature in the child.

In the example used here, both the *make* and the *display* routines in *PERSON* can be renamed and used as part of the *make* and *display* routines in class *WORKER*. The *make* routine in *WORKER* gets the personal details, then gets the pay rate for the new worker. The *display* routine in *WORKER* shows the personal details, then shows the other fields added in the class. New routines have to be added to set the number of hours worked, and to calculate the pay and tax. The client structure of these classes is shown to the left below; here, the boss uses the services of a worker, so an arrow connects the client to the supplier. The client chart contains the class *WORKER* and not the class *PERSON*, because an object of type *WORKER* is declared and used in the client, not an object of type *PERSON*. The inheritance structure is shown to the right, where the arrow connects the child to the parent.

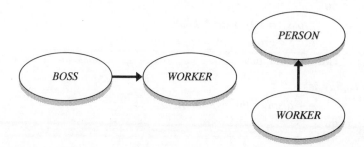

The full code for class *WORKER* is

```
class WORKER
inherit
    PERSON
        rename
            make as make_person,
            display as display_person
        end
creation {BOSS}
    make

feature {NONE}
    pay_rate, hours, gross, tax: REAL
    tax_rate: REAL is 22.5

feature {BOSS}
    make is
            -- get and store the name, sex, address, and pay rate
        do
            make_person
            io.putstring ("%NEnter pay rate: ")
            io.readreal
            pay_rate := io.lastreal
        end -- make

    has_worked (today: REAL) is
            -- update the total hours worked
        do
            hours := hours + today
        end -- has_worked

    find_pay is
            -- calculate the gross pay and the tax
        do
            gross := pay_rate * hours
            tax := gross * tax_rate / 100
        end -- find_pay

    display is
            -- display the worker fields
        do
```

```
            display_person
            io.putstring ("%NPay rate: ")
            io.putreal (pay_rate)
            io.putstring ("%NHours worked: ")

            io.putreal (hours)
            io.putstring ("%NGross pay: ")
            io.putreal (gross)
            io.putstring ("%NTax on gross: ")
            io.putreal (tax)
            io.new_line
        end - - display
    end - - class WORKER
```

An object of type *WORKER* has 17 features, eight inherited and nine immediate. The eight inherited features may be divided into public and private features, so three exported attributes and two exported routines are inherited from the parent class *PERSON*, plus three private routines; exported features are shown in bold face below. The two public routines have different names in the child, because they are inherited and renamed. Five additional attributes are defined in the class, plus four routines that use the new attributes. The features of *PERSON* and of *WORKER* are shown below.

PERSON features	rename	WORKER features
name		name
address		address
sex		sex
make	make_person	make_person
get_sex		get_sex
valid_gender		valid_gender
display	display_person	display_person
print_title		print_title
		pay_rate
		hours
		gross
		tax
		tax_rate
		make
		has_worked
		find_pay
		display

The class *BOSS* is a client of class *WORKER*, because a boss uses the services of the worker. The client declares an object of type *WORKER*, and then uses the services or features of this class. The code in class *BOSS* then calls features of class *WORKER*, which may be inherited unchanged from the parent, defined as immediate routines in the child, or defined in the child but using code from the parent; the source of the features is invisible to the client. The definition for the simple class *BOSS* is

```
class BOSS
creation
    make

feature
    me: WORKER

    make is
            -- make, work, and display the worker
        do
            !!me.make
            me.has_worked (40)
            me.find_pay
            me.display
        end    make

end -- class BOSS
```

Renaming applies the open–closed principle to OO systems, because it allows a feature to be inherited and used as part of another routine. The existing code is unchanged so the system is closed, and the new class provides new functionality so the system is open. When a feature is inherited and renamed, it has the same feature body and signature as before, but it has a new name in the new class. Because inheritance is transitive, this new name is inherited by any children of the new class.

9.8   System structure chart

A feature may be located in the parent, and used in the child, or the child may use both inherited and immediate code in a single routine. A system structure chart shows the location of the code in a system, so a plan may use parent code, child code, or both. In a system structure chart, a parent is written before the child, and the location of each node is shown.

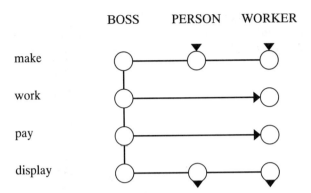

BOSS   PERSON   WORKER

make

work

pay

display

The system structure chart for the *BOSS* system is shown above. When a worker is created, code in both class *PERSON* and class *WORKER* is executed. The fact that a worker works and is paid is captured purely by code in class *WORKER*. Finally, the attributes in both classes are displayed, and code is executed in each class to show the relevant details.

In this example every plan terminated at the child, but this does not always happen. A check account and a savings account, for example, both have the same rules for depositing money. The *deposit* routine is therefore contained completely in the parent class, class *ACCOUNT*, and the plan for depositing terminates at the parent.

9.9   Export

When a class inherits a feature, the export policy comes along with the feature. The child can retain the existing policies, or define a new policy for a feature. All the parent features are there if the child wishes to export them, but the child can define its own, different exports and thus its own behavior.

A feature inherits its export status from the parent. The child class can use the inherited export policy, or it can override the inherited policy by using the **export** clause. The **export** clause lists the new export policy using the familiar {. . .} notation, and this policy is then applied to each feature listed after the policy. If there are multiple export policies, each policy is placed on a single line, separated by a semi-colon. The form of the export clause is

> **export**
> *{classes} feature, feature, . . . feature;*
> *{classes} feature, feature, . . . feature*

Each line of the clause consists of an export policy, followed by the list of features that use the export policy. The format is the same as that used for features and for creation, a list of classes separated by commas. Feature names in the feature list are separated by commas, and terminated by a semi-colon. The keyword **all** may be used instead of a feature list, to denote all the inherited features; the keyword may be used only once within an export clause. The export clause **export** *{NONE}* **all**, for example, hides all the features inherited from a parent.

9.10   Redefine

A child may use features inherited from its parent in three main ways. It may use an inherited feature unchanged. It may rename an existing feature; this retains the feature definition, but gives it a new name. Finally, a child may redefine a feature it inherits; this option retains the name and signature, but changes the implementation of the feature. These three alternatives allow a class to take its pick of the features offered by the parent; some may be kept as they are, others renamed and used as part of a new feature, while others may be redefined and overwritten by more appropriate features.

A feature is redefined by the keyword **redefine** followed by the name of the feature, inside the **inherit** clause; if multiple features are redefined, then each name is separated by a comma. The **rename** clause precedes the **redefine** clause if both are present in an inherited definition. The **inherit** statement is procedural, so each clause is executed in sequence. This means that a feature can be renamed in the **rename** clause, then the feature with this new name can be redefined in the **redefine** clause. The format of the redefine clause is

```
class A
inherit
    B
        rename
            . . .
        redefine
            x, y, z
        end
```

The redefine clause breaks the link between the name of a feature and its content; the name is retained in the child, but the child defines a new version of the feature. The feature in the parent class is called the precursor of the redefined feature. A feature defined in the current class is called an immediate feature. The feature used in the current class is called the active or final feature.

A function with no arguments can be redefined as an attribute, but an attribute cannot be redefined as a function. A feature preceded by the keyword **frozen** cannot be redefined. Freezing the name of a feature is used for system-level features that will never be changed, and can be used by all the classes in a system. The standard system features *clone*, *standard_copy*, and *is_equal* are frozen, because they are Eiffel-defined features that can be used everywhere and will never change. The routine header for *copy* lists a name that can be redefined, *copy*, and a name that is frozen and cannot be redefined, *standard_copy*. The full feature interface (with the frozen name shown) is

---

copy, **frozen** *standard_copy (other:* **like** *Current) is*
         – – Copy every field of other onto
         – – corresponding field of current object
     require
         other_not_void: other /= *Void*
     ensure
         is_equal (other)
     end – – copy

The feature has two names, *copy* and *standard_copy*. The name *copy* can be redefined for specific classes, so each class can define its own copy routine, but the feature *standard_copy* cannot be redefined and is the same for all classes.

9.11   Redefine example: class *CONTRACTOR*

Consider the example of a worker who is an independent contractor, not a full-time employee. The salary of a contractor is not taxed each week; instead, the full salary is paid by the employer and the contractor pays the tax in their income tax each year. For this reason, the standard method for calculating gross pay is incorrect, and has to be redefined. The rest of the information about the worker is the same, so the existing class can be reused except for the feature that calculates gross pay and tax. A new class *CONTRACTOR* may be defined as

---

class *CONTRACTOR*
inherit
     WORKER
         redefine *tax_rate*
         end
creation
     make
feature
     tax_rate: REAL **is** 0.0
end – – class *CONTRACTOR*

An object of type *CONTRACTOR* has 17 features, with the same feature names and signatures as the features in its parent, class *WORKER*. Sixteen of these features are inherited, and one is defined in the child as an immediate feature. The content of the immediate feature *tax_rate* is different from the version in the parent class *WORKER*.

9.12   Case study: the *BANK* system

The existing *BANK* system is restructured by inheritance to separate out the components of a customer. A customer is a person who has a bank account, plus a user identifier and a password. Two classes can be defined to capture this distinction, where the class *CUSTOMER* inherits the class *PERSON*. The personal features are the person's name, sex, and address, plus routines that use this data. The additional customer features are the unique customer identifier, the password and the account, plus routines that use this data.

The design and code for this extension are shown in the case study (see Part E, Section 5). There is no new specification, because the change is made to increase reuse and modularity of the system, not to add new functionality. The separation of person from customer allows other types of customer to be easily added in the future, such as corporations or customers with a joint account.

Summary

- A class can be reused by inheritance, as well as by the client relationship.
- When a class is inherited, the existing, original and reused class is called the parent and the new, inheriting class is called the child class.
- A child **inherits** all the features of the parent, and may add new features of its own. A feature call does not distinguish between parent and child features; all features are used exactly as though they were defined in the child.
- A feature may be **renamed** by the child, to retain the feature definition but change its name.
- The export status of a feature is inherited with the feature, but may be changed by listing the new export policy of the feature in the **export** clause.
- The creation routine is inherited, but not its **creation** status. It is the responsibility of the child to choose its creation routine.
- The **expanded** status of a class is not inherited.
- A feature **redefined** in the child retains its name and signature, but receives a new body.

Exercises

1. How is code reused by inheritance? Give an example, showing the client and inheritance charts, and parent, child, and client code. How does inheritance affect a client of the child?
2. Draw an inheritance chart from amoeba to human (you may gloss over some of the stages). On each node of the chart, write the new features for each child.
3. There are three main clauses within an **inherit** clause. What are they? What does each do? What is the format of each clause? What order are they listed in?
4. Consider the following Eiffel class headers:

```
class A
creation
    make
feature

    a, b: M
    c is
    d: BOOLEAN is
    e (a: X) is
end -- class A

class B
inherit
    A
            rename
                a as aye,
                c as cee

            redefine
                aye, d
            end
creation
    make
feature
    a, f, g: N
    h is
    i (a: O) is
end -- class B

class C
inherit
    B
            rename
                aye as eh,
                a as aiee,
                b as bee,
                i as eye
            redefine
                h, eye
            end
creation
```

```
            make
   feature
            k, l: Q
            a is
   end  -- class C
```

Draw a table with the classes listed down the left side, in inheritance order. Write the names of each feature in the first class (class *A*) along the top of the table, then write the name of that feature in the child. If the definition of the feature has changed in the child, mark it with an asterisk.

5. Consider the following specification:

A bank offers four types of account: savings, check, scrooge, and investment. The first three types can be accessed through an ATM, so they offer the services deposit, withdraw, and show balance. For each type of account, the rules for each service are slightly different.

Any amount may be deposited in an account. A withdrawal from a savings account decrements the balance by the amount withdrawn. A successful withdrawal from a check account costs 50 cents. An unsuccessful withdrawal from a check account costs $5. There are no charges or penalties for a savings account. The balance of an account cannot be negative.

A savings account gets daily interest; the interest rate is 4.5 percent a year. A check account gets no interest. An investment account is created with an initial balance, and accrues daily interest for a period of three, six, or 12 months. A three-month investment account has an annual interest rate of 5.5 percent, a six-month account has a 6.0 percent rate, and a 12-month account 6.5 percent. When the account matures at the end of the period, the total amount is transferred into the customer's check account. If there is no check account, then one is created specially to receive the investment funds.

A scrooge account allows money to be deposited, but not withdrawn. A scrooge account is set up for some period with an interest rate of 6.0 percent, and the balance increases over the period due to interest and deposits. Interest is paid daily. At the end of the period, the money is transferred into a check account.

Write the inheritance hierarchy for this fragment of the system. First, build a table that shows the unique and common parts of the system, then convert this table to an inheritance hierarchy. List the classes across the top of the table, the parent classes last; list the goals down the side of the table. In the table, write the action for each goal in each class; if the action is the same for all child classes, write the action in the parent. The detailed steps are as follows:

(a) Give a name to each class.
(b) Write down the attributes for each class on the table.
(c) Write down the routines for each class on the table.
(d) Capture the common behavior in an inheritance hierarchy.
(e) Define the inheritance hierarchy by writing the feature header code in each class.

(f) Implement each feature.

The problem given here is complex, so it can be decomposed into smaller pieces. A simpler problem is to consider only two classes. Write the class definition for a single class, then choose another class and design the inheritance hierarchy for those two classes. When you believe that your solution works, add a third class. Finally, add the last class.

CHAPTER 10

Polymorphism

Keywords

conformance
deferred
effective
static type
dynamic type
polymorphism

A class in an inheritance hierarchy has many types, from the current type to the most abstract type at the top of the hierarchy. At each level, the appropriate behavior for that level is defined. A common pattern is to define the feature interface at a high level in the hierarchy, and to defer the body or action of a feature until a later, descendant class. Such a **deferred** feature has its name and signature defined in a parent, but the definition or body of the feature is given in the child. The child effects or gives an effective definition for the feature, so each child can define its own specific action. Objects of the various child types can be treated identically by calling the feature on the object; the feature interface is identical, but the content of the feature is specific to each class. This technique is called polymorphism, because it allows the same code to use objects of many shapes or types.

10.1   The Eiffel type hierarchy

Every object is an instance of a class. Eiffel uses a class hierarchy to define the very top and the very bottom levels of any user-defined inheritance structure. At the top of the Eiffel hierarchy is the class *GENERAL*, which defines the generic routines *clone*, *copy*, and *is_equal*. Below that is the class *PLATFORM*, which defines the specific features needed to tailor the Eiffel language to run on a specific platform or computer system, such as the number of bits used to store numbers of type *INTEGER*, *REAL*, and *DOUBLE*. Below that is the class *ANY*, which is the ancestor of every user-defined class, so all user-defined classes sit below *ANY* in the hierarchy.

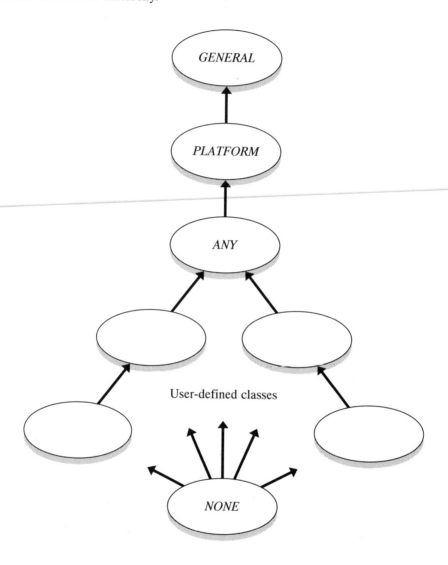

Every class written by a user inherits from the Eiffel class *ANY*, without the need for an explicit inheritance clause. The class *ANY* allows features to be defined that work for any class; more formally, that work for all classes of type *ANY*. System-wide features can be defined once at the appropriate level, and used by all the children of class *ANY*; in particular, the generic features *clone*, *copy*, and *is_equal* are defined once and used in any class. No class is of type *NONE*, by definition. Class *NONE* defines the bottom node in the inheritance hierarchy, so by definition no class can inherit it. The special value *Void* is of type *NONE*.

With the introduction of inheritance, what is meant by the type of an object has to be defined in more detail. A worker is a person; more formally, an object of type *WORKER* is also an object of type *PERSON*, because *WORKER* inherits *PERSON*. The base class of a specific class is defined to be the top-level user class, at the top of the user-defined hierarchy. The inheritance hierarchy for a class may be many levels deep, so a class can be of many types, from its current type all the way up to type *ANY*. In the previous chapter, an inheritance hierarchy was defined for a *CONTRACTOR*, who is a *WORKER*, who is a *PERSON*, who is of type *ANY*. This reflects the real world: I am a worker, a person, a human being, an animal, a living being, and a thing (in some languages, the top level of the inheritance hierarchy is a class *THING*). An object that is an instance of a class in an inheritance hierarchy is of many types. A class has an immediate type, as well as one or more inherited types. A generic class can generate many types, one type for each actual parameter.

Given the Eiffel class hierarchy, in particular the two classes *ANY* and *NONE*, it can now be seen that there is a single, consistent rule for export policies: a feature is exported to the classes listed in its export policy. A feature exported to objects of type *ANY* is thus available to all classes; a feature exported to objects of type *NONE* is available to no classes. A feature exported to one or more specific classes is available to those classes, and to descendants of those classes, because a descendant of class *X* is of type *X*, as well as more specific types.

10.2   Conformance

Inheritance in the Eiffel type system provides a way to define one type in terms of another. It also determines when one type can replace another, and ensures that the type system works in an intuitively reasonable manner. Consider an example where you go into a restaurant and ask for a salad. For this request, it is reasonable that any type of salad will be acceptable, such as a garden salad, a fruit salad, a chef's salad, and so on. These are specific types of salad, so they conform to the definition of a salad. On the other hand, receiving a hamburger would be a surprise, because a hamburger is not a type of salad. The notion of conformance makes this expectation explicit.

In an assignment statement, the type of the right-hand side of the assignment must be the same as the type of the variable on the left-hand side. Because a variable may have many types due to inheritance, this rule must be stated more formally: the type of the expression on the right of the assignment must conform to the type on the left. Class B conforms to class A if they are the same class, or class B is a descendant of A; A cannot also conform to B because inheritance is directed.

Consider the classes *CONTRACTOR*, *WORKER*, and *PERSON*, a hierarchy of three classes. A contractor is a specific type of worker, and a worker is a specific type of person. If I need a job done and advertise for the services of a worker, then there is no surprise if I use a contractor, because a contractor can take the place of a worker. On the other hand, I would be surprised if a person who is not a worker answered the ad; I want a more specific class. In the same way, an Eiffel variable can store an object of its defined type (*WORKER*) or an object of any sub-type (*CONTRACTOR*), because the child conforms to the parent. Examples of correct and incorrect conformance are

p: PERSON	
w: WORKER	
c: CONTRACTOR	
p := c	*-- valid; a contractor is a person*
p := w	*-- valid; a worker is a person*
w := p	*-- invalid; a person is not a worker*
w := c	*-- valid; a contractor is a worker*
c := p	*-- invalid; a person is not a contractor*
c := w	*-- invalid; a worker is not a contractor*

When a feature is redefined, the signature of the new version must conform to its precursor in the parent class. The signature of a feature lists the number, order, and type of the values passed as arguments to the routine, and the type of any value returned from the routine. To ensure that redefinition works in a reasonable manner, the signatures of any old and new versions of a feature must conform; more formally, each type in the signature of the new version must conform to the corresponding type in the old version. A redefined feature often keeps the original signature; conformance allows descendants to replace their ancestors in the signature.

An expanded type conforms directly to its base type, and indirectly to other classes through the base type. Consider the two declarations and the assignment

ref_type: T
exp_type: **expanded** *T*
ref_type := exp_type

This assignment is valid, and has the effect of copying the values of *exp_type* into the variable *ref_type*. Expanded types are discussed in more detail in *Eiffel: The Language* (Meyer, 1992).

10.3   Deferred features

The foundation of reusable software is to define a feature once, and use the feature as needed. A feature is placed in a class in the hierarchy and can then be used by inheritance; in system design, a great amount of time is often spent working out the best place to store a feature so that it can be reused. One of the most powerful inheritance techniques is to define the feature interface for a general class of objects in a general class, and then leave each specific, inheriting class to define its own specific action or body of the feature. Every child plays the same role and has similar behavior, but the exact, internal details of the behavior are different.

A routine header defines the external interface or signature of the routine, and the routine body defines the action. A routine may be defined with a header, but no body; such a routine has only a defined interface, so its body cannot be executed. The interface is defined in a parent class, and the body is deferred; a child class then inherits the routine and defines the body. The parent defines a deferred routine, and the child makes this routine effective; such a process is called effecting the routine.

A deferred routine is defined by replacing the keyword **do** with the keyword **deferred**, and leaving the body of the routine empty. A deferred routine to find an area, for example, is

---

deferred class *X*
feature
    area: REAL **is**
        – – area
      deferred
      end

A class with a deferred routine is called a deferred class; this must be stated in the class header, as shown above. An instance of a deferred class cannot be created, because Eiffel cannot find a routine body to connect to the feature header. A deferred class therefore does not contain a creation clause.

10.4   A deferred example: class *POLYGON*

Consider a system that implements a graphics library. Classes in the library define geometric shapes such as points, lines, circles, triangles, squares, and rectangles. A polygon is a general name for closed geometric objects made of straight lines, such as triangles and squares. An abstract class *POLYGON* may therefore be defined to capture the general properties and behavior of polygons; this class is then inherited by specific types of polygon.

Operations on polygons include computing the area and perimeter of a shape, moving the shape around, or changing the size of the shape. These behaviors can be defined in the abstract class *POLYGON* as effective or as deferred routines. A polygon has a perimeter, and the length of this perimeter can be easily calculated for arbitrary polygons, so an effective routine to calculate the perimeter is defined in this class. A polygon has an area, but it is difficult to define a method for finding the area of an arbitrary polygon, so the body of this feature is deferred. Defining the function *area* as a deferred routine says that all polygons have an area, but the effective routine to calculate the area is left for more specific classes to define.

The code for the deferred class *POLYGON* looks like

---

deferred class *POLYGON*

feature *{NONE}*

```
            vertices: LINKED_LIST[POINT]

feature {ANY}
    make is
                -- get the points that define the polygon
        deferred
        end -- make

    perimeter: REAL is
                -- the length of the perimeter of the polygon
        local this, previous: POINT
        do
            from
                vertices.start
                this := vertices.value
            until vertices.islast
            loop
                previous := this
                vertices.forth
                this := vertices.value
                Result := Result + this.distance (previous)
            end
            Result := Result + this.distance (vertices.first)
        end -- perimeter

    area: REAL is
                -- return the area of the figure
        deferred
        end -- area

    display is
                -- display the location of the vertices
        do
            from vertices.start
            until vertices.off_right
            loop
                vertices.item.display
                vertices.forth
            end
        end -- display

    move (delta_x, delta_y: REAL) is
                -- move by delta_x horizontally and delta_y vertically
```

```
      do
            from vertices.start
            until vertices.off_right
            loop
                  vertices.item.move (delta_x, delta_y)
                  vertices.forth
            end
      end -- move

end -- class POLYGON
```

Specific types of polygon, such as triangles, rectangles, and squares, define effective versions for each deferred routine. A deferred routine is not redefined in the child, because it was never defined; the child defines an effective routine. An effective parent routine may be used by the child as written, or it may be redefined to more specific versions.

10.5   An effective example: class *RECTANGLE*

A rectangle is a polygon with four sides, where the sides meet at right angles. Rectangles are created, moved, and displayed like any other polygon, and have an area and a perimeter. On the other hand, a rectangle has special features of its own (matching sides, four vertices, right angles) which may result in better ways of doing some of the operations. *RECTANGLE* can thus be defined as a child of *POLYGON*, the inherited features can be effected or changed, and new features can be added as needed. To create a rectangle, all the *RECTANGLE* routines have to be effective, because it is impossible to create an object of a deferred type. One possible way to implement the class *RECTANGLE* is

```
class RECTANGLE
inherit
    POLYGON
        redefine perimeter
        end
creation
    make

feature {NONE}
    number_of_vertices: INTEGER is 4
    side1, side2: REAL

feature {ANY}
    make is
```

```
                    -- make a rectangle, store the lengths of the sides
            local
                i: INTEGER
                p: POINT

            do
                !!vertices.make
                io.putstring ("%NEnter the four points of the rectangle")
                from
                until i = number_of_vertices
                loop
                    !!p.make_input
                    i := i + 1
                    vertices.put (p, i)
                    vertices.forth
                end
                side1 := vertices.item(1).distance (vertices.item(2))
                side2 := vertices.item(2).distance (vertices.item(3))
            end -- make

        perimeter: REAL is
                    -- length of the perimeter of a rectangle
            do
                Result := 2 * (side1 + side2)
            end -- perimeter

        area is
                    -- area of the rectangle
            do
                Result := side1 * side2
            end -- area

    end -- class RECTANGLE
```

Because *RECTANGLE* is a descendant of *POLYGON*, all the polygon features are features of the new class. The features in the two classes are shown below, first those defined in the parent class, then the routines inherited, defined, or redefined in the child. Exported features are shown in bold face.

Polygon			Rectangle
vertices			*vertices*
make	effect		**make**
perimeter	redefine		**perimeter**

area	effect	*area*
display		*display*
move		*move*
		number_of_vertices
		side1
		side2

Inheritance is transitive, so a class that inherits from *RECTANGLE*, such as *SQUARE*, has all the *POLYGON* features as well as all the additional *RECTANGLE* features.

A function can be redefined or effected as an attribute. It is not possible to redefine an attribute as a function, because an attribute value can be and often is assigned where a function cannot be assigned. For the same reason, it is not possible to redefine or effect an attribute as a constant; the attribute can be changed but the constant cannot, so the behavior is not equivalent.

10.6   Dynamic types

With the use of inheritance and conformance, it is now possible for a variable to be declared as one type (such as *WORKER*) and to actually contain an object of another type (such as *CONTRACTOR*). A contractor is a type of worker, so a *CONTRACTOR* object can be stored in a *WORKER* variable because the child conforms to the parent. This flexibility means that we must be careful about stating the type of an object; more formally, we must be careful about the type of the object pointed to by a variable. In particular, we must distinguish between a variable's static and dynamic type. The static type is the type that was used in the variable declaration, and the dynamic type is the current type of the object stored in the variable. These may be the same type for a particular variable, or they may be different.

Consider the example used in the last chapter, where three variables of different types were defined by the declarations and the creations

p: PERSON	– – static type of *p* is *PERSON*
w: WORKER	– – static type of *w* is *WORKER*
c: CONTRACTOR	– – static type of *c* is *CONTRACTOR*
!!p.make	
!!w.make	
!!c.make	

With the existing inheritance hierarchy, the static and dynamic types of *c* must be the same, because *CONTRACTOR* has no children, so the only thing that can be stored in *c* is an object of type *CONTRACTOR*. On the other hand, we can store workers and contractors in the variable *p*, because both of these classes conform to the class *PERSON*. The following assignments are valid by conformance, and change the type of the object pointed to by the name.

$p := w$	— — dynamic type of p is *WORKER*
$p := c$	— — dynamic type of p is *CONTRACTOR*
$w := c$	— — dynamic type of w is *CONTRACTOR*

Changing the type of a variable at run-time can be done by assignment, in which case we refer to the process as dynamic assignment. The same effect can occur during variable binding in a procedure call, when the formal argument is replaced by a conforming actual argument. The type can also be changed by dynamic creation, described below. The general term for the process is dynamic binding, in which the type of a variable is changed at run-time.

10.7   Dynamic creation

Eiffel has the ability to specify the type of an object when the object is created, as well as when the variable is declared. An explicit type is given in the creation command for the object, and must conform to the static or declared type of the variable. The syntax of the dynamic creation command is

> *!CLASS!object.make*

where the creation type (the class between the bangs) is a child of the object's type.

An example of this technique is provided by a graphics system in which the user can dynamically create objects using an interactive menu. The menu requests the type of object to create, the user types in a single character, and the system then creates an object of the appropriate type. A bad implementation of this scenario is

```
class GRAPHIC
creation
    make

feature
    poly: POLYGON

    . . .

    do_choice (choice: CHARACTER) is
            — — create an object of the appropriate type
            — — THIS IS THE WRONG WAY TO DO THE TASK
        local
            t: TRIANGLE
            r: RECTANGLE
            s: SQUARE
```

```
            do
                inspect choice
                    when 'T' then
                        !!t.make
                        poly := t
                    when 'R' then
                        !!r.make

                        poly := r
                    when 'S' then
                        !!s.make
                        poly := s
                end -- inspect
            end -- do_choice
```

In this implementation, a set of local variables are declared, one of them is created, and the new object is then assigned to the attribute *poly*. There is no need for all these variables, because the type can be dynamically defined when the object is created. A good implementation of the menu feature *do_choice* is much shorter and simpler than the version shown above; it is

```
    poly: POLYGON
    . . .
    do_choice (choice: CHARACTER) is
            -- create an object of the appropriate type
        do
            inspect choice
                when 'T' then !TRIANGLE!poly.make
                when 'R' then !RECTANGLE!poly.make
                when 'S' then !SQUARE!poly.make
            end -- inspect
        end -- do_choice
```

An explicit type for the object is defined in the creation command, so no local variables are required; an object of the explicit type is simply created. The declared type of the object is the static type, here a *POLYGON*. The type of the object when it is created is the dynamic type; here, the dynamic type of *poly* is one of *TRIANGLE*, *RECTANGLE*, or *SQUARE*. When dynamically created types are used by a client, they must appear in the client chart.

This example introduces a new form of the creation command, in which an explicit type is defined in the instruction. There are two additional forms of creation needed with inheritance; the complete list of creation forms is shown on the next page.

Creation command	Creation clause
!!p	none
!!p.make	**creation** *{<exports>}* *make*
!<type>!.make	**creation** *{<exports>}* *make*
none	**creation**

An object may have no creation routine (case 1), or it may have a routine, possibly with arguments (case 2). An object may be dynamically typed (case 3), which affects the creation command but not the creation clause. If the creation clause is empty (case 4) as opposed to absent (case 1), then an object of that type cannot be created. Objects of a deferred class cannot be created, so a deferred class contains no creation clause. In the case where all features of a class are defined, but the class is not useful by itself, the creation clause is left empty. The class can still be used by inheritance, but not by a client as a stand-alone entity.

10.8   Polymorphism

Polymorphism means the ability to take several forms (poly = many, morph = shape), where each form can be treated identically. The mechanisms that allow polymorphism are overloading, in which an operator can have several meanings, and dynamic binding, in which a variable can have several types. These techniques allow the same symbol (operator or variable) to be used in different ways, and support polymorphism.

As an example, consider a list that contains many different kinds of graphical objects, such as *TRIANGLEs*, *RECTANGLEs*, *SQUAREs*, and *HEXAGONs*. In this example, the list is statically defined to be a list of *POLYGONs*. Any object that conforms to *POLYGON* can be inserted into this list, because the objects are all polygons, so the list is indeed a list of polygons. An example of inserting "different" types of objects on a list is given by the code

```
shapes: LINKED_LIST[POLYGON]
poly_filler is
        -- insert objects of different types into the list
    local
        p: POLYGON
    do
        !!shapes.make
        !!p.make
        shapes.insert_right (p)
        !SQUARE!p.make
        shapes.insert_right (p)
        !HEXAGON!p.make
```

```
        shapes.insert_right (p)
    end -- poly_filler
```

Polymorphism allows extremely compact and flexible code to be written, because the same line of code can do different things! In the list of polygons, for example, each object can be displayed by calling the *display* routine for that object:

```
    display_shapes is
            -- show each of the elements on the list
        do
            from shapes.start
            until shapes.after
            loop
                shapes.item.display
                shapes.forth
            end
        end -- display_shapes
```

If the names and signatures of the child features are the same, then the code can simply call a feature for that object. To execute the feature call, Eiffel examines the type of object to the left of the dot, looks up the relevant class, and executes the feature with that name in that class. As far as the client is concerned, it is simply displaying each object; how the object is actually displayed is an internal detail of each class.

The client chart shows the classes declared in the client, so it shows both the polymorphic list and any static classes, but no dynamic classes. The client chart for the code shown above, assuming that the code is contained in class *GRAPHIC*, is thus

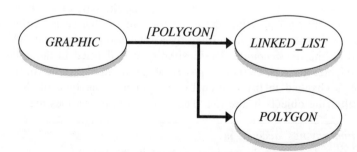

Polymorphism means that the type of an object is not usually tested at all. A common parent is defined, objects of the various child types are created, and from then on the various objects are treated identically by the client code. Any complexity is hidden inside the features of the children. There may be cases, however, where the type of an object does have to be used; in the case study, for example, a customer can request access to their savings account, or to their check account. The type of an object can be found using the conditional assignment operator.

The conditional assignment, or assignment attempt statement, uses the symbol "?=" in place of the assignment symbol ":=". If the type of the right-hand side conforms to the type of the left-hand side, then the assignment is successful and a useful value is assigned; if the types do not conform, then the value of *Void* is assigned. An object can be tested to see if it is of some type by trying to assign it to a name of the desired type by a conditional assignment of the form

```
type: TYPE
object: OBJECT
     type ?= object
```

After this code has been executed, the name *type* will contain either the value *Void*, or have the same value as *object*.

DESIGN PRINCIPLE 13: Don't explicitly test the type of an object. Use polymorphism to define a common interface. Use conditional assignment to find the desired type.

In the case study for this chapter, a customer may have up to three types of account: savings, check, and investment. When a customer uses the ATM, they are asked for the account type, and the reply is used to find the correct object; only savings and check accounts can be accessed via the ATM. A polymorphic solution is to store the three accounts in a list, and then scan through the list to find the desired object. Once the objects have been stored on the list, however, we have "lost track" of exactly where the object was stored. The standard method to find an object from a polymorphic list is to scan the list matching on a conditional assignment; this method uses the defined type hierarchy to find the type of an object.

The code shown below has the basic form of the list scan routine presented in Chapter 8, but the match is defined by a successful assignment. The accounts are stored on the list *accounts*. The desired type is defined in the code below as a local variable; the type cannot be passed as an argument to the routine, because the value is changed in the routine by assignment. The type of the variable is used to filter the objects in the list. The matched scan routines are

```
find_savings_account is
        -- find the savings account in the list
    local account: SAVINGS
    do
        from accounts.start
        until accounts.after or else account =/ Void
```

```
            loop
                    account ?= accounts.item
                    accounts.forth
            end
        end – – find_savings_account

    found_savings: BOOLEAN is
                – – was a savings account found on the list?
            do
                    Result := not accounts.after
            end – – found_savings
```

The loop scans through the objects on the list, attempting to assign each one. If an object on the list has the same type as the variable (more formally, conforms to the variable), then the assignment succeeds and the loop terminates with the cursor pointing to the desired object. If no object of the desired type is found, then the cursor is left pointing after the list.

10.9   Case study: the *BANK* system

The *BANK* system is extended to use three types of account: savings, check, and investment accounts. A customer may have one account of each type. The extra specification for this part of the case study is

> There are three types of bank account: savings, check, and investment. A customer may have one account of each type. Savings and check accounts are accessed through the ATM. Savings and investment accounts accrue daily interest.
>
> A successful withdrawal from a check account costs 50 cents. An unsuccessful withdrawal from a check account (a bounced check) costs $5. There are no charges or penalties for a savings account. A savings account gets daily interest; the interest rate is 4.5 percent a year. A check account gets no interest. The balance of an account cannot be negative.
>
> An investment account may not be accessed through the ATM. It is created with an initial balance, and accrues daily interest for a period of three, six, or 12 months. A three-month investment account has an annual interest rate of 5.5 percent, a six-month account has a 6.0 percent rate, and a 12-month account 6.5 percent. When the account matures at the end of the period, the total amount is transferred into the customer's check account. If there is no check account, then one is created specially to receive the investment funds.

This part of the case study shows the detailed analysis and design of an inheritance hierarchy, through several iterations. For each version, the analysis and design that led to that solution are presented, then evaluated. The analysis, design, evaluation, and solution code for this extension are shown in Section 6 of the case study.

Summary

- The body of a routine may be **deferred** in a parent class. An effective definition is supplied by descendants of the class. A class with a deferred routine is called a deferred class; objects of a deferred class cannot be created.
- The declared type of an object is called the static type, and the actual or run-time type is called the dynamic type of the variable.
- A child class conforms to the parent class, so an object can be assigned to a variable of its own type, or to a variable of its parent type.
- The type of an object may be changed at run-time by dynamic assignment, binding, or creation; the general process is called dynamic binding.
- Dynamic binding allows a variable to contain objects of different types, and overloading allows an operator to have different actions, depending on its arguments.
- Children of a common parent with identical behavior can be treated identically by a client. The client calls a feature, and the action of that feature is defined by each child. This technique is called polymorphism (many shapes).

Exercises

1. Describe what is meant by each of the following terms. Give the format and the effect of the corresponding Eiffel clause:
   - inherit
   - rename
   - redcfine
   - defer.

2. What is meant by an effective feature? an immediate feature? an inherited feature?

3. How are two features joined? What must be true before the two features can be joined?

4. What is the difference between a static and a dynamic type? Compare and contrast static and dynamic types in dynamic creation, dynamic assignment, and dynamic binding.

5. What is polymorphism? Do polymorphic classes have to have the same class interface? How does polymorphism replace explicit selection in the code?

6. The game of battleships is a two-player game, played on two boards. Each board is a two-dimensional array, containing empty squares (sea) and occupied squares (ships). Each player in turn guesses a location on the opponent's board; if there is a ship at that location, then the ship is destroyed and the player gets another turn. Play continues until all of a player's ships have been destroyed.

   The most basic version of this game has a small board and a single ship which does not move. Write a system in which you play against the computer. To simplify the system, use a 3x3 board, a single ship that takes up one square, a random number generator for the computer's guesses, no memory of previous guesses, and no validation of the user input. Design a system to play the game of battleships. *Hint:* The only difference between the two players (person and computer) is the source of the guess (input versus generated).

7. Consider the specification in the previous chapter, which described four kinds of bank account: savings, check, scrooge, and investment. Examine your previous solution and see if your solution can be improved by the use of deferred features.

8. Consider the following specification:

A bank offers six types of account: savings, check, scrooge, minimum, debit, and investment. The first five types can be accessed through an ATM, so they offer the services deposit, withdraw, and display. For each type of account, the rules for each service are slightly different.

Any amount may be deposited in an account. A withdrawal from a savings account decrements the balance by the amount withdrawn. A successful withdrawal from a check account costs 50 cents. An unsuccessful withdrawal from a check account costs $5. There are no charges or penalties for a savings account. The balance of an account cannot be negative.

A savings account gets daily interest; the interest rate is 4.5 percent a year. A check account gets no interest. An investment account is created with an initial balance, and accrues daily interest for a period of three, six, or 12 months. A three-month investment account has an annual interest rate of 5.5 percent, a six-month account has a 6.0 percent rate, and a 12-month account 6.5 percent. When the account matures at the end of the period, the total amount is transferred into the customer's check account. If there is no check account, then one is created specially to receive the investment funds.

A scrooge account allows money to be deposited, but not withdrawn. A scrooge account is set up for some period with an interest rate of 6.0 percent, and the balance increases over the period due to interest and deposits. Interest is paid daily. At the end of the period, the money is transferred into a check account.

The balance of a minimum account is not allowed to fall below $20 000. It has an interest rate of 7.5 percent.

A debit account is like an always available bank loan. The account is set up with an initial value of at least $5000. If the balance goes below this, interest is charged on the difference at 9.5 percent per annum, calculated daily. Note that this is negative interest deducted from the balance; the customer has to pay for the money that was used. Interest deductions are stopped when the balance returns above the initial amount.

Write the inheritance hierarchy for this fragment of the system:

(a) Give a name to each class.
(b) Write the inheritance chart.
(c) For each class, show the feature names.
(d) Indicate which features are inherited, and which are immediate.
(e) Write polymorphic code (caller and called) to create a list of accounts.
(f) Write polymorphic code to add interest at the end of every day.

CHAPTER 11

Complex inheritance

Keywords

multiple inherit
join
undefine
repeated inherit
select
constrained genericity

Three topics are addressed in this chapter: multiple inheritance, repeated inheritance, and constrained genericity. A class may inherit from one or many parents. A common pattern is to have two features with the same name and signature, where one is deferred and defines the interface, and the other, effective feature defines the action. These features are automatically merged or joined during inheritance. If both features are effective, one version may be converted to a deferred feature by **undefine**, so the two features are automatically joined. With multiple inheritance, there may be a name clash in the inherited features, which is resolved by **rename**, **undefine**, or by a clause that tells the class to **select** a particular feature as the active feature. A class may inherit from the same parent one or more times, showing repeated inheritance. Finally, the type of parameter passed to a generic class can be constrained in the generic class header, so a constrained generic class only accepts a parameter that conforms to the constraint.

11.1   Multiple inheritance

A class may inherit from more than one parent, and the child can use features from both parents. This is a very common practice in OO systems, because it allows each class to define a constellation of useful features that a child class can inherit and combine. Multiple inheritance is implemented by listing multiple class names in the child's inherit clause, such as

```
class A
inherit
      B; C; D
```

The inherited class names are separated by semi-colons; if there are sub-clauses within each class, then these are listed within each class, such as

```
class A
inherit
    B
          rename
                p as q,
                r as s
          redefine
                t
          end;
    C;
    D;
```

With multiple inheritance, all the features from all the parents are now features of the child. While the code to inherit multiple classes is simple, care must be taken if there are two or more inherited features with the same name and signature. If one feature is deferred and one effective, then the two features are automatically joined or merged in the child to define one effective feature. If both features are effective, then the name clash must be resolved.

11.2   Multiple inheritance example: a storable list

To illustrate the power of multiple inheritance, consider a system that uses complex data structures such as lists. Every time this system is started, the list structures have to be created from scratch, so the user has to type in the same input again and again. It would be much simpler if the list could be stored in a file between sessions, then read in at the start of each session. The class *STORABLE* offers features to store an object to and retrieve an object from a file, but that class has nothing to do with lists. The desired class can be defined by inheriting from both class *LINKED_LIST* and from class *STORABLE*.

11.2.1 Class STORABLE
The Eiffel Library class *STORABLE* allows an object to be stored to a file and retrieved from a file. The class offers many services; a shortened version of the class interface is

```
class interface STORABLE exported features
      store_by_name (filename: STRING)
```

```
                    -- Produce an external representation of the entire object structure
                    -- reachable from current object.
                    -- Write this representation onto file of name filename
        require
            filename_not_void: filename /= Void

    retrieve_by_name (filename: STRING)
                    -- Retrieve an object structure from external representation
                    -- previously stored in file of name filename
        require
            filename_not_void: filename /= Void

    retrieved: like Current
                    -- Last object retrieved by one of the retrieval procedures

end interface -- class STORABLE
```

The *store_by_name* routine stores a single object to file. The routine starts at the name of the object and traces any links or pointers through the object's data structure to all parts of the object. This is what is meant by "reachable from the current object", so file storage is thus a deep operation. In the *BANK* system, for example, the bank contains all the data in the entire system, every customer and every account for every customer. The single bank object thus contains all the permanent data for this system, so only that object has to be stored. The routines *retrieve_by_name* and *retrieved* are a matched pair of features; the first is a command to get the object, and the second returns a pointer to the retrieved object. Some versions of Eiffel combine the two routines into a single function called *retrieve_by_name*.

11.2.2 Class STORE_LIST

A class that inherits from both *LINKED_LIST* and *STORABLE* can create an object that is a list when the system is running, and is stored away in a file between sessions. The definition of such a class is extremely simple, because no features are added or changed; the class exists only to combine the features of both its parents. The complete class definition is shown below; the need to undefine two features is discussed in a later section of this chapter. The formal parameter *T* in the class header is replaced by the actual parameter passed from the client when the system is compiled.

```
class STORE_LIST[T]
inherit
    STORABLE
        undefine
            is_equal,
            copy
```

```
          end;
       LINKED_LIST[T]
   creation
       make

   end -- class STORE_LIST
```

All the features of both parents are inherited by this class, so a client can now declare an object to be of type *STORE_LIST*, retrieve the stored version of the list, use, change, delete, and add elements to this list during a session, then store the list at the end of a session.

11.2.3 Retrieving and storing a list

A client declares and uses objects of type *STORE_LIST*. The first time a list is needed, it is created by the client; every other time, the client simply retrieves the list from file.

When an object is stored, the object must inherit *STORABLE*. An object is stored by a command of the form *x.store_by_name (filename)*, so *x* must be a storable object. In the bank system, the list of customers must be a storable object.

When the list is retrieved, however, there is no object *x* to use in a feature call, because the name *x* does not have a value; if it did, the name would already point to the list! The retrieve command is thus called on the current object (the client, here the bank) by a command of the form *retrieve_by_name (filename)*, and the *retrieved* value is assigned. In the bank system, both classes *BANK* and *STORE_LIST* must inherit the class *STORABLE*; the list so that it can be stored, and the bank so that it can retrieve the list. The inheritance charts for this part of the system are shown below.

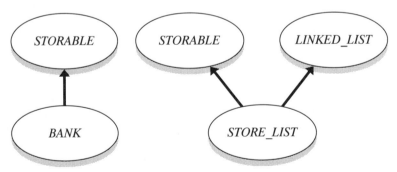

The client chart for this part of the system is shown below, where the bank uses a storable list instead of just a list of customers. As always, client and inheritance charts capture different kinds of links, so they are shown separately.

The client code to retrieve and store a list of customers is shown below. The client passes the actual parameter *CUSTOMER* to *STORE_LIST* in the declaration, and this type is bound to the formal parameter *T* in the class header. The creation routine for the class retrieves and assigns the object if it exists, and creates an empty list if it does not. The code shown below retrieves the object by its filename, and assigns the retrieved object to the name if the file contained an object with the same structure, using a conditional assignment. If a file of the right type with the right name existed, then the assignment succeeds; note that the assignment may fail (and a value of *Void* be assigned) if the file does not exist, or if the file contains the wrong type of object. The store routine stores the list to the named file.

```
class BANK
inherit
    STORABLE
creation
    make

feature {NONE}
    patrons: STORE_LIST[CUSTOMER]
    filename: STRING is "patrons.dat"

feature
    make is
            -- create or retrieve from file the list of customers
        do
            retrieve_by_name (filename)
            patrons ?= retrieved
            if patrons = Void then !!patrons
            end
        end -- make
    ...
    store is
            -- store the updated list to file
        do
            patrons.store_by_name (filename)
        end -- store
end -- class BANK
```

This example of multiple inheritance took two separate classes, and combined them dynamically to give the desired functionality. The same technique can be used to store and retrieve arrays, trees, graphs, or any type of data structure, because the data structure and the file access have been separated into two classes. The example nicely shows the 'mix and match' philosophy of reuse in Eiffel; new code does not have to be written, because all the desired features already exist and can simply be used.

11.3   Joining features

Eiffel automatically joins or merges a deferred feature with an effective feature that has the same name and signature. One common use of this technique is to define an interface in one class as a set of deferred features, define the effective features in another class, and join the two sets of features in a child that inherits both classes. In this way, the interface to a class is separate from the class itself, but the two can be combined to form a single class that is used by a client; the separation is made through the inheritance structure, and is thus invisible to the client.

As an example, consider the account menu interface in the banking system case study. A class *MENU* can be defined which contains all the code to interact with the user, and then calls a deferred feature when the input is complete. A separate class *ACCOUNT* is defined with a set of effective features, and a child class inherits from both parents and joins the features. If the account details change, then the class *ACCOUNT* can be modified without changing the menu interface. If the menu changes from character-based to some other form of menu, then class *MENU* can be modified without affecting the account actions. The interactive account class *INTERACCT* inherits its interactive features from *MENU*, and the account features from *ACCOUNT*. The inheritance chart for these classes is shown below.

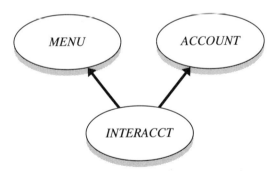

The code for one of the menu choices and one of the account actions might look like the code shown below. The user interface and deferred features are given in the class *MENU*. Because this class contains a deferred feature, it must be defined as a deferred class.

```
deferred class MENU
creation

feature
    . . .
```

```
        do_choice is
                -- execute the choice made by the user
            do
                inspect io.lastchar
                    when 'D', 'd' then
                        io.putstring ("Enter the amount to deposit: ")

                        io.readreal
                        deposit (io.lastreal)
                        . . .
            end -- do_choice

        deposit (amount: REAL) is
                -- add amount to the balance
            deferred
            end

end -- class MENU
```

An effective feature for *deposit* is defined in the class *ACCOUNT*. This class contains no deferred features, but an object of this type should never be created, only instances of the specific types of account. For this reason, class *ACCOUNT* is defined with an empty creation clause which stops any client from creating an instance of this type. The effective code is

```
class ACCOUNT
creation

feature
    deposit (amount: REAL) is
            -- add amount to the balance
        do
            balance := balance + amount
        end
    . . .
end -- class ACCOUNT
```

The child class *INTERACCT* inherits from both parents, getting the feature interface from class *MENU*, and the feature definition from class *ACCOUNT*. The complete code for the child class is

```
class INTERACCT
inherit
    MENU; ACCOUNT
```

```
creation
    make
end -- class INTERACCT
```

All the features in both classes are inherited, and the deferred and effective features are joined, because these features have the same name and signature. The child class has to nominate its own creation routine, as always. The full code for the menu and account classes is shown in Section 7 of the case study.

11.4   Undefine

If a class inherits two effective features with the same name, then they cannot be joined and create a name clash. The name clash can be resolved by converting one of the features from effective to deferred, so that the (now) deferred feature is joined with the (single) effective feature. The format of the **undefine** clause is

```
class A
inherit
    B
        undefine
            x, y, z
        end
```

The keyword **undefine** is followed by the names of all features in the inherited class to be undefined. Multiple undefined features have their names separated by commas.

In the storable list example above, there was a name clash because the effective features *is_equal* and *copy* were inherited from both *STORABLE* and *LINKED_LIST*. The banking system simply stores and retrieves files, so there is no need to compare or copy files and these features can be undefined from *STORABLE* to resolve the name clash. The effective versions of the routines *is_equal* and *copy* in the class *STORE_LIST* are thus the two routines from the class *LINKED_LIST*. The full code in class *STORE_LIST* is

```
class STORE_LIST[T]
inherit
    STORABLE
        undefine
            is_equal,
            copy
        end
    LINKED_LIST[T]
```

```
    creation
        make
    end -- class STORE_LIST
```

A feature's signature can be changed to a conforming signature if the feature is first undefined and then redefined in the same inheritance clause. The code to do this is

```
    class A
    inherit
        B
            undefine
                x

            redefine
                x
            end
        feature
            x (m: N) is . . .
```

This dual change allows the signature of an inherited feature to be changed, because the feature is first made deferred and then redefined by the feature definition in the child. The new definition of the feature must conform to the previous definition, so each type in the new signature must conform to the corresponding type in the inherited feature.

11.5   Repeated inheritance

Repeated inheritance occurs when a class inherits from the same parent more than once. Repeated inheritance occurs every time a class inherits from two user-defined classes, because both parents inherit from class *ANY*, and the child thus has repeated inheritance from class *ANY*. Repeated inheritance may occur at a single level, but more often occurs via different inheritance paths in the inheritance hierarchy.

There are two cases to consider in which a feature is repeatedly inherited. If the feature has not been changed in any path from its parent, then the different versions are merged into a single feature. If the feature has been changed in one of the paths, then each of the different versions is retained in the child, and care must be taken to avoid a name clash.

All the features are inherited from both parents, so repeated inheritance could produce a whole series of name clashes because each of the parents has features with the same name. Many of the features in the new child often refer to exactly the same feature in both parents, however. Eiffel simply combines features with the same names and signatures when the features are inherited by repeated inheritance. On the other hand, some features will have to be different, and these are renamed to prevent them being merged. The shared features in the child are joined into a single feature, while those that have been changed are stored as separate features.

Consider the example of a joint bank account. A joint account is an account that can be used by more than one person; for simplicity, let's consider an account with only two users. The two customers have different names, but the same user identifier, password and, of course, the same account. This situation could be set up as two customers who both own the single account, or as a new class of customer that is two people, not a single person. Two separate customers does not model reality here, because the bank deals with a single customer that is two people.

A joint account can be modelled by repeated inheritance. A customer that is two people is implemented by a class *JOINT*, which inherits *PERSON* twice. The two people have their own name and sex, but share the same address, user id, and account. The inheritance hierarchy for the class *JOINT* is shown below; here, the repeated inheritance occurs at a single level.

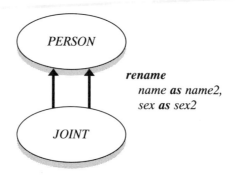

The code for class *JOINT* is shown below.

```
class JOINT
inherit
    PERSON;
    PERSON
        rename
            name as name2,
            sex as sex2,
            make as make_person,
            display as display_person
        redefine
            make,
            display
        end

feature
    make is
```

```
                        - - set the personal details for both people
            do
                make_person
                . . .
            end

        display is
                - - display the personal details for both people
            do
                display_person
                . . .
            end - - display

    end - - class JOINT
```

The attributes in class *JOINT* are the joined and changed attributes from both parents, here the attributes name, name2, sex, sex2, and address. The creation and display routines have to be changed to set and display two names and one address, but all other routines are the same. All the features that were unchanged on the path from the parent are joined, while those features that were changed have their own, different names and definitions.

11.6   Select

If different versions of a feature are inherited from the same parent, then the feature to be used in the child can be stated in the **select** clause of the inheritance clause. The other, unselected versions are discarded, solving the name conflict. A feature is selected by writing the keyword **select** as part of the inheritance clause for that class, followed by the name of the selected feature. The format of the select clause is

```
class A
inherit
    B
        select x, y, z
        end
```

If there are multiple features selected from the same class, then the feature names are separated by commas. **Select** is used in repeated inheritance, where **undefine** is used to decide between competing versions of a feature in multiple inheritance.

11.7   The inheritance clause

A class may inherit from a single parent, from multiple parents, or from the same parent repeatedly. Name clashes due to inheritance can be avoided by **rename**,

undefine, or **select**, followed by the automatic joining of a deferred and an effective version. The signature or body of a feature can be changed by a **redefine**. The export status of a feature is changed by the **export** clause. The format of the full inheritance clause is shown below. The sub-clauses are executed in order, so the same feature may be renamed, and then redefined under that new name.

---

class A
inherit
    B

        rename $--$ new name in child
            m **as** n
        export $--$ new export policy in child
          $\{C, D\}\ o,\ p$
        undefine $--$ no definition in child
            q
        redefine $--$ new body in child
            $r,\ s$
        select $--$ select active feature
            t
        end

A feature can be divided into four parts: a name, a type, a value, and an export policy. The name is simply the name of the routine, the type is defined by the signature, the value is defined by the routine body, and the export policy by the **feature** exports. A **rename** clause changes the name, but does not affect the signature or the body. An export clause changes the export status. A feature is changed from effective to deferred by the **undefine** clause. A **redefine** clause allows the designer to change the signature of a feature, so long as the new signature conforms to the old, and the content of the feature body may also be redefined. If there are competing effective features inherited repeatedly from the same parent, then one of these versions is **select**ed to be the active version in the child.

The action of each inheritance clause is shown below. Each part of a feature is listed across the top of the table, the clauses are listed down the side of the table, and the effect of the clause on the feature is indicated in the body of the table.

	Name	Signature	Body	Export
rename	new name			
export				new policy
undefine			deferred	
redefine		conforms	new body	
select	active	active	active	

The select clause does not change the definition of a feature: it simply selects the competing feature, from the repeated parent, that is active in the child class.

11.8   Genericity

The classes *ARRAY* and *LINKED_LIST* are generic classes, because they can use objects of any type. A generic class is passed an actual parameter in the variable declaration. The actual parameter is then bound to the formal parameter when the system is compiled. A declaration for an array of customers, and the class header for the class *ARRAY*, are shown below.

```
bank: ARRAY[CUSTOMER]

class ARRAY[T]
             – – define the features for an array of objects of type T
```

In the class definition, formal parameters are written after the name of the class, enclosed in square brackets; multiple parameters are separated by commas. The names "T" (for Type) and "G" (for Generic) are common names for formal parameters. Parameter binding occurs at compile time, while argument binding (in routines) occurs at run-time.

A generic class may be inherited, just like any other class. It may be inherited with the formal parameters bound or unbound. A storable array of customers may be defined by

```
class SAC
inherit
    STORABLE;
    ARRAY[CUSTOMER]
creation
    make
end – – class SAC
```

The actual parameter *CUSTOMER* is passed to class *ARRAY*, but it is hard-coded in the class *SAC*. *SAC* is not a generic class, because it only defines a class that uses customers. A generic class may be defined by giving a formal parameter in the class header:

```
class STORE_ARRAY[T]
inherit
    STORABLE
    ARRAY[T]
creation
    make
end – – class STORE_ARRAY
```

The class *STORE_ARRAY* is generic, because it can handle any type of object passed as an actual parameter from a client. An actual parameter is passed from a client, and bound to all occurrences of the formal parameter.

A generic class is powerful because it makes no assumptions about the objects that it uses; formally, it makes no assumption except that the object is of type *ANY*. An array and a list manipulate complete objects and never "look inside" an object. There are many cases, however, where a generic class needs to use features of the object. An example of this is a list, where each element has a unique key. The key can be used to search the list and find the desired object, but such a comparison has to be done by the client of the list, and has to be done by every client of a list with a key. The list class cannot assume that all objects it uses have a unique key, because such an assumption is not true for generic lists.

A special class can be defined for a list of objects with unique keys, by inheriting the list class and adding facilities to check the key of each object in the list. Such a class, however, can only handle certain types of objects: those with a key field. The type of object that can be passed as a parameter to this class must be constrained to have a key. This can be done by constraining the parameter list so that only certain types of objects can be passed as parameters.

11.9   Constrained genericity

A generic class can specify that only certain types should be used by the class, by placing a constraint on the type of the formal parameter. This technique is called constrained genericity, because the parameter type is constrained by the class header. Because the type of parameter is constrained, specialized classes can be defined that make use of the features of the constrained type. A constraint is defined on the formal parameter in the class header by stating that the formal parameter must be of some specific type; the only valid actual parameters are then classes of this type. The mechanism is more general than it might at first appear, because any actual parameter that conforms to the constraint is valid.

A generic class header is constrained by listing the formal parameter, the constraint indicator "->", and the name of the constraining class. The form of a constrained class header is

```
class G [T -> C]
```

which means, "In the generic class G, the class bound to T must be of type C."

Consider the class *CUSTOMER* in the *BANK* system. It would be nice to define a keyed list class that could search a list of customers, and look inside each element to see if it matched a given key value. Class *CUSTOMER* has to contain a key, and an exported routine *match* that receives a test key and returns true if the test key matches the key of the current object. The code in class *CUSTOMER* would look like

```
class CUSTOMER
feature
    key: INTEGER
    match (test: INTEGER): BOOLEAN is
            -- does the current object match this key?
        do
            Result := test = key
        end -- match
```

The constrained generic class, which is a list of keyed objects, may then be defined as

```
class KEY_LIST [T -> CUSTOMER]
inherit
    LINKED_LIST [T]
creation
    make
feature
    find (target: INTEGER) is

            -- position the cursor at the element with key value target
            -- or after if no matching element is in the list
        do
            from start
            until after or else item.match (target)
            loop forth
            end
        end -- find
```

The name of the list is not contained in the code above, because the code refers to the current object; the object is a list, because it inherits class *LINKED_LIST*. The code looks inside an object because it uses a feature called *match* that takes an integer and returns a Boolean value, so the class must use constrained genericity.

To use the power of matching arbitrary keys, the constraint in the class header is loosened so that any keyed class can be passed as a parameter. This constraint can be enforced by using the inheritance hierarchy to define a deferred class *MATCHABLE* which contains a deferred feature *match*, and making this the constraint. A *CUSTOMER* can then inherit *MATCHABLE* and effect the deferred routine. The inheritance (top) and client (bottom) structure for such a system is shown on the next page.

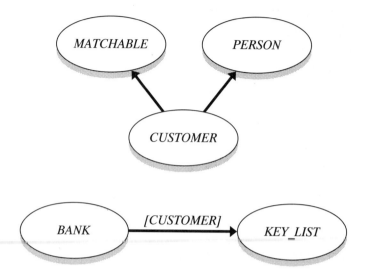

The code for such a system could look like

```
deferred class MATCHABLE
feature
    match (target: INTEGER): BOOLEAN is

            -- does the key match the target?
            deferred
            end -- match
end -- class MATCHABLE

class CUSTOMER
inherit
    MATCHABLE;
    PERSON
feature
    match (target: INTEGER): BOOLEAN is
            -- does the key match the target?
        do
            Result := key = target
        end -- match
    . . .
end -- class CUSTOMER

class KEY_LIST [T -> MATCHABLE]
inherit
```

```
      LINKED_LIST [T]
creation
      make
feature
      find (target: INTEGER) is
                  -- position the cursor at the element with key value target
                  -- or off_right if no matching element is in the list
            do
                  from start
                  until after or else item.match(target)
                  loop forth
                  end
            end -- find
      found: BOOLEAN is
                  -- was the target found?
            do
                  Result := not after
            end -- found
end -- class KEY_LIST
```

The general mechanism for constrained genericity can thus be defined in four steps:

1. Define a deferred parent (*MATCHABLE* here).
2. Inherit the parent class and effect the deferred feature (*match* in class *CUSTOMER* here).
3. List the parent as the generic constraint (*KEY_LIST* here).
4. Pass the base class (*CUSTOMER* here) as the actual parameter.

The use of a keyed list for customer lookup is illustrated in Section 7 of the case study.

11.10   Reuse in Eiffel

A traditional programming language, such as Pascal or C, supports code reuse by routines. A routine is defined once and then called as needed, with any needed data being passed as arguments to the routine. Eiffel supports code reuse in four ways: routine, client, inherit, and generic.

An Eiffel routine is defined to do a single thing, and complex actions are achieved by calling a series of routines. A set of preconditions can be defined on each routine, to define the values that can be passed as arguments; if the precondition is true when the routine is called, then the routine guarantees the effect or postcondition of the routine.

The class provides the basic unit of reuse in OO programming, because it encapsulates a set of related data and routines. In Eiffel, both data and routines are treated equally as features of the class, so we can simply talk about the behavior of the class. The use of a feature outside the class is explicitly controlled by the export policy; it is usual to export selected routines, and to hide the data inside the class. The simplest form of reuse is provided by the client relation, in which a client of the supplier class creates an object of that type, and then uses the services of that object. The creation of an object is controlled by the export policy on the creation routine.

A class can be reused by the inheritance relation. Inheritance occurs when one class can be viewed as a more specific version of another class; client means "has", "uses", or "contains" where inherit means "is". All features in a parent class are available to the inheriting, child class, and more features are usually added by each child. A feature may be defined in the parent class, or deferred until the child. When a feature is inherited, it can be used unchanged, it can be effected, and its name, signature, body, and export status may be altered in the child. A class may use single, multiple, or repeated inheritance.

A class can be reused by passing it to a generic class, which contains generic code to handle any object passed as a parameter to the class. If there is a need to use a feature of the object, then the inheritance hierarchy can be used to constrain the type of parameter passed to the constrained generic class. This allows type-specific code to be added to the new constrained class, so code can be written once inside the new class and used by a client of the generic class.

The price of reuse is a distributed system. In a traditional system, it is possible and common to write a long series of statements that are executed as a single chunk. This can produce very short and efficient code, but it does not support reuse. If any part of this code changes, then the whole routine has to be amended and recompiled. If a similar task needs to be done, then the existing code can offer a template for the new, similar code, but new code has to be written. If one part of the code needs to be done separately, then the existing code has to be rewritten to separate out this part, or the code has to be rewritten in a separate routine.

In a distributed system, each unit of action has been given its own routine, so a user can simply combine the existing behavior to achieve a new goal. The unit of action is a node, and the exact nodes that occur in a system are determined by the interaction between the plans and objects in the system. The goals of a system are defined to be its outputs, which are defined in the problem specification. The code in the system can then be analyzed as a set of plans, one plan for each goal. Plans and objects are orthogonal, because a plan can use many objects and an object can be used in many plans. The plan defines the essential, necessary actions that must occur to achieve the goal, and shows the essential links between these actions.

The process of analysis can be seen as the process of finding the plan actions, and finding how each action depends on a previous action; this is shown in a plan structure diagram. Given the necessary actions and links, a designer has immense freedom in how to implement the plan, both in choosing the language constructs that are used, and in deciding how to chunk the code and where to place the chunks. The process of design can be seen as taking the minimal, essential links and using them to build the structure of the solution, which is shown in a client chart, an inheritance chart, and a system structure diagram.

Analysis reveals the structure of the problem, and design creates the structure of the solution.

Summary

- A class may inherit from multiple parents. If one parent feature is deferred and the other is effective, they are automatically joined to provide an effective feature in the child.
- A common pattern in multiple inheritance is to have one class define the interface, and another class the action or implementation, so that each role can be changed independently.
- A feature may be **undefine**d when inherited, if two effective routines have a name clash.
- A class may inherit repeatedly from a parent. Common features are merged, and altered features are kept separate. When two effective versions of a repeated feature create a name clash, one of them may be **select**ed as the active version when it is inherited.
- A generic class handles objects of any type, passed as a parameter through the parameter list in the class header; such a process is called genericity. A generic class makes no assumptions about the behavior of its objects.
- Constrained genericity allows a generic class to use features of a parameter, by limiting or constraining the type of the parameter. A constraining parent class is defined, inherited by a child class, and listed as the constraint in the generic class. Only actual parameters of this type can then be passed.

Exercises

1. How are name clashes resolved in multiple inheritance? in repeated inheritance?
2. What happens when two features are joined? What must be true to join two features? Can two effective features be joined?
3. Genericity gives one way of reusing code. How does it do this?
4. Why do we need constrained genericity? What does the word "constrained" mean? What is constrained? How is it constrained?
5. What are the main steps in constrained genericity?
6. Build a constrained generic class:
   (a) Write code to display an ARRAY of POINTs.
   (b) Write code to display an ARRAY of PERSONs.
   (c) Write a generic class SHARRAY (show array) that displays all items in the array.
   (d) Write the code that uses class SHARRAY to replace (a) and (b).
7. List the ways that code is reused in Eiffel.

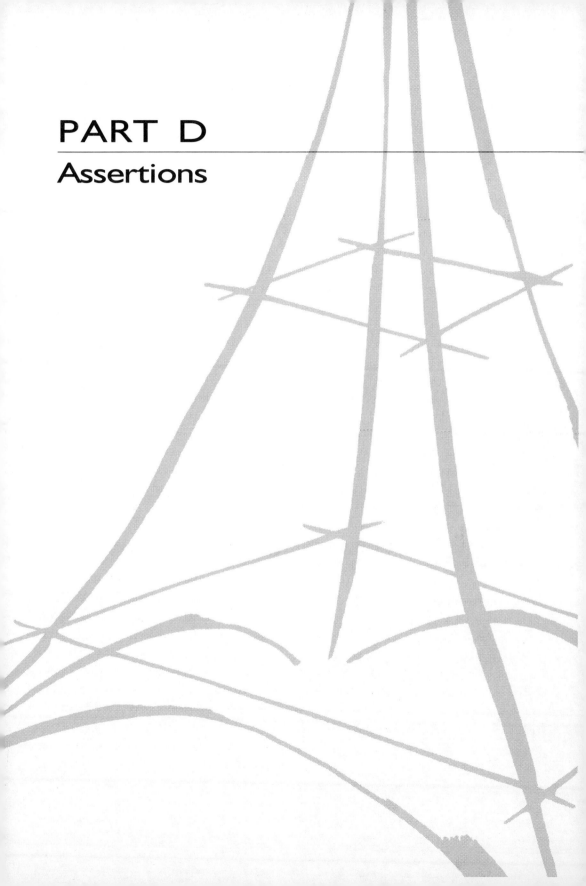

PART D
Assertions

CHAPTER 12

Programming by contract

contract
rights
obligations
assertions
pre- and postconditions
exceptions

Contracts govern the interactions between parties; ideally, they describe both the rights and obligations of all the persons involved. Assertions are logical expressions that precisely describe software; for example, the precondition for a procedure defines the conditions necessary before the routine's invocation, while the postcondition describes what must hold after execution is complete. Assertions can be used to write contracts for software components, which can also be monitored at run-time. If an assertion evaluates to false, then an exception is raised indicating that the contract has been violated.

12.1   Introduction

Experience has shown that software development is an error-prone activity. One of the major difficulties is defining exactly what a software component does or should do. Imagine the problems you would face if you didn't know what to expect from the machines, services, and organizations in your daily life. What if sometimes your boss gave you your paycheck, and other times he didn't for no reason? What if an ATM debited your account, but didn't give you any money? What if instead of replacing the defective parts, an automobile shop took your car apart and returned all the non-defective parts to you? Life would be complex and error prone indeed. Unfortunately, this is the current state of the art in some aspects of software development. It is very difficult to precisely specify software requirements.

In the day-to-day conduct of human affairs, contracts govern the interactions between parties. Ideally, a contract precisely defines the interactions between individuals, organizations, and machines. Contracts may be explicit or implicit. For example, an explicit contract governs the interactions between employers and labor unions. The wages to be paid, working conditions, and fringe benefits are all explicitly determined and agreed on by both parties before work begins. In contrast, an implicit contract governs the operation of ATMs. It is assumed that the machine will both dispense money and debit the corresponding account. If the machine malfunctions, the party who profited from the error can be called to remedy the situation based on general principles of banking and commerce.

Implicit and explicit contracts have different strengths and weaknesses. Implicit contracts save time and trouble as long as all the parties involved understand the unstated assumptions; however, they may cause considerable trouble for the uninformed. Explicit contracts eliminate many misunderstandings, but take time and trouble to create. Typically, implicit contracts are used in common situations, while explicit agreements are made in more unique circumstances. Some situations are governed by both explicit and implicit contracts. For example, in an auto repair shop the customer signs a very small explicit contract before the job is begun. It may list the work known to be necessary and give a preliminary estimate. However, as work progresses, further problems may be uncovered which will increase the overall cost, and of course the work must be done to prevailing (implicit) professional standards.

To illustrate, consider a very simple device that dispenses just one kind of soft drink: a coke machine. At one level, the interaction between customer and machine is quite simple: the customer puts a coin into the machine and takes a coke out. We can understand the implicit contract governing this situation in terms of the rights and obligations of both the customer and the machine. On one hand, the customer has an obligation to put a coin into the machine. This gives him the right to take a coke from it. On the other hand, the machine has an obligation to give the customer a coke, but has the right to wait until a coin has been received. These rights and obligations are conditional. The customer is only obligated to put a coin into the machine if they want a coke; if they are not thirsty then the contract does not apply. Similarly, the machine is not obligated to give a coke if a coin has not been received. The customer activates the contract with its duties and obligations when he puts a coin into the machine.

At present, most software systems are governed by implicit contracts; unfortunately, in many cases at least one of the parties involved doesn't understand the unstated assumptions. By extending the idea of explicit contracts into the world of software, we create a method of programming by contract.

One of the major goals of object-oriented programming languages, and of Eiffel in particular, is to provide significant support for software reuse. Ideally, this allows components to be applied in many different situations and systems, thereby lowering their overall cost. However, to fully realize the potential benefits it must be relatively easy to determine if a component is suitable for a proposed use. It must be possible to quickly understand what services the component performs and what conditions are necessary for its correct operation. Ideally, we should be able to understand the operation of the component in an abstract way, without all the unnecessary detail that might change over time. A software contract, then, should describe what is to be done, not how it is to be accomplished. It should state the conditions necessary for correct operation of a routine, as well as the results of the routine's execution.

To illustrate, suppose we are constructing a simulation of the coke machine discussed earlier. Assume it has a routine called *put_in_money* that the customer calls to put a coin into the machine. The procedure takes a *COIN* as a parameter and does not return a value.

---

put_in_money (coin: COIN) **is**
         −− put a coin in the machine
         −− machine must register coin entered

The routine header and comments constitute a contract between the routine and its caller. The caller must use a valid coin; this is ensured by the parameter's type. The machine must register that a coin has been entered; this is stated in the comments. The routine header and the comments define the visible properties of the routine, but give no details about how the code will actually run. They define the behavior of the routine in an abstract and informal way.

Assume that the coke machine has another routine, *take_out_coke,* which the user calls to obtain his coke once he has paid. The function takes no arguments and returns a *COKE* to the caller.

---

take_out_coke: COKE **is**
         −− take a coke from the machine
         −− caller must have already paid

The second comment line states that the caller must have already paid, and the function's return value ensures that an object of type *COKE* will be returned.

It seems as if this contract is sufficient. After all, our simulation of the coke machine is an extremely simple piece of software. However, as usual, there are hidden problems.

12.2   Assertions

One of the primary limitations of current software engineering methods is the use of natural language to describe requirements. At one level, natural language requirements are easy to understand. Everyone who reads them will probably feel they have some understanding of what should be done. On the other hand, natural language is by its very nature ambiguous. It is quite easy for different people to understand requirements in different ways. Consider the coke machine. Our informal contract for the *put_in_money* routine states that the "machine must register coin entered", and that for *take_out_coke* states that the "caller must have already paid". Now, what exactly does this mean? Do we only need to put in one coin to obtain a coke, or is more than one coin necessary before a coke can be obtained? What would cause the entry of a coin to become unregistered? Must a coin be entered for each coke, or can we put in one coin and take as many cokes as we want? Even in this simple case, we cannot resolve all our uncertainties easily. Our common sense tells us that we have to pay once for each coke we take (although we might wish it were otherwise), but without more information we cannot be absolutely sure that one coin is enough for a coke.

The problems of ambiguous contracts become much more significant for large systems. In the case of a large application in a complex domain, many different interpretations are possible for the simplest of sentences. In many areas of human commerce, specialized notations have been developed to eliminate the ambiguity in contracts. Blueprints, for example, are commonly used in the construction of buildings. The elements of these drawings are precisely defined so that all readers will gather the same meaning. We can carry this idea into the software domain by writing contracts using logical (or Boolean) expressions called assertions. Assertions give our contracts a precise meaning that must be acknowledged by all; they formally define the behavior of the software. Since Boolean expressions can be tested to see if they are true or false, assertions can be monitored at run-time to ensure that the contract is obeyed, thereby enhancing testing and debugging.

The idea of assertions sounds wonderful, because we can use them to precisely define and enforce contracts; however, we need to make things a bit more specific to accomplish anything useful. Exactly where do assertions appear? What information is necessary to describe the operation of a routine or a class? Let us begin with routines.

To the caller, the routine acts like a black box; it is called, does something internally, and then returns. The caller only sees this external behavior, and so the contract must be defined on this behavior. To the caller, there are two significant interactions with a routine. Before the routine is called, the caller must ensure that all the conditions necessary for its correct operation have been established. After the call has completed, the caller expects that the routine has correctly performed its function. We can formalize this with the notion of pre- and postconditions.

The precondition for a routine is an assertion that must be true whenever the routine is called. It states the conditions necessary for the routine's correct operation, thereby defining the caller's obligations and the routine's rights. The postcondition for a routine is an assertion that must be true whenever the routine's execution has completed. It defines the properties that will hold when the routine has performed its designated operation, thereby defining the routine's obligations and the caller's rights. In Eiffel, preconditions are designated by the keyword **require**, and postconditions are designated by the keyword **ensure**.

Let us reconsider the *put_in_money* routine for the coke machine. The caller puts in a coin, and has then paid; this gives them the right to a coke. A coke may not always be provided, however; what if the machine has run out of cokes? The formal contract for the procedure can thus be written in assertions as

```
    put_in_money (coin: COIN) is
            -- put a coin in the machine
            -- machine must register coin entered
```

```
          require
              not paid and
              not empty
          ensure
              paid and
              not empty
```

We have now defined the important aspects of the machine's condition (or state) in terms of two Boolean variables. *Paid* is true when a coin has been entered and therefore a coke may be obtained. *Empty* is true when there are no cokes left in the machine. The precondition states that both *paid* and *empty* must be false; in other words, the machine has cokes to offer, but a coin must be put in to obtain one. The postcondition states that *paid* must be true and *empty* false; in other words, the machine has cokes to offer, and a coin need not be entered to obtain one.

The contract for *take_out_coke* is similar. The precondition requires that the variables *paid* and *empty* must respectively be true and false when the routine is called, while the postcondition ensures that *paid* will be false when the routine returns.

```
      take_out_coke: COKE is
              -- take a coke from the machine
              -- caller must have already paid
          require
              paid and
              not empty
          ensure
              not paid
```

These pre- and postconditions define a contract that binds both the *put_in_money* and *take_out_coke* routines and their callers. The coke machine says in effect to its clients: if you promise to call *put_in_coin* only when *empty* and *paid* are both false, I, in return, promise to set *paid* to true and to leave *empty* unchanged. Furthermore, if you promise to call *take_out_coke* only when *paid* is true and *empty* is false, I, in return, promise to set *paid* to false. The precondition for a routine defines the caller's obligation and the routine's rights. For example, the precondition for *put_in_money* both constrains the caller and guarantees the routine that it will only be called when the machine is not empty and money needs to be put in. The postcondition for a routine defines the routine's obligations and the caller's rights. For example, the postcondition for *put_in_money* both constrains the routine and guarantees the caller that *paid* will be true when the routine returns.

It is important to realize that if its precondition is not satisfied, a routine is not bound by the other terms of the contract; in other words, it does not have to leave a state that satisfies the postcondition. This frees the routine from the task of checking for and responding to erroneous input and requires the caller to do so. It furthermore reduces the risk of the checks not being done, or being done multiple times. Performing multiple checks increases complexity as well as needlessly consuming run-time resources. Not performing checks is dangerous and leads to fragile implementations. Pre- and postconditions produce a clear delineation of responsibility that results in clean, well-structured systems.

12.3   An example class: *COKE_MACHINE*

We can now examine the code for the entire coke machine class. The condition of our *COKE_MACHINE* is described by three variables. We define a Boolean called *paid* which is true whenever a coin has been entered and a coke can be taken. We keep track of the coins in the machine using a *LIST* called money which holds *COINs*. We represent the cans left to be sold as a *LIST* of *COKEs*.

The class *LIST* implements a simple kind of list. The make procedure for *LIST* takes a single argument, which is the maximum number of elements. The *COKE_MACHINE* class has a feature *size* which is used to initialize the *LISTs* cokes and money. The *LIST* class has the operations *insert, delete, first,* and *empty*. *First* references the first item in the *LIST,* while *delete* removes it. *Insert* puts an item on the front of the *LIST,* while *empty* returns true only if there are no elements present. The complete code for the *COKE_MACHINE* is shown below, together with the assertions on each routine.

The *make* procedure for *COKE_MACHINE* initializes both *money* and *cokes*. Its precondition is **true** (which is always satisfied), while its postcondition ensures that the machine is empty when it is initialized. The function *empty* returns true whenever there are no more cokes in the machine. Its precondition is also **true**, while its postcondition ensures that the function result is set correctly.

The procedure *put_in_money* takes a coin as a parameter, adds the coin to *money,* and sets *paid* to true. The precondition presented in the previous section has been extended to eliminate the possibility of calling *put_in_money* with a void reference. The improved precondition requires that cokes are available for sale, that no coin has been entered since the last coke was removed, and that the input coin is valid. The postcondition for *put_in_money* ensures that the machine records that a coke has been paid for, and that the availability of cokes has not been changed.

The function *take_out_coke* returns the first coke in *cokes* to the customer, removes that coke from the list of those still to be sold, and sets *paid* to false. Its precondition requires that money has been paid for a coke not yet received, and that cokes are available to dispense. The postcondition presented in the previous section has been extended to eliminate the possibility of *take_out_coke* returning a void reference. The improved postcondition ensures that a coke is returned to the caller, and that the fact that a coke was taken is recorded.

```
class COKE_MACHINE
creation
    make
```

```
feature {NONE}
    money: LIST [COIN];
    cokes: LIST [COKE];
    size: INTEGER is 100
feature {ANY}
    paid: BOOLEAN
    make is
                -- initialize coke machine
        require
            true
        do
            !! money.make (size);
            !! cokes.make (size)
        ensure
            empty
        end -- make
    empty: BOOLEAN is
                -- is machine out of cokes?
        require
            true
        do
            Result := cokes.empty
        ensure
            Result = cokes.empty
        end -- empty
    put_in_money (coin: COIN) is
                -- put a coin in the machine
                -- machine must register coin entered
        require
            not paid and
            not empty and
            not coin.Void
        do
            money.insert (coin);
            paid := true
        ensure
            paid and
            not empty
        end -- put_in_money
    take_out_coke: COKE is
```

```
                -- take a coke from the machine
                -- caller must have already paid
        require
            paid and
            not empty
        do
            Result := cokes.first;
            cokes.delete;
            paid := false
        ensure
            not paid and
            not Result.Void
        end -- take_out_coke
    end -- class COKE_MACHINE
```

We have now seen a simple example of programming by contract. The pre- and postconditions of each routine define both the obligations and rights of both the routine and its caller. We might be tempted to believe that the problems of software development have been solved. However, there are still more problems remaining.

12.4   Exceptions

We have ignored a rather important point in our discussion of contracts: in practice, they are not always honored. In society at large, the police and courts provide the means of redress when obligations are not performed or rights not honored. This is necessary not only to put the fear of reprisal into the hearts of villains, but also to wake up well-meaning, but somewhat inattentive, citizens. Contracts are sometimes broken intentionally, but are many times simply neglected or forgotten. The policeman giving traffic tickets not only generates revenue for the district, but also reminds people how speed affects one's ability to drive safely.

The same situation prevails in the world of software. While a few unscrupulous vendors may intentionally sell low-quality components, the vast majority desire to produce quality products that conform to their customer's expectations. Unfortunately, this is quite difficult to do in practice. While writing contracts using pre- and postconditions makes the expectations of both parties explicit, it alone does not guarantee that these expectations will be met—especially initially. Run-time monitoring of assertions can be a powerful tool for improving software quality. Whenever the program reaches a point in its execution where an assertion applies, that assertion is evaluated like any other Boolean expression. If it evaluates to true, then everything is fine so execution can continue. If it evaluates to false, there is a problem: a contract has been violated and the problem needs to be corrected. This simple process can be a tremendous aid to software construction and testing.

In Eiffel, the implementation can be instructed to either check or not check assertions at run-time. If an assertion is violated—in other words, evaluates to false—an exception is raised. An exception interrupts the program's normal execution and transfers control to an exception handling routine. Violation of an assertion is not the only reason an exception can be raised. Hardware and operating system errors are also handled by the same general mechanism. The default response is for the system to terminate and print a message describing where the problem occurred. In general, this message includes a list of all the modules active at the time the problem occurred. It also describes the type of exception; in the case of an assertion violation, this would include whether a pre- or postcondition evaluated to false. Exception handling is discussed more fully in a later chapter.

To make our current discussion more concrete, let us return to the class *COKE_MACHINE* described in the previous section. Consider the following implementation of the routine *put_in_money*.

```
put_in_money (coin: COIN) is
        -- put a coin in the machine
        -- machine must register coin entered
    require
        not paid and
        not empty and
        not coin.Void
    do
        money.insert (coin)
    ensure
        paid and
        not empty
    end -- put_in_money
```

This is a machine that cheats its users! *Put_in_money* does not satisfy its contract because it does not set *paid* to true; therefore, the postcondition evaluates to false when the routine terminates. This causes an exception to be raised and the entire system to terminate. An error message is printed designating the postcondition of *put_in_money* as the failed assertion. A similar situation occurs if *put_in_money* is called when *empty* is true (in other words, when the machine is out of cokes). In this case the precondition evaluates to false when the routine is called, and again an exception is raised. The system terminates and prints a message stating that the precondition of *put_in_money* has been violated.

As another example, consider the routine *take_out_coke* from the *COKE_MACHINE* class.

```
take_out_coke: COKE is
        -- take a coke from the machine
        -- caller must have already paid
```

```
        require
            paid and
            not empty
        do
            cokes.delete;
            paid := false
        ensure
            not paid and
            not Result.Void
        end – – take_out_coke
```

This implementation is incorrect because it does not return a *COKE* to the caller, although it does remove one from the available list. When the routine terminates, the postcondition evaluates to false because *Result* is void. Therefore, an exception is raised, the program terminates, and the system prints a message stating that the postcondition of *take_out_coke* has been violated. An exception also occurs if *take_out_coke* is called when *paid* is not true or the machine is empty. In this case, when the call is attempted the precondition evaluates to false, an exception is generated, and the system terminates with a message stating that the precondition for *take_out_coke* was the location of the problem.

Summary

- Assertions are Boolean (logical) expressions used to describe the properties of software.
- Assertions can be used as a documentation aid, and as the basis for an exception mechanism.
- Routines are specified using pre- and postconditions. The precondition describes the properties that must hold when a routine is invoked. The postcondition states the properties that will be true when it returns.
- The pre- and postconditions for a routine specify a contract between the routine and its caller. The caller fulfills the contract by establishing the precondition before each call. The routine fulfills the contract by establishing the postcondition before it returns.
- An exception is triggered when an assertion is violated at run-time. The default response is for the system to print the location of the error and terminate.

Exercises

Consider a slightly more complex machine for dispensing soft drinks. *TWO_COIN_MACHINE* is identical to the *COKE_MACHINE* described previously, except that the customer must put two coins in before they can receive their coke. The feature *paid* from *COKE_MACHINE* has been replaced with two

Boolean variables: *one_paid* and *two_paid*. *Two_paid* is true only if two coins have been paid and a coke has not been taken, while *one_paid* is true if either one or two coins have been entered.

```
class TWO_COIN_MACHINE
creation
    make
feature {ANY}
    one_paid: BOOLEAN;
    two_paid: BOOLEAN;
    . . .
    empty: BOOLEAN is
            -- is machine out of cokes?
    put_in_money (coin: COIN) is
            -- put a coin in the machine
            -- machine must register coin entered
        . . .
    take_out_coke: COKE is
            -- take a coke from the machine
            -- two coins must have been paid
        . . .
end -- class TWO_COIN_MACHINE
```

1. Write a procedure body for the *put_in_money* routine.
2. Write pre- and postconditions for the *put_in_money* routine.
   (*Hint:* You may not be able to specify everything you would like.)
3. Write a procedure body for the *take_out_coke* routine.
4. Write pre- and postconditions for the *take_out_coke* routine.

CHAPTER 13

Assertions on routines

Keywords

Pre- and postconditions
require
ensure
old
strip

Pre- and postconditions are designated by the keywords **require** and **ensure** respectively. The precondition states the conditions necessary for successful invocation of the routine; therefore, it may reference only features available to all potential callers. The postcondition describes both the routine's effects as seen by the user and the implementor's assumptions; therefore, it may reference features not exported from the enclosing class. The old and strip operators allow postconditions to be written more compactly. The phrase "**old** *expression*" references the value of *expression* upon invocation of the routine, while the phrase "**strip** *item*" refers to an array consisting of all the features of the enclosing class excluding *item*.

13.1   Syntax of pre- and postconditions

In Eiffel, pre- and postconditions are used to write contracts for the behavior of routines. The precondition states the properties that must be true when the routine is called, while the postcondition states what must be true when the routine returns. The precondition defines the caller's obligations and the routine's rights, while the postcondition states what the routine must accomplish and what the caller may expect.

In Eiffel, the precondition is designated with the keyword **require**. It follows the header for the associated routine and precedes the declarations of local variables. The postcondition is indicated by the keyword **ensure**. It follows the body of the routine and precedes the final **end**.

```
routine_name (parameters: TYPES) is
    require
        precondition
    local
        local_variables
    do
        routine_body
    ensure
        postcondition
    end
```

As an illustration, let us consider the class *LIST* used in the previous chapter by *COKE_MACHINE*. It exports five routines: *empty, full, first, insert,* and *delete.* The Boolean functions *empty* and *full* return true if the list contains no elements, or has no more free space respectively. The function *first* returns the element at the front of the list, while the procedures *insert* and *delete* put a new element at the front of the list and remove the first element respectively.

We can implement *LIST* using the *ARRAY* class from the Eiffel library. Each *LIST* consists of an array called *elements*, an index into the array called *count*, and an integer called *max_count* which provides an upper bound on the number of items. In our implementation, elements are both inserted and deleted from the front of the list; therefore, *count* is the next available location in *elements*, and the first element in the list is in location *count* minus one. In other words, when an element is inserted into a list, it becomes the *count*-th item in *elements*, and the *count* minus first item in *elements* is the first element in the list.

```
class LIST [T]
creation
    make
feature {NONE}
    elements: ARRAY [T];
    count: INTEGER;
    max_count: INTEGER
feature {ANY}
    make (size: INTEGER) is
    empty: BOOLEAN is
            -- is list empty?
        . . .
    full: BOOLEAN is
            -- is list full?
        . . .
    insert (elem: T) is
```

```
            – – put an element into the list
      . . .
first: T is
            – – return first element in list
      . . .
delete is
            – – remove first element from list
      . . .
end – – class LIST
```

The *make* procedure for *LIST* initializes *elements* with a lower bound of zero and an upper bound of *size* minus one; therefore, *count* can range from zero to *size*, and an empty list will have a *count* of zero. The postcondition for *make* requires that the list is empty at the end of the initialization. The precondition for the routine requires that *size* be greater than zero; in other words, it is not possible to create a list that will always be empty.

```
make (size: INTEGER) is
    require
        size > 0
    do
        !! elements.make (0, size – 1);
        max_count := size
    ensure
        empty
    end – – make
```

The function *empty* returns true when there are no elements in the list. It can be called when the list is in any state whatsoever; therefore, its precondition is true. The body of *empty* simply sets the return value to the equivalence of *count* and zero, and its postcondition states that *Result* has been set correctly.

```
empty: BOOLEAN is
            – – is list empty?
    require
        true
    do
        Result := (count = 0)
    ensure
        Result = (count = 0)
    end – – empty
```

While the precondition for *empty* is a valid use of assertions, it is somewhat redundant. Since true can never evaluate to false, it is unnecessary to explicitly state it. In other words, since the precondition is always satisfied, there is no reason to record it or check it at run-time. Therefore, we can write *empty* with no precondition; this is equivalent to writing a precondition of true.

```
empty: BOOLEAN is
        -- is list empty?
    do
        Result := (count = 0)
    ensure
        Result = (count = 0)
    end -- empty
```

Notice that the body of empty is a single assignment statement (denoted by ":="), while the postcondition is a Boolean expression (denoted by "="). The body of the routine sets *Result* to a value: true if *count* is 0 or false if *count* is not equal to zero. The postcondition states that *Result* satisfies a certain condition: if *count* is zero then *Result* must be true; if *count* is not zero then *Result* must be false.

The function *full* is similar to *empty*. It returns true only when there isn't room for more elements in the list. The body of the routine simply sets *Result* to the equality of *count* and *max_count*. It has no precondition, but its postcondition ensures that *Result* has been correctly set.

```
full: BOOLEAN is
        -- is list full?
    do
        Result := (count = max_count)
    ensure
        Result = (count = max_count)
    end -- full
```

For simple functions such as *empty* and *full*, the postconditions are quite redundant with the implementations: it is unlikely that they will detect any errors. However, they do provide the users of the routine with a precise, compact description of its operation. This description can remain constant, even as the implementation changes. For more complex implementations, the pre- and postconditions can provide a useful simplification, allowing the users to call a routine without understanding the details of its construction.

We can also describe the operation of the other routines using pre- and postconditions. For example, consider the procedure *insert*, which puts a new element into the list. The precondition for the routine requires that the list is not full; in other words, that there is room to insert the new element. The postcondition states that the list is not empty after the insertion is complete. Since *count* is the next available location in the list, the body of the procedure simply puts the item to be inserted at location *count* in *elements* and then increments *count* by one.

```
insert (elem: T) is
         -- put an element into the list
    require
        not full
    do
        elements.put (elem, count);
        count := count + 1
    ensure
        not empty
    end -- insert
```

Now let us consider the function *first*, which returns the element at the front of the list. Since in our implementation insertions and deletions both occur at the beginning of the list, and *count* is the next available location, the first element in the list is at location *count* minus one in *elements*. The body of *first* simply sets the return value to the correct item. The precondition for the function requires that the list is not empty when it is invoked, while the postcondition ensures that *Result* has been set to the correct object.

```
first: T is
         -- return first element in list
    require
        not empty
    do
        Result := elements.item (count − 1)
    ensure
        Result = elements.item (count − 1)
    end -- first
```

The *delete* procedure removes the first element from the list. Since the first element is in location *count* minus one in *elements*, the routine simply decrements *count*, thereby making that location inaccessible. In other words, since *first* returns the element in location *count* minus one, and *insert* puts a new element in location *count*, by decrementing *count* we ensure that the element in location *count* minus one will never be referenced again. The precondition for *delete* requires that the list not be empty when the routine is called, and the postcondition states that the list cannot be full when *delete* completes its execution.

```
delete is
         -- remove first element from list
    require
```

```
               not empty
         do
               count := count - 1
         ensure
               not full
         end -- delete
```

As we have seen, the basics of pre- and postconditions are quite straightforward; however, we must use some judgment to ensure that the maximum benefit can be derived from their use.

13.2 Writing contracts using pre- and postconditions

Pre- and postconditions are tools for writing software contracts; as such, we must be sure that the parties involved can evaluate the terms and conditions that apply to them. What purpose would be served by writing a contract that could not be read by one of the concerned persons? Even with the best of intentions it would be difficult to consistently meet the requirements. There is not much point requiring that certain conditions be met by a party if that party cannot evaluate whether the desired properties have been achieved. For example, it would be pointless to write a contract requiring delivery of material with 99.9999 percent purity if the most accurate test available could only measure the purity to an accuracy of 0.1 percent. In such a situation, there would be no way for the supplier to tell if he had met his end of the bargain; he could have the best of intentions but still fall short of his obligations.

The same situation can occur with assertions. What use is there writing a precondition that can't be checked by a caller of the routine? Before calling a routine, the caller should be able to check that the precondition is true. Run-time monitoring of assertions is a tool for catching unintentional violations of software contracts. It is not a tool for filtering the input to procedures. Ideally, assertions are never violated in correct programs (unfortunately, there is always some possibility of a hardware error). However, if a caller cannot evaluate the precondition beforehand, they may have no choice but to attempt the call and see what happens. Therefore, preconditions may only reference features that are available to all potential callers of the routine. This ensures that they can check the necessary conditions and thereby live up to their end of the contract.

To illustrate, let us return to the class *LIST*. The precondition for *insert* is that the list is not full.

```
     insert (elem: T) is
               -- put an element into the list
          require
               not full
          . . .
```

We could write this as *"count < max_count"*; however, this would not be a good idea. *LIST* does not make either *count* or *max_count* visible to its clients; therefore, they would not be able to directly evaluate the precondition before making the call. Since *full* is exported from *LIST*, the expression "**not** *full*" can be evaluated by the caller before *insert* is invoked. The caller should be able to evaluate the precondition for a routine exactly as it is written.

The situation is similar for *delete*. The precondition requires that the list not be empty.

---

delete **is**

    −− remove first element from list

  require

    not *empty*

  . . .

This could have been written as *"count = 0"*, but since *count* is not exported the expression could not be evaluated by potential callers. By using the externally visible feature *empty*, the caller can check the precondition exactly as it is written before making the call.

As another example, consider the *put_in_money* procedure from the class *COKE_MACHINE*. The precondition requires that both *paid* and *empty* be false when the routine is called.

---

class *COKE_MACHINE*

  . . .

feature {NONE}

  money: LIST [COIN];

  cokes: LIST [COKE];

  size: INTEGER **is** 100

feature {ANY}

  paid: BOOLEAN

  . . .

  empty: BOOLEAN **is**

    −− is machine out of cokes?

    . . .

  put_in_money (coin: COIN) **is**

    −− put a coin in the machine

    −− machine must register coin entered

    require

      not *paid* **and**

      not *empty* **and**

      not *coin.Void*

  . . .

Since the machine is empty exactly when *cokes* is empty, the precondition could have been written "*cokes.empty*"; however, since *cokes* is not an exported feature of the class, callers would not be able to evaluate the precondition as written before calling the routine. By using the exported feature *empty* to write the precondition, the ability of clients to check the precondition before attempting a call is guaranteed.

Pre- and postconditions serve different purposes in the contract between routine and caller; therefore, the rules governing what features may appear in them are also different. Preconditions serve only to record the caller's obligations to the routine. Postconditions have two different functions. First, they enumerate the routine's obligations to its callers, thereby completing the software contract. Second, they provide a check on the implementor's assumptions; in other words, they record changes to the object that are not visible to the caller. Being able to check these assumptions by monitoring assertions at run-time can significantly enhance debugging.

When postconditions are used to describe the routine's obligations to its clients, they should only reference features that are visible to the caller; however, when they are used to describe the implementor's assumptions, they may contain references to non-exported features. If a postcondition is being used to document the effects that will be visible to the caller of a routine, it can only reference exported features, because changes to non-exported features are not seen by the caller. On the other hand, if the implementor is using a postcondition to describe effects internal to an object, then non-exported features can be referenced. When assertions are used to communicate with callers, they must be written in a language callers can understand; however, this restriction does not apply if they are used to record the implementor's assumptions. Ideally, the users of class can understand it completely by reading its short form, which includes only those clauses of the pre- and postconditions which reference only exported features. Only the implementors would see the complete class, including those assertions which reference non-exported features.

As an example, consider the *insert* routine on class *LIST*. As previously stated, the postcondition for the procedure simply ensures that the list is not empty after the insertion is complete. From the client's view, this is probably sufficient; however, as an aid to the implementor, we might wish to check that *count* has not somehow been set to an erroneous value. The postcondition for *insert* now serves two purposes. The expression "**not** *empty*" describes the routine's obligation to its caller: the list must not be empty when *insert* terminates. The restrictions on the value of *count* serve as checks on the implementor's assumptions. Since *count* is not exported to the caller, they are not part of the contract with the caller. These restrictions imply that if *count* is somehow set to a value less than zero or greater than *max_count*, something has gone wrong. Run-time assertion monitoring will catch this and allow the problem to be corrected as quickly as possible.

> *insert (elem: T)* **is**
>   – – put an element into the list
>   **require**
>   **not** *full*

```
        do
              elements.put (elem, count);
              count := count + 1
        ensure
              not empty and
              0 <_ count and count <= max_count
        end -- insert
```

The *delete* routine is similar. As previously presented, the postcondition for the procedure simply ensures that the list is not full after the insertion is complete. As an aid to the implementor, we will also check that *count* has not somehow been set to an erroneous value. The postcondition now serves two purposes. The expression "**not** *full*" describes the routine's obligation to its caller, while the restrictions on the value of *count* serve as checks on the implementor's assumptions.

```
     delete is
              -- remove first element from list
        require
              not empty
        do
              count := count - 1
        ensure
              not full and
              0 <= count and count <= max_count
        end -- delete
```

13.3   Labeled assertion clauses

With the mechanisms presented so far, we can write software contracts using pre- and postconditions. If the system has been instructed to perform the appropriate level of checking, violations of these contracts at run-time will cause an exception to be raised. This will result in the system terminating with a message describing the location of the violation. While this information is beneficial, debugging can still prove difficult because assertions may check for more than one condition at a time.

For example, suppose an exception occurs during execution of the *insert* routine from the *LIST* class. When the program terminates, we are told that the postcondition of *insert* has been violated. How much do we really know? Well, since the postcondition is "**not** *empty* **and** $0 <= count$ **and** $count <= max\_count$", we know that either *empty* was true, *count* was less than zero, or *count* was greater than *max_count*. Ideally, we would like to know which of these three is the case.

We can achieve this by dividing the postcondition into three parts which are monitored independently at run-time.

Assertions, therefore, can be more than Boolean expressions. They can be sequences of clauses separated by semi-colons. Each clause can be preceded by an optional label (followed by a colon) which is used in the description of run-time violations. So, an assertion with one clause looks like this:

---

label: boolean_expression

---

and an assertion with two clauses would look like this:

---

label_1: expression_1; label_2: expression_2

By convention, we will write clause labels in all lower case letters. An assertion evaluates to true if and only if all the clauses in it evaluate to true; in other words, the semi-colon can be read as a logical "and". The clauses in an assertion are evaluated from left to right (top to bottom) until a clause evaluates to false and an exception is raised or the end of the assertion is reached.

Let us return to the *insert* routine. By dividing the postcondition into three parts and adding labels, we obtain the following:

---

insert (elem: T) **is**
       − − put an element into the list
   require
     not_full: **not** *full*
   do
     . . .
   ensure
     not_empty: **not** *empty*;
     count_greq_0: $0 <= count$;
     count_lseq_max: $count <= max\_count$
   end − − *insert*

The precondition consists of a single clause labeled *not_full*, while the postcondition contains three clauses labeled *not_empty*, *count_greq_0*, and *count_lseq_max*.

If assertions are being monitored at run-time, then when *insert* is called the clause *not_full* is evaluated. If it is true, then execution proceeds normally. If it is false, then an exception is raised, and the system terminates and prints a message stating that the clause *not_full* in the precondition for *insert* has been violated. When execution of the routine is complete, the clauses in the postcondition are evaluated in order. If the first clause is false, then an exception is raised and the system terminates, reporting that the condition *not_empty* in the postcondition for *insert* was not satisfied. If *not_empty* is true, then the second clause is evaluated. If this clause is false, then the system terminates, reporting that *count_greq_0* in the postcondition for *insert* has been violated. If *count_greq_0* is true, then the third clause is evaluated. If it is true, then *insert* terminates normally. If it is false, then an exception is raised and the system terminates, reporting that the clause *count_lseq_max* in the postcondition for *insert* was not satisfied.

As another example, recall the *put_in_money* procedure from the class *COKE_MACHINE*. The precondition for this routine has three parts: money must not have already been paid, the machine cannot be empty, and the input must be a valid coin. Likewise, the postcondition has two parts: the fact that money has been paid must be recorded, and the machine still must not be *empty*. We can divide the assertions into clauses and add labels to obtain the following:

---

     put_in_money (coin: COIN) **is**
           – – put a coin in the machine
           – – machine must register coin entered
     require
        not_paid: **not** *paid*;
        not_empty: **not** *empty*;
        coin_in: **not** *coin.Void*
     do
        . . .
     ensure
        paid: *paid*;
        not_empty: **not** *empty*
     end – – *put_in_money*

If assertions are being monitored at run-time, then when *put_in_money* is called the clauses in the precondition are evaluated from left to right (or top to bottom). If a clause evaluates to false, then an exception is raised and the system will terminate with a message stating that the specific clause in the precondition has been violated. If a clause evaluates to true, then evaluation continues. If all of the clauses are true, then so is the precondition. When execution of *put_in_money* is complete, the clauses in the postcondition are evaluated in order. If *paid* is false, then execution will terminate. If *paid* is true, then *not_empty* will be evaluated. If the result is true, then *put_in_money* will evaluate normally. If the result is false, then an exception will be raised, and the system will report that the clause *not_empty* in the postcondition for *put_in_money* was not satisfied.

13.4   Old expressions

While the facilities we have described so far can be used to write many useful contracts, unfortunately they are inadequate to the task of describing some very simple ones. For example, how do we describe a procedure which simply adds the value of its argument to a feature exported from its class?

```
    class EXAMPLE
    feature {ANY}
        x: INTEGER
        add_to_x (inc: INTEGER) is
            do
                    x := x + inc
            end -- add_to_x
    end -- class EXAMPLE
```

This is certainly a simple program, but at present we cannot use assertions to write a precise description of it. The problem is that we have no way of talking about the initial and final values of *x*. We would like the postcondition to say something like "the new value of *x* is equal to the old value plus *inc*", but we have no notation to do so.

We can solve this problem by providing a way to reference the value of an expression upon routine entry in the postcondition. This allows us to talk about both the "old" and "new" values in an assertion. Specifically, the **old** operator can appear only in postconditions. The phrase "**old** expression" references the value of expression when the routine began execution. This allows us to specify the *add_to_x* procedure as follows:

```
        add_to_x (inc: INTEGER) is
            do
                    x := x + inc
            ensure
                    x_increased: x = old x + inc
            end -- add_to_x
```

The expression "**old** *x*" refers to the value of *x* when execution of *add_to_x* began. The postcondition states that when the routine terminates, the value of *x* should equal the value when execution began plus *inc* (which cannot be changed by the procedure).

As another example, let us return to the *put_in_money* routine from *COKE_MACHINE*. The procedure takes a coin as a parameter and puts it into the machine's list of money. Therefore, the postcondition can state that the number of coins in *money* is one more than when the procedure began. The expression "**old** *money.count*" in the postcondition refers to the value of the *count* feature of *money* when *put_in_money* began execution; in other words, the number of coins in *money* when the routine started. Therefore, the clause labeled *more_money* in the postcondition states that the procedure has increased the number of coins in *money* by one. (Note that we are now assuming *count* is an exported feature of *LIST*.)

```
    put_in_money (coin: COIN) is
            -- put a coin in the machine
            . . .
        money.insert (coin);
            . . .
    ensure
            . . .
        more_money: money.count = old money.count + 1
    end -- put_in_money
```

The routine *take_out_coke* is similar. It removes a coke from the machine's list and returns it to the caller. The postcondition states that the number of cokes (in other words, *cokes.count*) is one less upon exit from the routine than it was on entry.

```
    take_out_coke: COKE is
            -- take a coke from the machine
            . . .
        cokes.delete
            . . .
    ensure
            . . .
        fewer_cokes: cokes.count = old cokes.count - 1
    end -- take_out_coke
```

As a final example, consider the *insert* routine from the class *LIST*. This procedure puts an element into the list and increments *count* to reflect this fact. The postcondition contains a clause *count_increased* which ensures that *count* has a value one greater when *insert* terminates than when it began.

```
    insert (elem: T) is
            -- put an element into the list
            . . .
        count := count + 1
    ensure
            . . .
        count_increased: count = old count + 1
    end -- insert
```

The old operator gives us the power to compare the initial and final states for a routine. In theory, this is all we need; however, in practice it still may be quite difficult to specify some things.

13.5   Strip expressions

The old operator can be used to describe what things have not been changed by a procedure. Unfortunately, this is quite tedious if the class has many features which are not modified. For example, consider the procedure *put_in_money* from *COKE_MACHINE*. This routine modifies the features *paid* and *money*, but leaves *cokes* and *size* unchanged. We could write an assertion for this as follows:

> *put_in_money (coin: COIN)* **is**
>   −− put a coin in the machine
>   . . .
>   **ensure**
>   . . .
>   *same_size*: *size* = **old** *size*;
>   *same_cokes*: *cokes* = **old** *cokes*
>   **end** −− *put_in_money*

While this will certainly work, it is a bit clumsy and will get more and more so as the number of features in the class increases. We can do much better by providing a notation for "everything but".

Specifically, in Eiffel the **strip** operator can be used to produce an array whose elements are all the features of the current object except those passed as arguments. For example, the expression "**strip** (*x, y*)" evaluates to an array whose elements are all the features of the current object except *x* and *y*. We can use the strip operator in a postcondition to designate the features that have not been changed. For example, the expression "equal (**strip** (*x, y*), **old strip** (*x, y*))" in a postcondition would indicate that the associated procedure only modifies the features *x* and *y*.

Returning to the *put_in_money* routine, we can now modify the postcondition to contain a clause ensuring that *money* and *paid* are the only features modified by the procedure.

> *put_in_money (coin: COIN)* **is**
>   −− put a coin in the machine
>   −− machine must register coin entered
>   **require**
>   *not_paid*: **not** *paid*;
>   *not_empty*: **not** *empty*;
>   *coin_in*: **not** *coin.Void*
>   **do**
>   *money.insert (coin)*;
>   *paid* := true
>   **ensure**
>   *paid*: *paid*;

```
        not_empty: not empty;
        more_money: money.count = old money.count + 1;
        no_extra_changes: equal (strip (money, paid),
                            old strip (money, paid))
    end -- put_in_money
```

The expression "**strip** (*money, paid*)" in the postcondition evaluates to an array whose elements are all the features in the class besides *money* and *paid*; in other words, an array with two elements: *cokes* and *size*. The *no_extra_changes* clause states that the value of this array is the same on exit from the routine as it was on entry. Therefore, the only features modified by the routine are *money* and *paid*.

As another example, let us recall the *take_out_coke* routine from the same class. This routine removes a coke from the machine and returns it to the caller. It modifies the features *cokes* and *paid*, but leaves *size* and *money* unchanged. We can now modify the postcondition for this procedure to include a clause ensuring that only the appropriate variables are changed by its execution.

```
    take_out_coke: COKE is
            -- take a coke from the machine
            -- caller must have already paid
        require
            paid: paid;
            not_empty: not empty
        do
            Result := cokes.first;
            cokes.delete;
            paid := false
        ensure
            not_paid: not paid;
            coke_out: not Result.Void;
            fewer_cokes: cokes.count = old cokes.count - 1;
            no_extra_changes: equal (strip (cokes, paid),
                                old strip (cokes, paid))
        end -- take_out_coke
```

The expression "**strip** (*cokes, paid*)" evaluates to an array whose elements are the values of all the features in the class except for *cokes* and *paid*; in other words, an array containing the values of *money* and *size*. The *no_extra_changes* clause states that the value of this array is the same on exit from the routine as it was on entry. Therefore, the procedure only modifies the features *cokes* and *paid*.

With the strip operator our notation for pre- and postconditions is complete. With it, we can write software contracts as well as document the implementor's

assumptions. With our full kit of tools in hand, let us return to the classes
COKE_MACHINE and *LIST* described previously.

13.6   An example class: *LIST*

We can now examine the code and assertions for the entire *LIST* class. *LIST*
exports the routines *empty, full, first, insert,* and *delete. Empty* and *full* return true
if the list contains no elements or has no more free space respectively. *First* returns
a pointer to the element at the front of the list, *delete* removes that element, and
insert puts a new element in the first position. Each list consists of an array called
elements, an index into the array called *count*, and an integer called *max_count*
which provides an upper bound on the number of items. Elements are both inserted
and deleted from the front of the list; therefore, *count* is the next available location
in *elements* and the first element in the list is at location *count* minus one.

The *make* procedure for *LIST* initializes *elements* with a lower bound of zero
and an upper bound of *size* minus one. Its precondition requires that *size* be greater
than zero, and its postcondition ensures that *elements* has been initialized, that
the list is empty, and that *max_count* has been set to *size*. The functions *empty*
and *full* do not have preconditions; in other words, they both have preconditions
of "**true**". Their postconditions ensure that the function's *Result* has been set
correctly, and that execution of the function has not changed the state of the list.
Specifically, the clause *no_changes* demands that an array consisting of the values
of all the features of the class ("**strip**") is equal to an array consisting of the
values of all the features of the class at the time routine execution began ("**old
strip**"). In other words, *no_changes* ensures that the values of *elements, count,*
and *max_count* are not changed by the function.

First returns the element at the front of the list; in our implementation this
is the item at location *count* minus one. The precondition for the routine requires
that the list not be empty when the routine is invoked. The postcondition ensures
that the *Result* is set correctly and that execution of the function does not change
the list in any way.

The *insert* procedure puts a new element at the beginning of the list. The body
of the routine simply puts the new item at location *count* in *elements*, then increases
count by one. The precondition requires that the list not be full when an insertion
is attempted, and the postcondition ensures that the list is not empty when the
procedure completes, that the number of elements in the list is one more when the
routine terminates than when it began, and that no extra changes were made to the
list. Specifically, the clause *no_extra_changes* demands that the array consisting of
the values of all the features of *LIST* except *elements* and *count* is equal to the array
consisting of the values of these same features when the routine began execution.

The *delete* procedure removes the first element from the list. Since the first
element is in location *count* minus one in *elements*, the routine simply decrements
count, thereby making that location inaccessible. The precondition for *delete*
requires that the list not be empty when the routine is called, and the postcondition
states that the list cannot be full when *delete* completes its execution, that the
number of items in the list is one less than it was when the routine began, and

that no extra changes were made to the list. Specifically, the clause *no_extra_changes* demands that *delete* only modifies *count*, leaving *elements* and *max_count* unchanged.

```
class LIST [T]
creation
    make
feature {NONE}
    elements: ARRAY [T];
    max_count: INTEGER
feature {ANY}
    count: INTEGER;
    make (size: INTEGER) is
        require
            size_big_enough: size > 0
        do
            !! elements.make (0, size − 1);
            max_count := size
        ensure
            elements_created: not elements.Void;
            empty: empty;
            max_count_eq_size: max_count = size
        end −− make
    empty: BOOLEAN is
            −− is list empty?
        do
            Result := (count = 0)
        ensure
            result_ok: Result = (count = 0);
            no_changes: equal (strip, old strip)
        end −− empty
    full: BOOLEAN is
            −− is list full?
        do
            Result := (count = max_count)
        ensure
            result_ok: Result = (count = max_count);
            no_changes: equal (strip, old strip)
        end −− full
    first: T is
            −− return first element in list
```

```
            require
                not_empty: not empty
            do
                Result := elements.item (count − 1)
            ensure
                return_first_item: Result = elements.item (count − 1);
                no_changes: equal (strip, old strip)
            end −− first
    insert (elem: T) is
                −− put an element into the list
            require
                not_full: not full;
            do
                elements.put (elem, count);
                count := count + 1
            ensure
                not_empty: not empty;
                count_increased: count = old count + 1;
                no_extra_changes:
                        equal (strip (elements, count),
                        old strip (elements, count))
            end −− insert
    delete is
                −− remove first element from list
            require
                not_empty: not empty
            do
                count := count − 1
            ensure
                not_full: not full;
                count_decreased: count = old count − 1;
                no_extra_changes:
                        equal (strip (count), old strip (count))
            end −− delete
    end −− class LIST
```

13.7   Class *COKE_MACHINE* revisited

With our expanded notion of assertion, we can produce much better pre- and
postconditions for the *COKE_MACHINE* class. As before, the condition of our

machine is described by three variables. The Boolean variable *paid* is true whenever a coin has been entered and a coke can be taken. We keep track of the coins in the machine using a list called *money* that holds *COINs*. The cans available for sale are represented as a list of *COKEs*.

The *make* procedure is as before, but the assertions describing its operation have been improved significantly. The single clause previously in the postcondition is now labeled *empty*, and two new clauses have been added. The clause *money_created* ensures that *money* has been initialized; specifically, it requires that *money* not be void. The *cokes_created* clause is similar, but references *cokes* instead of *money*. If any of these clauses are false when the procedure exits, an exception will be raised and the system will print a message saying that the appropriate clause in the postcondition for *make* has been violated.

The assertions for the *empty* function have also been changed significantly. The single clause previously in the postcondition has been labeled *result_ok*, and a new clause named *no_changes* has been added. This new clause makes explicit the fact that execution of *empty* does not change the state of the machine. Specifically, it states that an array consisting of the values of all the features of the class ("**strip**") is equal to an array consisting of the values of all the features of the class at the time routine execution began ("**old strip**").

The changes to *put_in_money* and *take_out_coke* are also significant; both routines have new clauses in their postconditions. For example, the postcondition for *put_in_money* now contains a clause labeled *more_money*, which states that the number of coins in *money* is increased by one during execution of the procedure. It also contains a clause labeled *no_extra_changes*, which states that *money* and *paid* are the only features modified by the routine. Specifically, *no_extra_changes* states that the array consisting of the values of all the features of *COKE_MACHINE* except *money* and *paid* is equal to the array consisting of the values of these same features when the routine began execution. The postcondition for *take_out_coke* contains a new clause labeled *fewer_cokes*, which states that the number of cokes is decreased by one during execution of the routine, and a new clause labeled *no_extra_changes*, which states that *cokes* and *paid* are the only features modified by execution of the function.

```
class COKE_MACHINE
creation
    make
feature {NONE}
    money: LIST [COIN];
    cokes: LIST [COKE];
    size: INTEGER is 100
feature {ANY}
    paid: BOOLEAN
    make is
            -- initialize coke machine
        do
```

```
            !! money.make (size);
            !! cokes.make (size)
        ensure
            empty: empty;
            money_created: not money.Void;
            cokes_created: not cokes.Void
        end -- make
empty: BOOLEAN is
            -- is machine out of cokes?
        do
            Result := cokes.empty
        ensure
            result_ok: Result = cokes.empty;
            no_changes: equal (strip, old strip)
        end -- empty
put_in_money (coin: COIN) is
            -- put a coin in the machine
            -- machine must register coin entered
        require
            not_paid: not paid;
            not_empty: not empty;
            coin_in: not coin.Void
        do
            money.insert (coin);
            paid := true
        ensure
            paid: paid
            not_empty: not empty;
            more_money: money.count = old money.count + 1;
            no_extra_changes: equal (strip (money, paid),
                                old strip (money, paid))
        end -- put_in_money
take_out_coke: COKE is
            -- take a coke from the machine
            -- caller must have already paid
        require
            paid: paid;
            not_empty: not empty
        do
            Result := cokes.first;
```

```
            cokes.delete;
            paid := false
        ensure
            not_paid: not paid;
            coke_out: not Result.Void;
            fewer_cokes: cokes.count = old cokes.count − 1;
            no_extra_changes: equal (strip (cokes, paid),
                                old strip (cokes, paid))
        end − − take_out_coke
end − − class COKE_MACHINE
```

With our complete notation for pre- and postconditions, we can write software contracts as well as document the implementor's assumptions. With the interface between the routine and its caller fairly well controlled, we may now turn our attention to describing the structures within routines in more detail.

Summary

- Pre- and postconditions are designated by the keywords **require** and **ensure** respectively.
- All the features necessary for the callers to evaluate the precondition must be available to them, but the postcondition may reference features not available to the clients.
- Assertions consist of (possibly) labeled clauses separated by semi-colons. The label precedes the corresponding assertion, and the two are separated by a colon.
- The **old** operator only appears in postconditions; "**old** *expression*" refers to the value of expression upon entry to the routine.
- The strip operator may be used to refer to all but certain features of an object. For example, "**strip** *(a, b)*" refers to all the fields of the current object except *a* and *b*.

Exercises

Consider the *TWO_COIN_MACHINE* developed in the exercises for the previous chapter.

1. Rewrite the pre- and postconditions for *put_in_money* with a separate, labeled clause for each logical expression.
2. Rewrite the pre- and postconditions for *take_out_coke* with a separate, labeled clause for each logical expression.
3. Add a clause containing an old operator to the postcondition for *put_in_money* describing how the number of coins in the machine is changed by execution of the routine.

4. Add a clause containing an old operator to the postcondition for *take_out_coke* describing how the number of cokes in the machine is changed by execution of the routine.

5. Add a clause to the postcondition for *put_in_money* describing how the final value of *two_paid* is related to the initial value of *one_paid*.

6. Add a clause containing a strip operator to the postcondition for *put_in_money* describing the features modified by the routine.

7. Add a clause containing a strip operator to the postcondition for *take_out_coke* describing the features modified by the routine.

CHAPTER 14

Assertions inside routines

Keywords

check instruction
loop invariant
loop variant
check
invariant
variant

Check instructions make the programmer's assumptions explicit. They can appear anywhere inside a routine, signifying that the enclosed assertion should evaluate to true. The correct operation of a loop is described by two special types of assertions. The invariant is a Boolean expression that must be true both before and after each iteration of the loop body, while the variant is a non-negative integer function that must be decreased by each execution. The invariant describes the properties common to each execution, while the variant is concerned with the differences between executions. Check instructions, loop variants, and invariants are designated by the keywords **check**, **variant**, and **invariant** respectively.

14.1   The check instruction

Pre- and postconditions describe the interactions between routines and their callers. This can allow the contracts between these parties to be made explicit, thereby enhancing program understanding, testing, and debugging. By monitoring pre- and postconditions at run-time, we can detect any problems that appear on routine entry or exit. While this is quite significant, we can gather even more information by allowing assertions to appear at arbitrary points inside routines. An assertion inside a routine documents the programmer's assumptions about the state of the object at the point where the assertion appears. By monitoring these assertions at run-time, we can potentially detect problems occurring at any point during a routine's execution, thereby gathering much more information than by checking pre- and postconditions alone.

Specifically, in Eiffel the check instruction signifies that an assertion should be true whenever the instruction is executed. A check instruction can appear anywhere inside a routine. It begins with the keyword **check** and is terminated with an **end**.

---

check

    assertion

end

Execution of a check instruction does not always cause the assertion it contains to be evaluated. As with pre- and postconditions, the system must be informed that run-time monitoring is to be enabled. If assertions (specifically check instructions) are not being monitored at run-time, then executing a check instruction will have no more effect than executing a comment. On the other hand, if run-time monitoring is enabled, then executing a check instruction will cause the assertion it contains to be evaluated. If the result is true, then execution proceeds normally; however, if the assertion is false, then an exception will be raised and the system will terminate with a message stating that a check assertion has been violated.

As an illustration, consider the *make* routine from the *COKE_MACHINE* class. The body of the procedure first initializes the list of coins (*money*), then initializes the list of cokes (*cokes*). After the *make* routine for *money* is called, we know that the entity should not be void. We can record this assumption with a check instruction following the call to *money.make*.

```
    make is
            - - initialize coke machine
        do
            !! money.make (size);
            check
                money_created: not money.Void
            end
            !! cokes.make (size)
        ensure
            empty: empty;
            money_created: not money.Void;
            cokes_created: not cokes.Void
        end - - make
```

When the *make* procedure for the *COKE_MACHINE* is executed, the *make* routine for *money* is first called with *size* as an argument. If check assertions are monitored at run-time, then when this call completes, the check instruction is executed and the clause *money_created* is evaluated. If it evaluates to true, then everything is as it should be and execution proceeds normally. If the assertion evaluates to false, then there is a problem. An exception will be raised and the system will terminate, printing a message stating that the clause *money_created* in the check instruction has been violated.

As another illustration, consider the function *take_out_coke* from the *COKE_MACHINE* class. The body of the function consists of three commands. First, the result variable is set to the first available coke; second, this coke is deleted from the available list; and third, *paid* is set to false, recording the fact that a coke has been taken. We can use a check instruction to record the fact that after the first instruction, *Result* should be equal to the first coke on the list.

```
take_out_coke: COKE is
        -- take a coke from the machine
        -- caller must have already paid
    require
        paid: paid;
        not_empty: not empty
    do
        Result := cokes.first;
        check
            result_is_first_coke:
                Result = cokes.first
        end
        cokes.delete;
        paid := false
    ensure
        not_paid: not paid;
        coke_out: not Result.Void;
        fewer_cokes: cokes.count = old cokes.count − 1;
        no_extra_changes:
                    equal (strip (cokes, paid),
                        old strip (cokes, paid))
    end -- take_out_coke
```

When the *take_out_coke* function is executed, *Result* is first set to the first coke on the list. If check assertions are monitored at run-time, then after this operation is complete, the check instruction is executed and the clause *result_is_first_coke* is evaluated. If it is true, then everything is as it should be and execution proceeds normally. If the clause evaluates to false, then an exception will be raised and the system will terminate with an appropriate error message.

As another example, consider a routine simulating a user of the *COKE_MACHINE*. The user must first put a coin into the machine and then take a coke out; this is accomplished by a call to the procedure *put_in_money* followed by a call to the function *take_out_coke*. After the call to *put_in_money* has completed, the machine should recognize that the cost of a coke has been paid and that the machine has a coke to give to the user. These conditions are signified by the *COKE_MACHINE* feature *paid* and by the negation of the feature *empty* respectively. We can document these facts about the functioning of the user routine with a check instruction following the call to *put_in_money*.

```
machine: COKE_MACHINE
. . .
user is
    local
        coin: COIN;
        coke: COKE
    do
        . . .
        machine.put_in_money (coin);
        check
            paid: machine.paid;
            not_empty: not machine.empty
        end
        coke := machine.take_out_coke
        . . .
    end -- user
```

During a call to this routine, if check assertions are monitored at run-time then the check instruction is executed after the call to *put_in_money* is complete. If *machine.paid* is false, then *put_in_money* has not performed as expected. An exception will be raised, and the system will terminate with a message stating that the *paid* clause has been violated. If *machine.paid* is true, then *not_empty* is evaluated. If the clause is true, then execution proceeds normally. If it is false, then an exception will be raised, and the system will terminate with a message stating that the clause has been violated.

In the above example, the check instruction actually serves two purposes. First, it documents the programmer's assumptions about the effects of executing *put_in_money*; after the call is complete, both *paid* and not *empty* should be true. Second, it records the programmer's assumptions about the precondition for *take_out_coke*; before the routine is invoked, *paid* should be true and *empty* should be false. The latter is a common use of check instructions: to document the precondition for a call in the code for the caller. The check instruction makes the interaction between routines explicit from the caller's point of view. This can enhance understanding and reduce errors when modifying the procedure.

For example, whatever changes are made to *user*, the routine must still ensure that the precondition for *take_out_coke* is true before the function is invoked.

These requirements are formalized in the check instruction preceding the call. Without this explicit information in *user*, a programmer might inadvertently modify the routine in a manner that caused the precondition for *take_out_coke* to be violated. This should never happen. In general, assertions are not violated in correct programs. The caller should be sure that the appropriate precondition is true before calling a routine. This can be accomplished with an explicit test, or if the precondition is known to be true then this fact can be documented with a check instruction.

A common instance of this general situation is division by zero. The result of division by zero does not have a simple mathematical definition, and on most machines division by zero will generate an exception; therefore, it is usually advisable to avoid the situation entirely. This can be accomplished in the two ways discussed previously. First, an explicit test can immediately precede the division.

```
if not x = 0 then
    y := z / x
else
    -- handle divide by zero
    . . .
end
```

This ensures that division by zero will never occur, but it does require an explicit check. On the other hand, if the programmer knows that the denominator cannot be zero, the comparison can be eliminated and the assumption can be recorded with a check instruction.

```
    . . .
    check x_not_zero: not x = 0 end
    y := z / x
    . . .
```

Since the assumption is now explicit, it is less likely that the routine will be modified so as to violate the condition, and run-time monitoring of assertions can be used to enhance debugging.

As another illustration, consider the function *first*, which returns the element at the front of a list. The precondition for this routine requires that the list not be empty when the routine is called. The simplest way to ensure that this is true is with an explicit test immediately before each call to first.

```
if not list.empty then
    x := list.first
else
    -- handle empty list
```

```
    . . .
  end
```

While this solution is adequate, checking *empty* before each call to *first* may consume run-time resources unnecessarily. If we know that the list cannot be empty, then we can eliminate the call to *empty* and document our assumption using a check instruction. For example, consider a loop that removes each element from a list and processes them in turn. If the termination condition for the loop is that the list is empty, then a call to *first* in the body will always find its precondition true. Therefore, we do not need an explicit test before the call, but will document our assumption with a check instruction.

```
  from
  until
      list.empty
  loop
      check not_empty: not list.empty end
      x := list.first;
      -- process x
      . . .
      list.delete
  end
```

The check instruction allows us to record our assumptions about the internal operation of procedures and functions. We can place assertions at arbitrary points in a routine body and use run-time assertion monitoring to detect problems occurring at any time during a program's execution. We can further enhance our capabilities with special constructs for difficult but common situations. Specifically, loops are particularly complicated and potentially difficult to understand. We can simplify the task of describing them significantly by providing special constructs for this purpose.

14.2   Loop variants and invariants

Loops provide many traps for the unwary. They are seemingly simple, easy to understand structures, but what experienced programmer has not spent at least one late night tracking down a subtle bug in an "obviously correct" loop? One of the difficulties is that loops are close to, but do not exactly match human intuitions about repetitive operations. A problem may be intuitively obvious, but its implementation with a loop can still provide a challenge. In light of our previous work with pre- and postconditions and the check instruction, it would seem that we should be able to use assertions to describe the operation of loops. At first we might think, why not just use the check instruction? Well we could, but the result would be very large and messy descriptions. Since loops are specialized constructs, we will need specialized assertions to easily describe them.

So where do we start? We will begin with a rather obvious, but important distinction. Unlike other simple constructs, a loop does not always terminate; it is possible for a program to go into an "infinite loop", executing the same instructions over and over to no one's benefit. Therefore, we will distinguish two separate, but equally important, properties of a correct loop. First, it must do the correct thing while it is running, and second, it must terminate (unless, of course, it is meant to be an infinite loop). Since there are two important properties, correctness and termination, we will need two special types of assertion, one for each.

First, we want to more precisely define the notion "the loop does the correct thing while it is running". To do so, we define a property called the invariant which is always true about the loop. It is unchanging (not varying) during the loop's execution. This idea is more intuitive than it might at first seem. A loop represents a number of executions of its body. Every execution of the body is in some way similar to the others; otherwise, how could we combine them all into a single construct? The invariant is simply a description of the similarities between the executions.

An illustration may be helpful. Consider a very simple loop that sums the integers from one to ten. The invariant for this loop is that the loop counter (call it k) is between one and ten, and that the current total is equal to the sum of all the integers from one to k.

```
from
    k := 1;
    total := 1
-- invariant:    1 <= k <= 10 and
--               total = sum of all integers from 1 to k
until
    k = 10
loop
    k := k + 1;
    total := total + k
end
```

The next step is to more precisely define the notion "it must terminate". To do so, we will define a property called the variant which is different for each execution of the loop. As with the invariant, this may sound strange at first, but is really quite logical. A loop represents a number of executions of the body. Each execution must be different, or there would be no point in multiple executions. In fact, each execution must be moving toward a goal; otherwise, why would the loop ever stop? The variant is simply a way of describing the distance of the current execution from the goal that signals termination. Continuing with the previous illustration, we know that k is different for every execution of the body of the sum loop. Further, we know that the goal is reached when k is equal to ten. Therefore, the variant for the loop (the distance to termination) is just the difference between ten and k. The variant of the loop should be steadily decreasing during execution of the loop; in other words, the loop should be steadily progressing toward termination.

```
from
    k := 1;
    total := 1
-- invariant:        1 <= k <= 10 and
--                   total = sum of all integers from 1 to k
-- variant:          10 - k
until
    k = 10
loop
    k := k + 1;
    total := total + k
end
```

We can now make the relationship between the effect of a loop and its assertions a little more precise. When the loop terminates, both the termination condition and the invariant will be true. The effect of the loop then is described by the combination of these two Boolean expressions. For example, the invariant for the sum loop is that k is between one and ten and *total* is the sum of all the integers from one to k. The termination condition for the loop is that k is equal to ten. The combination of these two is then that *total* is the sum of all the integers from one to ten, and this is the effect of the loop.

The variant does not really say much about what the loop will do, but is very important in determining that the loop will terminate; in other words, it has a lot to say about whether the loop will do anything. The variant must always be non-negative while the loop is running, and it must be decreased by each iteration of the loop. Since the variant cannot decrease indefinitely without reaching zero, its mere existence implies that the loop will terminate. For example, the variant for the sum loop is just ten minus k. Since we know this expression is positive, and that it is decreased by each iteration of the loop, we also know that the loop will terminate.

Specifically, in Eiffel the invariant is an assertion that must hold after loop initialization and that must be preserved by the loop body. The variant is an integer expression that must be non-negative while the loop is running and must be decreased by each iteration of the loop. The invariant is designated by the keyword **invariant** and immediately follows the loop initialization, while the variant is designated by the keyword **variant** and immediately follows the invariant.

```
from
    initialization
```

```
invariant
    assertion
variant
    integer expression
until
    termination condition
loop
    body
end
```

We can now make our example more precise. The invariant for the sum loop contains two clauses. They are that k is at least one and no more that ten respectively. The fact that the running total is the sum of all the integers from one to k is written as a comment, because our notation does not allow us to write it as a Boolean expression. The variant for the loop is just the difference between ten and k.

```
from
    k := 1;
    total := 1
invariant
    k_big_enough: 1 <= k;
    k_small_enough: k <= 10
    -- total = sum of all integers from 1 to k
variant
    10 - k
until
    k = 10
loop
    k := k + 1;
    total := total + k
end
```

The system can be notified that loop variants and invariants are to be checked at run-time. If loop assertions are monitored at run-time, execution will proceed as follows. First the loop initialization is executed, then the invariant is evaluated. If the invariant is false, then an exception is raised and the system will terminate with a message stating that the invariant has been violated. If the invariant is true, then things are as they should be and execution continues with evaluation of the variant. If the variant is less than zero, then an exception is raised and the system will terminate with a message stating that the variant is in error. If the variant is non-negative, then the value is stored and execution continues with evaluation of the termination condition. If the termination condition is true, then the loop terminates. If the termination condition is false, then execution continues with the loop body. After the loop body completes, then the invariant is again evaluated. If it is false, then an exception is raised. If it is true, then execution continues and the variant is evaluated. If the variant is less than zero, then an exception is raised. If not, then the current value is compared with the previous one. If execution of the loop body did not decrease the variant, then an exception is raised. If it did, then execution continues with an evaluation of the termination condition. If the termination condition is true, the loop terminates. If not, then execution continues with the loop body. This pattern continues, with both the invariant and variant being evaluated after every execution of the body, until the loop terminates.

More specifically, let us again consider the sum loop presented above. If loop assertions are monitored at run-time, then both the variant and invariant will be evaluated after loop initialization and after each execution of the loop body. The invariant must always be true. If it ever evaluates to false, then an exception will be raised and the system will terminate with a message stating that the appropriate clause in the loop invariant has been violated. Similarly, the variant must always be greater than or equal to zero. If k is ever greater than ten, then an exception will be raised and the system will terminate with a message stating that the loop variant is in error. Finally, the variant must be decreased by each execution of the loop body. The system will save the value of the variant before execution of the body and then compare it with the value afterwards. If there is no decrease, then an exception will be raised and the system will terminate with a message stating that the loop variant has been violated.

Let us continue with a rather elegant example of loop assertions: a program to approximate the square root of an integer. The function *sqrt* returns the largest integer less than or equal to the square root of its argument. In other words, it returns the largest integer whose square is no greater than the input. The precondition requires that the number in question be positive, and the postcondition states that the result is correct. More specifically, it states that the square of *Result* is no more than the input, and that the square of *Result* plus one is greater.

---

sqrt (n: INTEGER): INTEGER **is**
      – – approximate square root of *n*
  require
    n_greq_zero: *n* >= *0*
  do
    . . .
  ensure
    sqrt_small_enough: *Result* ^ *2* <= *n;*
    sqrt_big_enough: *n* < *(Result + 1)* ^ *2*
  end – – *sqrt*

The body of the function consists of a single loop. *Result* is initialized to zero, and is increased by one during each execution of the loop body until the desired value is reached. The loop terminates when the square of *Result* plus one is greater than *n* (the argument to the routine). The invariant for the loop is that *Result* squared is between zero and *n*, and the variant is the difference between *n* and *Result*.

```
from
    Result := 0
invariant
    a_squared_greq_zero: 0 <= Result ^ 2;
    a_squared_lseq_zero: Result ^ 2 <= n
variant
    n - Result
until
    (Result + 1) ^ 2 > n
loop
    Result := Result + 1
end
```

The variant for the above loop demonstrates an important property of variants: they do not have to be an exact count of the number of iterations remaining. In general, *n* minus *Result* will not reach zero during execution of the loop, but this is not a problem. The variant actually represents an upper bound on the number of iterations remaining for the loop, rather than an exact count. Similarly, the loop body can decrease the variant by more than one; in fact, it can reduce it by ten, or 100, or half its value. The only restrictions on the variant are that it must be non-negative at all times during the loop's execution, and that it must be decreased by each execution of the loop body.

Let us return to our consideration of *sqrt*. If loop assertions are monitored at run-time, both the variant and invariant will be evaluated after loop initialization and after each execution of the loop body. Both clauses of the invariant must always evaluate to true. If *Result* squared is either less than zero or greater than *n*, then an exception will be raised and the system will terminate with a message stating that the appropriate clause of the loop invariant has been violated. Similarly, the variant must always be non-negative. If *Result* is ever greater than *n*, then an exception will be raised and the system will terminate with a message stating that the loop variant is in error. Finally, the variant must be decreased by each execution of the loop body. Since the body increases *Result* by one, this is no problem; however, if something should go wrong, an exception will be raised and the system will terminate with an appropriate error message.

As a final illustration, let us consider a new routine for the *LIST* class. The function *member* returns true if its argument is in the list under consideration. The function can be called on any list; therefore, it has no precondition (in other words, its precondition is true). The postcondition ensures that if the function returns true, then the element in question is at the appropriate location in the list.

The body of the routine consists of a single loop. Each element of the list is examined in turn until all have been considered or the element in question has been found. The invariant for the loop is that the loop counter (k) is between zero and the number of elements in the list (*count*), and the variant is the difference between *count* and k.

```
      member (elem: T): BOOLEAN is
                -- is elem an element of list?
      local
          k: INTEGER
      do
          from
              k := 0
          invariant
              k_big_enough: 0 <= k;
              k_small_enough: k <= count
          variant
              count - k
          until
              k = count or Result
          loop
              if elements.item (k).Equal (elem) then
                  Result := true
              end
              k := k + 1
          end
      ensure
          result_ok:
              Result implies elements.item (k - 1).Equal (elem)
      end -- member
```

If loop assertions are monitored at run-time, then both the variant and invariant will be evaluated immediately after loop initialization. The invariant must evaluate to true, and the variant must be greater than or equal to zero. If either of these conditions is not met, then an exception will be raised and the system will terminate. As loop execution continues, both the variant and invariant will be evaluated after each iteration of the body. As before, the invariant must be true and the variant must be non-negative or an exception will be generated. The system will also check that the variant is decreased by each execution of the loop body. The values before and after each iteration are compared, and if the latter is not smaller than the former then an exception will be raised.

Summary

- Check instructions can be used to make the programmer's assumptions explicit. A check instruction signifies that an assertion should evaluate to true at a particular point during a routine's execution.
- Loops can be characterized by a variant and an invariant.
- The loop **variant** is a non-negative integer function that is decreased by each iteration of the loop body.
- The loop **invariant** is an assertion that is true after loop initialization and is preserved by each iteration of the body.
- The system can be instructed to monitor loop invariants and variants, as well as check instructions at run-time.

Exercises

1. Place check instructions after each statement in the following code fragments.

   Example: w := 3;

   check

       w_is_3: w = 3

   end

   x := 4;

   check

       w_is_3: w = 3;

       x_is_4: x = 4

   end

   (a) *a := y // z;*

      b := y \\ z;

      *c := a * b;*

   (b) *a := x * y / z;*

      *b := w / x * z;*

      c := a + b

2. Write an invariant and variant for the following loops.

   (a)

   > *prod (n: INTEGER): INTEGER* **is**
   >   −− product of first *n* positive integers
   >   **require**
   >   *n_greq_one: n >= 1*
   >   **do**
   >   **from**
   >   *k := 1;*

```
            total := 1
        until
            k = n
        loop
            k := k + 1;
            total := total * k
        end
    end -- prod
```

(b)

```
cbrt (n: INTEGER): INTEGER is
        -- approximate cube root of n
    require
        n_greq_zero: n >= 0
    do
        from
            Result: := 0
        until
            (Result + 1) ^ 3 > n
        loop
            Result := Result + 1
        end
    ensure
        cbrt_small_enough: Result ^ 3 <= n;
        cbrt_big_enough: n < (Result + 1) ^ 3
    end -- cbrt
```

CHAPTER 15

Assertions on classes

Keywords

class invariant
stable time
invariant

The clients of a class should see a consistent state at all stable times; in other words, both before and after each call on a visible feature. The class invariant is an assertion that describes the properties that must hold at all stable times; it does not have to hold at all points during a routine's execution, or when a routine is called from inside the class. In other words, the class invariant is added to both the pre- and postcondition of any client-invoked routine. The definition of the class invariant follows the features for a class and is designated by the keyword **invariant**.

15.1   Class invariants

Pre- and postconditions, check instructions, and loop assertions all provide powerful tools for describing programs. Run-time monitoring of these constructs can also significantly enhance testing and debugging. However, the reader may have already noticed that the assertions describing even small programs can become quite lengthy. Some might not consider this a problem; lengthy descriptions are a small price to pay for the increased understanding that may come from making all the assumptions underlying a routine explicit. None the less, we certainly don't want to make assertions any longer than necessary. One common, but non-optimal, situation is repeated clauses that appear in the pre- and postconditions for all the routines of a class. These clauses represent properties of the class that must be true at all stable times; in other words, that must be true both before and after each external call to any routine. We call these times stable because they represent the points at which a client can see the condition of the object, and clients should always see a stable, consistent state.

301

As an illustration, consider the class *LIST* discussed in previous chapters. The class exports a feature called *count*, which is the number of items currently in the list. From the caller's point of view, *count* should always be between zero and the maximum size of the list. This assumption can be documented by two clauses stating that *count* is greater than or equal to zero, and less than or equal to *max_count* respectively. To demand that these properties hold at all stable times, these two clauses could be added to the postcondition for *make* and to both the pre- and postconditions for each exported routine. However, this is both messy and redundant. There is really only one piece of information (*count* must be between zero and *max_count*), but it appears 11 times (in the postcondition for *make*, and in both the pre- and postconditions for each of the five other exported routines).

We can do much better by using a construct specifically designed for these situations. The class invariant describes the properties of a class that must be true at all stable times; in other words, the properties that must be true at both the beginning and end of each interaction between a client and the class. The class invariant can significantly shorten pre- and postconditions by allowing repeated clauses to be moved into it. For example, in the *LIST* class the restrictions on the value of *count* can be put into a class invariant. Class invariants also restrict the effects of routines not yet written for the class. They define "general principles of operation", analogous to the general procedures clauses in a legal contract. Not only are the pre- and postconditions shorter than if these clauses appeared explicitly, but any future routines on the class are required to maintain these constraints.

In Eiffel, the class invariant is an assertion, denoted by the keyword **invariant**, which appears at the end of the class definition. The class invariant can only reference the state of the object: it cannot refer to the parameters of routines or features of other classes.

```
class name

    . . .
invariant
    assertion
end - - class name
```

Continuing with our previous illustration, the invariant for the *LIST* class contains two clauses. *count_big_enough* requires that *count* always be at least zero, while *count_small_enough* demands that it never be more than *max_count*.

```
class LIST [T]

    . . .
invariant
    count_big_enough: 0 <= count;
    count_small_enough: count <= max_count
end - - class LIST
```

As with the other types of assertions, the system can be instructed that class invariants are to be monitored at run-time. If this is the case, then the invariant will be evaluated at both the beginning and end of each call originating from outside the class. As usual, the clauses in the invariant are evaluated from left to right, top to bottom. If all the clauses are true, then things are as they should be and execution proceeds normally. If a clause evaluates to false, then there is a problem; an exception is raised and the system terminates with a message stating that the responsible clause in the class invariant has been violated.

For example, if class invariants are being monitored at run-time, then the clauses in the invariant for *LIST* will be evaluated at all stable times: after execution of *make*, and both before and after any call to *empty, full, insert, delete,* or *first* from outside the class. Evaluation of the invariant begins with *count_big_enough*. If this clause is false, then an exception is raised and the system terminates with a message naming the clause in the class invariant that was violated. If it is true, then things are as they should be and execution continues with evaluation of *count_small_enough*. If this clause is true, then evaluation of the invariant is complete and execution continues normally; however, if it is false, then an exception is raised and the system will terminate with an appropriate error message.

As another illustration, consider the *COKE_MACHINE* discussed previously. This class contains two lists, *cokes* and *money*, consisting of cokes and coins respectively. At any stable point during the class's execution, both the number of cokes and coins should be between zero and the capacity of the lists. Specifically, *cokes.count* and *money.count* should both be between zero and *size*, where *size* is a feature of the class. Now, these facts could be recorded using pre- and postconditions; however, the amount of redundancy would be unacceptable. It is much more reasonable to make the restrictions on *cokes.count* and *money.count* part of the class invariant: pre- and postconditions are shortened and future routines must also obey the constraints.

Therefore, the invariant for *COKE_MACHINE* now contains four clauses: one each to demand that *cokes.count* be at least zero, that *cokes.count* be no more than *size*, that *money.count* be at least zero, and that *money.count* be no more than *size*.

```
class COKE_MACHINE

    . . .
invariant
    cokes_count_big_enough: 0 <= cokes.count;
    cokes_count_small_enough: cokes.count <= size;
    money_count_big_enough: 0 <= money.count;
    money_count_small_enough: money.count <= size
end - - class COKE_MACHINE
```

If class invariants are being monitored at run-time, then the invariant for *COKE_MACHINE* will be evaluated at both the beginning and end of every call to a routine from outside the class. If every clause in the invariant evaluates to true, then things are as they should be and execution proceeds normally. If any clause evaluates to false, then an exception will be raised and the system will terminate with a message stating that the appropriate clause in the class invariant has been violated.

The previous examples have demonstrated that more precise descriptions of classes can be created without increasing the size of the pre- and postconditions on routines. While this is significant, at times we can do even better: we can decrease the size of existing pre- and postconditions while maintaining their descriptive power. For example, in no situation should a coin be put into the *COKE_MACHINE* if there are no cokes available for sale (the machine does not have a coin return). We can document this fact by placing a clause in the class invariant stating that *empty* is false whenever *paid* is true.

---

class *COKE_MACHINE*

   . . .

invariant

   not_paid_when_empty: *empty* **implies not** *paid*;

   . . .

end – – class *COKE_MACHINE*

This allows us to simplify the pre- and postconditions for *put_in_money* and *take_out_coke* respectively. Currently, both these assertions require that a coin has been paid and that cokes are available for sale; specifically that the features *paid* and *empty* be true and false respectively. Now, since the class invariant is implicitly part of the pre- and postconditions for all exported routines, the postcondition for *put_in_money* and the precondition for *take_out_coke* can both be simplified to only demand that paid be true. Therefore, the class invariant has allowed us to decrease the size of already written pre- and postconditions without changing their meaning.

---

   put_in_money (coin: COIN) **is**

        – – put a coin in the machine

        – – machine must register coin entered

    require

       . . .

    ensure

       more_money: *money.count* = **old** *money.count + 1;*

       no_extra_changes:

          equal (**strip** (*money, paid*),

            old strip (*money, paid*));

       paid: paid

    end – – *put_in_money*

   take_out_coke: *COKE* **is**

        – – take a coke from the machine

```
                    -- caller must have already paid
        require
            paid: paid
        do
            Result := cokes.first;
            cokes.delete;
            paid := false
        ensure
            . . .
        end -- take_out_coke
```

This example brings up an important, but subtle point. The class invariant must be true at all stable times; it must hold after creation of each instance, and both before and after every external call to a routine. However, it may be violated during execution of a remote call or at any time during a local call. The class invariant has no effect on non-exported routines, and is implicitly "and"ed to the pre- and postconditions for exported routines only when they are called from outside the class.

Specifically, the class invariant for *COKE_MACHINE* requires that *empty* be false whenever *paid* is true, but when *take_out_coke* is executed to remove the last coke from the machine, the invariant will temporarily be false in the middle of the routine. Imagine that *take_out_coke* is invoked when there is one coke remaining in the machine. The precondition for the routine requires that *paid* be true. When the routine begins execution, *Result* is set to the one remaining coke, which is then deleted from the list of those available for sale. At this point, the machine is empty but *paid* is still true. This is fine, however, because the next statement sets *paid* to false and re-establishes the invariant before a stable state is reached. The class invariant does not have to hold at every point during execution of every routine. It need only hold at the beginning and end of every external invocation.

Class invariants add to our tool kit of pre- and postconditions, check instructions, and loop assertions. They allow us to write more precise descriptions of classes more concisely, as well as put constraints on the operation of future routines. With this in mind, let us examine the latest versions of the classes we have previously considered.

15.2   Class *LIST* revisited

First, let us again consider the entire description of the *LIST* class. As before, the class exports the routines *empty*, *full*, *first*, *insert*, and *delete*. *Empty* and *full* return true if the list contains no elements or has no more free space respectively. *First* returns a pointer to the element at the front of the list, *delete* removes that element, and *insert* puts a new element in the first position. Each list consists of an array called *elements*, an index into the array called *count*, and an integer called *max_count* that provides an upper bound on the number of items. Elements are both inserted and deleted from the front of the list; therefore, *count* is the next available location in *elements*, and the first element in the list is in location *count* minus one.

The *LIST* class now exports the *member* function, which returns true if a given item is an element of the list. The body of the routine consists of a single loop. *Result* is initialized to false, and each item in *elements* is examined in turn. If the item in question matches the argument to the routine, then *Result* is set to true and the loop terminates. If all the elements have been examined without finding a match, then the loop terminates with *Result* equal to false. The function may be called on any list, so it has no precondition. The postcondition for the routine ensures that if *member* returns true, then the element in question is at some location in the list.

The invariant for *LIST* contains three clauses. *count_big_enough* requires that *count* be at least zero, while *count_small_enough* demands that it be no more than *max_count*. The *max_count_ok* clause requires that *max_count* correctly reflect the size of the *elements* array; this prevents a routine from modifying these variables in an inconsistent manner. All three of these clauses must be true after the *make* procedure terminates, and both before and after each external call to any exported routine.

```
class LIST [T]
creation
    make
feature {NONE}
    elements: ARRAY [T];
    max_count: INTEGER
feature {ANY}
    count: INTEGER;
    make (size: INTEGER) is
        require
            size_big_enough: size > 0
        do
            !! elements.make (0, size − 1);
            max_count := size
        ensure
            elements_created: not elements.Void;
            empty: empty;
            max_count_eq_size: max_count = size
        end − − make
    empty: BOOLEAN is
        − − is list empty?
        do
```

```
            Result := (count = 0)
        ensure
            result_ok: Result = (count = 0);
            no_changes: equal (strip, old strip)
        end -- empty
full: BOOLEAN is
            -- is list full?
        do
            Result := (count = max_count)
        ensure
            result_ok: Result = (count = max_count);
            no_changes: equal (strip, old strip)
        end -- full
first: T is
            -- return first element in list
        require
            not_empty: not empty
        do
            Result := elements.item (count - 1)
        ensure
            return_first_item: Result = elements.item (count - 1);
            no_changes: equal (strip, old strip)
        end -- first
insert (elem: T) is
            -- put an element into the list
        require
            not_full: not full
        do
            elements.put (elem, count);
            count := count + 1
        ensure
            not_empty: not empty;
            count_increased: count = old count + 1;
            no_extra_changes:
                equal (strip (elements, count),
                    old strip (elements, count))
        end -- insert
delete is
            -- remove first element from list
```

```
        require
            not_empty: not empty
        do
            count := count − 1
        ensure
            not_full: not full;
            count_decreased: count = old count − 1;
            no_extra_changes:
                equal (strip (count), old strip (count))
        end −− delete
    member (elem: T): BOOLEAN is
            −− is elem an element of list?
        local
            k: INTEGER
        do
            from
                k := 0
            invariant
                k_big_enough: 0 <= k;
                k_small_enough: k <= count
            variant
                count − k
            until
                k = count or Result
            loop
                if elements.item (k).Equal (elem) then
                    Result := true
                end
                k := k + 1
            end
        ensure
            result_ok:
                Result implies elements.item (k − 1).Equal (elem)
        end −− member
    invariant
        count_big_enough: 0 <= count;
        count_small_enough: count <= max_count;
        max_count_ok: max_count = elements.count
    end −− class LIST
```

15.3   Class *COKE_MACHINE* for the third time

Finally, let us again consider the entire description of the *COKE_MACHINE*. As before, the condition of our machine is described by three variables. The Boolean variable *paid* is true whenever a coin has been entered and a coke can be taken. We keep track of the coins in the machine using a list called *money*, while the cans available for sale are represented as a list called *cokes*. The machine also exports three routines. *Empty* returns true if there are no more cokes available for sale, while *put_in_money* and *take_out_coke* allow the customer to put in a coin and take out a coke respectively.

COKE_MACHINE has been changed by the addition of a class invariant which ensures that the number of cokes and coins are both between zero and *size*, and that *paid* is never true when the machine has no more cokes for sale. The invariant is written as five clauses. *not_paid_when_empty* requires that if *empty* is true, then *paid* must be false. *cokes_count_big_enough* ensures that the number of cokes is greater than or equal to zero, and *cokes_count_small_enough* requires that there are no more than *size* cokes in the machine. *money_count_big_enough* and *money_count_small_enough* place the same restrictions on the number of coins the machine holds. These five clauses must all be true after the *make* procedure terminates, and both before and after any external call to *empty, put_in_money*, or *take_out_coke*.

The *make* and *empty* routines are exactly as before: both the bodies and the pre- and postconditions which describe them have not been changed. However, both of these routines may now assume that the class invariant is true when they begin execution, and are required to leave a state where the class invariant holds.

The use of a class invariant has allowed us to improve the assertions describing *put_in_money* and *take_out_coke*. The precondition for *put_in_money* is the same as before; however, the postcondition has been simplified. Previously, it required both that *paid* be true and that the machine was not empty. Now, the class invariant requires that the machine not be empty whenever *paid* is true; therefore, the new postcondition just requires this single condition. The precondition for *take_out_coke* has been changed in a similar manner. Previously, it required that *empty* evaluate to false and *paid* to true. The new version takes advantage of the class invariant to reduce this to the truth of *paid*.

```
class COKE_MACHINE
creation
    make
feature {NONE}
    money: LIST [COIN];
    cokes: LIST [COKE];
    size: INTEGER is 100
feature {ANY}
    paid: BOOLEAN
    make is
```

```
                    -- initialize coke machine
        do
            !! money.make (size);
            !! cokes.make (size)
        ensure
            empty: empty;
            money_created: not money.Void;
            cokes_created: not cokes.Void
        end -- make
empty: BOOLEAN is
            -- is machine out of cokes?
        do
            Result := cokes.empty
        ensure
            result_ok: Result = cokes.empty;
            no_changes: equal (strip, old strip)
        end -- empty
put_in_money (coin: COIN) is
            -- put a coin in the machine
            -- machine must register coin entered
        require
            not_paid: not paid;
            not_empty: not empty;
            coin_in: not coin.Void
        do
            money.insert (coin);
            paid := true
        ensure
            more_money: money.count = old money.count + 1;
            no_extra_changes:
                equal (strip (money, paid),
                    old strip (money, paid));
            paid: paid
        end -- put_in_money
take_out_coke: COKE is
            -- take a coke from the machine
            -- caller must have already paid
        require
            paid: paid
        do
```

```
            Result := cokes.first;
            cokes.delete;
            paid := false
        ensure
            fewer_cokes: cokes.count = old cokes.count − 1;
            no_extra_changes:
                    equal (strip (cokes, paid),
                        old strip (cokes, paid));
            not_paid: not paid;
            coke_out: not Result.Void
        end −− take_out_coke
    invariant
        not_paid_when_empty: empty implies not paid;
        cokes_count_big_enough: 0 <= cokes.count;
        cokes_count_small_enough: cokes.count <= size;
        money_count_big_enough: 0 <= money.count;
        money_count_small_enough: money.count <= size
    end −− class COKE_MACHINE
```

Summary

- Class invariants describe properties that must be true of all instances of a class.
- Class invariants allow shorter pre- and postconditions because the pre- and postconditions implicitly include the invariant.
- Class invariants must be satisfied both before and after every remote (but not local) call to a routine. The class invariant may be invalidated during a routine's execution.
- The *make* procedure must initialize the class invariant.

Exercises

1. Consider the *TWO_COIN_MACHINE* developed in the exercises for earlier chapters.

```
class TWO_COIN_MACHINE
creation
    make
feature {ANY}
    one_paid: BOOLEAN;
    two_paid: BOOLEAN;
```

```
    . . .
    put_in_money (coin: COIN) is
            -- put a coin in the machine
            -- machine must register coin entered
        . . .
    take_out_coke: COKE is
            -- take a coke from the machine
            -- two coins must have been paid
        . . .
end -- class TWO_COIN_MACHINE
```

(a) Which clauses of the class invariant for *COKE_MACHINE* given in Section 15.3 above are also appropriate for *TWO_COIN_MACHINE*?

(b) Write class invariant clauses for *TWO_COIN_MACHINE* that describe the relationship between *one_paid*, *two_paid*, and *empty*. (*Hint:* Remember that *two_paid* is true only if two coins have been paid and a coke has not been taken, while *one_paid* is true if either one or two coins have been entered.)

2. Must the class invariant for *TWO_COIN_MACHINE* be true at the beginning of the *make* procedure?

3. Must the class invariant for *TWO_COIN_MACHINE* be true when the *make* procedure has completed its execution?

4. Must the class invariant for *TWO_COIN_MACHINE* hold when *put_in_money* begins execution?

5. Must the class invariant for *TWO_COIN_MACHINE* hold when *put_in_money* completes?

6. Must the class invariant for *TWO_COIN_MACHINE* hold all during *put_in_money*'s execution?

CHAPTER 16

Assertions and inheritance

Keywords

inheritance
class invariants
pre- and postconditions
require else
ensure then

Inheritance of assertions guarantees that the behavior of a class is compatible with that of its ancestors. For example, a class should not assume a state that would be invalid for any of its predecessors; therefore, it must satisfy all their invariants. Similarly, a class must be able to perform (at least) all the functions of its ancestors; therefore, the redefinition of a routine may only weaken the precondition and strengthen the postcondition. The pre- and postconditions for a routine redefinition are designated by the keywords **require else** and **ensure then** respectively. The precondition for a redefined routine is equivalent to the new precondition **or else** the precondition from the original routine, while the postcondition is equivalent to the new postcondition **and then** the original.

16.1   Introduction

We now have a powerful set of tools with which to formally describe programs. Pre- and postconditions, check instructions, loop assertions, and class invariants allow us to describe many properties of software components. We can use these assertions to write software contracts which may be monitored at run-time to ensure compliance. However, we need to realize that these tools are embedded in a language which supports inheritance; therefore, classes can redefine routines inherited from their parents. To complete our understanding of assertions and their use, we must now examine how the tools presented so far interact with inheritance.

The inheritance mechanisms provided by Eiffel are powerful, and if used correctly can lead to smaller, more elegant systems consisting of easily reusable components. However, these mechanisms can also lead to chaos if misused. If redefinition and dynamic binding are allowed to arbitrarily change the behavior of operations, clients will be unable to depend on stable, predictable outcomes. Assertions can provide an answer to this problem. Briefly, in Eiffel descendants inherit the class invariants of their parents, and any redefinition of a routine must satisfy the original pre- and postconditions; therefore, if client code relies only on properties specified using assertions, all descendants are guaranteed to perform all functions required of their ancestors.

We can extend our contracting metaphor to view the inheritance of assertions as programming by sub-contract. In the real world, a general contractor may hire any number of others to perform parts of the original job; however, these sub-contractors must perform the work up to the standards required in the overall contract, and must do it cheaply enough so that the general contractor can complete the entire job for the agreed-upon price. In Eiffel, descendants can only do more, cheaper than their ancestors. Specifically, any redefinition of a routine may only change the postcondition by making it stronger (more difficult to satisfy); therefore, all descendants are guaranteed to perform (at least) all the functions of their ancestors. Similarly, any redefinition may only change the precondition by making it weaker (easier to satisfy); therefore, all descendants are guaranteed to perform in (at least) all cases their ancestors would accept.

16.2   Class invariants

To begin, let us consider the inheritance of class invariants. In Eiffel, a class inherits the invariants of all its ancestors; therefore, each instance of the descendant class must satisfy the invariant of each ancestor class. For example, if the class *HOUSE_CAT* is a descendant of both *CAT* and *PET*, and *CAT* is a descendant of *ANIMAL*, then any instance of *HOUSE_CAT* must satisfy the class invariants of *CAT*, *PET*, and *ANIMAL*. In other words, the invariant for *HOUSE_CAT* consists of its own invariant "and"ed with the invariants of all its ancestors. If class invariants are being monitored at run-time, then the invariants of all the ancestors of a class will be evaluated before the invariant of the class itself. For example, if class invariants are being checked, then the invariants for *CAT*, *PET*, and *ANIMAL* will all be evaluated before the invariant for *HOUSE_CAT*.

As a more concrete example, let us consider the problem of maintaining an ordered list. An ordered list is simply a list in which every element is greater than or equal to all those preceding it; in other words, the first element in the list is the smallest, the second is the next to smallest, and so on. We can use the *LIST* class described previously to maintain an ordered list by defining a descendant class with an appropriate invariant. The first thing we must do is define the Boolean function *ordered*, which returns true if and only if the elements of the list have the correct relationship. The function is defined on any list, so it has no precondition (in other words, it has a precondition of true). The postcondition requires that if the function returns false, then the last two items examined were in the incorrect order.

The routine consists of a single loop. *Result* is initialized to true because an empty list is always ordered. Each pair of elements in the list is compared, starting at the front of the list and continuing until the end is reached or the result is known to be false. When a pair of elements is compared, the *Result* is set to false if they are out of order. The invariant for the loop requires that *k* be within the proper range, and that if *Result* has been set to false then the last two items examined were out of sequence. The loop variant is just the value of the loop counter (*k*).

```
ordered: BOOLEAN is
    local
        k: INTEGER
    do
        from
            Result := true;
            k := count
        invariant
            k_big_enough: 0 <= k;
            k_small_enough: k <= count;
            correct_result:
                not Result implies
                elements.item (k - 1) < elements.item (k)
        variant
            k
        until
            k < 2 or not Result
        loop
            k := k - 1;
            if elements.item (k - 1) < elements.item (k) then
                Result := false
            end
        end
    ensure
        not Result implies
        elements.item (k - 1) < elements.item (k)
    end -- ordered
```

We can now define the class *ORDERED_LIST* as a descendant of *LIST* that exports the same features. The major difference between the two is that *ORDERED_LIST* has a class invariant requiring that the items be ordered both before and after each external call to any routine. Another difference is that the elements in an *ORDERED_LIST* must belong to a descendant of the kernel library class *COMPARABLE*; this guarantees that the necessary comparison operators are defined. An *ORDERED_LIST* must be able to perform all the functions of a *LIST* from the client's point of view. While most of the operations will be identical, the *insert* routine must be modified to maintain the ordering relation when a new element is added.

```
class ORDERED_LIST [T -> COMPARABLE]
inherit
    LIST [T] redefine insert;

    . . .

feature {ANY}

    . . .

    insert (elem: T) is
                    -- must maintain order

        . . .

    ordered: BOOLEAN is

        . . .

invariant
    ordered: ordered
end -- class ORDERED_LIST
```

16.3   Pre- and postconditions

In Eiffel, the inheritance of pre- and postconditions supports programming by sub-contract; any redefinition of a routine must satisfy a precondition that is at least as easy to satisfy as the original, and a postcondition that is at least as demanding as the original. In other words, a sub-contractor may weaken the precondition and strengthen the postcondition, but not vice versa.

Specifically, if pre- and postconditions are present in the redefined routine, they are designated with the keywords **require else** and **ensure then** respectively.

```
    routine_name (parameters: TYPES) is
        require else
            new-precondition
    . . .
        ensure then
            new-postcondition
        end -- routine_name
```

The new pre- and postconditions are evaluated before the originals. In other words, the above assertions are equivalent to the following, where the original pre- and postconditions are from the definition of the routine in the parent class. The default new precondition is **false**, and the default new postcondition is **true**.

```
routine_name (parameters: TYPES) is
    require
        new-precondition or else original-precondition
    . . .
    ensure
        new-postcondition and then original-precondition
    end -- routine_name
```

Specifically, if pre- and postconditions are being monitored at run-time, then the new precondition is evaluated at the beginning of each call to the routine. If it is true, then execution continues with the body of the routine. If the new precondition is false, then the original precondition is evaluated. If the original precondition is also false, then an exception is raised and the system terminates with an appropriate message. If the original precondition is true, then execution continues with the routine body. After execution of the routine body completes, the new postcondition is evaluated. If it is false, then an exception is raised and the system terminates with an appropriate message. If the new postcondition is true, then the original postcondition is evaluated. If it is true, then everything is as it should be and the call completes normally. If it is false, then an exception is raised and the system terminates with an appropriate message.

As an illustration, consider the *insert* procedure for the *ORDERED_LIST* class. The original precondition for *insert* required that the list was not full, and the postcondition ensured that the list was not empty, that *count* was increased by one, and that *elements* and *count* were the only features changed by the operation.

```
insert (elem: T) is
        -- put an element into the list
    require
        not_full: not full
    do
        . . .
    ensure
        not_empty: not empty;
        count_increased: count = old count + 1;
        no_extra_changes:
            equal (strip (elements, count),
                old strip (elements, count))
    end -- insert
```

In *ORDERED_LIST*, the class invariant requires that the list be ordered at the beginning of insert; therefore the precondition need not be changed, and so none appears in the redefined routine. While the original postcondition for *insert* is also acceptable, we will strengthen it by requiring that *elem* be a member of the list when the procedure terminates.

---

insert (elem: T) **is**

      −− put an element into the list

do

    . . .

ensure then

    elem_member: *member (elem)*

end *−− insert*

The pre- and postconditions for the redefinition of *insert* are equivalent to the following. Since there is no new precondition, the original is used unchanged, while the new postcondition is "and"ed onto the beginning of the original. Notice that we save considerable duplication by inheriting the pre- and postconditions for the *insert* routine in the *LIST* class, rather than rewriting them in the pre- and postconditions for the new routine explicitly.

---

insert (elem: T) **is**

      −− put an element into the list

require

    not_full: **not** *full*

do

    . . .

ensure

    elem_member: *member (elem);*

    not_empty: **not** *empty;*

    count_increased: *count* = **old** *count* + *1;*

    no_extra_changes:

        equal (**strip** *(elements, count),*

            old strip *(elements, count))*

end *−− insert*

If pre- and postconditions are being monitored at run-time, the precondition for *insert* will be evaluated at the beginning of each attempt to add a new element to an *ORDERED_LIST*. The new precondition is false, so evaluation precedes directly to the original precondition (from *LIST*). If it is false, then an exception is raised and the system terminates with a message stating that the precondition for insert has been violated. If the original precondition (*not_full*) is true, then everything is as it should be and execution continues with the procedure body. When the body completes, the postcondition is evaluated. The new postcondition (*elem_member*) is evaluated first. If it is false, then an exception is raised and the system terminates with a message stating that the postcondition for insert has been violated. If the new postcondition is true, then the original postcondition is evaluated. If it is false, then an exception is raised and the system terminates with a message stating that the postcondition for insert has been violated. If the original postcondition is also true, then everything is as it should be and the call terminates normally.

While the external behavior of the *insert* procedure for *ORDERED_LIST* is quite simple, its implementation is reasonably complex; therefore, we will examine it in the context of the entire class definition.

16.4   An example class: *ORDERED_LIST*

ORDERED_LIST is a descendant of *LIST* with a class invariant requiring that the elements in the list be ordered both before and after each external call. The class defines a *BOOLEAN* function *ordered* that returns true if and only if the elements of the list have the correct relationship. The items in an *ORDERED_LIST* must belong to a descendant of the kernel library class *COMPARABLE* so that the necessary comparison operators are defined. *ORDERED_LIST* exports the same features as its parent *LIST*. Most of the operations are inherited with no modifications, but the *insert* routine is redefined to maintain the ordering relation when a new element is added.

The *insert* routine for *ORDERED_LIST* inherits both pre- and postconditions from its parent. The redefinition leaves the precondition unchanged, but strengthens the postcondition by requiring that the new element be a member of the list when the routine completes. The body of *insert* consists of two loops and two assignments. The first loop finds the proper location for the new element. The chosen element will follow the new item in the resultant list. The second loop moves all the elements, from the selected one to the beginning, up one location; this frees up the space for the new addition (remember that the items in a list are stored in reverse order, so that the first element has the largest index). Finally, the new item is inserted and the number of elements in the list is incremented.

```
insert (elem: T) is
    local
        k: INTEGER
    do
        < first_loop >
        -- found correct location
        -- all previous elements smaller
        -- all succeeding elements greater
        < second_loop >
        -- all preceding elements moved up one
        elements.put (elem, location + 1);
        count := count + 1
    ensure then
        elem_member: member (elem)
    end -- insert
```

The variable *location* (roughly, the location of the new element in the list) is a feature of the *ORDERED_LIST* class, rather than local to the *insert* routine. While this is not necessary for our present purposes, it does no harm and will prove necessary for the example given in the next chapter.

The first loop finds the proper location for the new element to be added to the list. The loop initialization sets *location* to the index of the first item in the list. Each element is then considered in turn until the end of the list is reached or one greater than or equal to the item to be inserted is found. The invariant for the loop states that *location* is within the range of valid indices, that the list is still ordered, and that the element to be inserted is greater than all the items previous to *location* in the list. The variant is just *location*, with one added so that it always remains non-negative.

```
from
      location := count − 1
invariant
      location_big_enough: − 1 <= location;
      location_small_enough: location < count;
      ordered: ordered;
      greater_than_previous:
            location = count − 1 or else
            elem > elements.item (location + 1)
variant
      location + 1
until
      location = − 1 or
      elem <= elements.item (location)
loop
      location := location − 1
end
```

The second loop moves all the elements, from the selected one to the beginning, up one location in *elements*; this frees up the space for the new addition. The loop initialization sets the loop counter (*k*) to one more than the highest valid index. Each iteration of the loop then moves an item up one location and decrements *k*. The invariant for the loop requires that *k* be within the range of valid indices, and that the list still be ordered. The variant is the number of elements still to be moved to their new locations; in other words, the difference between the loop counter and the location for the new element.

```
from
      k := count
invariant
      k_big_enough: location < k;
```

```
        k_small_enough: k <= count;
        ordered: ordered
    variant
        k – location
    until
        k = location + 1
    loop
        elements.put (elements.item (k – 1), k);
        k := k – 1
    end
```

We can now examine the class in its entirety.

```
class ORDERED_LIST [T -> COMPARABLE]
inherit
    LIST [T] rename make as list_make
            redefine insert
creation
    make
feature {ANY}
    location: INTEGER;
    make (size: INTEGER) is do
        !! list_make (size)
        end – – make
    insert (elem: T) is
        require
            not_full: not full
        local
            k: INTEGER
        do
            from
                location := count – 1
            invariant
                location_big_enough: – 1 <= location;
                location_small_enough: location < count;
                ordered: ordered;
                greater_than_previous:
                    location = count – 1 or else
                    elem > elements.item (location + 1)
            variant
                location + 1
```

```
        until
            location = - 1 or
            elem <= elements.item (location)
        loop
            location := location - 1
        end
        -- found correct location
        -- all previous elements smaller
        -- all succeeding elements greater
        check
            location_big_enough: - 1 <= location;
            location_small_enough: location < count;
            ordered: ordered;
            greater_than_previous:
                location = count - 1 or else
                elem > elements.item (location + 1);
            less_than_remaining:
                location = - 1 or else
                elem <= elements.item (location)
        end
        from
            k := count
        invariant
            k_big_enough: location < k;
            k_small_enough: k <= count;
            ordered: ordered
        variant
            k - location
        until
            k = location + 1
        loop
            elements.put (elements.item (k - 1), k);
            k := k - 1
        end
        check
            location_big_enough: - 1 <= location;
            location_small_enough: location < count;
            ordered: ordered;
            greater_than_previous:
                location = count - 1 or else
```

```
                    elem > elements.item (location + 1);
                less_than_remaining:
                    location = - 1 or else
                    elem <= elements.item (location)
            end
        elements.put (elem, location + 1);
        count := count + 1
    ensure
        elem_member: member (elem);
        not_empty: not empty;
        count_increased: count = old count + 1;
        no_extra_changes:
            max_count = old max_count and
            position = old position
    end -- insert
ordered: BOOLEAN is
    local
        k: INTEGER
    do
        from
            Result := true;
            k := count
        invariant
            k_big_enough: 0 <= k;
            k_small_enough: k <= count;
            correct_result:
                not Result implies
                elements.item (k - 1) < elements.item (k)
        variant
            k
        until
            k < 2 or not Result
        loop
            k := k - 1;
            if elements.item (k - 1) < elements.item (k) then
                Result := false
            end
        end
    ensure
        not Result implies
```

$$elements.item\ (k-1) < elements.item\ (k)$$
> **end** – – *ordered*
>
> **invariant**
>> *ordered*: *ordered*
>
> **end** – – class *ORDERED_LIST*

Summary

- Inheritance of assertions guarantees that the behavior of a class does not differ in unpredictable ways from that of its ancestors.
- The invariants of all the ancestors of a class apply to the class itself.
- Programming by sub-contract implies that a routine redefinition may only weaken the precondition or strengthen the postcondition.
- The pre- and postconditions for a routine redefinition are designated by the phrases **require else** and **ensure then** respectively.
- The precondition for a redefined routine is equivalent to the new precondition **or else** the original precondition. The default new precondition is **false**.
- The postcondition for a redefined routine is equivalent to the new postcondition **and then** the original postcondition. The default new postcondition is **true**.

Exercises

Consider the problem of maintaining a strictly ordered list of integers. In such a list, each element is exactly one more than the item preceding it. For example, "1, 2, 3" is a strictly ordered list, but "1, 3, 4" and "1, 2, 4" are not. The empty list is strictly ordered, as is any list with only one element.

Strictly_ordered is a Boolean function which returns true if and only if a list is strictly ordered. The precondition is simply **true**, while the postcondition ensures that if the function returns false then the list is not strictly ordered. The loop counter, k, is initialized to reference the first element in the list, while *Result* is initialized to true. The loop examines every pair of elements in turn until the end of the list is reached. If a pair is not in the correct relationship, then *Result* is set to false; otherwise, nothing is done. The invariant for the loop requires that k be within the valid range, and that if *Result* is false then the last pair of elements examined were in the incorrect relationship.

> *strictly_ordered*: *BOOLEAN* **is**
>> **local**
>>> *k*: *INTEGER*
>>
>> **do**
>>> **from**
>>>> $k := count - 1;$

```
                  Result := true
              invariant
                  k_big_enough: - 1 <= k;
                  k_small_enough: k < count;
                  correct_result:
                      not Result implies
                      elements.item (k - 1) + 1 /= elements.item (k - 2)
              variant
                  k + 1
              until
                  k <= 0 or not Result
              loop
                  . . .
              end
          ensure
              correct_result:
                  not Result implies
                  elements.item (k - 1) + 1 /= elements.item (k - 2)
          end - - strictly_ordered
```

1. Write a body for the above loop which correctly completes the definition of
    strictly_ordered.

    We can now define the class *STRICT_LIST* as a descendant of
    ORDERED_LIST; the main difference is that *STRICT_LIST* has a class invari-
    ant requiring that the list be strictly ordered. For the sake of clarity, the *make*
    and *insert* routines from *ORDERED_LIST* are renamed *ordered_make* and
    ordered_insert respectively. *STRICT_LIST* exports the routines *empty, full,
    first*, and *member*, which are inherited from *ORDERED_LIST* with no modi-
    fications. *Empty* and *full* return true when the list has no elements or no free
    space respectively, *first* returns the item at the beginning of the list, and
    member returns true when an item is already in the list. *STRICT_LIST* defines
    the exported features *last* and *strict_insert*. *Last* returns the element at the
    end of the list, while *strict_insert* places a new element into the list if possible.
    The Boolean function *strictly_ordered* returns true if and only if the list is
    strictly ordered; it is used in the class invariant.

```
    class STRICT_LIST
    inherit
        ORDERED_LIST [INTEGER]
            rename make as ordered_make,
                   insert as ordered_insert
    creation
```

```
    make
    feature {ANY}
        make (size: INTEGER) is do
            !! ordered_make (size)
            end -- make
        last: INTEGER is
            require
                not_empty: not empty
            do
                Result := elements.item (0)
            end -- last
        strict_insert (elem: INTEGER) is
            . . .
            end -- strict_insert
        strictly_ordered: BOOLEAN is
            . . .
            end -- strictly_ordered
    invariant
        . . .
    end -- class STRICT_LIST
```

2. Write a clause which completes the class invariant for *STRICT_LIST*.

   We can only insert particular items into a strictly ordered list. Specifically, the element to be inserted must either be one less than the first item on the list, or one more than the last item. Therefore, we cannot simply redefine the *insert* procedure from *ORDERED_LIST* in *STRICT_LIST*.

3. Why can't we simply redefine the *insert* procedure in *STRICT_LIST*? (*Hint:* What are the allowable modifications to pre- and postconditions when redefining a function?)

   We will define a procedure *strict_insert* to insert an item into a *STRICT_LIST*. The routine takes the element to be inserted as an argument, and the precondition requires that space for a new item be available. The routine will insert the new element if it is possible to do so and maintain strict ordering; otherwise, it will leave the list unchanged.

```
    strict_insert (elem: INTEGER) is
        require
            not_full: not full
        do
            . . .
        ensure
```

```
            . . .
    end -- strict_insert
```

4. Write a postcondition for the procedure. (*Hint:* The *good* function returns true if it is possible to insert an element and maintain strict ordering, while *last* returns the value of the last item in the list.)

```
    good (elem: INTEGER): BOOLEAN is
    do
        Result := empty
                    or else elem = first - 1
                    or elem = last + 1
        end -- good
    last: T is do Result := elements.item (0) end -- last
```

CHAPTER 17

Exceptions

Keywords

exception
organized panic
resumption,
propagation
rescue clause
retry instruction

Exceptions are generated when an assertion is violated at run-time. There are two acceptable responses. In an organized panic approach, a stable state is generated before the executing routine terminates signaling failure to its caller. In a resumption approach, the conditions that precipitated the violation are corrected and the routine is restarted from the beginning. Exceptions will propagate from routine to caller until the problem can be corrected, or the top level is reached and the system terminates. Control passes to the rescue clause when an exception is generated during execution of a routine. The clause then produces a stable state before signaling failure to the caller, or re-invoking the routine by executing a retry instruction. Rescue clauses are designated by the keyword **rescue**, and retry instructions consist of the keyword **retry**.

17.1 Introduction

We have seen how assertions can be used to describe the properties of programs in a way that supports the idea of programming by contract. We have also seen how the run-time monitoring of assertions can aid in the enforcement of these contracts and thereby enhance testing and debugging. We have learned that in Eiffel, an exception is raised when an assertion is violated at run-time, and that the default response to an exception is termination of the entire system with a message describing the location of the problem. While this response is satisfactory in many instances, it may have occurred to the reader that in some situations a different approach would be more appropriate. If a routine executes a component which fails (and thereby generates an exception), execution cannot precede as if nothing had happened; however, system termination is not always necessary. Sometimes, other plans can be made.

The general solution is to provide language constructs for processing exceptions. Ideally, this allows the problem which caused the exception to be corrected and execution to continue normally. When an exception has been raised, the contract between routine and caller has been violated. It is not acceptable to simply terminate silently with an error; the caller must be informed that the contracted work could not be completed. There are two acceptable responses to an exception. In organized panic, a stable state is generated before the routine terminates signaling failure to its caller. In resumption, the conditions that caused the problem are corrected and the routine is restarted from the beginning. Properly, routines must either fulfill their contracts or fail; there is no middle ground.

In general, exceptions will propagate from routine to caller until a level is found where the problem can be corrected, or the top level is reached and the entire system terminates. The action taken when an exception is triggered depends on whether the currently executing routine can discover and correct the underlying problem. If possible, the routine uses a resumption strategy; it corrects the problem and completes its execution successfully. If this is not possible, the routine uses organized panic; it generates a stable state and then signals failure to its caller. Failure of the called routine triggers an exception in the caller and the entire process repeats. In this manner, control is passed in a systematic way from routines to their callers until a way is found to correct the problem, or until the original program invocation is reached, at which point the entire system terminates.

Specifically, in Eiffel the rescue clause and retry instruction provide the necessary facilities for exception handling. Each routine may have a rescue clause which is executed when an exception is triggered during execution of the body. The rescue clause performs the actions necessary to produce a stable state before the routine terminates. If the conditions that caused the exception can be discovered and corrected, a retry instruction may be executed in the rescue clause, which will restart the routine at the beginning. Eiffel supports only the disciplined use of exceptions; routines must either satisfy their pre- and postconditions or notify their callers of the discrepancy.

Eiffel supports both organized panic and resumption strategies. Organized panic can be implemented using only a rescue clause, while a resumption approach also requires a retry instruction. Specifically, when an exception is triggered, the rescue clause associated with the current routine is first executed. If the rescue clause implements an organized panic approach, then it simply restores a stable state before the routine terminates signaling failure to the caller. This raises an exception in the caller and the entire process repeats. The default is for this process to continue until failure of the top-level call causes the system to terminate with a message describing the location of the problem. On the other hand, if the clause implements a resumption strategy, then it corrects the underlying problem and executes a retry instruction to restart the routine. If this strategy is successful, then the caller will never know that an exception occurred.

17.2   Rescue clauses

Ideally, certain processing should be performed whenever an exception occurs during a routine's execution. The object containing the routine should be restored to a stable state, whether an organized panic or resumption strategy is being used. A stable state should be established before the routine terminates and signals an error to its caller, because leaving the object in an inconsistent state complicates further processing. A stable state should be established before the routine is restarted, because correct execution of the routine depends on this assumption.

In Eiffel, the rescue clause allows the results of a partial execution to be cleaned up and a stable state to be restored before the routine terminates or is restarted. For example, the clause may contain instructions to restore data structures that were modified during the partial execution. This allows the caller to view an invocation of the routine as an "all or nothing" proposition; either the routine terminates normally, fulfilling the contract specified in the postcondition, or an exception is raised with no visible effects of the call.

In Eiffel, the rescue clause is designated by the keyword **rescue** and follows the body and postcondition for the routine.

```
    routine_name (arguments: TYPES) is
        require
            precondition
        local
            local_variables
        do
            routine_body
        ensure
            post_condition
        rescue
            rescue_clause
        end
```

To illustrate, consider a simple class that simulates a folding ruler. Such a ruler is hinged in the middle so that it can be used in either collapsed or expanded form. For example, if the ruler is six inches long folded, it would be 12 inches long unfolded. The class *FOLDING_RULER* exports the features *length*, *sections*, and *section_length*, which are the length, the number of sections in use, and the length of a ruler section respectively. It also provides the operations *fold* and *unfold*, which respectively reduce or increase the number of sections in use. The class has an invariant that requires the length of the ruler to be equal to the number of sections in use times the length of a section.

```
    class FOLDING_RULER
    feature {ANY}
        length: INTEGER;
```

```
        sections: INTEGER;
        section_length: INTEGER is 6;
        . . .
invariant
        consistent: length = sections * section_length
end -- class FOLDING_RULER
```

To illustrate the use of rescue clauses, let us consider the *unfold* routine from this class. The precondition for this procedure requires that the ruler is currently folded, while the postcondition ensures that both *length* and *sections* are increased by the proper amount. The rescue clause for the routine simply sets the length of the ruler to the length of a single section and the number of sections to one.

```
unfold is
    require
        folded: sections = 1
    do
            . . .
    ensure
        longer: length = old length + section_length;
        more_sections: sections = old sections + 1
    rescue
        length := section_length;
        sections := 1
    end -- unfold
```

In Eiffel, the rescue clause is executed whenever an exception is triggered during execution of the routine body, including violation of the postcondition. When the rescue clause executes to completion, the routine terminates and an exception is triggered for the caller. Since the call may have originated from outside the object, the rescue clause should always restore the class invariant.

To illustrate, let us again consider the *unfold* procedure for *FOLD-ING_RULER*. Suppose the postcondition for *unfold* is violated and an exception is raised. The rescue clause is executed before the routine terminates and an exception is triggered in its caller. The rescue clause sets *length* and *sections* to *section_length* and one respectively. This restores the class invariant and ensures that the caller of *unfold* will see a stable state for *FOLDING_RULER*. Therefore, the caller can view *unfold* as an all-or-nothing operation; either *unfold* completes with the postcondition true, or it fails with no visible effects.

As a more complex illustration, consider the problem of maintaining an ordered list with no duplicates. We will define a class *NODUP_LIST* as a descendant of *ORDERED_LIST* and have it export roughly the same operations. The main difference is that *NODUP_LIST* has a class invariant requiring that no two elements in the list are identical.

Unfortunately, we cannot simply redefine the insert operation in the class. If we insert an element already present into a *NODUP_LIST*, then we will invalidate the class invariant. We could avoid this situation by strengthening the precondition for insert (on *NODUP_LIST*) to require that the new element not already be present, but this violates our rule that redefinition can only weaken the precondition for a routine. Similarly, we could weaken the postcondition so that a *NODUP_LIST* would simply be unchanged by an attempt to insert a duplicate element, but our rules require that redefinition only strengthen postconditions. Therefore, we will define a new procedure, *nodup_insert*, which inserts an item into a *NODUP_LIST*. For the sake of clarity, the insert routine from *ORDERED_LIST* will be renamed as *ordered_insert*.

```
class NODUP_LIST [T -> COMPARABLE]
inherit
    ORDERED_LIST [T]
        rename insert as ordered_insert
creation
    make
feature {ANY}
    . . .
invariant
    no_duplicates: no_duplicates
end -- NODUP_LIST
```

NODUP_LIST defines a Boolean function *no_duplicates* which returns true only if each element in the list is unique. *No_duplicates* has a precondition of **true**, and its postcondition requires that if the function returns false then the last two elements examined are identical. The body of the routine consists of a single loop. The function return value is initialized to true, and each pair of elements in the list is examined in turn. If the pair is equal, then *Result* is set to false; otherwise nothing is done. The invariant for the loop states that the loop counter (k) is between one and *count* plus one, and that if *Result* is false then the last two elements examined were duplicates.

```
no_duplicates: BOOLEAN is
    local
        k: INTEGER
    do
        from
            Result := true;
            k := 1
        invariant
            k_big_enough: 1 <= k;
```

```
            k_small_enough: k <= count + 1;
            correct_result:
                not Result implies
                    elements.item (k – 1).Equal (elements.item (k – 2))
        variant
            count – k + 1
        until
            k >= count or not Result
        loop
            if elements.item (k).Equal (elements.item (k – 1))
                then Result := false end;
            k := k + 1
        end
    ensure
        correct_result:
            not Result implies
                elements.item (k – 1).Equal (elements.item (k – 2))
    end – – no_duplicates
```

To illustrate the use of rescue clauses, consider a routine that attempts to insert an element into a *NODUP_LIST*. The procedure *try_insert* takes the element to be inserted as an argument. Its precondition requires that space be available in the list, while its postcondition ensures that the element has been inserted, but is not a duplicate. The body of the routine simply calls the *insert* routine from *ORDERED_LIST*. Specifically, the new element is inserted at position *location* plus one by *ordered_insert*. If an element with the same value was already present, then it will be at position *location*. The postcondition ensures that this possibility has not occurred, and the rescue clause for the procedure removes the duplicate element if necessary.

For our present purpose, we will assume that *ordered_insert* either inserts the element in question, or fails leaving the original list unchanged. Therefore, the postcondition for *try_insert* can be violated in two different ways. If *ordered_insert* succeeds, but inserts a duplicate element, then an item must be removed from the list. On the other hand, if *ordered_insert* fails, then the new element is not a member of the list and no further action is possible. Therefore, the body of the rescue clause for *try_insert* consists of an *if* statement which branches on the presence of a duplicate element in the list. The code to remove the duplicate element consists of a single loop and an assignment. The loop starts at the duplicate element and moves each element up one location until the front of the list is reached. The assignment then reduces the number of valid elements in the list by one.

```
    try_insert (elem: T) is
        require
```

```
            not_full: not full
local
    k: INTEGER
do
    ordered_insert (elem)
ensure
    is_member: member (elem);
    not_duplicate:
        location = - 1 or else
        not elements.item (location).Equal (
            elements.item (location + 1))
rescue
    if location >= 0 and then
        elements.item (location).Equal (
        elements.item (location + 1)) then
        from
            k := location + 1
        invariant
            k_big_enough: location < k;
            k_small_enough: k <= count
        variant
            count - k
        until
            k = count - 1
        loop
            elements.put (elements.item (k + 1), k);
            k := k + 1
        end
        count := count - 1
    end
end -- try_insert
```

To better understand the operation of this routine, we will consider two cases. In both instances, assume that pre- and postconditions are being monitored at run-time, and that the precondition for *try_insert* evaluates to true. First, suppose we call *try_insert* with an element that is not a member of the current list. The body of *try_insert* first calls *ordered_insert*, which successfully inserts the element at position *location*, and then the postcondition for *try_insert* is evaluated. Both the *is_member* and *not_duplicate* clauses evaluate to true, so the procedure terminates normally.

On the other hand, suppose we call *try_insert* with an element that is already a member of the current list. As before, the body of the procedure first calls *ordered_insert* which successfully inserts the element at position *location*. Then, the postcondition for *try_insert* is evaluated. The *is_member* clause evaluates to true, but the *not_duplicate* clause evaluates to false as the items at positions *location* and *location* plus one are identical. Therefore, an exception is raised and the rescue clause for *try_insert* is executed. The condition of the *if* statement evaluates to true, so the code to remove a duplicate element is executed. The loop begins with the duplicate element and moves each item up one position until the front of the list is reached. This eliminates the duplicate entry, and so when the assignment corrects *count* a stable state has been produced. At this point, the rescue clause terminates without having executed a retry instruction; therefore, execution of the routine is complete and *try_insert* terminates signaling failure to its caller.

17.3   Retry instructions

Rescue clauses allow the restoration of a stable state before a routine terminates signaling failure to its caller. In many situations this is all that can be accomplished; however, in some cases, it is possible to discover and correct the cause of the exception at run-time. In these cases, we would like to use a resumption strategy: make the necessary adjustments and then restart the routine to run to completion. In Eiffel, the retry instruction provides this capability. It consists of the single keyword **retry** and may only appear in a rescue clause.

To illustrate, consider the *nodup_insert* routine from *NODUP_LIST*. This procedure takes the element to be inserted as a parameter. The precondition for the routine requires that space be available for the new element, while the postcondition ensures that the element is a member of the list, and that only elements and count have been changed during the execution. The body of *nodup_insert* consists of a single *if* statement which branches on the Boolean variable *already_tried*. If *already_tried* is false (the first time through the body), then *try_insert* is called with the new element as an argument; otherwise (the second time), nothing is done. The routine has a rescue clause consisting of a single *if* statement. If *already_tried* is false and the new element is already a member of the list (first try failed because element is already a member), then *already_tried* is set to true and the routine is restarted.

```
    nodup_insert (elem: T) is
        require
            not_full: not full
        local
            already_tried: BOOLEAN
        do
            if not already_tried then
                try_insert (elem)
            end
        ensure
```

```
            is_member: member (elem);
            no_extra_changes:
                    equal (strip (elements, count),
                        old strip (elements, count))
        rescue
            if not already_tried and member (elem) then
                already_tried := true;
                retry
            end
        end -- nodup_insert
```

When a retry instruction is executed, it causes the routine that contains it to restart at the beginning; therefore, both the precondition and the class invariant should be true before it is invoked. Local variables are not reinitialized before the restart, but the precondition may be rechecked. Use of the retry instruction does not guarantee successful execution of the routine. New exceptions may be generated and must be handled as before.

To illustrate, let us again consider the *nodup_insert* routine. To better understand the operation of this procedure, we will consider three cases. In all instances, assume that pre- and postconditions are being monitored at run-time. Furthermore, assume that space is available to insert the new element into the list; therefore, the preconditions for *nodup_insert* and *try_insert* both evaluate to true. First, suppose that we call *nodup_insert* with an item that is not presently a member of the list in question. When the routine is invoked, *already_tried* is initialized to false; therefore, *try_insert* is called with the new element as an argument. *Try_insert* successfully inserts the new element into the list; therefore, the postcondition for *nodup_insert* evaluates to true, and the procedure terminates normally.

Second, suppose that we call *nodup_insert* with an item that is already a member of the list. Execution proceeds as before, and *try_insert* is called with the new element as an argument; however, in this case *try_insert* fails and an exception is generated. *Try_insert* produces a stable state before terminating; the rescue clause ensures that the list is the same as before the routine was invoked. When *try_insert* terminates, the rescue clause for *nodup_insert* is invoked. At this point, *already_tried* is false and the item is a member of the list; therefore, *already_tried* is set to true and the retry instruction restarts *nodup_insert* from the beginning. This time *try_insert* is not executed, the body of *nodup_insert* terminates normally, the postcondition evaluates to true, and the routine successfully completes its execution.

Third, suppose we call *nodup_insert* with an item that is not already a member of the list, but will cause *try_insert* to fail (for some mysterious reason, *try_insert* cannot add the element, but it will leave the list unchanged). In this case, execution proceeds as in the previous example until the rescue clause for *nodup_insert* is executed. Since the item in question was not originally a member of the list, and *try_insert* failed leaving the list unchanged, the item is currently not a member of the list. Therefore, the condition of the *if* statement in the rescue clause evaluates to false, the instructions inside the *if* statement are not performed, the rescue clause completes without executing a retry, and *nodup_insert* terminates signaling failure to its caller.

In all three cases, exceptions are used in a disciplined manner; *nodup_insert* either satisfies the contract defined by its pre- and postconditions, or notifies its caller of the discrepancy. In Eiffel, the rescue clause and retry instruction provide a powerful, elegant system for run-time exception handling.

17.4   An example class: *NODUP_LIST*

We can now examine the code for the entire *NODUP_LIST* class. *NODUP_LIST* is a descendant of *ORDERED_LIST*; therefore, the elements in the list are kept in ascending order. *NODUP_LIST* exports the routines *empty*, *full*, *first*, *nodup_insert*, *delete*, and *member*; all but *nodup_insert* are inherited from *ORDERED_LIST* with no modifications. *Empty* and *full* return true if the list has no elements or no free space respectively. *First* returns the element at the front of the list, *nodup_insert* puts an item into its correct position in the list (if it is not already present), *delete* removes the element at the front of the list, and *member* returns true if an item is already present in the list. For the sake of clarity, *NODUP_LIST* renames the *insert* routine from *ORDERED_LIST* as *ordered_insert*.

NODUP_LIST has an invariant requiring that no two elements in the list are identical. For this purpose, it defines a Boolean function *no_duplicates* which returns true only if each element in the list is unique. *No_duplicates* has a precondition of **true**, and its postcondition requires that if the function returns false then the last two elements examined are identical. The body of the routine consists of a single loop. The function return value is initialized to true, and each pair of elements in the list is examined in turn. If the pair is equal, then *Result* is set to false; otherwise nothing is done.

NODUP_LIST defines a procedure *try_insert* which attempts to add an element to the list. The precondition for *try_insert* requires that space be available in the list, while the postcondition ensures that the element has been inserted, but is not a duplicate. Specifically, the new element is inserted at position *location* plus one by *ordered_insert*. If an element with the same value was already present, then it will be at position *location*. The postcondition for *try_insert* ensures that this possibility has not occurred, and the rescue clause for the procedure removes the duplicate element if necessary.

The postcondition for *try_insert* can be violated in two distinct ways. If *ordered_insert* adds a duplicate element, then an item must be removed from the list. On the other hand, if *ordered_insert* fails to add the new element and it is not already a member of the list, then no further action is possible. Therefore, the rescue clause for *try_insert* consists of an *if* statement on the presence of a duplicate element in the list. The code to remove the duplicate element consists of a single loop and an assignment. The loop starts at the duplicate element and moves each element up one location until the front of the list is reached. The assignment then reduces the number of valid elements in the list by one.

The *nodup_insert* procedure takes the element to be inserted as a parameter. The precondition requires that space be available for the new element, while the postcondition ensures that the element is a member of the list, and that only *count* and *elements* were changed by the procedure. The body of *nodup_insert* consists of an *if* statement on the Boolean *already_tried*. If *already_tried* is false (the first time through the body), then *try_insert* is called with the new element as an argument; otherwise (the second time) nothing is done. The routine has a rescue clause consisting of a single *if* statement. If *already_tried* is false and the new element is already a member of the list (first time failed because already present), then *already_tried* is set to true and the routine is restarted.

```
class NODUP_LIST [T -> COMPARABLE]
inherit
    ORDERED_LIST [T]
        rename insert as ordered_insert
creation
    make
feature {ANY}
    make (size: INTEGER) is do
        !! list_make (size)
        end -- make
    try_insert (elem: T) is
        require
            not_full: not full
        local
            k: INTEGER
        do
            ordered_insert (elem)
        ensure
            is_member: member (elem);
            not_duplicate:
                location = - 1 or else
                not elements.item (location).Equal (
                    elements.item (location + 1))
        rescue
            if location >= 0 and then
                elements.item (location).Equal (
                elements.item (location + 1)) then
                from
                    k := location + 1
                invariant
                    k_big_enough: location < k;
                    k_small_enough: k <= count
```

```
                    variant
                        count − k
                    until
                        k = count − 1
                    loop
                        elements.put (elements.item (k + 1), k);
                        k := k + 1
                    end
                    count := count − 1
            end
        end −− try_insert
    nodup_insert (elem: T) is
        require
            not_full: not full
        local
            already_tried: BOOLEAN
        do
            if not already_tried then
                try_insert (elem)
            end
        ensure
            is_member: member (elem);
            no_extra_changes:
                equal (strip (elements, count),
                    old strip (elements, count))
        rescue
            if not already_tried and member (elem) then
                already_tried := true;
                retry
            end
        end −− nodup_insert
    no_duplicates: BOOLEAN is
        local
            k: INTEGER
        do
            from
                Result := true;
                k := 1
            invariant
                k_big_enough: 1 <= k;
```

```
                    k_small_enough: k <= count + 1;
                    correct_result:
                        not Result implies
                        elements.item (k - 1).Equal (elements.item (k - 2))
                variant
                    count - k + 1
                until
                    k >= count or not Result
                loop
                    if elements.item (k).Equal (elements.item (k - 1))
                        then Result := false end;
                    k := k + 1
                end
            ensure
                correct_result:
                    not Result implies
                    elements.item (k - 1).Equal (elements.item (k - 2))
            end - - no_duplicates
    invariant
        no_duplicates: no_duplicates
    end - - class NODUP_LIST
```

17.5 Discussion

Exceptions are an extremely powerful mechanism, and as such should be used sparingly. They are not a technique for dealing with uncommon (but acceptable) cases. They should be reserved for unpredictable events, untestable preconditions, and protection against errors remaining in software. The programs in this chapter are not examples of the ideal use of exceptions; they simply illustrate the exception mechanism in Eiffel. In general, exception handlers should be simple. They should contain the minimum code necessary to restore a stable state and terminate or restart the routine. Complex algorithms for unusual cases should be placed in the routine body rather than in the rescue clause. Exceptions are ideal for a situation such as an "out of memory" error on attempted object creation. Checking before each operation would be extremely expensive, and failure of the operation is unusual; therefore, it is an ideal situation to be handled in a rescue clause.

Summary

- Exceptions are generated when an assertion is violated at run-time and when the hardware or operating system signals an error.

- Exceptions should be used sparingly. They should be reserved for unpredictable events, untestable preconditions, and protection against errors remaining in software.
- There are two acceptable responses to an exception. Either achieve a stable state and signal failure, or change the conditions that caused the problem and retry.
- The rescue clause for a routine defines the actions to be taken when an exception occurs during its execution.
- The retry instruction may be used in a rescue clause to re-invoke the routine. The routine fails if the rescue clause terminates without executing a retry.
- The rescue clause should establish both the routine precondition and the class invariant before executing a retry. It should establish the class invariant before terminating in any case.
- The rescue/retry mechanism guarantees that a routine will only terminate by executing its body to normal completion or by signaling failure to its caller.

Exercises

Consider the class *STRICT_LIST* developed in the exercises for the previous chapter. We will define a routine *just_insert* which simply calls the insert routine from *ORDERED_LIST*. The precondition requires that the new element can be inserted while maintaining strict ordering.

```
just_insert (elem: INTEGER) is
    require

        . . .

    do
        ordered_insert (elem)
    end -- just_insert
```

1. Write a precondition for *just_insert*. (*Hint:* The *good* function returns true if it is possible to insert an element and maintain strict ordering.)

```
good (elem: INTEGER): BOOLEAN is do
    Result := empty
                or else elem = first - 1
                or  elem = last + 1
    end -- good
```

The *strict_insert* procedure inserts a new element into a *STRICT_LIST*. The routine takes the element to be inserted as an argument, and the precondition requires that space for a new item be available. The postcondition ensures that either the new element is a member of the list, or the insertion was not possible and the list is unchanged. The body of the routine consists of an *if* statement on the Boolean *already_tried*. If *already_tried* is false (the body is being executed for the first time), then *just_insert* is called with the item to be inserted; otherwise (the second time) nothing is done. The rescue clause for the routine also consists of an *if* statement on *already_tried*. The first time the rescue clause is executed, *already_tried* is set to true and the routine is restarted; the second time, nothing is done.

```
    strict_insert (elem: INTEGER) is
        require
            not_full not full
        local
            already_tried: BOOLEAN
        do
            if not already_tried then just_insert (elem) end
        ensure
            member_if_possible: member (elem) or not good (elem)
        rescue
            if not already_tried then

                . . .

            end
        end -- strict_insert
```

2. Write a body for the above *if* statement that correctly completes the definition of *strict_insert*.
3. Does the rescue clause for *strict_insert* have to restore the class invariant? Which class invariants are involved? (*Hint:* Which classes are ancestors of *STRICT_LIST*?)
4. What must be true before a retry instruction is executed in the rescue clause for *strict_insert*?

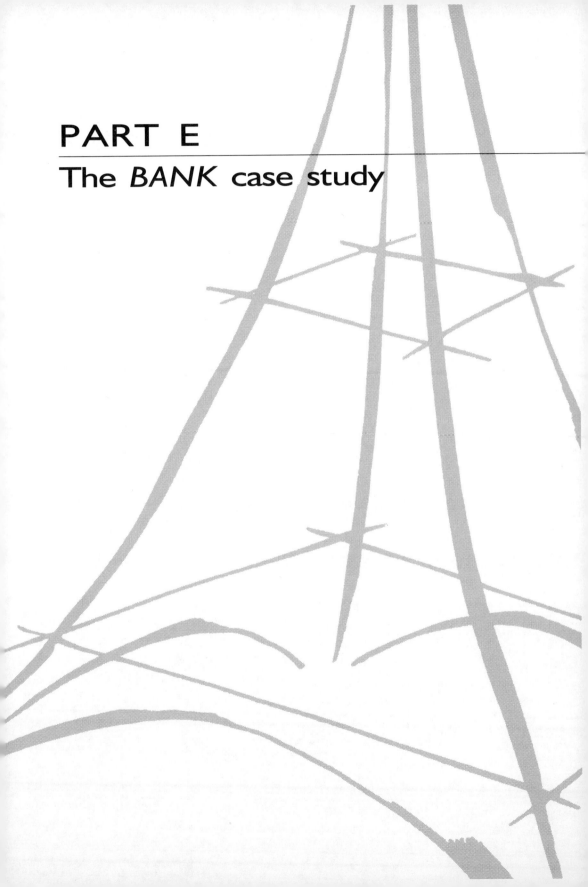

PART E
The *BANK* case study

1 A class: *ACCOUNT*

1.1 Specification

Money is deposited into and withdrawn from a bank account, and the balance
can be displayed. Interest is added daily on the current balance; the interest rate
is 4.5 percent a year.

1.2 Analysis

There is only a single object in this system, an instance of class *ACCOUNT*. The
data in an account are the balance and the interest rate. The three stated goals
are to deposit, withdraw, and show the balance. The routines to deposit and
withdraw receive a single argument, the amount of money to be added or
subtracted from the balance. For all this to happen, an account must be created
in the first place. We have added a display routine to help with debugging.

The public features are exported to class *CUSTOMER*, the client of this class.

1.3 Design

The client and system structure charts for this system are shown below; because
there is only a single class defined in this first version of the system, the charts
are extremely simple. The client chart for the single class *ACCOUNT* is

In a system structure (sS) chart, the classes are listed across the top of the

347

figure, and the system goals along the left-hand side. The goals in a system are identified by asking, "What does the system do?", and grouping the plan for each goal into a set of routines; goals are always verbs. The objects in the system can be identified by asking, "What data does the system use?" and grouping the data into objects; an object is always a noun.

The plan to add interest has been separated into two parts: a function that returns the daily interest rate, and a procedure that calculates the daily interest and adds it to the balance. Private features are usually not shown on a sS chart, because the chart captures only the external data flow. The node and its data flow have been shown in the chart below, because the system is very simple; for larger systems, internal features are not shown. The sS chart showing the system goals, classes, and data flow for each exported feature of the *ACCOUNT* class is shown below.

ACCOUNT

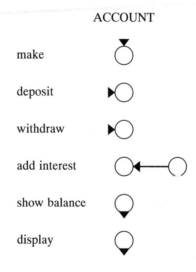

make

deposit

withdraw

add interest

show balance

display

1.4   **Solution code**

```
class ACCOUNT
creation
    make
feature {NONE}
    balance: REAL
    interest_rate: REAL is 4.5
feature {CUSTOMER}
    make is
            -- set the initial balance
        do
            io.putstring (" Initial account balance: ")
            io.readreal
            balance := io.lastreal
        end -- make
    display is
            -- show the balance and interest_rate
        do
            io.putstring ("%NThe balance is: ")
            io.putreal (balance)
            io.putstring ("%NThe interest rate is: ")
            io.putreal (interest_rate)
        end -- display
    deposit (amount: REAL) is
            -- add this amount to the balance
        do
            balance := balance + amount
        end -- deposit
    withdraw (amount: REAL) is
            -- subtract this amount from the balance
        do
            balance := balance - amount
        end -- deposit
    show_balance is
            -- display the balance
        do
            io.putstring ("%NThe current balance is ")
            io.putreal (balance)
        end -- show_balance
```

```
    add_interest is
                -- add the daily interest to the balance
        do
            balance := balance + balance * day_rate
        end -- add_interest
feature {NONE}
    day_rate: REAL is
                -- daily interest rate
        do
            Result := (interest_rate / 100.0) / 365.25
        end -- day_rate
end -- class ACCOUNT
```

2 A system: *BANK, CUSTOMER,* and *ACCOUNT*

2.1   Specification

Build a complete, simple, banking system that uses the class *ACCOUNT* developed in the previous chapter, by adding a customer and a root class *BANK* for the system. A customer has a name, sex, address, and a bank account. For this version of the banking system, the customer executes a single transaction of each type: deposit, withdraw, show balance, and add interest.

2.2   Analysis

When an OO system is extended, no code should be rewritten. Code is added to implement the new goals, and the calling structure may be changed, but no existing code should be changed. This is the meaning of reuse: you don't rewrite code, just pick up the existing code and reuse it. This is not always possible, because it is not always possible to decompose the task correctly into small pieces, but it should happen most of the time. If you find yourself continually changing code, then your original design was not decomposed enough. In the case study developed in this book, new code is added for each extension.

A customer has four attributes: the name, sex, address, and account. The code to set and use these attributes should be placed with the data, in class *CUSTOMER*. The root class for the system, class *BANK*, creates a customer, and then forces the customer to use the account. The customer thus has a *make* routine and a *use* feature, which are called directly from the class *BANK*.

2.3   Design

The customer has to be created by a creation routine which sets the customer attributes and creates an account for the customer. The customer has an account, so the account is an attribute of class *CUSTOMER*. Once the customer has been created, a transaction of each type is executed on the account. The global structure of the class *CUSTOMER* is thus a creation routine, and another routine to execute the transactions. A root class *BANK* is needed to call these two routines in *CUSTOMER*, and to add interest to the account. The root class *BANK* contains a single, simple creation routine to create the customer, force a series of transactions, and add interest to the account.

A customer has an account, and uses the services provided by that account. The class *BANK* is the root module, which drives the whole system. The client chart is

Each node in a sS chart represents one or more routines. The control flow (feature calls) between classes is shown by a horizontal line, and sequence within a class is shown by a vertical line. A circle at the left of the chart is the initial call to a routine which starts the plan for that goal; nodes within a plan contain both the called code and the call to the next class; and nodes at the right of the chart are terminal features, which define the basic actions and call nothing else.

The sS chart for this version of the *BANK* system is shown on the next page. The bank creates a customer, the customer creates an account, and the customer and account are displayed. The bank then forces the customer to use the account by executing one transaction of each type. Interest is then added to the account.

The new nodes in the system that are added in this part of the case study are indicated by a star next to the node. No change has been made to class *ACCOUNT*. Two classes have been added to the system.

BANK   CUSTOMER ACCOUNT

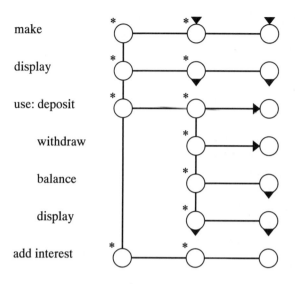

The routines to deposit, withdraw, and show the balance are called by the customer. The bank creates the customer and account first, uses the customer, and adds interest to the account. Adding interest to the account is not under the control of the customer.

2.4   Solution code

The solution code for this version of the banking system is shown below, in client chart order. When listing code, it is normal to show the code in client order, by listing the calling code before the code that is called. The listing order is *BANK*, then *CUSTOMER*, then *ACCOUNT*. There is no change to the class *ACCOUNT*; the code is included here to show a complete system. Each class is shown on a separate page in this part of the case study.

```
class BANK
creation
    make
feature {NONE}
    patron: CUSTOMER
    make is
            -- create and use a customer
        do
            !!patron.make
            patron.display
            patron.use
            patron.add_interest
        end -- make
end -- class BANK
```

```
class CUSTOMER
creation {BANK}
    make
feature {NONE}
    name: STRING
    sex: CHARACTER
    address: STRING
    account: ACCOUNT
feature {BANK}
    make is
            -- create the customer by getting data from the user
        do
            io.putstring ("%NEnter the customer details%N")
            io.putstring (" %N Name: ")
            io.readline
            name := io.laststring
            io.putstring (" Sex (M/F): ")
            io.readchar
            sex := io.lastchar
            io.putstring (" Address: ")
            io.readline
            address := io.laststring
            !!account.make
        end -- make
    display is
            -- show the customer details
        do
            io.new_line
            io.putstring (name)
            io.putstring (" of sex ")
            io.putchar (sex)
            io.putstring (" lives at ")
            io.putstring (address)
            account.display
        end -- display
    use is
            -- deposit, withdraw, show balance, display the account
        do
            account.deposit (2000.0)
            account.withdraw (5.0)
```

```
                account.show_balance
                account.display
        end -- use
    add_interest is
                -- add interest to the account
        do
                account.add_interest
        end -- add_interest
    end -- class CUSTOMER
```

```
class ACCOUNT
creation {CUSTOMER}
    make
feature {NONE}
    balance: REAL
    interest_rate: REAL is 4.5
feature {CUSTOMER}
    make is
                -- set the initial balance
        do
            io.putstring (" Initial account balance: ")
            io.readreal
            balance := io.lastreal
        end -- make
    display is
                -- show the balance and interest_rate
        do
            io.putstring ("%NThe balance is: ")
            io.putreal (balance)
            io.putstring ("%NThe interest rate is: ")
            io.putreal (interest_rate)
        end -- display
    deposit (amount: REAL) is
                -- add this amount to the balance
        do
            balance := balance + amount
        end -- deposit
    withdraw (amount: REAL) is
                -- subtract this amount from the balance
        do
            balance := balance - amount
        end -- withdraw
    show_balance is
                -- display the balance
        do
            io.putstring ("%NThe current balance is ")
            io.putreal (balance)
        end -- show_balance
    add_interest is
                -- add the daily interest to the balance
```

```
        do
                balance := balance + balance * day_rate
            end -- add_interest
feature {NONE}
    day_rate: REAL is
                    -- daily interest rate
            do
                Result := (interest_rate / 100.0) / 365.25
            end -- day_rate
end -- class ACCOUNT
```

3 Selection and iteration

Extend the *BANK* system by adding a password to login to the system, and a menu-based interface to the account; these additions simulate an automatic teller machine (ATM).

The system starts up, creates a single customer, and waits for the customer to enter their password. The customer is allowed three attempts to enter a valid password. If no correct password is entered after three attempts, then the system terminates. If the password is correct, then a menu of account choices is shown, and the system reads and executes the customer's choice. Any number of transactions may be made; processing on the account continues until the customer chooses to exit the system. Interest is then added to the account for the customer.

The valid menu choices (upper or lower case) for the customer are

D, d	Deposit
W, w	Withdraw up to the total amount in the account
B, b	Show the balance
Q, q	Quit the system
H, h	Help: Show the menu choices

The existing code in the *ACCOUNT*, *CUSTOMER*, and *BANK* classes is changed as little as possible; it is just used in a different way in the new system. New classes have to be added for the *PASSWORD* and perhaps for the menu, and code has to be added to existing routines to use these new classes. Code is reused when an OO system is modified, not rewritten.

Password processing looks like a good candidate for a class, because the password has to be stored and tested. The key data that defines the object is the stored password. There are three obvious features: the password, a *make* routine to store the password, and a *login* routine to compare the user input to the stored password. The user is allowed three attempts to input the correct password. If the correct password is input, then the system proceeds to the user menu; otherwise the system exits immediately.

The menu could be an object, although the situation is not as clear. A menu prompts the user for a choice, validates the user's reply, and then executes the valid choice. These operations (get choice, execute choice) are enclosed in a loop so that the customer can perform multiple transactions on the account. The menu choice is at the heart of the menu, but this choice is not stored; choices are made and executed, but need not be stored. The menu thus encapsulates a series of operations, but does not encapsulate any stored data.

3.3   Design

The menu is concerned with interface details that are not central to an account, so it should be separate from class *ACCOUNT*. There are many ways to access an account, such as a character-based menu, a graphics interface, or a special ATM machine, so the interface should be kept separate. For this version of the system, the menu is implemented as a client of *ACCOUNT* and a supplier to class *CUSTOMER*, because the customer uses the menu to use the account. The correct way to implement the menu is to use an inherited class *MENU*, but that solution cannot be presented until Section 7 of the case study.

Some of the menu choices require the account to be used or modified, so these choices need to call code in class *ACCOUNT*. Other choices, such as the choice to show the menu and exit from the system, do not use the account.

The rules for withdrawing from an account have been changed, so the withdraw routine in the *ACCOUNT* has to be changed. The new version of the *BANK* system has an extra class for the *PASSWORD* and *MENU*, and added code for testing the amount before money is withdrawn from an *ACCOUNT*.

The client chart for this version of the system is shown on the next page. The bank has a single customer, who has a single account. The customer must enter a correct password before getting access to the account menu, then the menu has control of how the account is used. At the end of processing, the bank adds interest to the account, via the customer.

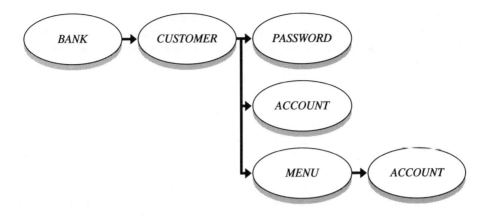

The system structure for this version of the system is shown below, where the new parts of the system are starred. An object for the bank's single customer is made initially, then the system waits for the user to arrive. To use the system, the customer logs into the system and is presented with the account menu. The menu reads and executes choices until the customer exits the system, when interest is added by the bank and the system exits.

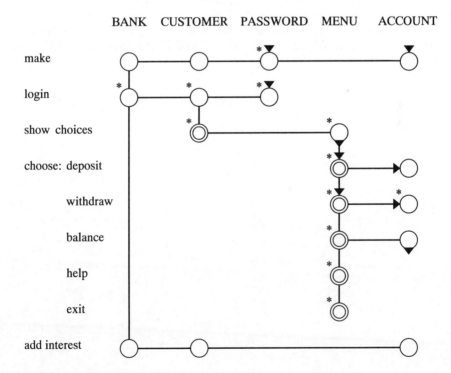

The order in which events happen in the system can be read directly from the system structure chart, by tracing through the control flow shown there. Feature calls between classes are shown by horizontal lines; sequence within a class is shown by vertical lines.

Goal selection is shown by a double circle in a node. The customer has to login before they can use their account. The code to read the password at login is contained in class *PASSWORD*. If the customer successfully logs in, then the menu choices are shown and the menu starts. A choice then has to be made for the menu option, shown by the set of alternate nodes in the menu; the choice is shown by the data input on the first of the alternate choices. For deposit and withdraw, an amount also has to be supplied by the customer. The amount is read in by code in class *MENU* and passed to the appropriate account routine. Two inputs are thus indicated by the first data arrow on the selection node in class *MENU*, one input to make the choice and another input for the first choice, *deposit*.

Two new classes have been added in this part of the case study. Within class *ACCOUNT*, a single feature has been added to check the balance before a withdrawal. The routines to display an object have been omitted from the chart for simplicity, because *display* is used for debugging and is not a system goal defined in the specification.

3.4   Solution code

The code for the new classes *PASSWORD* and *MENU* is shown on the next page. The code in the classes *BANK* and *CUSTOMER* is also shown, both the existing and the new code. A single feature is shown for class *ACCOUNT*, because the rest of the class code is unchanged and is listed in previous parts of the case study.

```
class BANK
creation
    make
feature {NONE}
    richie: CUSTOMER
    make is
                -- make the single customer
                -- get the customer to login and use the ATM
                -- add interest to their account
        do
            !!richie.make
            richie.login
            richie.add_interest
        end -- make
end -- class BANK
```

```
class CUSTOMER
creation {BANK}
    make
feature {NONE}
    name, address: STRING
    sex: CHARACTER
    password: PASSWORD
    account: ACCOUNT
    menu: MENU
feature {BANK}
    make is
            -- set the customer details
        do
            io.putstring ("%NEnter the customer details%N")
            io.putstring (" %N Name: ")
            io.readline
            name := io.laststring
            get_sex
            sex := io.lastchar
            io.putstring (" Address: ")
            io.readline
            address := io.laststring
            !!password.make
            !!account.make
        end -- make
feature {NONE}
    get_sex is
            -- loop until the user enters a valid gender
        do
            from
                io.putstring (" Sex (M/F): ")
                io.readchar
            until valid_gender
            loop
                io.putstring ("Invalid sex code. Valid codes are M, m, F,
                f. Try again%N")
                io.putstring (" Sex (M/F): ")
                io.readchar
            end
        end -- get_sex
```

```
        valid_gender: BOOLEAN is
                -- has a valid sex code been entered?
            do
                inspect io.lastchar
                when 'M', 'm', 'F', 'f' then Result := true
                else Result := false
                end
            end -- valid_gender
feature {BANK}
    display is
                -- show the customer's personal details
            do
                print_title
                io.putstring (name)
                io.putstring (" lives at ")
                io.putstring (address)
                io.new_line
                account.display
            end -- display
    login is
                -- if the customer enters the valid password
                -- then start the ATM menu
            do
                password.login
                if password.valid then !!menu.make (account)
                else io.putstring ("Login failure. Exiting system%N")
                end
            end -- login
    add_interest is
                -- add interest to the account
            do
                account.add_interest
            end -- add_interest
feature {NONE}
    print_title is
                -- be polite
            do
                inspect sex
                when 'M', 'm' then io.putstring ("%NMr. ")
                when 'F', 'f' then io.putstring ("%NMs. ")
```

```
            end
        end -- print_title
    end -- class CUSTOMER
```

```
class PASSWORD
creation {CUSTOMER}
    make
feature {NONE}
    password: STRING
    tries: INTEGER
    max_tries: INTEGER is 3
feature {CUSTOMER}
    make is
                -- set the password
        do
            io.putstring (" Password: ")
            io.readword
            password := io.laststring
        end -- make
    login is
                -- attempt to get a valid password
        do
            from get_word
            until valid or failure
            loop
                io.putstring ("Incorrect password. Try again%N")
                get_word
            end
        end -- login
    valid: BOOLEAN is
            -- is the input word the password?
        do
            Result := io.laststring.is_equal (password)
        end -- valid
    failure: BOOLEAN is
            -- has the password been tried too many times?
        do
            Result := tries = max_tries
        end -- failure
feature {NONE}
    get_word is
            -- read in a password, add 1 to the number of
            attempts
        do
```

```
            io.putstring ("%NPlease enter the password: ")
            io.readword
            tries := tries + 1
        end -- get_word
end -- class PASSWORD
```

```
class MENU
creation {CUSTOMER}
    make
feature {NONE}
    account: ACCOUNT
feature {CUSTOMER}
    make (acc: ACCOUNT) is
                -- store the account, display the menu
                -- get and execute menu choices
        do
                account := acc
                from show_choices
                until end_chosen
                loop
                    get_choice
                    do_choice
                end
                io.putstring ("%NY'all have a nice day, hear%N")
        end -- make
feature {NONE}
    get_choice is
                -- get a valid menu choice from the user
        do
                from
                    io.putstring ("%NEnter menu choice: ")
                    io.readchar
                until valid_choice
                loop
                    io.putstring ("That is not a valid choice. Try again%N")
                    io.putstring ("The valid choices are D, W, B, Q, and
                    H%N")
                    io.putstring ("%NEnter menu choice: ")
                    io.readchar
                end
        end -- get_choice
    valid_choice: BOOLEAN is
                -- has the user entered a valid choice?
        do
                inspect io.lastchar
                when 'D', 'd', 'W', 'w', 'B', 'b', 'Q', 'q', 'H', 'h' then
```

```
                    Result := true
             else Result := false
             end
      end -- valid_choice
do_choice is
      -- execute the choice made by the user
   do
      inspect io.lastchar
      when 'D', 'd' then
         io.putstring ("Enter the amount to deposit: ")
         io.readreal
         account.deposit (io.lastreal)
      when 'W', 'w' then
         io.putstring ("Enter the amount to withdraw: ")
         io.readreal
         if account.enough (io.lastreal)
         then account.withdraw (io.lastreal)
         else io.putstring ("Sorry. You don't have that much%N")
         end
      when 'B', 'b' then
         account.show_balance
      when 'H', 'h' then
         show_choices
      when 'Q', 'q' then
         io.putstring ("%NThanks for the monies%N")
      end -- inspect
   end -- do_choice
end_chosen: BOOLEAN is
      -- has the user chosen to finish?
   do
      Result := io.lastchar = 'Q' or io.lastchar = 'q'
   end -- end_chosen
show_choices is
      -- show the valid menu choices
   do
      io.putstring ("%N Menu choices%N")
      io.putstring ("D Deposit money%N")
      io.putstring ("W Withdraw money%N")
      io.putstring ("B Show the balance%N")
      io.putstring ("Q Quit the system%N")
```

```
                io.putstring ("H Help: Show the menu choices%N")
        end -- show_choices
end -- class MENU
```

```
class ACCOUNT
. . .
feature
    . . .
    enough (amount: REAL): BOOLEAN is
        -- does the account contain this amount?
        do
            Result := balance >= amount
        end -- enough
end -- class ACCOUNT
```

4 Data structures

4.1 **Specification**

The bank can have many customers. Each customer has a unique integer key; successive integers are used for every new customer.

The bank runs over an extended period. At the start of each day, a bank teller adds interest to every account and then creates new customers; customers are never deleted. The ATM then runs all day, handling multiple customers. To use the ATM, a customer enters their unique key and password. Any number of transactions may be made on the account, until the customer is tired of playing with their money and exits the system. The ATM then waits for the next customer, until a special key of 666 is entered; this exits the ATM system for the day. The cycle then resumes for the next day: the teller adds interest and new customers, and the ATM system runs. Entry of the special key value of 999 into the ATM shuts down the whole system.

4.2 **Analysis**

There are two main changes to the banking system: the system runs continually, and the bank has many customers. There are now two sub-systems in the bank, one where the teller adds interest and creates accounts, and a second where the customers access their accounts through the ATM. The two sub-systems are candidates for new objects, because they encapsulate different functions in the system and may contain their own data: both the teller and ATM systems use the same set of customers. The teller has to add customers to the set, and scan through it to add interest for every customer. The ATM has to find a customer given the input identifier, and transfer control to that customer.

The system executes daily, until the special end-of-system sentinel (666) is input to the ATM. The top-level code will thus look something like

```
from
until system_exit
loop daily_cycle
end
```

The daily cycle has two parts, the teller and the ATM. The teller functions are performed, then the teller exits and starts up the ATM. The ATM continues until either the day-end sentinel (666) is input, or the system-end sentinel (999) is input. The top level of the daily cycle is thus

```
from
until day_exit or system_exit
loop
    teller
    ATM
end
```

The teller system contains two separate main loops, one for paying interest to the existing customers, and one to create new customers. The ATM system contains two embedded loops. There is a loop around customers, because the ATM handles multiple customers, one at a time. Within each customer there is a loop around transactions, because the customer can issue as many commands as they desire.

The ATM system gets the customer identifier and password, and checks to see if they are valid. If they are valid, the account menu is then presented and the customer uses their account. If the key or password are invalid, then the customer has to input new values. The key input to the ATM has three functions: it may identify a customer, it may signal that the ATM is to be shut down for the day (value 666), or it may close the whole system down (value 999).

4.3   Design

The set of customers can be implemented as a *LINKED_LIST*. This list is initially created by the *BANK*, and passed to the teller and ATM sub-systems. Because these two functional sub-systems now contain data (the list of customers), they can be defined as separate classes. The *BANK* system thus initially makes an empty list, and passes the list as an argument to each sub-system when they are created. The top-level control loop then cycles between the two systems, calling the teller and then the ATM.

The *TELLER* first scans through the list of customers and adds interest to each account. It then adds any new customers to the list, and exits. The ATM then starts, and waits for customers to arrive. The top-level control loop in the ATM class gets a customer identifier, acts on it, and waits for the next customer. If the identifier indicates a system shutdown (999) or an ATM shutdown (666), then the loop exits. If the identifier indicates a valid customer, then the customer is found and control is passed to that customer. Processing within a customer is the same as before. The additional objects in this version of the system are thus the separate *TELLER* and *ATM* classes, which use a *LINKED_LIST* of customers. The other classes are not changed, or changed only to use these new classes.

The client chart for this version of the system is shown below. The *BANK* creates and uses a *LINKED_LIST* of *CUSTOMER*s and the two classes *TELLER* and *ATM*. These two classes also use the list of customers. A customer uses a password and their account.

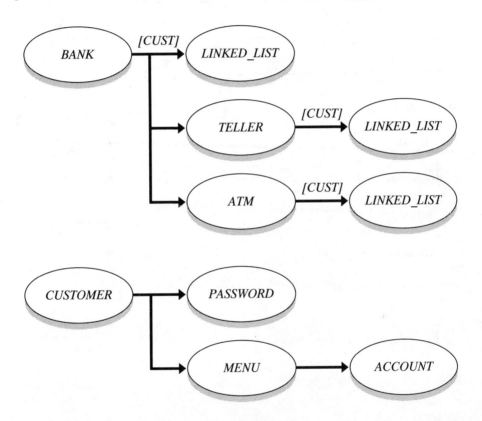

The structure chart for the system is shown below. When the system starts up, it creates an empty list of customers, and passes it to the teller and ATM. The teller first adds interest to every account, then adds new customers to the system, and exits. The ATM system then starts up and waits for a customer to login to the system and use the menu to show the menu choices, deposit, withdraw, and show the account balance.

The new system code added in this extension is starred. The *TELLER* and *ATM* classes have to be added, the *BANK* class changed to use these classes, and the *CUSTOMER* class extended to store the customer key and match the input against the stored key when the customer logs into the ATM.

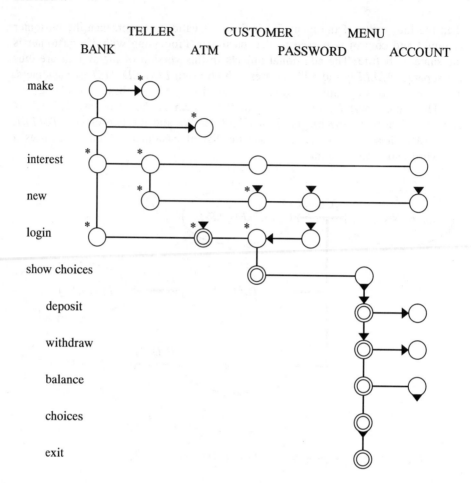

4.4

Solution code

The new code for this version of the system is shown below.

```
class BANK
creation
    make
feature {NONE}
    patrons: LINKED_LIST[CUSTOMER]
    teller: TELLER
    atm: ATM
    make is
                -- make the list of customers
                -- pass it to the ATM and TELLER
                -- run the ATM and teller until system is shut down
        do
            !!patrons.make
            !!teller.make (patrons)
            !!atm.make (patrons)
            from
            until atm.system_finished
            loop
                teller.run
                atm.run
            end
            io.putstring ("%NExit banking system%N")
        end -- make
end -- class BANK
```

```
class TELLER
creation {BANK}
    make
feature {NONE}
    patrons: LINKED_LIST[CUSTOMER]
feature {BANK}
    make (customers: LINKED_LIST[CUSTOMER]) is
            -- set the patrons to the list of customers
        do
            patrons := customers
        end -- make
    run is
            -- add interest to all accounts
            -- create new customers
        do
            add_interest
            new_customers
        end -- run
feature {NONE}
    add_interest is
            -- add interest for every customer
        do
            from patrons.start
            until patrons.after
            loop
                patrons.item.add_interest
                patrons.forth
            end
        end -- add_interest
    new_customers is
            -- add any new customers, with unique customer key
        local patron: CUSTOMER
        do
            io.putstring ("%NAdd new customers%N")
            from
                io.putstring ("%NAny customers to add (Y/N)? ")
                io.readchar
            until io.lastchar = 'N' or io.lastchar = 'n'
            loop
                !!patron.make (patrons.count + 1)
```

```
                    patrons.finish
                    patrons.put (patron)
                    io.putstring ("%NMore new customers (Y/N)? ")
                    io.readchar
                end
            end -- new_customers
    end -- class TELLER
```

```
class ATM
creation {BANK}
   make
feature {NONE}
   patrons: LINKED_LIST[CUSTOMER]
   end_atm: INTEGER is 666
   end_system: INTEGER is 999
feature {BANK}
   make (customers: LINKED_LIST[CUSTOMER]) is
            -- set the patrons to the list of customers
      do
         patrons := customers
      end -- make
   run is
            -- run the ATM menu until the bank shuts it down
      do
         from
            greeting
            get_id
         until
            atm_finished or system_finished
         loop
            serve_customer
            get_id
         end
            io.putstring ("%NExiting ATM system%N")
      end -- run
feature {NONE}
   greeting is
            -- welcome the user
      do
         io.putstring("%N**************************%
            %*************")
         io.putstring ("%N* Welcome to myBank,")
         io.putstring (" where your money is my money *")
         io.putstring("%N**************************%
            %*************")
      end -- greeting
   get_id is
            -- get a customer's user identifier
```

```
            do
                    io.putstring ("%NEnter user id: ")
                    io.readint
            end -- get_id
    atm_finished: BOOLEAN is
                    -- has the ATM finished for the day?
            do
                    Result := io.lastint = end_atm
            end -- atm_finished
    system_finished: BOOLEAN is
                    -- has the system shutdown code been input?
            do
                    Result := io.lastint = end_system
            end -- system_finished
    serve_customer is
                    -- find the customer with the current input id
                    -- if the customer exists, transfer control
            do
                    find (io.lastint)
                    if found then patrons.item.login
                    else io.putstring ("%NThat is not a valid user id")
                    end
            end -- serve_customer
    find (id: INTEGER) is
                    -- set the cursor at the person with this key
                    -- if no such person, cursor is offright
            do
                    from patrons.start
                    until patrons.after or else patrons.item.match (id)
                    loop patrons.forth
                    end
            end -- find
    found: BOOLEAN is
                    -- is the cursor in the list?
            do Result := not patrons.after end -- found
end -- class ATM
```

```
class CUSTOMER
    . . .
feature {NONE}
    . . .
    key: INTEGER
feature {TELLER}
    make (id: INTEGER) is
            -- set the customer details
        do
            . . .
            key := id
        end -- make
    display is
            -- show the customer's personal details
        do
            io.putstring ("%NCustomer #")
            io.putint (key)
            io.putstring (": ")
            . . .
        end -- display
feature {ATM}
    match (id: INTEGER): BOOLEAN is
            -- does the customer key match this id?
        do
            Result := id = key
        end -- match
    . . .
end -- class CUSTOMER
```

5 Single inheritance

  Description

The class *CUSTOMER* is split into two classes in order to separate behavior that belongs to a *PERSON* from that which belongs to a *CUSTOMER*. This allows other types of customer to be easily added in the future, such as corporations or customers with a joint account.

5.2   **Analysis**

The general attributes of a person are placed in a parent class, and the routines that set and use this data are placed in the same class. As the remaining attributes and routines are specific to a customer, they are placed in the child class.

5.3   **Design**

A *PERSON* has a name, address, and sex. A *CUSTOMER* is a *PERSON* who has a bank account; to use this account, the customer also requires a unique identifier and a password. Thus, a customer is a person who has an account, a unique identifier, and a password. The routines associated with these three attributes live in the class *CUSTOMER*. In the banking system, an object of type *PERSON* is never created, only customers. Class *PERSON* has thus been defined with an empty creation routine, so objects of this type cannot be created. For the same reason, all the features are private.

The inheritance chart for *CUSTOMER* and *PERSON* is shown on the next page; the client chart is unchanged.

In a sS chart, parent classes are listed before their children, in left-to-right order. The chart for this version is shown below; nodes which differ from the previous version are starred.

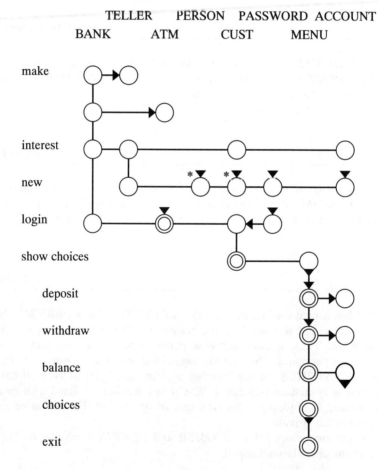

From the structure chart, it may be seen that the personal details are not used by any other part of the system; in fact, they are only used to display a customer.

For this single system defined by the current specification, there is no need to separate a customer from a person, because a customer is always a person in this system. The two roles are separated so that each can be used separately in future versions of the system and in other systems.

5.4   Solution code

No new code is required; instead, the existing code is divided into the two classes *PERSON* and *CUSTOMER*. The new code for this version is shown below; where a routine is moved as a unit and thus unchanged, only the routine header is shown.

```
class PERSON
creation
feature {NONE}
    name, address: STRING
    sex: CHARACTER
    make is
            -- set the personal details
        do
            io.putstring ("%NEnter the personal details%N")
            io.putstring (" Name: ")
            io.readline
            name := io.laststring
            get_sex
            sex := io.lastchar
            io.putstring (" Address: ")
            io.readline
            address := io.laststring
        end -- make
    display is
            -- show the personal details
        do
            io.putstring ("%N ")
            show_title
            io.putstring (name)
            io.putstring (" lives at ")
            io.putstring (address)
        end -- display
feature {NONE}
    get_sex is
```

```
                          -- loop until the user enters a valid sex
      . . .
      valid_gender (code: CHARACTER): BOOLEAN is
                      -- has a valid sex code been entered?
      . . .
      show_title is
                  -- be polite
      . . .
   end -- class PERSON
```

```
class CUSTOMER inherit
    PERSON
        rename
            make as person_make,
            display as person_display
        end
creation {TELLER}
    make
feature {TELLER}
    make (id: INTEGER) is
            -- set the customer details
        do
            io.putstring ("%NEnter the customer details%N")
            person_make
            . . .
        end -- make
    display is
            -- show the customer details
        do
            person_display
            io.putstring ("%NThe account details are:%N")
            account.display
        end -- display
    add_interest is
            -- add interest to the account
feature {ATM}
    match (id: INTEGER): BOOLEAN is
            -- does the customer key match this id?
    login is
            -- if the customer enters the valid password
            -- then start the ATM menu
end -- class CUSTOMER
```

6 Polymorphism

Specification

The additional specification for this part of the system is:

There are three types of bank account: savings, check, and investment. A customer may have one account of each type. Savings and check accounts are accessed through the ATM. Savings and investment accounts accrue daily interest.

A successful withdrawal from a check account costs 50 cents. An unsuccessful withdrawal from a check account (a bounced check) costs $5. There are no charges or penalties for a savings account. A savings account gets daily interest; the interest rate is 4.5 percent a year. A check account gets no interest. The balance of an account cannot be negative.

An investment account may not be accessed through the ATM. It is created with an initial balance, and accrues daily interest for a period of three, six, or 12 months. A three-month investment account has an annual interest rate of 5.5 percent, a six-month account has a 6.0 percent rate, and a 12-month account 6.5 percent. When the account matures at the end of the period, the total amount is transferred into the customer's check account. If there is no check account, then one is created to receive the investment funds.

6.2 Analysis

The focus of the analysis is the inheritance hierarchy for the types of account, and this part of the system is discussed in detail below. The ability of a customer to have multiple accounts affects three other parts of the system, however: customer creation, account creation for an existing customer, and account selection in the ATM menu.

The class *CUSTOMER* has to be extended to store up to three accounts, and its creation routine has to be extended to create up to three accounts. The account menu has to be extended to ask the customer to select one of the accounts. Finally, the class *TELLER* has to be extended to create new accounts for an existing customer; this is a new, implicit goal for the system. These three parts are essential for the system to work, but the code for them uses no new Eiffel constructs, and the details of these three parts are omitted from this part of the case study. The code to create each account is part of customer processing, and is contained in class *CUSTOMER* or lower. The *TELLER* code only needs to be changed when an existing customer has a new account, because the teller has to choose to add an account or not. The teller initiates the command to add a new account, but the code to effect the command is contained in the *CUSTOMER* and *ACCOUNT* classes. This hides the complexity by pushing the code down the client chart.

The design and coding of the account inheritance hierarchy is the central topic of this section of the case study. Before the hierarchy can be designed, however, data must be collected on the common and different behavior of each account.

All accounts have a balance and an interest rate, although the exact rate differs for each account and for each period of an investment account. All accounts are created with an initial balance, but an investment account also requires the period. Savings and check accounts can receive deposits. Money can also be withdrawn from each type of account, but the rules are slightly different, both for how much is enough and for the cost of a transaction. Both savings and check accounts only display the balance, but a separate routine to display the period must be written for the three investment accounts. Interest is added to all accounts in the same way, daily. Finally, the investment account has to keep some kind of counter to check if the account has matured; this involves an attribute, and a test of the attribute value. The table from this analysis is shown below, where a cross indicates the same content across classes, and a circle indicates a different content.

	Savings	Check	Investment
balance	x	x	x
rate	o	o	o
make	x	x	o
deposit	x	x	
withdraw	o	o	
show balance	x	x	
display	o	o	o
left			x
mature?			x
interest	x	x	x

The table shows the interaction between goals and objects at a high level, and can be used as a basis for the high-level design of the account inheritance hierarchy. The hierarchy structure forms a basis for design, but it may be changed later when a more detailed analysis is made of parts of the system that are unclear, or for which the design is ugly.

An interesting design issue in polymorphism is how to stop things from happening; as an example, a check account does not receive any interest. This could be implemented by not calling *add_interest* on a check account, or by calling it and adding zero money. The first solution (control the call in the client) means we have to check the type of an account, before using it; this is ugly, because you should not test the type of an account. By setting the interest rate to zero, we can just add interest to all accounts equally using polymorphism. The calling code is now simple, because the savings and check accounts have the same interface; the consequence is that we have a routine that essentially does nothing, and exists only because some other class executes that command.

6.3 First design

An abstract class *ACCOUNT*, containing the balance, the rate, an interest routine, and a deferred display routine, can be defined. The class *INVEST* can then inherit from the general class, and add features to count each day, and to check if the account is mature. The other two types of account have the same behavior for make, deposit, and show balance, so an abstract class can be defined for them; call this class *INTERACCT* (interactive account). Different classes are needed for the *SAVINGS* and *CHECK* accounts in order to deal with the different rules for withdrawing money. At this point in design, the inheritance hierarchy looks like that shown on the next page, where each class is drawn with the class name, attributes, and routines shown in that order in each box. In the diagram, a deferred feature has been starred.

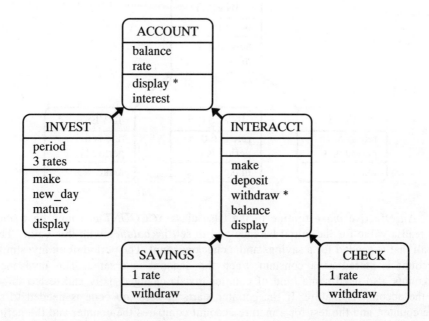

In this solution, the variable *rate* is stored in the parent class *ACCOUNT*. The individual rates for each type of specific account are stored as constants in each type of account, and the value is assigned to the variable when the object is created.

6.4   Focus: making an account

The solution design for the account inheritance hierarchy given above is, in one part at least, ugly. It violates process guideline 5 (Chapter 3), which holds that a feature should be placed as high in the inheritance hierarchy as possible. Every account has to be created, but the creation routines are placed in the specific types of account, and not in the parent. With the current design, even a deferred feature cannot be placed in the parent, because the signatures of the child features are different: the creation routine for savings and check accounts has no argument, but the creation routine for an investment account has one argument, the period. A common creation routine should be in the parent, because all accounts have to be created; this is a general feature of accounts. The obstacle is the different arguments to the routines.

One solution is to have the same signature for all the creation routines. The three types of investment account each have a different period and interest rate, and can be defined, literally, as three types of investment account: *INVEST_3*, *INVEST_6*, and *INVEST_12*. The common parent *INVEST* contains everything except the *make* routine, which differs for each type of investment account. The inheritance hierarchy for this part of the system is shown below.

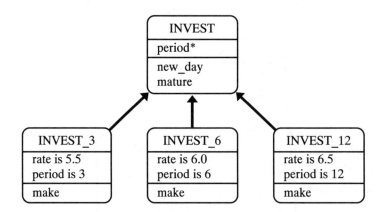

An effective *make* routine in the base class *ACCOUNT* can now be written to read a value for the initial balance and to set the *balance* with this value. This is all that is needed for a savings and a check account. The period of an investment account is stored as a constant when the account is created. The investment accounts also need some kind of counter that is changed daily and tested to see if the account is mature. If the counter starts at zero, no code is needed to set the counter, and the test for a mature account compares the counter and the period times 30; the acccount is mature if the number of days are the same. The base class *ACCOUNT* now contains a simple creation routine that sets the initial balance. This routine is effective and sufficient for all five types of specific account, with the inheritance hierarchy and contents shown above. The latest version of the investment account inheritance hierarchy is shown on the next page.

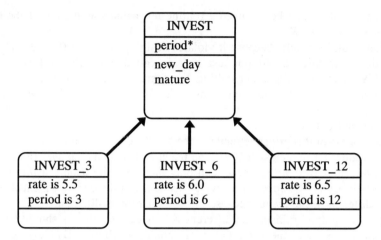

This is the third version of the system; each version was designed, evaluated, and improved. Each version was driven by a flaw in the existing solution, by a piece of the solution that was not as simple as possible. No code was written during this process. Instead, diagrams were used to record the shape of the design, and easily changed as the design evolved from a first idea to an elegant solution.

6.5   Focus: withdraw

The only remaining difficulty is the withdrawal code for the savings and check accounts. Money can be withdrawn from both types of account, so the central or basic action of withdrawing money (*balance := balance − amount*) should be placed in the common parent, class *INTERACCT*. However, the location of the remaining parts of the plan to withdraw money is unclear.

The basic code for the two accounts is shown below, with the control flow and routine names shown, but the rest of the details left vague. If this code was placed in a routine in each class, it would be called something like *try_withdraw*.

```
SAVINGS                          CHECK
if enough (money)                if enough (money)
then withdraw (money)            then withdraw (money)
                                 else penalty
```

Both accounts need a test to see if there is enough money in the account before the money is withdrawn, but the test value differs: for a savings account the withdrawal has to be less than or equal to the balance, but for a check account we have to test for the amount plus 50 cents. If there is enough, then a different amount has to be withdrawn (that 50 cents again). Finally, if the balance is too small, then the check account incurs a penalty of $5, but nothing happens to the savings account. The control flow cannot be captured in a single routine, because a single selection statement is used, and the statements are different for each case.

At this point, it looks like we need a routine *try_withdraw* in each of the classes *SAVINGS* and *CHECK*.

This solution is ugly, because it violates design principle 3 (Chapter 7), which holds that a feature should not test if it is called correctly. A feature of the *ACCOUNT* class is called, but calling the feature may or may not result in a withdrawal. The client should only call a feature when the action will succeed. Think of a feature as a kind but grumpy uncle, who says, "Call me when you're ready, but not before."

Application of this principle removes the test for enough money from the account class, and moves it into class *MENU*. The menu code gets the amount from the user, tests if the withdrawal will succeed, and only then calls the feature *withdraw* in the class *INTERACCT*. The code for a savings account and the code for a check account will be different in the menu, because the control flow is different.

By using polymorphism, the differences between the classes should be hidden inside each class, and the same behavior should be offered. By moving the test outside the class, we can no longer treat the different types of account in the same way. Perhaps the most elegant solution is to make the role of the menu more abstract, and to have the menu perform the same actions for all types of transaction. The generic *MENU* code to execute each user choice would then look something like

---

if *can* **then** *do* **else** *recover* **end**

---

where the details of *can*, *do*, and *recover* are provided by each class. Class *SAVINGS* would always reply **true** to the query *can*, and have an empty routine for the action *recover*, while class *CHECK* would have code in the routines for each of the three roles. This keeps the design elegant and obeys all the design guidelines, but each class now has to supply code for each role, code that in many cases does nothing. This is inefficient, but conceptually clean; menu system design is discussed in more detail in Meyer (1988), Chapter 12. In the interests of simplicity, we have chosen to place a routine *try_withdraw* inside the classes *SAVINGS* and *CHECK*.

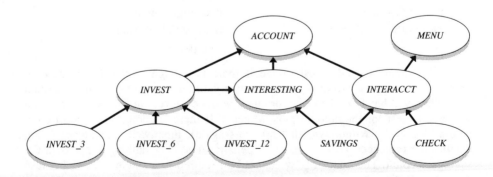

The final inheritance structure for the accounts is shown above. The class *INTERESTING* has been defined for interest-bearing accounts which contain the code to add interest to the balance. The class *INTERESTING* is used to scan through the polymorphic list and to add interest to the correct types of account. Similarly, the class *INTER_ACCT* is used to find the interactive accounts i.e. those accounts that can be accessed through an ATM.

It should now be clear how the design guidelines indicate a bad system design, and support one choice in system design over another. It should also be clear that making the right choice can be difficult, because a solution is evaluated on a set of criteria that often lead to conflicting choices. Design is hard; for this reason, you need to develop expertise in making a design choice and evaluating the results of your choice.

6.6   Final solution

The only change to the client chart for this part of the case study is that a customer uses all three accounts; this part of the client chart is shown below. Because this change is hidden inside the customer, the rest of the client chart is not affected. The five types of accounts are stored on a polymorphic list of accounts. The client chart shows the list declaration, as well as any other declarations; dynamic types are not clients, because there is no declaration of those types.

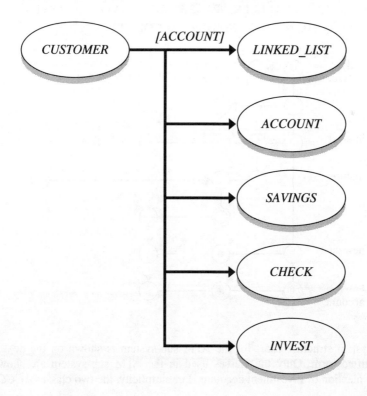

The system structure for the complete system is shown below in two parts: the teller sub-system, then the ATM sub-system. The new code required for this version of the *BANK* system is starred; existing code that has been moved into the new classes is not new code, and hence is not starred. The classes *PERSON*, *INVEST_3*, *INVEST_6*, and *INVEST_12* are omitted for simplicity. The common behavior is captured in a parent class, so the code to implement an action in a plan may be contained in a parent class or in a child. The connected set of nodes that indicate a plan may thus terminate at a parent, or go all the way to the child.

The system structure chart for the *TELLER* sub-system is shown below. When the bank starts up, it creates an empty list of customers and passes it to the teller. The teller is then called to add interest to all existing accounts. If an investment account is mature (the test is defined in class *INVEST*), then the account balance is deposited in a check account and the investment account is deleted. When a new customer is created, they may have from one to three accounts; the code to create multiple accounts is contained in class *CUSTOMER*. The bank teller selects an object to create, so the same goal (create an account) is applied to different objects (savings, check, invest). The creation code is contained purely within class *ACCOUNT*, so there is no link to the children classes for creation. The existing customers are then scanned, and one or more new accounts may be added; again, the object selection code is contained in the class *CUSTOMER*, and the code to create an account is in class *ACCOUNT*.

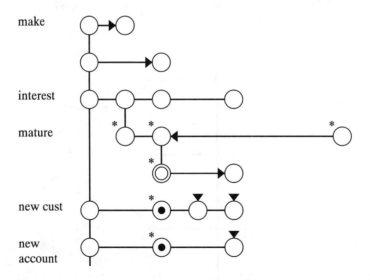

The system structure chart for the ATM sub-system is shown on the next page, in a simplified form. Only the classes used in the ATM sub-system are shown, so there is no mention of investment accounts. For simplicity, the two classes *ACCOUNT*

and *INTERACCT* (interactive account) have been collapsed into one column in the chart, shown under the heading *ACCOUNT*.

The bank initially creates an ATM, and passes it the list of customers. The ATM service then starts when the teller has finished. A customer has to login to the ATM system by entering a customer identifier; this corresponds to the action of placing your card in the ATM machine. The ATM system uses this id to find the customer's account, and transfers control to the customer. The customer enters their password, and is then given access to the interactive menu. The menu reads and executes customer choices, for multiple accounts, until the customer leaves the ATM.

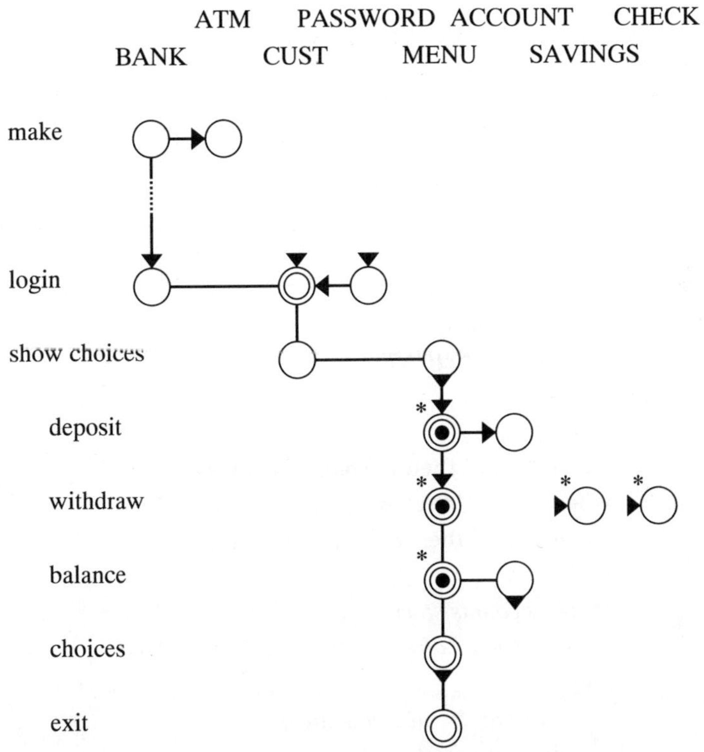

ATM   PASSWORD ACCOUNT   CHECK
BANK   CUST   MENU   SAVINGS

make

login

show choices

deposit

withdraw

balance

choices

exit

The customer enters their user id and password into the system; if the login is successful (shown by a selection node), then they enter the menu system. The menu system offers a choice of goals for the customer, shown by the series of choices within the *MENU* class. Some of these goals can be handled within the menu class, while others require the user to choose a type of account. These nodes contain a double selection, because there is a selection of goals, and then a selection of objects within a goal, such as asking to see the balance in a check account. A goal selection is indicated by a double circle, and an object selection by a filled centre in the circle; three nodes in the chart contain both symbols.

The code to deposit money is contained in the parent class *ACCOUNT*. When money is withdrawn, part of the code is in the parent, and part in each of the children. The code to show the balance of an account is contained in the parent.

6.7   Solution code

The polymorphic code for the accounts in class *CUSTOMER*, and the complete account class definitions, are shown below.

```
class CUSTOMER
feature {NONE}
    accounts: LINKED_LIST[ACCOUNT]
    . . .
    find_account (type: CHARACTER) is
            -- set the cursor at this type of account
            -- if no such account, cursor is after
        local
            savings: SAVINGS
            check: CHECK
            invest: INVEST
            account: ACCOUNT
        do
            inspect type
            when 'S', 's' then account := savings
            when 'C', 'c' then account := check
            when 'I', 'i' then account := invest
            end
            from accounts.start
            until accounts.after or else account /= Void
            loop
                account ?= accounts.item
                accounts.forth
            end
        end -- find_account
    found_account: BOOLEAN is
            -- is the cursor in the list?
        do
            Result := not accounts.after
        end -- found_account
    add_account (type: CHARACTER) is
            -- add an account of this type to the customer
```

```
            local account: ACCOUNT

        do
                inspect type
                when 'S', 's' then !SAVINGS!account.make
                when 'C', 'c' then !CHECK!account.make
                when 'I', 'i' then
                    io.putstring ("Enter period (3/6/12): ")
                    io.readint
                    inspect io.lastint
                    when 3 then !INVEST_3!account.make
                    when 6 then !INVEST_6!account.make
                    when 12 then !INVEST_12!account.make
                    end
                end
                accounts.put (account)
            end -- add_account
        . . .
        use_account (choice: CHARACTER) is
                -- if the customer has this account, start the menu
            local account: INTERACCT
            do
                find_account (choice)
                if found_account then
                    account ?= accounts.item
                    account.menu
                else io.putstring ("%NYou don't have that type of account")
                end
            end -- select_account
    feature {TELLER}
        add_interest is
                -- add interest to any savings or investment account
            local account: INTERESTING
            do
                from accounts.start
                until accounts.after
                loop
                    account ?= accounts.item
                    if account /= Void then account.add_interest end
                end
```

```
        end -- add_interest
new_day is
        -- add a day to the investment account counter
        -- if the investment account is mature
        -- transfer the balance to the check account
        -- and delete the investment account
local
        invest: INVEST
        check: CHECK
do
        from accounts.start
        until accounts.after or else invest /= Void
        loop
                invest ?= accounts.item
                if invest /= Void then
                    invest.new_day
                    if invest.mature then
                        find_account ('C')
                        if not found_account then !!check.make end
                        check.deposit (invest.balance)
                        accounts.remove
                    end -- mature

                end -- invest
        end -- loop
    end -- add_interest
end -- class CUSTOMER
```

```
class ACCOUNT
feature {NONE}
    balance: REAL
feature {TELLER}
    make is
                -- set the initial balance
        do
            io.putstring ("%NEnter initial balance: ")
            io.readreal
            balance := io.lastreal

        end -- make
    display is
                -- show the balance
        do
            io.putstring ("%N The balance is $")
            io.putreal (balance)
        end -- display
end -- class ACCOUNT
```

```
deferred class INTERESTING
inherit
    ACCOUNT
feature {CUSTOMER}
    add_interest is
            -- add the daily interest to the balance
        do
            balance := balance + balance * day_rate
        end -- add_interest
feature {NONE}
    day_rate: REAL is
            -- daily interest rate
        do
            Result := (interest_rate / 100) / 365.25
        end -- day_rate
    interest_rate: REAL is
            -- yearly interest rate
        deferred
        end -- interest_rate
end -- class INTERESTING
```

```
deferred class INVEST
inherit
   ACCOUNT
      rename
         display as display_basic
      export
         {CUSTOMER} balance
      end;
   INTERESTING
      redefine display
      end
feature {NONE}
   period: INTEGER is
            -- period of account in months
      deferred
      end
   days: INTEGER
feature {TELLER}
   new_day is
            -- increment the day counter
      do
         days:= days + 1
      end -- new_day
   mature: BOOLEAN is
            -- is the account mature?
      do
         Result := days = period * 30
      end -- mature
   display is
            -- show the balance, interest rate, period, and day counter
      do
         io.putstring ("%N***Investment account***")
         display_basic
         io.putstring ("%N The period is ")
         io.putint (period)
         io.putstring (" months")
         io.putstring ("%N The account has run for ")
         io.putint (days)
```

```
                    io.putstring (" days")
            end -- display
    end -- class INVEST
```

```
class INVEST_3
inherit
    INVEST
creation {CUSTOMER}
    make
feature {NONE}
    period: INTEGER is 3
    interest_rate: REAL is 5.5
end -- class INVEST_3

class INVEST_6
inherit
    INVEST
creation {CUSTOMER}
    make
feature {NONE}
    period: INTEGER is 6
    interest_rate: REAL is 6.0
end -- class INVEST_6

class INVEST_12

inherit
    INVEST
creation {CUSTOMER}
    make
feature {NONE}
    period: INTEGER is 12
    interest_rate: REAL is 6.5
end -- class INVEST_12
```

```
deferred class INTERACCT
inherit
    ACCOUNT;
    MENU
creation
feature {CUSTOMER}
    deposit (amount: REAL) is
            -- add amount to balance
        do
            balance := balance + amount
        end -- deposit
    enough (amount: REAL): BOOLEAN is
            -- does the account contain this amount?
        do
            Result := balance >= amount
        end
    withdraw (amount: REAL) is
            -- subtract this amount from the balance
        do
            balance := balance - amount
        end
    show_balance is
            -- display the current balance
        do
            io.putstring ("%NThe current balance is ")
            io.putreal (balance)
        end -- show_balance
end -- class INTERACCT
```

```
class SAVINGS
inherit
    INTERACCT;
    INTERESTING
creation {CUSTOMER}
    make
feature {NONE}
    interest_rate: REAL is
            -- interest rate for savings account
        do
            Result := 4.5
        end -- interest_rate
feature {CUSTOMER}
    try_withdraw (amount: REAL) is
            -- withdraw this amount if there is enough money
        do
            if enough (amount) then withdraw (amount)
            else io.putstring ("%NInsufficient funds")
            end
        end -- deposit
end -- class SAVINGS
```

```
class CHECK
inherit
    INTERACCT
creation {CUSTOMER}
    make
feature {NONE}
    interest_rate: REAL is
            -- interest rate for savings account
        do
            Result := 0.0
        end -- interest_rate
    charge: REAL is 0.50          -- charge for good
                                     transaction

    penalty: REAL is 5.00         -- penalty for bouncing a
                                     check
feature {CUSTOMER}
    try_withdraw (amount: REAL) is

            -- if there is enough money, withdraw the amount
            -- if not, charge a penalty for bouncing a check
        do
            if enough (amount + charge)
            then withdraw (amount + charge)
            else
                io.putstring ("%NInsufficient funds")
                apply_penalty
            end
        end -- try_withdraw
    apply_penalty is
            -- apply the penalty for bouncing a check
            -- account balance cannot go negative
        do
            if balance >= penalty
            then balance := balance - penalty
            else balance := 0
            end
        end -- apply_penalty
end -- class CHECK
```

7 Complex inheritance

Specification

Read the system data from file every morning when the system starts up, and write it to file every night when the system shuts down.

7.2   **Analysis**

Three changes are made to the system in this last part of the case study, one that affects the functionality of the system, and two that make the code more reusable. The first change adds file storage and retrieval. The second change uses multiple inheritance to separate the menu from the account classes. The third change takes the list lookup code in the *TELLER* and *ATM* classes, and places the repeated code inside a *KEY_LIST* class using constrained genericity.

There is no analysis in this section of the case study, because the new specification does not require detailed analysis. The problems lie in implementing the solution, not in an analysis of the problem structure. List lookup and storage require changes to the list class, as well as other classes, so the two changes have been combined in the code shown below. The changes to the system for a deferred *MENU* class are then presented.

7.3   **Design: list storage and retrieval**

The list of customers is stored and retrieved by inheriting the class *STORABLE* in the *BANK* (to retrieve the list) and in the list class (to store the list). The inheritance chart for this part of the system is shown below, where the new class that is both a list and storable has been called class *STORE_LIST*.

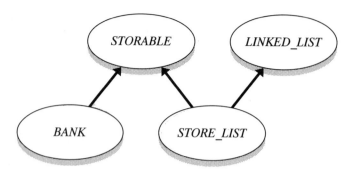

7.4   Design: a keyed list

The construction of a class that is a keyed list requires a deferred class that has a key and a match routine (class *KEY*), a child that inherits this parent and effects the match routine (class *CUSTOMER*), and a constrained generic class (class *KEY_LIST*). The constrained class has *KEY* as its constraint in the class header, and contains code to look up an element of the list using a key. The inheritance chart for this part of the system is shown below.

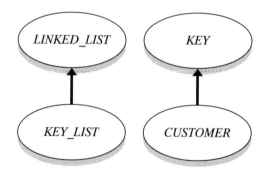

The client chart for the keyed list class is shown below. The constraint on the generic class is inside the *KEY_LIST* class definition, and so is not shown on the client chart.

7.5   Design: a keyed, storable list

A keyed, storable list class is created by combining the inheritance hierarchies from the two applications, and moving the lookup code from the clients (*TELLER* and *ATM*) into the keyed class. The inheritance hierarchy for the keyed, storable list class is shown below.

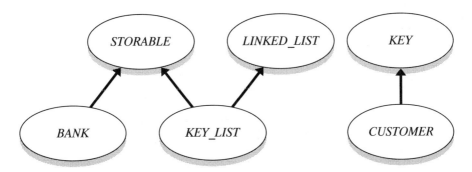

No system structure charts are shown in this part of the case study; the complete charts and code are shown in the next section.

7.6   Solution code: a keyed, storable list

The new code for the definition and use of the keyed, storable list is shown below. The name of the lookup command in class *KEY_LIST* is *find*, and its matched query is *found*. If the customer with a given key is found, then the object is returned from the list using *item*.

```
class BANK
inherit
    STORABLE
...
feature {NONE}
    filename: STRING is "patrons.dat"
    patrons: KEY_LIST[CUSTOMER]
    make is
            -- make or retrieve the list of customers
            -- make the ATM and TELLER, pass the customer list
            -- run the ATM and teller until system shuts down
            do
                start_up
                ...
                store_patrons
            end -- make
    start_up is
            -- make or retrieve the list of customers
        do
            retrieve_by_name (filename)
            patrons ?= retrieved
            if patrons = Void then !!patrons.make end
        end -- start_up
    store_patrons is
            -- store the list of customers
        do
            patrons.store_by_name (filename)
        end -- store
end -- class BANK
```

```
class TELLER

. . .

feature {NONE}
    patrons: KEY_LIST[CUSTOMER]
feature {BANK}
    make (customers: KEY_LIST[CUSTOMER]) is
            -- set the patrons to the list of customers
        do
            patrons := customers
        end -- make
    new_accounts is
            -- add any new accounts for existing customers
        do
            from
                io.putstring ("%NNew accounts for customers (Y/N)? ")
                io.readchar
            until io.lastchar = 'N' or io.lastchar = 'n'
            loop
                patrons.get_id
                patrons.find (io.lastint)
                if patrons.found
                then add_accounts (patrons.item)
                else io.putstring ("%NThat's not a valid user id")
                end
                io.putstring ("%NMore new accounts (Y/N)? ")
                io.readchar
            end
        end -- new_accounts
    . . .
end -- class TELLER
```

```
class ATM
feature {NONE}
    patrons: KEY_LIST[CUSTOMER]
feature {BANK}
    make (customers: KEY_LIST[CUSTOMER]) is
            -- set the patrons to the list of customers
        do
            patrons := customers
        end -- make
    . . .
    serve_customer is
            -- find the customer with a key matching the input id
            -- if the customer exists, transfer control
        do
            patrons.find (io.lastint)
            if patrons.found then patrons.item.login
            else io.putstring ("%NThat is not a valid user id")
            end
        end -- serve_customer
end -- class ATM
```

```
class KEY_LIST [T -> KEY] inherit
    STORABLE
        undefine
            is_equal,
            copy
        end;

    LLIST[T]
creation {BANK}
    make
feature {TELLER, ATM}
    get_id is
            -- get a customer's user identifier
        do
            io.putstring ("%NEnter user id: ")
            io.readint
        end -- get_id
    find (id: INTEGER) is
            -- set the cursor at the person with this key
            -- if no such person, cursor is offright
        do
            from start
            until after or else item.match (id)
            loop forth
            end
        end -- find
    found: BOOLEAN is
            -- is the cursor in the list?
        do Result := not after end -- found
end -- class KEY_LIST
```

Design: an inherited *MENU*

The last extension to the case study is to separate the menu from the account actions that are called by the menu. This is done simply by defining the actions as deferred routines in class *MENU*, defining effective features in the appropriate account, and joining the deferred and effective features by multiple inheritance.

There is already a class that represents an interactive account, class *INTER-ACCT*. This class can just inherit the deferred menu class, because it already contains the needed account routines, either deferred or effective. The final inheritance hierarchy for the account sub-system is shown on the next page.

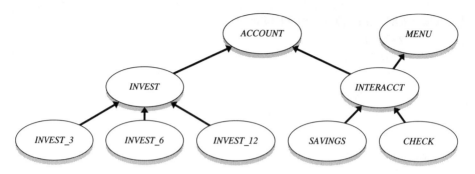

7.8   Solution code: an inherited *MENU*

The new code for class *MENU* is shown below; the code that is not changed from
the existing class is not shown here.

```
deferred class MENU
. . .
feature {NONE}
    do_choice is
                -- execute the choice made by the user
        do
            inspect io.lastchar
            when 'D', 'd' then do_deposit
            when 'W', 'w' then do_withdraw
            when 'B', 'b' then show_balance
            when 'H', 'h' then show_choices
            when 'Q', 'q' then exit_menu
            end -- inspect
        end -- do_choice
    do_deposit is
                -- get the amount to deposit, then deposit it
        local amount: REAL
        do
            io.putstring ("Enter the amount to deposit: ")
            io.readreal
            deposit (io.lastreal)
        end -- do_deposit
```

```
    do_withdraw is
            -- get the amount to withdraw
            -- if there is enough money, withdraw the amount
        local amount: REAL
        do
            io.putstring ("Enter the amount to withdraw: ")
            io.readreal
            amount := io.lastreal
            try_withdraw (amount)
        end -- do_withdraw
    try_withdraw (amount: REAL) is
            -- withdraw this amount if there is enough money
        deferred
        end -- withdraw
    exit_menu is
            -- say bye bye
        do io.putstring ("%NY'all have a nice day, now%N")
        end
feature
    deposit (amount: REAL) is
            -- add the amount to the balance
        deferred
        end -- deposit
    show_balance is
            -- display the current balance
        deferred
        end -- show_balance
end -- class MENU
```

8 The complete *BANK* system

A banking system has multiple customers. Each customer may have a savings account, a check account, and an investment account, but may only have one account of each type. The bank offers access to check and savings accounts through an interactive menu like that seen in an automatic teller machine (ATM); an investment account cannot be accessed through the ATM. Savings and investment accounts accrue daily interest, paid on the current balance; check accounts do not accrue interest.

Any amount may be deposited in an account. A withdrawal from a savings account decrements the balance by the amount withdrawn. A successful withdrawal from a check account costs 50 cents. An unsuccessful withdrawal from a check account costs $5. There are no charges or penalties for a savings account. The balance of an account cannot be negative.

A savings account gets daily interest; the interest rate is 4.5 percent a year. A check account gets no interest. An investment account is created with an initial balance, and accrues daily interest for a period of three, six, or 12 months. A three-month investment account has an annual interest rate of 5.5 percent, a six-month account has a 6.0 percent rate, and a 12-month account 6.5 percent. When the account matures at the end of the period, the total amount is transferred into the customer's check account. If there is no check account, one is created to receive the investment funds.

The bank system runs for an extended period of many days. At the start of each day, the bank adds interest to every account and creates new customers, and new accounts for existing customers. Each customer has a unique integer key; successive integers are used for each new customer. Customers and accounts are never deleted from the bank. The ATM then runs all day, handling multiple customers. To use the ATM, a customer enters their unique key (this simulates putting a card into the ATM) and their password, chooses an account, then chooses commands from the menu. These commands are read and executed, until the customer finishes; the ATM then waits for the next customer. A special key of 666 exits the ATM system for the day, and the cycle then resumes for the next day. Entry of the special key value of 999 into the ATM shuts down the whole system. The bank data is stored to file when the system shuts down, and is retrieved from file when the system starts up again.

A customer is allowed three attempts to login to the ATM by entering a valid password. If no correct password is entered after three attempts, then the ATM system rejects the login attempt and asks for a new customer identifier. If the password is correct, then the customer is shown a menu of account choices, and the system reads and executes the choices. Any number of transactions may be made; processing on the account continues until the customer chooses to exit that account. Multiple accounts may be chosen and used within a single ATM session.

The ATM menu choices (upper or lower case) are

D,d	Deposit
W,w	Withdraw up to the total amount in the account
B,b	Show the balance
Q,q	Quit the system
H,h	Help: Show the menu choices

8.2   Inheritance charts

The inheritance charts for the complete banking system are shown on the next page. The first chart shows the inheritance for a storable, keyed list, and for an element of that list, a customer. The second inheritance chart shows the inheritance structure of the bank accounts.

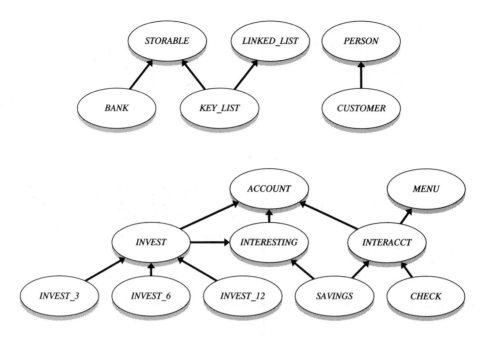

8.3   Client charts

The client chart for the complete banking system is shown below.

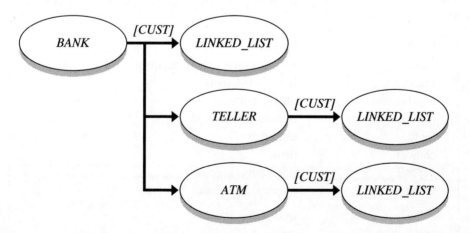

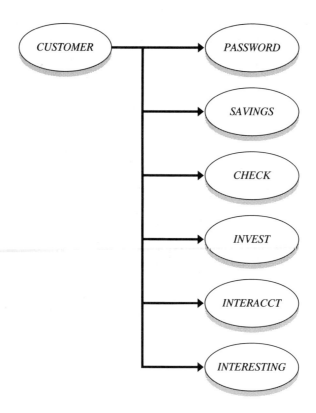

The system goals are all given in the specification. The goals and their objects are

Goal	Objects
make	new customers, new accounts
retrieve	list of customers
pay interest	all accounts
mature account	investment account
login	customer
choices	menu
deposit	interactive account
withdraw	interactive account
balance	interactive account
exit	menu
store	list of customers

For each goal, a plan is defined. The code in the plan is then divided among the objects in the plan, in order to define the system structure.

8.5   System structure charts

The system structure charts for the *BANK* system are shown below. The first chart shows the *BANK* (retrieve and store) and *TELLER* sub-system, and the second chart shows the *ATM* sub-system. The Eiffel library classes *STORABLE* and *LINKED_LIST* have been omitted for the sake of simplicity, as have several user-defined classes, and the names of some classes have been abbreviated in the chart. The names of all the user-defined classes in the system are shown to the left of the table below, and the name of the class used in the chart is shown to the right.

Full class name	Name in chart
BANK	BANK
TELLER	TELLER
ATM	ATM
KEY_LIST	KLIST
PERSON	
KEY	
CUSTOMER	CUST
PASSWORD	PASS
ACCOUNT	ACCT
INVEST	INV
INVEST_3	
INVEST_6	
INVEST_12	
MENU	MENU
INTER_ACCT	INTER
SAVINGS	SAV
CHECK	CHECK

The *TELLER* sub-system is shown in the system structure chart on the next page, as well as the *BANK* storage and retrieval. The account inheritance structure has been collapsed for simplicity in the chart, from nine to four classes. The *BANK* starts up each morning and retrieves the customer details from file using class *KEY_LIST*, unless this is the first day, when an empty list of customers is created. At the end of each day, the updated customer list is stored to file.

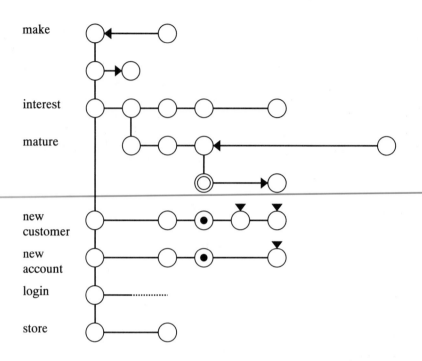

The *TELLER* is passed the list of customers. First, interest is added to every account for every customer; the code to add interest sits in class *ACCOUNT*. If an investment account is mature (test in *INVEST*), then the money is deposited into a check account (the deposit code is in class *INTERACCT*) and the investment account is deleted. Any new customers are added to the list, then any new accounts are added for existing customers; both these tasks use the common account creation routine defined in class *ACCOUNT*. The *TELLER* sub-system then exits and control passes to the *ATM* sub-system.

The system structure chart for the *ATM* system is shown on the next page. The ATM system starts up and waits for a customer to login. If the customer enters a correct user id (read in *ATM*, used in *KEY_LIST* and *CUSTOMER*) and password (read and tested in *PASSWORD*), then the customer is asked to choose an account, the menu choices are listed, and the ATM menu is presented (*MENU*). The customer then has to choose first an account (savings or check), and then a command for that account (*MENU*) and the chosen command is executed on the chosen account. This is both a goal and an object selection, shown by a double filled node.

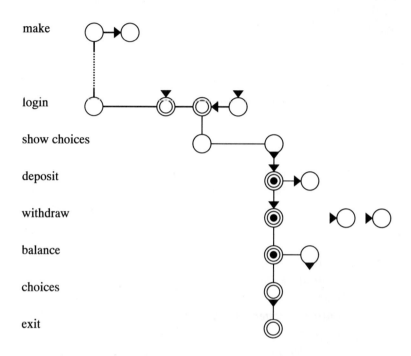

The ATM system remains active until a special user id of 999 is entered into the ATM. This code tells the system to write its data to file and exit.

8.6   Eiffel code

The complete Eiffel code for the *BANK* system is shown on the next page. Every user input has been tested and validated before it is used in the system. Each class listing begins on a new page, unless several complete classes can be placed on the same page.

```
class BANK
inherit
    STORABLE
creation
    make
feature {NONE}
    filename: STRING is "patrons.dat"
    patrons: KEY_LIST[CUSTOMER]
    teller: TELLER
    atm: ATM
    make is
            -- make or retrieve the list of customers
            -- make the ATM and TELLER, pass the customer list
            -- run the ATM and teller until system shuts down
        do
            start_up
            !!teller.make (patrons)
            !!atm.make (patrons)
            from
            until atm.system_finished
            loop
                teller.run
                atm.run
            end
            store_patrons
            io.putstring ("%N%NExit banking system%N")
        end -- make
    start_up is
            -- make or retrieve the list of customers
        do
            retrieve_by_name (filename)

            patrons ?= retrieved
            if patrons = Void then !!patrons.make end
        end -- start_up
    store_patrons is
            -- store the list of customers
        do patrons.store_by_name (filename) end -- store
end -- class BANK
```

```
class TELLER
creation {BANK}
    make
feature {NONE}
    patrons: KEY_LIST[CUSTOMER]
feature {BANK}
    make (customers: KEY_LIST[CUSTOMER]) is
            -- set the patrons to the list of customers
        do
            patrons := customers
        end -- make
    run is
            -- add interest to all accounts
            -- create new customers
            -- create new accounts for existing customers
        do
            new_day
            show_header
            new_customers
            new_accounts
        end -- run
feature {NONE}
    new_day is
            -- add interest for every customer
            -- tell the investment accounts that it is a new day
        do
            from patrons.start
            until patrons.after
            loop
                patrons.item.add_interest
                patrons.item.new_day
                patrons.forth
            end
        end -- add_interest
    show_header is
            -- show the teller a nice message
        do
            io.putstring ("%N")
            io.putstring
            ("%N***********************************")
```

```
                    io.putstring ("%N* Add new customers and new accounts
                    *")
                    io.putstring
                    ("%N***********************************")
            end
    new_customers is
                    -- add any new customers with their initial accounts
            local patron: CUSTOMER
            do
                    from
                            io.putstring ("%NAny customers to add (Y/N)? ")
                            io.readchar
                    until io.lastchar = 'N' or io.lastchar = 'n'
                    loop
                            !!patron.make (patrons.count + 1)
                            add_accounts (patron)
                            patrons.finish
                            patrons.put (patron)
                            io.putstring ("%NMore new customers (Y/N)? ")
                            io.readchar
                    end
            end -- new_customers
    new_accounts is
                    -- add any new accounts for existing customers
            do
                    from
                            io.putstring ("%NNew accounts for customers (Y/N)? ")
                            io.readchar
                    until io.lastchar = 'N' or io.lastchar = 'n'
                    loop
                            patrons.get_id
                            patrons.find (io.lastint)
                            if patrons.found then add_accounts (patrons.item)
                            else io.putstring ("%NThat is not a valid user id")
                            end
                            io.putstring ("%NMore new accounts (Y/N)? ")
                            io.readchar
                    end
            end -- new_accounts
    add_accounts (patron: CUSTOMER) is
```

```
                    -- add one or more accounts to this customer
        local reply, type: CHARACTER
        do
            from
            until reply = 'N' or reply = 'n'
            loop
                get_account_type
                type := io.lastchar
                patron.find_account (type)
                if patron.found_account
                then io.putstring ("%NCustomer has that type. Try
                again")
                else patron.add_account (type)
                end
                io.putstring ("%NMore accounts (Y/N)? ")
                io.readchar
                reply := io.lastchar
            end
        end -- add_accounts
    get_account_type is
                    -- get a valid type of account identifier
        local type: CHARACTER
        do
            from
            until valid_account_type (type)
            loop
                io.putstring ("%NEnter type of account (S/C/I): ")
                io.readchar
                type := io.lastchar
                if not valid_account_type (type) then
                    io.putstring ("%NThat is not a valid type. Try
                    again")
                end
            end
        end -- get_account_type
    valid_account_type (type: CHARACTER): BOOLEAN is
                    -- is this a valid type of account to create?
        do
            inspect type
            when 'C', 'c', 'S', 's', 'I', 'i' then Result := true
```

```
            else Result := false
            end
      end -- valid_type
end -- class TELLER
```

```
class ATM
creation {BANK}
    make
feature {NONE}
    patrons: KEY_LIST[CUSTOMER]
    end_atm: INTEGER is 666
    end_system: INTEGER is 999
feature {BANK}
    make (customers: KEY_LIST[CUSTOMER]) is
            -- set the patrons to the list of customers
        do
            patrons := customers
        end -- make
    run is
            -- run the ATM menu until a bank officer shuts it down
        do
            from
                greeting
                patrons.get_id
            until atm_finished or system_finished
            loop
                serve_customer (io.lastint)
                patrons.get_id
            end
            io.putstring ("%NExiting ATM system%N")
        end -- run
    atm_finished: BOOLEAN is
            -- has the ATM finished for the day?
        do
            Result := io.lastint = end_atm
        end -- atm_finished
    system_finished: BOOLEAN is
            -- has the system shutdown code been input?
        do
            Result := io.lastint = end_system
        end -- system_finished
feature {NONE}
    greeting is
            -- welcome the user
        do
```

```
                    io.putstring("%N***********************")
                    io.putstring ("%N* Welcome to myBank, where your money
                    is my money *")
                    io.putstring("%N***********************")
            end -- greeting
        serve_customer (input_id: INTEGER) is
                    -- find the customer with the input id
                    -- if the customer exists, transfer control
            do
                    patrons.find (input_id)
                    if patrons.found then patrons.item.login
                    else io.putstring ("%NThat is not a valid user id")
                    end
            end -- serve_customer
    end -- class ATM
```

```
class KEY_LIST [T -> CUSTOMER]
inherit
    STORABLE;
    LINKED_LIST[T]
creation {BANK}
    make
feature {TELLER, ATM}
    get_id is
            -- get a customer's user identifier
        do
            io.putstring ("%NEnter user id: ")
            io.readint
        end -- get_id
    find (id: INTEGER) is
            -- set the cursor at the person with this key
            -- if no such person, cursor is offright
        do
            from start
            until after or else item.match (id)
            loop forth
            end
        end -- find
    found: BOOLEAN is
            -- is the cursor in the list?
        do Result := not after end --  found
end -- class KEY_LIST
```

```
class PERSON
creation
feature {NONE}
    name, address: STRING
    sex: CHARACTER
feature {TELLER}
    make is
            -- set the personal details
    do
        io.putstring ("%NEnter the personal details%N")
        io.putstring (" Name: ")
        io.readline
        name := io.laststring
        get_sex
        sex := io.lastchar
        io.putstring (" Address: ")
        io.readline
        address := io.laststring
    end -- make
feature {NONE}
    get_sex is
            -- loop until the user enters a valid sex
        do
            from
            until valid_gender
            loop
                io.putstring (" Sex (M/F): ")
                io.readchar
                if not valid_gender then
                    io.putstring ("Valid codes are M, m, F, or f. Try
                    again%N")
                end
            end
        end -- get_sex
    valid_gender: BOOLEAN is
            -- has a valid sex code been entered?
        do
            inspect io.lastchar
            when 'M', 'm', 'F', 'f' then Result := true
            else Result := false
```

```
                    end
           end -- valid_gender
    print_title is
               -- be nice
           do
               inspect sex
               when 'M', 'm' then io.putstring ("%NMr. ")
               when 'F', 'f' then io.putstring ("%NMs. ")
               end
           end -- print_title
feature
    display is
               -- show the personal details
           do
               io.putstring ("%N ")
               print_title
               io.putstring (name)
               io.putstring (" lives at ")
               io.putstring (address)
           end -- display
end -- class PERSON
```

```
class CUSTOMER
inherit
    PERSON
        rename
            make as person_make,
            display as person_display
        end
creation {TELLER}
    make
feature {NONE}
    key: INTEGER
    password: PASSWORD
    accounts: LINKED_LIST[ACCOUNT]
feature {TELLER}
    make (id: INTEGER) is
            -- set the customer details
        do
            person_make
            key := id
            !!password.make
            !!accounts.make
        end -- make
    find_account (type: CHARACTER) is
            -- set the cursor at this type of account
            -- if no such account, cursor is after
        local
            savings: SAVINGS
            check: CHECK
            invest: INVEST
            account: ACCOUNT
        do
            inspect type
            when 'S', 's' then account := savings
            when 'C', 'c' then account := check
            when 'I', 'i' then account := invest
            end
            from accounts.start
            until accounts.after or else account /= Void
            loop
            account ?= accounts.item
```

```
                    accounts.forth
                end
        end -- find_account
    found_account: BOOLEAN is
                -- is the cursor in the list?
        do
            Result := not accounts.after
        end -- found_account
    add_account (type: CHARACTER) is
                -- add an account of this type to the customer
        local account: ACCOUNT
        do
            inspect type
            when 'S', 's' then !SAVINGS!account.make
            when 'C', 'c' then !CHECK!account.make
            when 'I', 'i' then
                io.putstring ("Enter period (3/6/12): ")
                io.readint
                inspect io.lastint
                when 3 then !INVEST_3!account.make
                when 6 then !INVEST_6!account.make
                when 12 then !INVEST_12!account.make
                end
            end
            accounts.put (account)
        end -- add_account
feature {ANY}
    display is
                -- show the customer details
        do
            person_display
            io.putstring ("%NThe customer id is ")
            io.putint (key)
            io.putstring (". The accounts are:")
            from accounts.start
            until accounts.after
            loop
                accounts.item.display
                accounts.forth
            end
```

```
            end -- display
    feature {ATM}
        login is
                    -- if the customer enters the valid password
                    -- then get them to choose an account
            do
                password.login
                if password.valid then use_accounts
                else io.putstring ("Login failure. Exiting system%N")
                end
            end -- login
    feature {KEY_LIST}
        match (id: INTEGER): BOOLEAN is
                    -- does the customer have this id?
            do
                Result := key = id
            end -- match
    feature {NONE}
        use_accounts is
                    -- select an account to use, show the account menu
                    -- loop until user decides to leave
            do
                from get_atm_type
                until finished
                loop
                    use_account (io.lastchar)
                    get_atm_type
                end
                io.putstring ("Y'all have a nice day, hear?%N")
            end -- use_accounts
        get_atm_type is
                    -- get a valid account type that can be accessed via ATM
                    -- or get the exit command
            local reply: CHARACTER
            do
                from
                    io.putstring ("%NEnter type of account, or quit (S, C,
                    Q): ")
                    io.readchar
                    reply := io.lastchar
```

```
                    until
                         valid (reply)
                    loop
                         io.putstring ("Sorry, that was not a valid choice")
                         io.putstring ("%NYou can only use a savings or a check
                         account")
                         io.putstring ("%NEnter type of account, or quit (S, C,
                         Q): ")
                         io.readchar
                         reply := io.lastchar
                    end
               end -- get_atm_type
          finished: BOOLEAN is
                    -- has the user decided to finish?
               do
                    Result := io.lastchar = 'Q' or io.lastchar = 'q'
               end -- finished
          use_account (choice: CHARACTER) is
                    -- if the customer has this account, start the menu
               local account: INTERACCT
               do
                    find_account (choice)
                    if found_account then
                         account ?= accounts.item
                         account.menu
                    else io.putstring ("%NYou don't have that type of account")
                    end
               end -- select_account
     feature {TELLER}
          add_interest is
                    -- add interest to any savings or investment account
               local account: INTERESTING
               do
                    from accounts.start
                    until accounts.after
                    loop
                         account ?= accounts.item
                         if account /= Void then account.add_interest end
                    end
               end -- add_interest
```

```
    new_day is
            -- add a day to the investment account counter
            -- if the investment account is mature,
            -- transfer the balance to the check account
            -- and delete the investment account
    local
        invest: INVEST
        check: CHECK
    do
        from accounts.start
        until accounts.after or else invest /= Void
        loop
            invest ?= accounts.item
            if invest /= Void then
                invest.new_day
                if invest.mature then
                    find_account ('C')
                    if not found_account then !!check.make end
                    check.deposit (invest.balance)
                    accounts.remove
                end -- mature
            end -- invest
        end -- loop
    end -- add_interest
end -- class CUSTOMER
```

```
class PASSWORD
creation {CUSTOMER}
    make
feature {NONE}
    password: STRING
    tries: INTEGER
    max_tries: INTEGER is 3
feature {CUSTOMER}
    make is
            -- set the password
        do
            io.putstring (" Password: ")
            io.readword
            password := io.laststring
        end -- make
    login is
            -- attempt to get a valid password
        do
            from get_word
            until valid or failure
            loop
                io.putstring ("Incorrect password. Try again%N")
                get_word
            end
        end -- login
feature {NONE}
    get_word is
            -- read in a password, add 1 to the number of attempts
        do
            io.putstring ("%NPlease enter the password: ")
            io.readword
            tries := tries + 1
        end -- get_word
feature {CUSTOMER}
    valid: BOOLEAN is
            -- is the input word the password?
        do
            Result := io.laststring.is_equal (password)
        end -- valid
    failure: BOOLEAN is
```

-- has the password been tried too many times?
do
    Result := tries = max_tries
end -- failure
end -- class *PASSWORD*

```
deferred class ACCOUNT
feature {NONE}
    balance: REAL
feature {CUSTOMER}
    make is
            -- set the initial balance
        do
            io.putstring ("%NEnter initial balance: ")
            io.readreal
            balance := io.lastreal
        end -- make
    display is
            -- show the balance and the interest rate
        do
            io.putstring ("%N The balance is $")
            io.putreal (balance)
        end -- display
end -- class ACCOUNT
```

```
deferred class INTERESTING
inherit
    ACCOUNT
feature {CUSTOMER}
    add_interest is
            -- add the daily interest to the balance
        do
            balance := balance + balance * day_rate
        end -- add_interest
feature {NONE}
    day_rate: REAL is
            -- daily interest rate
        do
            Result := (interest_rate / 100) / 365.25
        end -- day_rate
    interest_rate: REAL is
            -- yearly interest rate
        deferred
        end -- interest_rate
end -- class INTERESTING
```

```
deferred class INVEST
inherit
    ACCOUNT
        rename
            display as display_balance
        export
            {CUSTOMER} balance
        end;
    INTERESTING
        undefine
            display
        end
feature {NONE}
    days: INTEGER
    period: INTEGER is
            -- period of account in months
        deferred
        end
feature {CUSTOMER}
    new_day is
            -- increment the day counter
        do
            days:= days + 1
        end -- new_day
    mature: BOOLEAN is
            -- is the account mature?
        do
            Result := days = period * 30
        end -- mature
    display is
            -- show the balance, interest rate, period, and day counter
        do
            io.putstring ("%N***Investment account***")
            display_balance
            io.putstring ("%N The period is ")
            io.putint (period)
            io.putstring (" months")
            io.putstring ("%N The account has run for ")
            io.putint (days)
            io.putstring (" days")
        end -- display
end -- class INVEST
```

```
class INVEST_3
inherit
    INVEST
creation {CUSTOMER}
    make
feature {NONE}
    period: INTEGER is 3
    interest_rate: REAL is 5.5
end -- class INVEST_3

class INVEST_6
inherit
    INVEST
creation {CUSTOMER}
    make
feature {NONE}
    period: INTEGER is 6
    interest_rate: REAL is 6.0
end -- class INVEST_6

class INVEST_12
inherit
    INVEST
creation {CUSTOMER}
    make
feature {NONE}
    period: INTEGER is 12
    interest_rate: REAL is 6.5
end -- class INVEST_12
```

```
deferred class MENU
feature {CUSTOMER}
    menu is
                -- display the menu
                -- get and execute menu choices
        do
            from show_choices
            until end_chosen
            loop
                get_choice
                do_choice
            end
        end -- menu
feature {NONE}
    get_choice is
                -- get a valid menu choice from the user
        do
            from
                io.putstring ("%NEnter menu choice: ")
                io.readchar
            until valid_choice
            loop
                io.putstring ("That is not a valid choice. Try again%N")
                io.putstring ("The valid choices are D, W, B, Q, and
                H%N")
                io.putstring ("%NEnter menu choice: ")
                io.readchar
            end
        end -- get_choice
    valid_choice: BOOLEAN is
                -- has the user entered a valid choice?
        do
            inspect io.lastchar
            when 'D', 'd', 'W', 'w', 'B', 'b', 'Q', 'q', 'H', 'h'
            then
                Result := true
            else Result := false
            end
        end -- valid_choice
    end_chosen: BOOLEAN is
```

```
                    -- has the user chosen to finish?
            do
                    Result := io.lastchar = 'Q' or io.lastchar = 'q'
            end -- end_chosen
    do_choice is
                    -- execute the choice made by the user
            do
                    inspect io.lastchar
                    when 'D', 'd' then do_deposit
                    when 'W', 'w' then do_withdraw
                    when 'B', 'b' then show_balance
                    when 'H', 'h' then show_choices
                    when 'Q', 'q' then exit_menu
                    end -- inspect
            end -- do_choice
    show_choices is
                    -- show the valid menu choices
            do
                    io.putstring ("%N Menu choices%N")
                    io.putstring ("D Deposit money%N")
                    io.putstring ("W Withdraw money%N")
                    io.putstring ("B Show the balance%N")
                    io.putstring ("Q Quit the system%N")
                    io.putstring ("H Help: Show the menu choices%N")
            end -- show_choices
    do_deposit is
                    -- get the amount to deposit, then deposit it
            local amount: REAL
            do
                    io.putstring ("Enter the amount to deposit: ")
                    io.readreal
                    deposit (io.lastreal)
            end -- do_deposit
    do_withdraw is
                    -- get the amount to withdraw
                    -- if there is enough money, withdraw the amount
            local amount: REAL
            do
                    io.putstring ("Enter the amount to withdraw: ")
                    io.readreal
```

```
                    amount := io.lastreal
                    try_withdraw (amount)
            end -- do_withdraw
        try_withdraw (amount: REAL) is
                    -- withdraw this amount if there is enough money
            deferred
            end -- withdraw
        exit_menu is
                    -- say bye bye
            do io.putstring ("%NY'all have a nice day, now%N") end
feature {CUSTOMER}
        deposit (amount: REAL) is
                    -- add the amount to the balance
            deferred
            end -- deposit
        show_balance is
                    -- display the current balance
            deferred
            end -- show_balance
    end -- class MENU
```

```
deferred class INTERACCT
inherit
    ACCOUNT;
    MENU
feature {CUSTOMER}
    deposit (amount: REAL) is
            -- add amount to balance
        do
            balance := balance + amount
        end -- deposit
    enough (amount: REAL): BOOLEAN is
            -- does the account contain this amount?
        do
            Result := balance >= amount
        end
    withdraw (amount: REAL) is
            -- subtract this amount from the balance
        do
            balance := balance - amount
        end
    show_balance is
            -- display the current balance
        do
            io.putstring ("%NThe current balance is ")
            io.putreal (balance)
        end -- show_balance
end -- class INTERACCT
```

```
class SAVINGS
inherit
    INTERACCT;
    INTERESTING
creation {CUSTOMER}
    make
feature {NONE}
    interest_rate: REAL is
                -- interest rate for savings account
        do
            Result := 4.5
        end -- interest_rate
feature {CUSTOMER}
    try_withdraw (amount: REAL) is
                -- withdraw this amount if there is enough money
        do
            if enough (amount) then withdraw (amount)
            else io.putstring ("%NInsufficient funds")
            end
        end -- deposit
end -- class SAVINGS
```

```
class CHECK
inherit
    INTERACCT
creation {CUSTOMER}
    make
feature {NONE}
    charge: REAL is 0.50        -- charge for good transaction
    penalty: REAL is 5.00       -- penalty for bouncing a check
feature {CUSTOMER}
    try_withdraw (amount: REAL) is
            -- if there is enough money, withdraw the amount
            -- if not, charge a penalty for bouncing a check
        do
            if enough (amount + charge)
            then withdraw (amount + charge)

            else
                io.putstring ("%NInsufficient funds")
                apply_penalty
            end
        end -- try_withdraw
    apply_penalty is
            -- apply the penalty for bouncing a check
            -- account balance cannot go negative
        do
            if balance >= penalty then balance := balance - penalty
            else balance := 0
            end
        end -- apply_penalty
end -- class CHECK
```

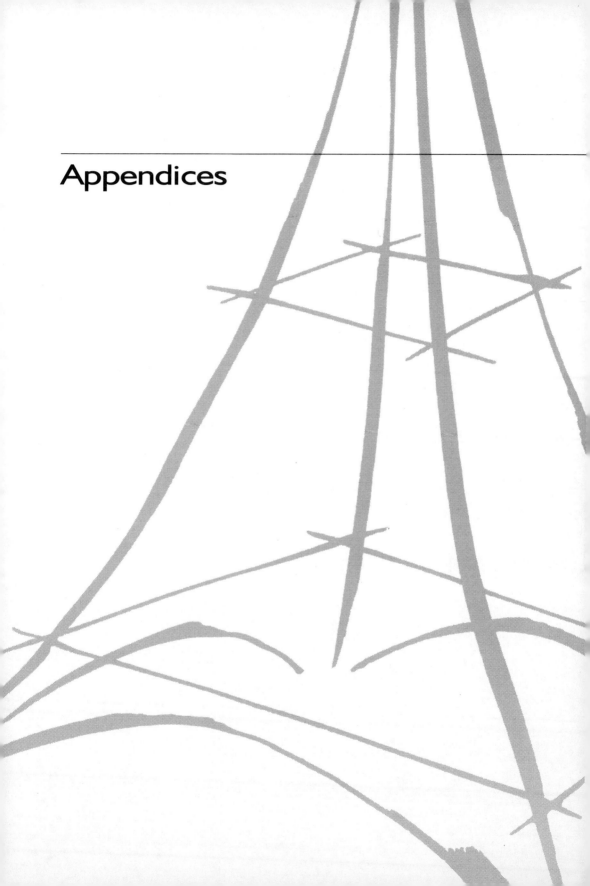

Appendices

APPENDIX A

Eiffel syntax

The syntax of each statement in the Eiffel language is shown below, in the order used in the book.

A.1 Class

The basic format of an Eiffel class is the class header, followed by the class body. The header gives the name of the class, and the name of its creation routine. The body consists of a list of features, which may be data (attributes) or routines (functions and procedures). All features are indented equally. All indenting is done with the same step size, in steps of four spaces. A space is placed before each comma, colon, and semi-colon, and around assignments.

```
-- class header comment
class NAME
creation
    make
feature
    attribute_name: type
    function_name (arguments): TYPE is
            -- header comment
        require
            preconditions
        local
            local variables
        do
            routine body
            Result := value
        ensure
```

```
            postconditions
        end – – function_name
  procedure_name (arguments) is
            – – header comment
        require
            preconditions
        local
            local variables
        do
            routine body
        ensure
            postconditions
        end – – procedure_name
  end – – class NAME
```

The export policy of a feature lists the classes that can call or use that feature. The policy is set in a **feature** clause, and remains in force until the next **feature** clause. The types of export policy are

Export clause	**Meaning**
feature	exported to all classes
feature {ANY}	exported to all classes
feature {X, Y, Z}	exported to classes X, Y, Z
feature {}	exported to no class
feature {NONE}	exported to no class

The creation status of a routine is separate from its export status, so a routine may be called as a creator or as a normal routine. The format of the export policy on the creator is the same as the normal export policy, such as

```
creation {X, Y, Z}
    make, setup
feature {ANY}
    make is . . .
    setup is . . .
```

A creation routine is called to create an object, indicated by *!!*. The same routine may be called to change an existing object by calling the routine without creation (no *!!*). The two uses of the same routine are

!!object.make	– – create new object
object.make	– – alter existing object

A.2   Sequence

Declaration:	*length: REAL*	attribute variable
	local *length: REAL*	local variable
	length: REAL **is** *4.5*	constant
	Red, Orange, Yellow: *INTEGER* **is unique**	unique constants
Input:	*io.readint*	read an integer value
	io.lastint	last integer value read
	io.readreal	read a real value
	io.lastreal	last real value read
	io.readdouble	read a double precision real value
	io.lastdouble	last double precision real value read
	io.readchar	read a character
	io.lastchar	last character read
	io.readline	read a line
	io.readstream (n)	read a stream of *n* characters
	io.readword	read a word
	io.laststring	last string read
	io.next_line	read from a new line
Output:	*io.putreal*	write a real value
	io.putdouble	write a double precision real value
	io.putint	write an integer value
	io.putchar	write a character value
	io.putstring	write a string value
	io.new_line	start a new line for output
Assignment:	*variable :=* *expression*	store the value of expression in the variable

A class can be expanded by placing the keyword **expanded** in the class definition, or in the variable declaration. The keyword *Current* returns the value of the current object, either an immediate value (for an expanded type) or a reference value.

Procedure: *name (argument list)* **is**
                 – – header comment
          require
               preconditions
          local
               local variables
          do
               routine body
          ensure
               postconditions
          end – – name

An argument list is a list of declarations, separated by semi-colons. Actual and formal arguments must agree in number, order, and type; name is irrelevant.

Function: *name (argument list): TYPE* **is**
                 – – header comment
          require
               preconditions
          local
               local variables
          do
               routine body
               Result := expression
          ensure
               postconditions
          end – – name

Infix operator: **infix** *name (arguments): TYPE* **is** . . .
Prefix operator: **prefix** *name: TYPE* **is** . . .

In a once routine, the keyword **do** is replaced by the word **once**. A once routine is executed only once, the first time it is called. Further calls to a once procedure do nothing, and further calls to a once function return the same value as the first call.

The keyword **like** can be used in the form **like:** *name* to define a type that is the same as the named variable.

A.3   Selection

If: **if** *condition1* **then**
                    action1

```
                elseif condition2 then
                    action2
                . . .
                else
                    default_action
                end
Inspect:        inspect expression
                when values then
                    action
                when values then
                    action
                . . .
                else
                    action
                end
```

Values in an **inspect** statement may be specified in three ways:
(i)   A single value: **when** *3* **then** . . .
(ii) A set of values: **when** *'a', 'e', 'i', 'o', 'u'* **then** . . .
(iii) A range of values: **when** *1. .12* **then** . . .

A.4   Iteration

```
Loop:       from
                initializations
            until
                exit_condition
            loop
                action
            end
```


A.5   Inheritance

The format of an inheritance clause is shown below. The sub-clauses are executed
in sequence, so that the effect of an early clause can be used in a later clause.

```
class A
        inherit B
            rename                              -- new name in child
```

```
             m as n
          export                          -- new export policy in child
             {C, D} o, p
          undefine                        -- no definition in child
             q
          redefine                        -- new body in child
             r, s
          select                          -- select active feature
             t
          end
```

Multiple classes can be inherited, separated by semi-colons, such as

```
class A inherit
   B; C; D
```

The class *ANY* is the implicit parent of all user-defined classes. The class *NONE* defines the bottom of the Eiffel inheritance hierarchy; by definition, no class can inherit *NONE*. The special value *Void* is of type *NONE*.

A.6   Genericity

A generic class receives a class name as a parameter and uses objects of that type. The formal parameter (usually called *"T"* for type or *"G"* for generic) is defined in the class header, and actual parameters are bound at compile time. An example of a generic class header is provided by class *ARRAY*, shown below. Multiple actual and formal parameters are separated by commas.

```
class ARRAY [G]
```

A formal parameter can be constrained or limited to be of the type given in the class header. The constraint operator is "->", so a constrained class header looks like

```
class GIRLS [T -> FUN]
```

and only actual parameters of type *FUN* can be passed to *GIRLS*.

APPENDIX B

Reserved words, special characters, and operators

A small set of reserved words have special meanings in Eiffel. You are not allowed to use them as names. The reserved words are

alias	all	and	as	*BIT*	*BOOLEAN*
CHARACTER	check	class	creation	*Current*	debug
deferred	do	*DOUBLE*	else	elseif	end
ensure	expanded	export	external	false	feature
from	frozen	if	implies	indexing	infix
inherit	inspect	*INTEGER*	invariant	is	like
local	loop	*NONE*	not	obsolete	old
once	or	*POINTER*	prefix	*REAL*	redefine
rename	require	rescue	*Result*	retry	select
separate	*STRING*	strip	then	true	undefine
unique	until	variant	when	xor	

B.2   **Special characters**

Character	Code	Mnemonic name
@	%A	At-sign
BS	%B	Backspace
^	%C	Circumflex
$	%D	Dollar
FF	%F	Form feed
\	%H	backslasH

~	%L	tiLda
NL	%N	Newline
'	%Q	(back) Quote
CR	%R	(carriage) Return
#	%S	Sharp
HT	%T	(horizontal) Tab
NUL	%U	nUll character
|	%V	Vertical bar
%	%%	Percent
'	%'	Single quote
"	%"	Double quote
[	%(	Opening bracket
]	%)	Closing bracket
{	%<	Opening brace
}	%>	Closing brace

B.3   Operator precedence order

The precedence order for all Eiffel operators is shown below; highest precedence is at the top of the table, lowest precedence is at the bottom. Operators at the same precedence level are shown together; these operators are evaluated left to right in an expression. Brackets override the default precedence order. A free operator (levels 10 and 11) is an operator whose name begins with one of the characters '@', '#', '|', or '&'.

Level	Operators
12	. (Dot notation for client feature calls)
11	**old strip**
	not unary + unary −
	All free unary operators
10	All free binary operators
9	^ (power)
8	* / // (integer division) \\ (integer remainder)
7	binary + binary −
6	= /= (not equal) < > <= >=
5	**and and then**
4	**or or else xor**
3	**implies**
2	<< >> (for manifest arrays)
1	; (semicolon separator between assertion clauses)

APPENDIX C

Charts

Three main types of charts are used in this book to describe an Eiffel system: client, inheritance, and system structure charts. Several other types of diagram are also used, to show the plan dependencies and the data structure of a system. The rules for constructing these five types of chart are given in this section. The rules for building a top-down calling chart and a control flow diagram are not given here, because there is already a large literature on these topics, and the charts are not used to describe an OO system.

The structure of a system is defined first by the plan dependencies in the system, and then by the decisions about how to order and organize the plan actions. A plan structure chart shows the essential dependencies between actions, which may be thought of as the problem structure; whatever the form of the solution, it has to obey these essential constraints. Analysis of the problem reveals the problem or plan structure. A system structure chart shows the order in which the actions are executed in the final solution, and may be thought of as the solution structure. Design of the solution creates the solution or system structure.

A chart or diagram describes the final form of the system, so it is a form of system documentation. Any chart must be a true and accurate reflection of the structure it describes. Diagrams can also be used as conceptual tools for designing the structure of a system, because they provide a picture of the system at a level higher than the code or even the behavior of the system. Diagrams can be used to design a system, and to show the structure of the final solution.

C.1   Client chart

A client chart shows the client–supplier or calling links in the system, where a client is a class that "has", "uses", or "contains" an instance of the supplier class. A link from a client class C to a supplier class S is defined whenever class C contains a declaration of the form $s: S$. By this definition, the client chart for dynamic creation only shows the static supplier class.

Each class is shown as an oval that contains the class name. The calling or using relation is shown by an arrow from the client to the supplier; a supplier cannot know in advance who will use its services, so the link is from the client. The client is shown to the left, and the supplier to the right. The client relation between a customer who has an account is shown as

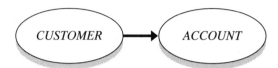

A generic class takes one or more classes as generic parameters; generic classes are often container classes. The generic client relationship is shown by writing the name of the parameter class in square brackets, between the client and the generic, container class. A customer with a list of accounts is shown as

For simplicity, the basic Eiffel classes *INTEGER*, *REAL*, *DOUBLE*, *CHAR-ACTER*, *BOOLEAN*, and *STRING* are not shown on a client chart.

C.2   Inheritance chart

An inheritance chart shows the inheritance links in the system. A class is shown as an oval containing the class name. A single arrow is drawn from the child to the parent; a class cannot know in advance who will inherit it, so the link is drawn from the inheriting class, from the child. A parent is drawn above a child. The diagram for three abstract and five specific types of account is shown below.

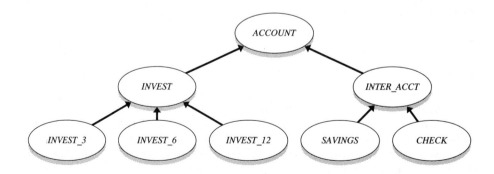

Multiple inheritance is shown by drawing an arrow from the child to every parent class. A storable list class *STORE_LIST*, which inherits its storable features from *STORABLE* and its list features from *LINKED_LIST*, is shown below.

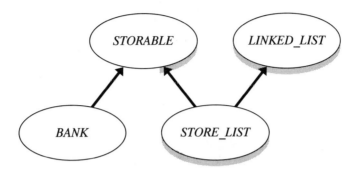

Repeated inheritance is shown by extending the inheritance hierarchy through as many levels as needed.

C.3   System structure chart

A system structure (sS) chart shows two things. First, it shows the location of the code; more formally, it shows which class contains the code that is used to achieve each specific system goal. Second, it shows the order in which events happen in the system.

The high-level structure of the chart is built by listing the classes across the top of the chart, and the goals down the left side. Class and attribute names are always nouns, and goal names are always verbs. For each goal, the system contains a plan to achieve that goal; more formally, it contains the code that implements the plan. This code is normally spread over several classes. Whenever a class and a plan intersect, that class contains some code in the plan, and a circle is drawn to indicate the location of the code; such a circle is called a node of the chart. The goals are often explicitly listed in the system specification, but there may be additional, implicit goals.

Classes are listed across the top of the chart, first in client order, then in inheritance order; the parents of a class are listed before the children. A system in which an interactive customer uses three kinds of account is listed in the order (client, parent, children) shown below.

   CUSTOMER   MENU   ACCOUNT   SAVINGS   CHECK   INVEST

A node in the chart corresponds to one or more features, and is drawn as a circle. The node shows that part of the plan for the goal lies in the object. This code may be implemented as a single routine or as many routines. Data flow into and out of a node is shown on the node as a triangle. Data flow to and from the user is shown above and below the node. Data flow from a routine (argument passing) is shown as a right-pointing arrow, and data flow returned to a routine (attribute or function) is shown as a left-pointing arrow. Data flow within an object, which occurs when a procedure sets an attribute, is not shown in a sS chart. The four types of data flow shown on a sS chart are listed below.

data from user   data to user   data to routine   data from routine

A node is written in the chart to show a unit of design. The boundaries of the unit are defined when control moves from one class to another, from one plan to another, or from one choice to another within a plan. A complete plan can be traced from the most basic operation or focus at the right of the chart, backward to the initial node in the top, left-hand corner of the chart. A node at the far left of a plan indicates the start of the plan (a routine call), a node in the middle of a plan indicates a routine definition that calls other features, and a node at the far right indicates the end of the line, a routine that does not use any other classes.

The order in which nodes are executed is shown by lines connecting the nodes on the chart. The order of events can be seen by starting from the top, left-hand corner of the chart and following the lines. The lines thus indicate the control flow through the system; control normally flows from left to right and top to bottom of the chart. Sequence and selection at the plan and object level are shown in the chart. Iteration is not shown in a system structure chart, nor is data flow.

Control flow between classes is shown by a horizontal line between two nodes. Such a link shows that one node is called by another, usually in left to right order based on the client chart. A line to the right of a node indicates a feature call from that node. A line to the left of a node indicates that that node is called.

Sequence within a class is shown by a vertical line between two nodes, where the lower node follows the upper node in execution order. In rare cases, a series of function calls within an object (but across goals) may be indicated by a vertical line, where the connected links start at the bottom and are traced backward through the calls.

Selection is shown by a circle within the node, so the symbol is a double circle. A selection node is shown for every optional path, so a single choice (**if then**) has a single node, a choice of two alternatives (**if then else**) has two nodes, and a multiple choice is shown by a set of multiple, connected nodes.

Object selection is shown by a filled circle at the center of the node. In polymorphism, an object is selected and the code within that object is executed. The different classes in the chart are shown to the right of the object selection node, with no control flow link; this pattern indicates that the objects are alternatives for that selection.

Symbol	Meaning
◯	node: one or more features
——	control flow between classes
│	sequence within a class
◎	goal selection
◉	object selection
◉	goal and object selection

Generic classes are shown in a system structure chart between the client and the parameter; note that this is not the order used in the client chart, where the parameter is placed between the client and the container classes. For simplicity, generic Eiffel library classes may be omitted from a sS chart.

C.4 Data structure chart

A data structure chart is built by tracing through the attributes from the class at the root of the data structure; for the complete system, this is the root class. The classes are listed from left to right in client chart order. Starting with the leftmost class, a pointer is drawn from the name of the object to the data array for that object.

A data array is a two-dimensional array consisting of a series of data records. A data record has three fields, listing the name, type, and value of the variable. Each record is shown across the page, in the order name, type, and value. The array is drawn down the page, one record per attribute, in the order given in the class definition. The value of a variable may be a simple or expanded value, or a reference value. For each reference value, a pointer is drawn to the data array for that object.

The data structure for a triangle is shown below.

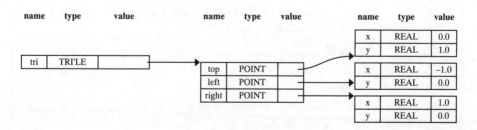

C.5   Plan structure chart

A plan structure or plan dependency chart shows the detailed data and control flow links between lines of code. Data flow occurs when one line of code produces or makes data which is consumed or used by another line; data flow is shown by a single line on the chart. The line of code that makes the data is drawn above the line that uses the data. Control flow occurs when one line controls another, by selection or iteration; each routine has its own, separate plan chart. Control flow is indicated by a double line between the two lines of code.

The links in a plan structure chart show which lines depend on other lines, and thus define the essential order in which lines of code have to be executed. Usually, no single or total order is defined, because the links are piecewise; there is great freedom in how a designer chooses to order the actions, so long as the essential, piecewise order is adhered to. The inputs to the plan are listed at the top of the chart, and the goal at the bottom. A system with multiple goals may have the individual plan structures merged, producing a single chart with multiple goals.

If the plan structure consists purely of data flow, then the diagram is called a data flow diagram; data flow charts are normally drawn with the arrows pointing down the page, from the place where a data value is made to where it is used.

Plan structure may be derived from program code by starting at each output or system goal, and tracing back through the links. Data flow links are traced first, then control flow links. To illustrate how plan structure can be derived, a simple Eiffel program is shown below (taken from Chapter 6) and its plan structure is then derived. The program finds the average rainfall for a particular period; the end of the period is indicated by a sentinel value of -999.

```
1.      rainfall, days: INTEGER
2.      end_of_input: INTEGER is -999
3.
4.      get_all_rainfall is
5.      -- get all the rainfall for the period
6.      -- record the sum and the interval
7.      do
8.          from
9.              io.putstring ("%NEnter the rainfall values for the
                period")
10.             io.putstring ("%NTo finish, enter the value – 999%N");
11.             get_rainfall (days)
12.         until
13.             io.lastint = end_of_input
14.         loop
15.             rainfall:= rainfall + io.lastint
16.             days := days + 1
```

```
17.                    get_rainfall (days)
18.              end
19.         end -- get_all_rainfall
20.
21.         get_rainfall (today: INTEGER) is
22.              -- prompt the user for today's rainfall value
23.         do
24.              io.putstring ("Enter the rainfall value for day ")
25.              io.putint (days + 1)
26.              io.putstring (": ")
27.              io.readint
28.         end -- get_rainfall
29.
30.         average_rainfall: REAL is
31.              -- average rainfall for the period
32.         do
33.              if days > 0
34.              then Result := rainfall / days
35.              end
36.         end -- average_rainfall
```

To make plan structure from code, all the code is unfolded to remove the classes and routines, because the plan structure is the basic, essential structure of the code. Starting with the average output in line 34 (actually, the output code would be in a client), the data flow may be traced back to where the *rainfall* and *days* values are produced. Pursuing the *rainfall* value first, it is produced by the code in lines 15 and 1. Line 1 is a terminal, but data flow may be traced backward from line 15, to itself and to the input command (line 27) called in lines 11 and 17. The input is a terminal, but the lines are controlled by the loop, so control flow can be traced back from these lines to line 13. This loop control line uses data produced by lines 11 and 17 (*io.lastint*), and by line 2. These three lines are all terminals, so that this branch of the plan structure is now complete.

Link tracing then recurs back until an empty link is found, in this case all the way back to line 34, which uses the variable *days*. Line 34 uses a data value made by lines 16 and 1. Line 1 is a terminal, but line 16 uses data produced by itself and by line 1. Line 16 is controlled by the loop, so a control link is traced back to line 13. The plan structure has already been traced from there, so tracing recurs back down the plan structure to line 34, which is controlled by line 33. Line 33 uses data produced by lines 16 and 1. All links have now been traced back from the goal, so the plan structure is complete. Prompts and labels do not contribute to the data or control flow, so they are not part of the plan structure.

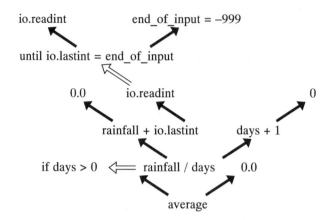

The plan structure for the code is shown above, where joins in the graph have been omitted from the diagram for simplicity. A filled arrow indicates data flow, while a hollow arrow shows control flow; the arrows shown are those created by the tracing algorithm, without showing the joins in the plan structure. In the pS, a routine call in a class is unfolded and replaced by the code. Classes are not shown in a plan structure diagram either, because both routines and classes are defined at the discretion of the designer, and are not part of the essential problem structure. The algorithm for building plan structure from code is given in Rist (1994), and a detailed model of the design process is given in Rist (in press).

APPENDIX D

Design principles

D.1 Planning

1. A plan is a set of actions which, when executed in the right order, achieve the goal of the plan.

D.2 Object-oriented programming

1. An object is designed around the data it stores.
2. A routine is small and does a single thing.
3. An object is an instance of a class.
4. A value can only be changed by code in its class.
5. The data and the code live in the same class.
6. Plans and objects are orthogonal: a plan can use many objects, and an object can be used in many plans.
7. Write code in a parent, and reuse it by inheritance.

D.3 Eiffel

1. A function returns a value and changes nothing.
2. A procedure changes value(s) and returns nothing.
3. The client is responsible for calling a routine correctly.
4. Export the behavior and hide the representation.
5. If you repeat code, your design is wrong.

D.4 The process of design

1. Decompose: solve a small part of the solution first.
2. Iterate: evaluate your solution, then improve it.
3. Abstract the code to define routines in classes.

4. Push the code as far right as is reasonable (client).
5. Push the code as high as is reasonable (inheritance).
6. Code and test part of the system at a time.

D.5   Design guidelines

1. Design by contract: behavior is defined by a contract, so the implementation is hidden.
2. A feature does a single thing.
3. The client is responsible for calling a routine, correctly.
4. Let the supplier do the work.
5. Hide the complexity inside a routine.
6. Routines that use an attribute live in that class.
7. Hide the attributes whenever reasonable.
8. Keep the number of attributes small; use local variables where possible.
9. Don't pass around a lot of data.
10. Names are clear, simple, and meaningful.
11. Use matched routines: a command to make a change, and a query to test the effect of the command.
12. Never repeat code. If code is repeated instead of reused, then the system design is wrong.
13. Don't explicitly test the type of an object:
    - Use polymorphism to define a common interface.
    - Use conditional assignment to find the desired type.

APPENDIX E

Run-time assertion monitoring

By definition, a program is correct only if all assertions evaluate to true during its execution; therefore, run-time monitoring of assertions does not affect the operation of correct programs. For incorrect programs, the effects depend on the compilation and execution options selected for particular classes. Although they may differ in details, all systems should support six different levels of assertion checking. Each level builds on the previous ones—for example, you can monitor only preconditions, or pre- and postconditions, but not postconditions alone.

1. No run-time monitoring of assertions.
2. Monitor preconditions only.
3. Monitor pre- and postconditions.
4. Monitor class invariants, as well as pre- and postconditions.
5. Monitor loop variants and invariants, as well as class invariants, and pre- and postconditions.
6. Monitor check instructions, class invariants, loop assertions, and pre- and postconditions.

The default is level two: monitor preconditions only. This prevents catastrophic failures resulting from routines called with incorrect arguments, while minimizing the cost of assertion monitoring.

If an assertion is being monitored at run-time, it should always evaluate to true (except for a loop variant, which should always be non-negative and be decreased by each iteration). If an assertion is false, then an exception is raised. For preconditions, the calling routine receives the exception. For all other assertions (postconditions, class invariants, loop assertions, and check instructions) the currently executing routine is the recipient.

REFERENCES

Booch, G. (1994), *Object Oriented Design*, Benjamin/Cummins, New York.

Coad, P. and Yourdon, E. (1990), *Object-oriented Analysis*, Prentice Hall, New York.

Henderson-Sellers, B. and Edwards, J.M. (1994), *BOOKTWO of Object-oriented Knowledge: The Working Object*, Prentice Hall, Sydney.

Meyer, B. (1988), *Object-oriented Software Construction*, Prentice Hall, New York.

Meyer, B. (1992), *Eiffel: The Language*, Prentice Hall, New York.

Norman, D.A. (1988), *The Psychology of Everyday Things*, Basic Books, New York.

Rist, R.S. (1994), "Search through multiple representations", in D.J. Gilmore, R.L. Winder, and F. Detienne (eds), *User-centred Requirements for Software Engineering Environments*, Springer-Verlag, Berlin, pp. 165–76.

Rist, R.S. (in press), "Program structure and design", to appear in *Cognitive Science*.

Rumbaugh, J., Blaha, M., Premerlani, W., Eddy, F., and Lorensen, W. (1991), *Object-oriented Modelling and Design*, Prentice Hall, Englewood Cliffs, N.J.

Russell, B.A.W. and Whitehead, A.N. (1913), *Principia Mathematica*, Cambridge University Press, Cambridge.

Schön, D.A. (1983), *The Reflective Practitioner*, Basic Books, New York.

Switzer, R. (1993), *Eiffel: An Introduction*, Prentice Hall, New York.

INDEX